Healthy Praise for *Diet for a Poisoned Planet*

"Read this book! *Diet for a Poisoned Planet* is among the nation's most important books on cancer prevention. It is a highly readable and scientifically well documented book that will clearly inform readers how to avoid the toxic and carcinogenic hazards in their food. I don't know of any other book which is likely to make such a valuable contribution to cancer prevention. No wonder the agrichemical and food industries and their hacks moved heaven and earth to try and block this important book's publication and distribution to the public."

> Samuel Epstein, M.D.
> Professor of Occupational and Environmental Medicine
> University of Illinois at Chicago

"Steinman's guide to safe food and drinking water and the nontoxic home is the protect-your-health book we needed years ago. It is important reading for anyone planning a pregnancy or family."

> Erik Jansson
> National Coordinator
> National Network to Prevent Birth Defects

"It took David Steinman, not responsible officials, to reveal that excessive levels of toxins were endangering people fishing in Santa Monica Bay. In this book, he persuasively warns against the pollutants poisoning our people—and offers personal and political remedies."

> Tom Hayden
> California Assemblyman

"*Diet for a Poisoned Planet* will succeed if it spurs readers to demand that government officials stand up to those who have allowed our food supply—and environment—to become tainted with potentially dangerous pesticides, additives, bacteria, and industrial chemicals."

> Michael F. Jacobson, Ph.D.
> Executive Director
> Center for Science in the Public Interest

"We agree with David Steinman when he says, 'People have an inalienable right to control their exposure to toxic chemicals.'"

> *Harrowsmith Country Life*

"Facing a contaminated food supply and environment, *Diet For a Poisoned Planet* helps us ask the right questions and offers provocative and useful solutions. It will open your eyes."

> Jay Feldman
> National Coordinator
> National Coalition Against the Misuses of Pesticides

DIET FOR A POISONED PLANET

How to Choose Safe Foods For You and Your Family

David Steinman

Ballantine Books • New York

This edition published by arrangement with Harmony Books, a division of Crown
Publishers, Inc.

Library of Congress Catalog Card Number: 91-92140

ISBN: 0-345-37465-7

Cover design by William Geller

Cover photo by George Kerrigan

Manufactured in the United States of America

First Ballantine Books Edition: April 1992

10 9 8 7 6 5 4 3 2

CONTENTS

FOREWORD

This book will change how you approach the food you eat every day. It may even change the methods used by our farm community to produce our food. Written in the tradition of Upton Sinclair's *The Jungle* and Rachel Carson's *Silent Spring*, *Diet for a Poisoned Planet* overturns the idea that our food supply is free of contamination from toxic chemicals. With great insight and clarity, David Steinman explains which foods promote good health and which foods are so burdened with poisons that they adversely affect your health.

To give you one indication of how far from safe our food is: when calculating the "acceptable" levels of carcinogenic pesticides in food, the Environmental Protection Agency treats each pesticide as if it were the only one to which people are exposed. This, of course, is far from the truth, and it permits a cumulative exposure to many pesticides that can be very dangerous. I feel that this is wrong, and it is my hope that this book will help persuade our government to address these issues of food safety.

Cancer, we are told, is decreasing. This is simply not true. As this book shows, cancer deaths have risen from less than 1 percent of all deaths in the nineteenth century to at least one out of five deaths (20 percent) in the U.S. today. Exposure to carcinogens can be divided into those about which one can make a choice and those that are obligatory. Exposure to carcinogenic pesticides and other toxins in foods is a choice and can be substantially lessened by simply following the suggestions contained in this book. *Diet for a Poisoned Planet* will help you choose the best possible foods that contribute least to your body's toxic burden.

I heartily recommend this book as required reading both because it can help you cut down your exposure to carcinogens and because by following the steps outlined here you can immediately and dramatically improve your health. Many food toxins have low-level neurotoxic effects. Once you follow these instructions, feelings of tiredness and lack of clarity of thought will diminish and feelings of general well-being will return once again. The quality of your life will be measurably improved.

William Marcus, Ph.D., Senior Science Advisor,
U.S. Environmental Protection Agency

The foreword by William Marcus is written in his capacity as a private citizen. Anything he has written is his own opinion and does not necessarily reflect the opinions or policies of his employer, the United States Environmental Protection Agency.

INTRODUCTION

I want to tell you a story. It's a true story, and it happened to me. It could happen to you, too.

I grew up near the ocean in Los Angeles, and I've loved fishing since I was a teenager. Pier fishing, surf casting, party boats—you name it, I did it. And like most fishermen I ate what I caught.

In April 1985, signs appeared at piers and on the beaches of the county of Los Angeles:

WARNING

**Eating fish caught
in Santa Monica Bay
may be harmful to your health
because of chemical contamination.
You should not eat the fish
called white croaker, king fish,
or tom cod.**

I was shocked. I'd been eating locally caught sport fish for years. I wanted to know more. How dangerous were these fish? Was I going to die from having eaten them? It was pretty upsetting. I felt like a victim.

Newspaper reports eventually revealed that DDT-laced waste sludge from a pesticide manufacturing plant had for years been dumped in the area of Santa Monica Bay. To keep the barrels containing waste from floating and creating navigation hazards, barge workers hacked them open before dumping them. The contents of those barrels had accumulated in the

1

bodies of fish feeding in these waters for years. Now they were accumulating in the bodies of people eating those fish.

At the time I was writing for the *L.A. Weekly*. I persuaded my editor there to support me in doing a study with a completely new approach by testing the blood of people who ate a lot of locally caught sport fish. My aim was to find out just how dangerous the fish were.

The answer was even worse than I expected. People who ate a lot of sport fish had serum DDT and PCB levels six to ten times higher than people who did not. I had my blood tested, too. Taking my age into account, I had one of the highest levels in the study group.

This news stunned me, as you may imagine. It started me wondering how many other poisons were in the foods I ate. It started me asking why government officials, who had known about the dumping for years, had withheld the information so long. It started me doing the research that eventually became this book.

I wanted to get rid of the poisons in my body. All the research I saw indicated that the higher the levels of pesticides and industrial pollutants in the blood, the higher the risk of cancer and other diseases. I didn't want to get sick from having unknowingly eaten tainted fish for years.

My first step in cleaning up my body was to determine how toxins get into it in the first place. Finding the answer to that question was not easy. In the past five years I've made hundreds of requests under the Freedom of Information Act for government studies about the safety of our food. I've looked at tens of thousands of chemical analyses of foods. I've analyzed government studies of hundreds of foods and sources of water to find out which have the highest levels of toxins in them, which the lowest. American farmers have used ever-increasing doses of pesticides for decades, and the combination of historical doses in the soil and fresh doses on every crop can make eating an undesirably risky business. But, fortunately, I was able to identify many low-toxin, safe foods that can be found in any supermarket. And I was able to single out the worst foods—the ones we must stay away from.

America's waters are polluted, too, by the runoff from pesticides and by industrial wastes. Fish caught in some waters are simply too dangerous to eat. But again, I was able to identify many seafoods of absolute purity.

As I published the results of my research in magazines and journals, I was thrilled by the responses I got. People were eager to know what I was learning. Across the country, people knew they were ingesting toxins from their diets, but there was no way for them to find out which were the safe foods and which ones were dangerous. I began to see how I could help other people relieve their food anxiety and take the same steps I was taking for safety.

After switching to a diet consisting of the safe foods I had learned about from my studies, I felt better than I ever had before. I lost weight; I had more energy and was in consistently better spirits; I could concentrate longer on my work without fatigue. I rarely got sick. It was a wonderful feeling.

But I couldn't stop wondering whether the toxins lodged in my body years before were still in there, possibly setting the stage for diseases. So I created an active detoxification program, and it worked wonders. After detoxing, the level of DDT in my body was reduced by 70 percent. The level of PCBs decreased 90 percent. This is astonishing when you consider how high the levels had been, and that only a couple of years ago most scientists believed it was impossible to rid your body of these toxic chemicals once they had accumulated in your fat. The active detox program worked for me. It can help you, too. I'll show you how.

How to find safe foods and detox a lifetime's accumulation of toxic chemicals—that is basically what I've put in this book. I think of it as a message of hope. Combining careful food decisions with active detox has changed my life. It can change yours, too. You will feel different. Let your body do the talking.

There's a lot of bad news in here about poisons in our food. It may seem discouraging. But I've got to tell you what's dangerous in order to point you to the foods that are safe.

And there *is* lots of great, safe, delicious food. Believe me, I love to eat, and what's in here is not a deprivation diet. If you follow the principles of what I call the low-toxin high-energy diet, you'll eat food that tastes wonderful and that's great for your body and your mind as well as for our planet. You'll have the extra assurance of knowing that you're not accumulating more twentieth-century poisons with every bite you take. And you'll know that by spending your food dollars on safe foods you're sending a message to industry in support of nontoxic farming and animal-raising methods. It's a liberating feeling.

1. AN END TO FOOD ANXIETY

It seems like we've heard nothing but bad news about foods for the past few years. You know the whole sad litany—dangerous pesticides on apples and other produce, industrial toxins in tap water and bottled water, pesticides and sulfa drugs in milk and some kinds of meat, ethylene dibromide in grains, toxins in fish. Sometimes it seems that nothing is safe to eat, and that we live in a constant state of food anxiety.

But you must not feel helpless. There *is* plenty of safe, delicious food to eat. And for your own well-being you need to find it. That's why I've written this book—to make it easy for you to provide safe meals for yourself and for your family and friends.

Based on five years of research on toxins in food, I've learned that it's possible to cut down significantly the amount of toxins we take in, and by doing so to reduce our chances of serious illness that these toxins can cause. This can be done through what I call the low-toxin high-energy diet. This is a program I have designed to help you eliminate many dangerous chemicals from your diet, avoid the diseases these toxins can cause, improve your health, and increase your energy level.

The basic idea of the diet is very simple. The best way to reduce your intake of dangerous chemicals is to identify the foods that have the highest levels of pesticides and other toxins and cut them right out of your life. In the chapters ahead I analyze hundreds of foods and tell you which ones are toxin free or low in toxins, and which ones are so high in toxins that you should avoid eating them.

Animal fats are a primary route by which many toxins enter our bodies, so the low-toxin high-energy diet is high in plant foods and low in fatty meats and dairy foods. By eating lots of fruits, vegetables, and grains, cutting down on meat and dairy foods, and learning to pick the safest,

4

lowest-toxin foods in all food groups, you can cut down the amount of pesticides and other toxins in your diet. People who are eating a reduced-cholesterol diet will find that they have already started down the road to toxin reduction, as some of the basic principles are the same. The low-toxin high-energy diet will even help most people lose weight! And it helps you feel better, mentally and physically.

Why is the low-toxin high-energy diet necessary? Are toxins in foods really that dangerous? Food-industry lobbyists and government officials constantly tell us that all our foods are safe, so you may be tempted to believe that the minuscule amounts of toxins in your food are too small to harm you. I know—that is the attitude I took for years. I assumed that government regulations would protect my health. Now I know better. Government regulations are much too lenient. They allow foods to be sold in the United States that the government's own scientists know are dangerous. *You* must take responsibility for ensuring the safety of your food.

Many of the toxins affecting us are chemicals used by farmers. Chemicals are used to fertilize the soil, to kill plants that inhibit crop growth, to kill insects and other living things that attack the crops, and to protect the crop from mold, fungus, and insects after harvest. Farmers have been using these chemicals for decades, and the chemicals have built up in the soil from repeated doses year after year. They get inside the crops and onto their outer coverings. They get into water supplies and into the fish who live in them. And they build up in the bodies of animals whose feed has been grown using these chemicals. These chemicals are biological poisons as adept at slowly damaging our cells and organs as they are at killing insects.

Modern agriculture isn't the only culprit. Industrial pollution of air and water is widespread. Auto exhaust and cigarette smoke take their toll. Toxic chemicals linger in tens of thousands of waste dumps across the nation, seeping into water supplies. From all these sources and more, our bodies accumulate toxic chemicals in our tissues.

How do we know these chemicals are dangerous? Study after study shows that chemicals in the actual amounts found in our food and water cause thousands of deaths throughout the population. Just eating the foods and drinking the water of late twentieth-century America can kill you. (I'll discuss some of these studies below. For a more complete discussion of the relationship between pesticides and human cancer, see the Postscript: Pesticides in Our Food.)

More than twenty-five years ago author Rachel Carson awakened America with her book *Silent Spring*. That story of America's growing dependence on pesticides depicted a nation whose landscape had been ravaged by their use. In its wake, several dangerous pesticides were banned.

Ironically, the volume of pesticides applied today is four times more than was used then. Farmers and ranchers have some 50,000 pesticide formulations and 700 chemical ingredients from which to choose.

Our chemical dependency has had tremendous human health consequences. In 1971, when President Richard Nixon declared war on cancer, 337,000 people died annually from the disease. In 1986 472,000 died from it, a 40 percent increase. Of course, not all of this increase can be attributed to toxic chemicals. We must also look at the increased number of women dying from lung cancer due to more women smoking, as well as population increases and the aging of our population. But our cumulative exposure to cancer-causing chemicals dumped in our food, water, and air is also playing a contributing role. Our war against cancer is a long way from being won.

It is interesting to note that only 100 years ago, cancer caused a little more than 3 percent of all deaths in Europe and less in America. And 100 years earlier than that, at the beginning of the nineteenth century, cancer was responsible for less than 1 percent of all deaths. Now cancer kills one out of four American men and one out of five women. Many explanations can be advanced for this huge increase in cancer deaths, including changes in infectious diseases, changes in diagnostic procedures in medicine, changes in exposure to known carcinogens such as tobacco smoke, and changes in life expectancy. But the increasing presence of man-made carcinogens in our food supply is surely a contributing factor.

More cases of cancer than ever are being linked with poisonous man-made chemicals. Cancers of all kinds have been linked with exposure to industrial pollutants and pesticides in food and water. My studies for a variety of organizations including the *Arizona Republic* newspaper and the National Academy of Sciences show that thousands of people potentially will get cancer from insecticides lodged in meat and poultry alone and that thousands more cancers could result just from insecticides lodged in dairy foods and fish.

According to the National Cancer Institute, between 1950 and 1985 in the United States:

• Cancer incidence among children under 15 (who provide an early warning system of problems that will afflict the overall population as it ages) increased 32 percent. Exposure to toxic chemicals in the womb can initiate childhood cancer.

• Urinary bladder cancer incidence increased 51 percent. Scientists have linked increased incidence to exposure to toxic chemicals that taint tap water.

ronmental factors play an important role in its onset. The British medical journal *Lancet* recently reported that widely used fungicides can form stable, fat-soluble compounds with toxic metals and then penetrate the blood-brain barrier. The report's author speculates that these compounds could be linked with the onset of Parkinson's disease. We also know that viruses, methyl-mercury, which is found at high levels in some fish, and a naturally occurring substance in food may also cause Parkinson's. Indeed, there may be multiple causes of Parkinson's disease, including toxic chemicals; that's why exposure reduction is essential.

Even coronary heart disease is, in part, caused by exposure to toxic chemicals. There is strong evidence from several studies that an association exists between elevated blood pressure and heart disease and elevated concentrations of PCBs and other toxic chemicals. Researchers reporting in the journal *Environmental Contamination and Toxicology* noted in a study of pesticide-related jobs and human disease, "There were apparent associations between high serum pesticide [levels] . . . and the subsequent appearance of hypertension, arteriosclerotic cardiovascular disease, and possibly diabetes. This could imply a causal role of any of the pesticidal and other environmental stresses to which these workers were exposed." How could industrial pollutants and pesticides cause coronary heart disease? Some may overstress the liver, which regulates cholesterol, such stress preventing the liver from keeping cholesterol at its proper level in the bloodstream.

Toxic chemicals may well play an even more significant role in the formation of arterial plaque in the human body, which leads to both stroke and coronary heart disease. Researchers have reported in *Scientific American*, "In the past 15 years it has become clear that [arterial] plaque is characterized by an accumulation of smooth muscle cells. The important question is: Why do the cells accumulate? Some of us now think the cells of a plaque are the progeny of a single mutated smooth-muscle cell from near the site of the plaque. If that is so, the plaque is comparable to a benign tumor of the artery wall. And if it is comparable then the search for initiating factors should be directed toward the genetic and environmental factors that cause mutation—the same kinds of agents and conditions that transform cells and thus initiate cancers." It is known that atherosclerotic plaques can be produced in the arteries of laboratory animals by the administration of toxic chemicals such as dimethylbenz[a]anthracene. Other toxic chemicals, experts strongly suspect, play the same role.

Cancer, Alzheimer's disease, Parkinson's disease, and heart disease are late consequences of exposure. Researchers on the cutting edge of chemical toxicology have established that among the first consequences of exposure to common toxic chemicals is neurotoxicity: reduced mental functioning, decreased IQ and mental acuity, inability to concentrate, and loss of feeling. Cancer, which has gotten much of the attention, is one of the last consequences to appear. Most people today have no conception of true mental clarity. We have all been exposed to low-level chemical residues for so long that it is difficult to conceive of life without their subtle neurotoxic effects.

Other insidious conditions, including diabetes, Epstein-Barr syndrome, chronic fatigue syndrome, weakened immunity, and anxiety, may result from a buildup of industrial pollution and pesticides. A child who has demonstrated antisocial and irrational behavior may slowly be driven crazy by food and drink laced with additives and preservatives and may be cured with a natural, wholesome diet of foods free of these toxic chemicals.

The bottom line is that industrial pollution and pesticides that come in drinking water and with breakfast, lunch, and dinner can accelerate cancer, increase chances of secondary disease, decrease mental clarity, and shave years from your life.

Unfortunately, most doctors know little about the impact of chemicals in food and water. Most have no training at all in chemical toxicology. In its landmark 1988 publication *Role of the Primary Care Physician in Occupational Environmental Medicine,* an expert committee of the National Academy of Sciences concluded that almost the entire medical field is functionally illiterate on the subject of the low-level toxicology of industrial pollution and pesticides. The committee also concluded that toxic chemicals are playing an increasingly significant role in the onset of disease and death. No wonder many persons whose illnesses are linked with a toxic chemical are never able to alleviate them; their doctors never think to check their blood or other bodily tissues for toxic chemicals. Yet, people are increasingly afflicted with chemical illnesses, and physicians must learn to recognize the symptoms that reflect industrial pollution and pesticide exposure through food and water. I believe that just as in the eighties many people checked their blood for cholesterol, in the nineties we will learn to have the toxic chemical levels of our blood checked. Fortunately, blood profiles are as easy to do as cholesterol tests. Many illnesses for which doctors can presently find no cure may be curable and manageable as we find their causes in toxic chemical burdens in our bloodstream and other tissues.

Little as they know about tracing environmentally caused diseases, doctors and scientists are even more dumbfounded when it comes to determining the effects of cumulative low-level exposures to many different toxic chemicals. The government's best scientists say they do not have the faintest idea how to test multiple chemicals in animal model systems. Experts know very little about how to test the effects of two chemicals together, let alone four, five, or ten.

When scientists have done studies on this chemical cocktail syndrome, it seems quite clear that they act synergistically. In one small 1976 study reported in the *Journal of Food Science,* a scientific team used three chemicals on a group of rats. The chemicals were tested one at a time on the rats without ill effect. When the scientists gave the rats two at a time, a decline in health was noted. When the rats were given all three chemicals at once, they all died within two weeks.

This is the kind of situation most of us face. We get several little bits of pesticides with our salad, different ones in our meat or fish, still others in the vegetables on the side, and a separate dose of additives and preservatives with dessert. Our wine has pesticides and for many of us our water, too. In addition our drinking water may contain solvents as well as lead. In a single meal we could easily consume residues of a dozen different neurotoxic or carcinogenic chemicals. Every meal, every drink of water, every day.

The EPA Office of Pesticide Programs does not even include all our potential exposures to the same pesticide when calculating permitted residue levels of a given compound on a single crop. The agency sets levels with "blinders" to the fact that people eat more than one product that has permitted residues of the same compound. EPA scientists have found that, at times, these residues, if totaled, exceeded 500 percent of the recommended daily intake.

We are told constantly that the level of a toxin in a certain food is "absolutely safe." But how many "absolutely safe" doses does it take before it's not safe anymore?

Most of the foods discussed in this book fall within the guidelines set by the government for toxins in our food. But the government's maximum contaminant levels are much too lenient. They are reached in conjunction with the food and chemical industries, and the standards do not take into account the fact that people are ingesting toxins from hundreds of sources. When the EPA sets a maximum contaminant level for a toxin in a particular food, it is based on the assumption that people will take in that toxin *only from that food.* This is convenient for scientific purposes, but patently false when dealing with the real world, where we all take in many toxins from many sources. Most chemicals in our food have not been adequately tested for human safety. And they have certainly not been tested with the chemical cocktail syndrome in mind. The EPA does not have a scientifically acceptable method for determining the risk for multiple chemical exposures from residues or any other environmental poisons.

No one knows whether regularly eating foods like salami, which a careful FDA study found to have a very high number of pesticide residues, will give a particular person cancer. But why add salami's toxins to all the other unavoidable toxins we breathe and drink and eat every day when so many other, far safer foods are available? Instead of a salami sandwich, why not have turkey breast, which has very few residues? That is the kind of choice

I want to help you make. There are hundreds of safe foods. So why eat unsafe ones when you don't have to?

The low-toxin high-energy diet outlined in these pages fits well within the guidelines put forward by the American Heart Association, the American Cancer Society, and the Surgeon General. It has been reviewed by nutrition experts and doctors, and I'm confident it presents a balanced, nourishing, and pleasing approach to food.

2. PLANT FOODS

You don't have to fall victim to chemical farming. Eating well is your best defense.

And eating plenty of plant foods is the key. It is the best way to gain an edge over toxic chemical pollution. Plant foods are the cornerstone of the low-toxin high-energy diet. If this book does nothing else but persuade you to increase the amount of plant foods you eat and cut down on animal foods, I will have accomplished a great deal.

This may seem surprising, since the chemicals applied to plant foods are among the major toxins that I'll come back to again and again in this book. But even the worst, most chemical-laced plant foods are much better for you than almost all animal foods. This is because plants are low on the food web. They consume nutrients from soil, water, and air. When you eat plant foods the only toxins you'll get are the ones that were freshly sprayed on the crop or that those plants pulled in from the limited span of their own root networks.

But cows, pigs, and other animals raised for slaughter concentrate in their flesh toxins from all the food they eat—thousands of plants laced with chemical pesticides. And the pesticides that accumulate in animal flesh are the same ones that can accumulate in human flesh. The higher up on the food web you eat, the greater concentration of toxins you are likely to consume. Humans, not surprisingly, are among the most poisoned creatures on earth.

It is important to avoid toxins everywhere you can, and I'll show you which plant foods have the highest and lowest concentrations of toxins. There are big differences, and you need to be able to tell safe from dangerous produce items. Some food crops usually receive heavy doses of pesticides; others get very little. But don't let the fact that there may be pesticides on plant foods deter you if there's nothing else around—always prefer plant foods to animal foods.

I am not a vegetarian, and I am not sure that I will ever swear off meat and poultry completely. But I eat them seldom, and as I show you the benefits of a diet high in plant foods and the dangers of a diet high in animal flesh, I hope you will make up your mind to do the same.

Fresh fruits, vegetables, grains, legumes, nuts, and seeds aren't just low in toxins. They also contain essential nutrients that actually help your body resist disease, prevent cancer, and resist the ravages of chemical pollution. This was summed up clearly and directly in a 1980 article in the *Journal of the American Dietetic Association:* "A growing body of scientific evidence supports a positive relationship between the consumption of a plant-based diet and the prevention of certain diseases."

In the low-toxin high-energy diet, plant foods should make up at least two-thirds of all your meals, preferably even more. I call this the two-thirds rule. Remember it daily! Nutritionists say you should eat at least four several-ounce servings daily of fruits and vegetables and four servings daily of beans, grains, and nuts; two servings daily of dairy foods for adults, three to four servings for children; and two servings a day of meat, poultry, fish, or eggs. I go beyond this conventional wisdom. I do not believe you need more than one flesh serving (meat, poultry, fish, or eggs) a day. Many days I eat no meat, poultry, fish, dairy, or eggs at all.

For snacks and desserts, keep plenty of fresh fruits and vegetables on hand instead of sweets and prepared foods. Because they are sustaining, satiating foods, fruits and vegetables provide an excellent snack in place of fatty animal foods. Fruits such as figs or oranges are a much better sweet snack for children than contaminant-loaded candy bars, which are extraordinarily high in cancer-causing pesticides such as BHC and lindane. When socializing, if you must decide between foods such as frankfurters, hamburgers, and prepared foods, or fresh fruits and vegetables, always choose fruits and vegetables. At a cookout, I'll make my entire meal from the crudité tray rather than eat hot dogs or hamburgers. The vegetables will be hugely lower in pesticide saturation than the meats, and their high fiber content will help your body rid itself of contaminants.

Do you need to lose a few pounds? Studies show that vegetarians are less likely to be overweight than meat eaters, and simply increasing the amount of plant foods you eat—with a corresponding decrease in animal foods, of course—will start you losing weight. People who love to eat but must lose weight can eat as much as they desire of simple whole-grain foods and water-heavy fresh fruits and vegetables such as grapefruit, strawberries, watermelon, asparagus, broccoli, cauliflower, and endive without conscience pangs.

Have you discovered that your cholesterol level is above 180 milligrams per deciliter? Are you the worried owner of an overstressed circulatory system hindered by high blood pressure? Perhaps you should eat a few extra spears of asparagus, a few more spoonfuls of kidney beans, and plenty of fresh fruit at your meals instead of chowing down on pesticide-saturated quarter-pound hamburgers, french fries, and milk shakes. Diets high in plant foods cut down mortality from coronary heart disease (probably regardless of their degree of pesticide contamination). Diets in which 60 to 70 percent of the calories come from starch, such as those consumed in Asian countries, are associated with low plasma cholesterol levels and low risk for coronary heart disease. Such diets tend to be very high in fiber and very low in saturated fat.

The beef industry would have us believe there is considerable debate about the role that diet has on lowering blood cholesterol levels. The meat industry has pointed out that some people eat a lot of meat and have very low cholesterol levels. Others eat very little meat and yet they have very high cholesterol. So, they say, how could animal flesh be implicated in plasma cholesterol concentrations? But these are the exceptions, not the rule. Overall, the numbers shake out very clearly: vegetarians have far lower cholesterol levels. One group of strict vegetarians from the Boston area who ate absolutely no animal products—not even dairy products or eggs—had an average blood cholesterol of about 125 milligrams per deciliter. Dr. William Castelli, director of the federal government's Framingham Heart Study in Massachusetts, said he has *never* seen anybody with a cholesterol level below 150 suffer a heart attack. Across the Atlantic, a study of more than ten thousand vegetarians and meat eaters in England reported similar results. For decades medical evidence has shown quite clearly that vegetarians and people who eat meat and poultry only a few times a month have far lower blood cholesterol levels.

Many people fear that if they cut down on meat they will not get enough protein. That is a myth. Animal protein is *not* superior to plant protein. Virtually all vitamins and minerals that animal foods provide are found in abundance in plant foods and seafood. The fact is that many of the healthiest, most long-lived persons on the planet are largely vegetarian.

Lately our knowledge of our protein needs has undergone a dramatic shift. We now know that a well-rounded diet combining a variety of fruits, vegetables, grains, legumes, nuts, and seeds will provide more than enough high-quality protein. As the noted British medical journal, the *Lancet,* editorialized more than thirty years ago: "Formerly, vegetable proteins were classified as second-class, and regarded as inferior to first-class proteins of animal origin, but this distinction has now been generally discarded."

We also now know that protein is not our primary source of energy.

Once we believed that persons involved in strenuous activity needed a great deal more protein than sedentary individuals. But now we know that complex carbohydrates, which we get in abundance from fruits, vegetables, beans, and grains, satisfy our energy needs.

Vegetable proteins are not always complete proteins alone. To create complete proteins containing all the amino acids necessary for human growth, you need to mix different vegetables with grains, beans, and seeds. This is called protein complementing.

Protein complementing is very simple. You can combine grains such as whole wheat, pasta, breads, oats, and rye with legumes such as soybeans and soy foods, kidney beans, navy beans, mung beans, bean sprouts, and peanuts. A sandwich made with whole wheat bread, organic peanut butter, and organic fruit conserve is an excellent high-protein pesticide-free snack. Or sprinkle walnuts, cashews, and other nuts on your whole grain cereal with dairy milk or soy milk to help create a high-quality protein. These are all complete protein meals.

The rule of thumb is this: grains combined with legumes equal a perfect protein. For example, a pasta main course with a side of kidney bean salad offers a complete protein. So does beans and rice. For excellent information on protein combining, read Frances Moore Lappé's classic, *Diet for a Small Planet*.

Registered dietician Elaine Grossman of the Nutrition Network, Los Angeles, has developed several charts, which I have reprinted here, that show many ways of combining plant foods to make complete proteins.

In addition to protein, plant foods provide a vast array of nutritional riches, from complex carbohydrates and fiber to virtually all the essential vitamins and minerals, including micronutrients, of which the body needs a minuscule amount for proper functioning. Together these nutrients protect the body against many diseases and cancer, including those caused by toxic chemicals.

Former Surgeon General C. Everett Koop has noted that a large body of evidence suggests that foods high in vitamin A help to protect the body against a variety of cancers. Green vegetables and orange-yellow vegetables are rich in vitamin A, and the Surgeon General has stated that these vegetables may contain many other protective components in addition to vitamin A. One study of an older population in Massachusetts has demonstrated that the risk for all cancers decreases with increasing intake of vegetables containing liberal amounts of vitamin A.

Foods containing vitamin A may help to protect women against cancer of the breast and cervix. Vitamin A–rich foods can also help prevent cancer of the bladder, colon, and stomach; each of these cancers, by the way, has been linked with exposure to toxic chemicals in food and water; bladder cancer and colon cancer can result, for example, from exposure to toxic

PLANT FOOD COMBINATIONS THAT MAKE COMPLETE PROTEINS

Whole Grains	with	Legumes, Greens, and Other Vegetables
Such as:		Such as:
Barley		Asparagus
Brown rice		Beet greens
Brown rice flour		Black-eyed peas
Buckwheat (buckwheat pancakes and soba noodles)		Broccoli
		Brussels sprouts
Bulgur wheat		Cauliflower
Corn on the cob		Collard greens
Cornmeal (cornbread and corn tortillas)		Garbanzo beans
		Green peas
Millet		Kidney beans
Oats (oat bran, oatmeal)		Lima beans
Rye (rye breads and rye crisps)		Navy beans
		Northern beans
Whole wheat (bagels, breads, breadsticks, cereal, crackers, graham crackers, lupini pasta, matzoh, muffins, pasta, pita bread, pretzels, tortillas, and triticale flour)		Okra
		Snap green beans
		Soybeans
		Spinach
		Tofu
		Tofu hot dogs
		Vegi-burgers (made with tofu)
		Peanuts
		Peanut butter
		Peanut oatmeal cookies

Potatoes	with	Greens and Other Vegetables
		Such as:
		Broccoli
		Collard greens
		Corn
		Mustard greens
		Okra
		Spinach

PLANT FOOD COMBINATIONS THAT MAKE
COMPLETE PROTEINS (*continued*)

Legumes	with	Greens and Other Vegetables
Such as:		Such as:
Black-eyed peas		Beet greens
Garbanzo beans		Collard greens
Green peas		Kale
Kidney beans		Mustard greens
Lima beans		Okra
Navy beans		Spinach
Northern beans		Sweet potatoes
Peanuts		Swiss chard
Peanut butter		Winter squash
Snap green beans		Yams
Soybeans		
Tofu		
Tofu hot dogs		
Vegi-burgers		
(made with tofu)		

chemicals in drinking water; stomach cancer may result from exposure to nitrites in cured meats and other cured foods.

Air pollution's toxic effects can also be mitigated with liberal amounts of vitamin A. Epidemiologic evidence correlates consumption of vegetables rich in vitamin A with decreased lung cancer. In fact, one study of nearly two thousand middle-aged men found that although animal foods and vegetables are both rich in vitamin A, dark yellow, orange, and green vegetables offered the best protection from lung cancer. Experts are not certain that it is the vitamin A in these vegetables that offers the cancer protection. It could be due to vitamin C or other unmeasured nutrients in the vegetables. But whether it was vitamin A or other nutrients, the message is the same: consumption of vegetables such as carrots, collards, broccoli, Brussels sprouts, and kale offers our bodies excellent protection against the formation of cancerous tissues, particularly in the alimentary tract.

Vitamin A–rich vegetables also contain antioxidant chemicals that protect against the formation of oxygen-free radicals. Oxygen-free radicals are formed in our bodies from a variety of environmental sources, including industrial pollutants and pesticides. They attach themselves to other molecules in the body and form cancer-causing compounds; this process is called oxidation. Experts compare cellular oxidation to rusting. Cellular oxidation is associated with damage to the cell's vital genetic material, DNA and RNA. This genetic material is responsible for providing instructions to your cells on how to repair or replace themselves. Because they can make the cell's genetic material go haywire, it is not surprising that these harmful oxidizing chemicals account for an increased risk of cancer. Those vitamins and minerals that prevent damage from cellular rusting are called antioxidants. Vitamin A also enhances our immune system response.

Vitamin A is also potentially toxic. People who consume large amounts of vitamin supplements (and, less commonly, animal livers) have experienced toxic effects such as headaches, skin and bone disorders, renal failures, and birth defects in their offspring. Vitamin A toxicity in children has been caused by taking over 50,000 IU a day. In adults, toxicity has been caused by taking over 100,000 IU a day. Getting vitamin A from plant foods is one way to avoid vitamin A toxicity. Excessive intake of plant foods that are rich sources of a form of vitamin A known as beta carotene is not known to cause toxic effects.

These vegetables are richest in vitamin A:

Carrots	Pumpkin
Chinese cabbage	Red peppers
Collard greens	Spinach
Dandelion greens	Sweet potatoes
Mustard greens	Turnip greens

These vegetables are also good sources:

Asparagus	Lettuce
Beet greens	Peas
Broccoli	Winter Squash
Brussels sprouts	Tomatoes
Endive	

These fruits are the richest in vitamin A:

Apricots	Mangoes
Cantaloupes	Peaches

These fruits are also good sources:

Avocados	Plantains
Cherries	Tangerines
Nectarines	Watermelons

A rule of thumb for selecting vitamin A–rich fruits and vegetables is to look for the most deeply colored produce.

Many vitamin A–rich fruits and vegetables are also rich in B vitamins.

The B vitamins are absolutely necessary for the body to function properly; they are invaluable during high-stress periods. The nutrients in the B vitamin complex help the brain function at top performance levels; these nutrients also fight depression.

Vitamin B_1—also known as thiamine—is an excellent antistress nutrient that the body needs in order to convert blood sugar into energy. Without thiamine, we would suffer severe brain disorders similar in effect to senile dementia. The B complex vitamins choline and lecithin are two nutrients that the body needs in order to produce acetylcholine, a neurotransmitting chemical that allows us to transmit messages from the brain to other nerve cells.

Vitamin B_{12} is the one nutrient that people who eat *no* animal foods have to be extra careful to get enough of. Vitamin B_{12} is an essential nutrient in our fight against pernicious anemia, stress, and fatigue. The richest sources of vitamin B_{12} are animal foods, including cheese, fish, liver, kidney, meat, milk, shellfish, whole eggs, and egg yolks, but many of these foods are saturated with pesticides. One 3-ounce serving of lean beef provides 79 percent of our daily vitamin B_{12} needs. Vegans—vegetarians who eat no dairy products or eggs—have to be especially careful: A British study of vegans reported that 35 percent had very low levels of B_{12} in their blood serum. However, there are other less abundant nonflesh sources of vitamin B_{12} such as soybeans, wheat germ, yeast, and comfrey leaves, and there are plenty of good seafood sources for vitamin B_{12}, plus skim (nonfat) milk and nonfat yogurt.

Good plant sources of other B vitamins include leafy vegetables, raw nuts, legumes, whole grains, and wheat germ.

Vegetables rich in B vitamins include:

> Black-eyed peas
> Brewer's yeast
> Green peas
> Jerusalem artichokes
> Lettuce
> Tomatoes

Fruits rich in B vitamins include:

> Avocados
> Oranges
> Pineapples
> Raisins
> Watermelons

Vitamin C is another antioxidant and a vital antipollution vitamin. It is found in greatest concentrations in fresh fruits and vegetables. Many studies have demonstrated vitamin C's cancer-deterring strengths. Biochemical studies suggest that vitamin C blocks the formation of carcinogens from cured meats such as bacon, ham, and smoked fish. Vitamin C has been shown to reduce bladder tumors induced by chemical carcinogens. Human studies have shown that foods containing vitamin C protect against cancers of the esophagus, stomach, and cervix. Supplements of vitamins C and E have been shown to reduce the formation of mutagenic chemicals in the gastrointestinal tract, which may be an important means of protection against cancers of the colon and intestines. Vitamin C protects experimental animals' lung cultures from the mutagenic effects of tobacco smoke. And biochemical studies show that vitamin C also prevents oxidation of certain chemicals to active carcinogenic forms. People living in heavily polluted areas need plenty of vitamin C.

Fresh fruits and vegetables are the main source of this essential vitamin. Animal foods have virtually none. It is best to get your vitamin C from fresh fruits and vegetables rather than from vitamin supplements, which are only imperfect imitations of their natural counterparts.

Fruits richest in vitamin C include:

Cantaloupes
Grapefruit
Lemons
Oranges
Papayas
Strawberries

Vegetables rich in vitamin C include:

Broccoli
Brussels sprouts
Cauliflower
Red peppers

Another antioxidant, vitamin E, appears to protect the body from cancer. Vitamin E, like vitamin C, blocks the formation of cancer-causing chemicals from the nitrites in cured meats. It can also help the body fight toxic chemicals, including cigarette smoke, in air pollution. Athletes should note that vitamin E is essential to the transport of oxygen into the bloodstream. Because aerobic exercise puts an extreme oxygen demand on the body, intense exercise puts greater vitamin E demands on the body, which could require supplementation.

Especially rich vitamin E sources include unfiltered cold-pressed vegetable oils, almonds, and peanuts. Be sure to buy organically grown peanuts, however, because there is significant pesticide contamination of chemically grown peanuts.

Did you know that every single cell in your body contains calcium? Did you know calcium regulates your heartbeat and that diets rich in calcium can help prevent coronary heart disease and hypertension? Calcium may even help prevent cancer by contributing to the orderly reproduction of your cells. Calcium is often used to help the body excrete heavy metals such as lead. A calcium-rich diet will prevent significant lead absorption in people who have an adequate iron intake. Since today we are bombarded with lead in our food, water, and air, this is especially vital.

Scientists have noted that calcium-rich diets actually alleviate the symptoms of anxiety, and they speculate that a calcium-deficient diet may result in anxiety disorders with symptoms such as heart palpitation, tremors, nausea, choking sensations, and blurred vision. The beneficial effects of vitamin A may also be enhanced by a diet rich in calcium.

Plant foods rich in calcium include:

Almonds	Figs
Beans	Kale
Beet greens	Oranges
Broccoli	Soybeans
Chinese cabbage	Tahini
Collards	Turnip greens
Dandelion greens	

Copper is another one of the trace minerals our bodies *must* have. Experts know very little about its contribution to our health, but they do know that copper plays a role in the production of blood hemoglobin. Indeed, some anemia can be cured only when iron is supplemented with copper. Copper helps the body use vitamin C. Copper is also able to prevent weakening of the walls of blood vessels, most notably the aorta, thus helping in the prevention of aneurysms and ruptures. Copper also helps in the prevention of heart disease. Copper helps prevent radiation damage, which may be in part why the pancreas, spleen, and white blood cells—all of which are naturally low in copper—are the organs most susceptible to radiation damage. Most Americans do get enough copper in their diets.

Fruits rich in copper include:

Apricots
Avocados
Currants

    Figs
    Prunes

Nuts rich in copper include:

    Almonds
    Brazil nuts
    Hazelnuts
    Peanuts
    Pecans
    Walnuts

Vegetables and legumes rich in copper include:

    Broccoli
    Kidney beans
    Lima beans
    Mushrooms
    Navy beans
    Peas

Selenium is another absolutely essential micronutrient. Working together with vitamin E, selenium enhances immune functions. It has been shown to prevent cancer, slow the aging process, and prevent heart and circulatory diseases. According to Dr. Michael Weiner, Ph.D., author of the excellent book *Reducing the Risk of Alzheimer's,* selenium together with vitamin E can play an instrumental role in prevention of Alzheimer's disease. Vegetables such as asparagus and garlic and many grains are rich in selenium. Seafood is also a rich source.

Once again, selenium in excess can be toxic. Be sure to vary your food sources; this will help eliminate any chance of ingesting toxic amounts of selenium from any one source. I don't advise unsupervised selenium supplementation because of the narrow range of safe levels.

Trying to remember which plant foods have which nutrients is pretty tough. You can make copies of these lists to use in planning your meals. But there is an easier way. When shopping for plant foods, try mixing colors. By eating lots of different fruits and vegetables with many shades of green, red, yellow, and orange, you know you are getting the full range of the nutrients these plant foods have to offer.

One of the best things about a diet high in plant foods is that it can actually help you undo the damage that pesticides and other dietary toxins have done to your body. Fiber is the key. Fiber binds toxic chemicals that are circulating in your body and moves them rapidly through your body. In addition, the spongelike nature of fiber helps scrub clean the thousands of nooks and crannies of your large intestine where carcinogens can pass through into the bloodstream. Fiber reduces the amount of time that chemical carcinogens spend in your body so they have less chance to damage cells. Fruits, vegetables, and especially grains are high in fiber. Animal foods have no fiber.

Of course, fiber also absorbs nutrients and moves them through the body, limiting absorption. But with a healthy diet that includes a wide variety of fruits, vegetables, and legumes and limited amounts of animal foods, you will have all the nutrients your body needs.

Even if you have been a heavy-duty carnivore for years, you can start to eat much larger quantities of grains, fresh fruits, vegetables, legumes, nuts, and seeds. This will start your detoxification process.

3. VEGETABLES AND FRUITS

In this world of chemically grown crops there are big differences in the way our favorite fruits and vegetables are grown. Some crops are sprayed with far more pesticides than others, and some absorb more pesticides than others into their edible parts. Some favorites such as apples, peaches, raisins, and spinach are drenched in pesticides. Other fruits such as the edible portions of oranges and bananas and vegetables including asparagus and cauliflower are usually far less tainted with chemicals. When I am in a market and have to choose between different chemically grown fruits and vegetables, I'm careful to choose nontoxic produce. I pretty much know which plant foods are relatively pesticide-free, and I remember, for example, that pineapples and watermelons have far fewer pesticide residues than cantaloupes; oranges and tangerines have fewer residues than apples; beans are nontoxic; and bananas and corn are fine.

In many cases, these differences in pesticide saturation are very significant. The bottom line for predicting health risks associated with any particular toxic chemical exposure is that the more frequently one is exposed and the higher the level of exposure, the greater the risk. Conversely, the less frequently one is exposed and the lower the concentration, the lower the risk. It is that simple.

Vegetable and Fruit Survival Guide

In order to determine which vegetables and fruits are safest, I examined detailed government food inspectors' reports and private studies of chemical residues in more than 150 fruits, vegetables, beans, nuts, and seeds. In this chapter and much of the book, the study I found most useful was a

25

huge research effort called the Total Diet Study, an ongoing study conducted by the Food and Drug Administration. It is the most accurate
assessment ever made of pesticide contamination of our food supply.

In the Total Diet Study, hundreds of common foods are analyzed each
year for more than one hundred different industrial chemicals and pesticides. The tests look for pesticides down to minute levels; the laboratory
detection limits used in this study are five to ten times more sensitive than
the methods used in laboratories that simply test items for regulatory
enforcement. Food samples are taken from four different geographic regions in the United States. These samples include the major name brands
of food that everyone buys, as well as local varieties. All the foods are
prepared as they would be in the home before they are analyzed, so the
residues detected are the ones that normal food preparation cannot eliminate. Often, studies focus on raw agricultural commodities fresh from the
fields, when pesticide levels are highest. To be as accurate as possible,
this study analyzes all foods exactly as they would be eaten, after preparation and cooking. If anything, this method slightly understates the pesticide saturation of foods.

The prepared foods are tested for more than one hundred different
chemicals. Some of the chemicals tested for have long since been banned,
but they persist in the soil or are still applied to crops in foreign countries
and are then imported and sold in American markets. Some of these pesticides have never been used in the United States but are used abroad and
show up on imported foods. But most of the chemicals tested for and found
are pesticides applied to crops by farmers across America.

For this book, I have used the Total Diet Study results for the most
recent four years available, ending in 1986. Since samples have been tested
from four geographic regions each year for four years, there are sixteen
samples for each food discussed.

The Total Diet Study measured the total number of residues found in
the sixteen samples. Common lettuce, for instance, had thirty-six residues
in sixteen samples. This means that, on the average, each of the sixteen
samples of lettuce analyzed had between two and three pesticide residues
in it. The study also listed the different kinds of pesticides found. In lettuce
there were nine. In addition, the study measured the concentration of each
pesticide in the food, in parts per million or parts per billion.

Fresh and canned fruits and vegetables were analyzed. Most canned
produce has far fewer pesticide residues than fresh. One reason for this
lower pesticide saturation is the additional processing that canned produce
undergoes, including extra washing and peeling, which help remove toxic
residues, particularly those on the surface of the fruit or vegetable. Another may be that additional pesticides are added to fresh produce throughout the distribution process. Unfortunately, canned produce may have

significantly more lead, to which we do not want to be exposed, and canned produce often has added salt or sugar. It also undergoes slight nutrient losses, especially of vitamins. Your best bet for good health is to purchase the least toxic fresh produce you can find. Fresh frozen produce is a good choice as well; it often has higher nutrient value than canned produce, and it can equal the nutrient value of fresh produce.

Organic fruits and vegetables are the safest, lowest-toxin fruits and vegetables available, and I strongly recommend that you seek out organic produce, especially as a substitute for the most pesticide-saturated foods. Organic farming is booming in this country as consumers demand safer, purer foods.

Organic foods are not readily available in many places, though, and for many people their higher cost is a burden. My goal in writing this book has been to show people which foods are safe and which foods are so high in toxins that organic or other substitutes are advisable.

Throughout this book, I've divided foods into "green light," "yellow light," and "red light" categories. I trust that what this means is obvious. Green light foods are your safest choices; you should eat them as often as you like. Yellow light foods are more saturated. Cut down on them; when possible, buy organic. And red light foods are dangerous. I've cut them out of my diet completely, or found organic substitutes for them. If you do eat them, try to do so seldom.

This division of foods into green light, yellow light, and red light groupings is a simplification of a huge amount of data. My goal in dividing foods this way has been to make it clear that there are significant differences in the toxicity of different foods. I have used two findings from the Total Diet Study as guidelines in dividing foods into these groups: which toxins were found in each food, and the total number of residues found.

In the section that follows, and throughout the book, I list the names of the toxins found in each food. Some of the names are probably familiar— DDT, dieldrin, and heptachlor, for example—and some are pretty arcane. I've listed them all, because I feel that it's important that we know our enemy. These are the poisons in our food! A short list of some of the most dangerous pesticides and other chemicals commonly found in food appears in the table below. In the back of the book I've provided a glossary where you can find out more about most of these toxins, what they are used for, and how dangerous they are.

I've told you the total number of residues found in each food because that number will give you a good idea of the relative safety of different foods. In most instances, the foods with the largest number of pesticide residues present the highest risk of cancer, and the foods with the fewest residues are the safest.

TABLE 1. COMMONLY FOUND CANCER-CAUSING
PESTICIDES AND THEIR CANCER POTENCY

Acephate	.0069
Azinphos-methyl	.00000015
Benomyl	.002065
Benzene hexachloride (BHC)*	6.3
Captafol	.025
Captan	.0023
Chlordane*	1.3
DDT*	.34
Dicofol	.44
Dieldrin*	16.0
Folpet	.0035
Heptachlor*	4.5
Hexachlorobenzene (HCB)*	1.7
Lindane*	1.3
Linuron	.328
Parathion	.0018
Permethrin	.03

Some of the most dangerous cancer-causing pesticides are ranked here according to their carcinogenic potency, a scale of relative carcinogenicity determined by the Environmental Protection Agency based on animal experiments. The larger the number, the more carcinogenically potent the chemical. Not all pesticides suspected to cause cancer have had a cancer potency number assigned, so many pesticides that may cause human cancer are not included in this list. Pesticides followed by an asterisk have been banned for use but are still present in the soil or are used on foreign crops, which are then imported into the United States.

I have not supplied information on the concentrations of each toxin because this information would have made the text much more complex without telling much more about how dangerous the foods are. With very few exceptions, the more total residues that are present in a food, the higher their concentrations. Conversely, those foods with the lowest number of residues usually have the lowest concentrations. In those few cases where this rule does not apply and a food with few residues has very high concentrations, I have pointed this out and placed such foods under the appropriate yellow or red light category.

For example, let's compare apples and oranges. Apples had eighty pesticide residues in the sixteen samples, oranges had twenty-three. Whereas apples had residues of several cancer-causing pesticides, including acephate, azinphos-methyl, BHC, captan, DDT, dicofol, and parathion, oranges had either no residues of these pesticides, or the residues had significantly lower concentrations. The concentration of parathion in apples was four times higher than in oranges. The concentration of dicofol was forty-two times higher in apples than in oranges. Knowing that apples had significantly more pesticide residues than oranges, we also know that apples had larger doses of the pesticides that were present. This logic applies in almost all cases.

In vegetables, contrast collard greens with lettuce. Collards contained eighty-seven pesticide residues, lettuce only thirty-six. Collards had far more carcinogenic pesticide residues. Of those pesticides found in both collards and lettuce, demeton-s sulfone, diazinon, dimethoate, endosulfan, methomyl, mevinphos, and methamidophos, the concentrations were all far higher on collards, except for methamidophos, which is not a carcinogen.

For about one-third of the foods evaluated in this book, I was able to perform relative cancer risk assessments using a standard government formula. Thus the placement of foods into green, yellow, and red light groups was based not only upon the number of total residues and their concentration in food but also on the outcome of these cancer risk assessments. These are all objective benchmarks.

Cancer risk assessments are performed using cancer potency figures assigned by federal agencies to some chemicals. Not all cancer-causing chemicals have been assigned a cancer potency factor. I was able to perform these assessments only for those foods that contained chemicals for which cancer potencies have been calculated. Cancer potency figures are based on animal experiments, and the higher the potency factor number the more carcinogenic the substance. I have used cancer potency factors that were developed by the EPA.

Cancer risk assessments take into account the potency factor, the amount of food ingested, the concentration of the chemical in the food, and the weight of the consumer. The number finally derived tells the number of cancers that one chemical alone can cause in one million persons eating the food containing that chemical. The formula does not take into account the cancer burden created by the combination of many carcinogens, or by other dietary sources of the same chemical. Still, cancer potency factors are useful as benchmarks for comparing relative risks.

In performing these analyses, I assumed that the same amounts of all foods would be eaten daily. Obviously we don't eat two ounces of everything daily. But this allows us to compare the foods objectively.

Generally, foods that would cause up to five excess cancers in one million persons were placed in the green group. Foods that would cause five to ten cancers were placed under yellow. Foods with risks beyond ten were placed under red.

Almost all of the foods discussed in this book, including green light foods, have some pesticide residues. By calling foods with pesticide residues green light foods, I do not mean to give the impression that it is absolutely and completely safe to eat foods with toxic residues in them. If I could, I would eat nothing but foods raised with no pesticides, herbicides, or other toxins. But that is simply not possible. So I do the best I can by limiting my consumption of yellow and red light foods and eating all the green light foods I can. The foods grouped under the green light heading are the safest foods in any supermarket.

At the end of this chapter (and all chapters) I've summarized the information in the survival guide into a safe shopping list you can refer to easily or have copied to take shopping with you.

You may notice, if you compare the survival guide in this chapter with survival guides in other chapters, that there is no hard line dividing green light foods, yellow light foods, and red light foods. A vegetable with fifty pesticide residues may be in the yellow light group, while a cut of meat with fifty residues is in the red light group. This is because different kinds of foods often concentrate different toxins, some of which are more harmful than others. I have taken these differences into account in dividing foods into different categories.

GREEN LIGHT

Green light means go! The fruits and vegetables listed below are the safest nonorganic foods available. Eat them as often as you like.

Alfalfa sprouts. Alfalfa sprouts had no detectable pesticide residues.

Applesauce. Canned sweetened applesauce had thirteen residues in sixteen samples, representing six different formulations. The most frequently detected pesticide was carbaryl, which was present in at least one-fourth of the samples. Less frequently detected industrial chemicals and pesticides included diazinon, dicloran, dimethoate, diphenyl 2-ethylhexyl phosphate, and phosalone.

Asparagus. In asparagus samples, residues of DDT, DCPA, and dicloran were infrequently found.

Avocados. Tests detected two pesticide residues in sixteen samples. Both were of the same pesticide, penta.

Adzuki beans. Adzuki beans had no detectable pesticide residues.

Bananas. Absolutely no pesticide residues were detected in samples of bananas. Bananas from throughout the world are among the safest of all common fruits. Bananas and other fruits that are harvested while still green are ripened with ethylene, a naturally occurring gas that is not known to cause any health problems.

Bean sprouts. Bean sprouts had no detectable pesticide residues.

Beets. Canned beets had one residue each of DDT, dieldrin, isopropyl-phenylphosphates, and tributyl phosphate. Fresh beets had occasional residues of DCPA and mevinphos.

Black-eyed peas (cowpeas). Black-eyed peas had eighteen pesticide residues in sixteen samples representing five different pesticide formulations: lindane, methamidophos, and pentachloroaniline most frequently; acephate and parathion less often.

Brussels sprouts. Brussels sprouts had very few detected pesticide residues including traces of DDT, endosulfan, and quintozene.

Cabbage. Seven pesticide residues were detected in sixteen samples of boiled cabbage, representing four different pesticide formulations: diazinon, dicloran, dieldrin, and methamidophos.

Carrots. Carrots are relatively low in pesticide saturation; thirty-two pesticide residues were detected in sixteen samples, representing eight different pesticide formulations. DDT and linuron were in at least one-fourth of the samples. Less frequently detected were chlorpropham, diazinon, dicloran, parathion, pentachloroaniline, and toxaphene. Organic carrots are widely available at progressive supermarkets and health food stores. They are reasonably priced, they taste better, and they are better for everybody. Be wary when Mexican carrots arrive in the United States from October through December.

Cauliflower. Cauliflower contained one residue each of DDT, diazinon, and methamidophos.

Chives. Chives had no detectable pesticide residues.

Corn. Two residues of the pesticide diazinon were detected in sixteen samples of fresh corn, an extremely safe food. The thick corn husk keeps sprays from edible portions. Canned corn had only one pesticide residue (diazinon) in sixteen samples. Cream-style canned corn had only one pesticide residue (penta) in sixteen samples.

Cranberry juice. Cranberry juice had no detectable residues.

Dates. Dates had no detectable pesticide residues.

Figs. Figs had few detectable pesticide residues, mainly malathion.

Fruit cocktail. Canned fruit cocktail had eleven pesticide residues representing four different pesticide formulations. Carbaryl was detected in at least one-fourth of the samples. Less frequently detected were DDT, dimethoate, and ethion. Fruit cocktail may contain red dye number 3.

Grape juice. Grape juice had sixteen pesticide residues in sixteen samples representing two pesticide formulations, carbaryl and dimethoate. Grape juice is safer than grapes; processing and pressing remove many residues.

Grapefruit. Sixteen pesticide residues were detected in sixteen samples of grapefruit, representing five pesticide formulations. Ethion was found most frequently, in at least one-fourth of the samples. Chlorobenzilate, dicloran, dicofol, and malathion were found less often.

Guavas. Guavas had few detectable pesticide residues, mainly dimethoate.

Hazelnuts. Hazelnuts had no detectable pesticide residues.

Lemonade (frozen reconstituted). Eight residues were detected in sixteen samples of lemonade, representing seven formulations: chlorobenzilate, dicofol, dimethoate, ethion, methidathion, omethoate, and tri (2-ethylhexyl) phosphate.

Lemons. Lemons had residues of chlorpyrifos, imazalil, and thiabendazole.

Lentils. Lentils had no detectable pesticide residues.

Lima beans (mature). Mature lima beans had nineteen pesticide residues representing nine formulations. Most frequently detected pesticides were lindane and methamidophos. Less frequently detected pesticides included BHC, chlorpyrifos, DCPA, dimethoate, penta, tecnazene, and toxaphene.

Limes. Limes had only infrequent detectable pesticide residues, particularly ethion.

Mixed vegetables. Canned mixed vegetables had twenty residues representing eight industrial chemical and pesticide formulations or their metabolites: acephate, captan, chlorpropham, methamidophos, tecnazene, tetrachloro (methylthio) benzene, tetrachlorobenzenes, and 2,3,5,6-tetrachloroaniline, a by-product of the breakdown of tecnazene.

Mushrooms. Canned mushrooms had thirty-one residues in sixteen samples representing seven different formulations. Most frequently detected pesticides (in at least one-fourth of the samples) included BHC, lindane, and penta. Less frequently detected industrial chemicals and pesticides were chlorpyrifos, diazinon, tributyl phosphate, and 2,3,5,6-tetrachloroaniline. Fresh mushrooms probably have slightly higher residues.

Navy beans. Navy beans had two pesticide residues, BHC and diazinon.

Onions. Onions had absolutely no pesticide residues.

Oranges. Navel and Valencia oranges had only twenty-three pesticide residues in sixteen samples. Considering the heavy pesticide saturation of many of our other favorite fruits (such as apples or peaches) a mark of twenty-three residues is relatively good. Most frequently detected were carbaryl and dicofol. Pesticides detected less often were carbophenothion, chlorpyrifos, dimethoate, ethion, methidathion, omethoate, and parathion. Food dye is often used to color the rinds of chemically grown oranges. Organic oranges are widely available and contain neither food dye nor pesticides.

Papayas. Papayas had no detectable pesticide residues.

Peaches (canned). Canned peaches in heavy syrup had only fourteen pesticide residues in sixteen samples, representing three pesticide formulations. Carbaryl was the most frequently detected pesticide; dieldrin and dimethoate were detected less frequently. If I were going to eat peaches, I would choose the canned product (in a lead-free can) without hesitation; processing and peeling can markedly reduce pesticide contamination. Fresh peaches are far more pesticide-saturated.

Pears (canned). Canned pears in heavy syrup had one pesticide residue, methamidophos.

Peas. Fresh green peas had twelve pesticide residues representing six pesticide formulations: acephate, carbaryl, diazinon, dimethoate, methamidophos, and parathion. Canned green peas had one pesticide residue, diazinon. The thorough cleaning as well as the processing of canned peas accounts for their lower pesticide levels.

Pecans. Pecans had fourteen residues in sixteen samples representing four different formulations. Diazinon and pentachlorobenzene were detected in at least one-fourth of the samples, malathion and tecnazene less frequently.

Pineapple juice. Absolutely no pesticide residues were detected in sixteen samples of pineapple juice.

Pineapples. Pineapples from Hawaii had no detectable pesticide residues; however, pineapples imported from Mexico contained residues of BHC, carbaryl, chlorpyrifos, and heptachlor. Buy domestically grown pineapples when possible.

Pinto beans. Pinto beans had two pesticide residues: BHC and penta.

Radishes. There were thirty-two pesticide residues in radishes, representing eleven pesticides. Detected in at least one-fourth of the samples were DCPA, DDT, endosulfan, and toxaphene. Less frequently detected pesticides included chlorpropham, chlorpyrifos, diazinon, dieldrin, heptachlor, omethoate, and parathion.

Rapini. Rapini had occasional residues of DCPA.

Red beans. Red beans had seven pesticide residues in sixteen samples representing seven pesticide formulations: BHC, diazinon, dieldrin, endosulfan, lindane, pentachloroaniline, and penta.

Sesame seeds. Sesame seeds occasionally had residues of endosulfan.

Shallots. Shallots had no detectable pesticide residues.

Snap green beans. Snap beans had thirty-four pesticide residues representing some twelve different pesticide formulations or metabolites. The most frequently detected pesticides included acephate, DDT, dicloran, endosulfan, and methamidophos. Less frequently detected pesticides included BHC, dicofol, parathion, pentachloroaniline, penta, quintozene, and vinclozolin. Canned snap beans had twelve pesticide residues in sixteen samples, representing four different pesticide formulations. Methamidophos was detected most frequently; acephate, dimethoate, and parathion less often. Again, the processing of canned produce probably is the reason for the presence of fewer pesticides.

Sunflower seeds. Sunflower seeds had no detectable pesticide residues.

Tangerines. Tangerines had slight residues of chlorpyrifos, ethion, imazalil, methidathion, and thiabendazole.

Tomatoes (canned). There were thirteen pesticide residues in sixteen samples of canned tomatoes, representing the pesticides carbaryl, endosulfan, and methamidophos.

Watercress. Watercress had no detectable pesticide residues.

Watermelon. Ten industrial chemical and pesticide residues were detected in sixteen samples of watermelon, representing four different pesticide formulations. The most frequently detected pesticide was methamidophos. Less frequently detected chemicals included dicloran, HCB, and tributyl phosphate.

Watermelon seeds. Watermelon seeds had no detectable pesticide residues, which is good news since children often devour them.

YELLOW LIGHT

The fruits and vegetables in this yellow light section have higher pesticide saturation than those in the green light section. You should still eat foods from this group but work extra hard to substitute organic fruits and vegetables for yellow light produce items. I want to emphasize once again that all plant foods, even the most pesticide-saturated, are better for you than the worst animal foods. For that reason the red light section of this chapter includes only two foods, and there is no red light heading at all in the next chapter, grains. You should go out of your way to find organic substitutes for the most saturated fruits and vegetables, such as raisins, peaches, potatoes, spinach, and peanuts. But in comparison to the most saturated and often the most popular animal foods, these plant foods are great for you.

Apple juice. Apple juice had fifteen pesticide residues in sixteen samples, representing three different pesticide formulations or their metabolites. Most frequently detected were carbaryl and dimethoate; omethoate occurred less frequently. The processing of apple juice removes many of the residues from fresh apples. Apple juice made from concentrate is a yellow light food because of the possible presence of radiation from the Chernobyl nuclear accident (more on this later in the chapter).

Apples. When the Natural Resources Defense Council (NRDC) undertook the task of informing consumers about the dangers of cancer-causing Alar to children and adults, their message created one of the major food-safety controversies of the decade. As many as six thousand young children may contract cancer as a result of the presence of Alar in apples and apple products, asserted the NRDC in its study. Alar is a growth regulator that enables apples to stay on trees longer. What made the use of Alar so tragic was that it was not needed and added so much risk. The industry claimed that cosmetically perfect apples could not be grown without this chemical. But I haven't noticed any shortage of apples or price increases this year, have you?

Alar may not be used any longer on domestic apples, but plenty of other cancer-causing and neurotoxic chemicals are. Red apples had eighty pesticide residues in sixteen samples, representing twenty different pesticide formulations. That's a lot of pesticides! And the FDA Total Diet Study didn't even check for Alar! Most frequently detected pesticides, in at least one-fourth of the samples, included azinphos-methyl, chlorpyrifos, DDT, dicloran, dicofol, endosulfan, and phosalone. Less frequently detected pesticides included acephate, BHC, captan, carbaryl, DCPA, diazinon, ethion, HCB, methamidophos, omethoate, parathion, penta, and phosmet. Chemical apples may still have Alar traces because of this chemical's long-lasting presence after orchards are sprayed.

If you do buy nonorganic apples, I recommend that you peel them or use a produce wash designed to remove wax, which is often laced with cancer-causing fungicides, and many pesticides from the fruit's surface. Simply spray a little produce wash on the apple, wipe with your hands, and rinse in pure water. Produce washes are usually available near the produce section of your supermarket and in health and natural food stores. But not all the pesticides in apples can be washed off; some are systemic and permeate the entire fruit. I highly recommend that you buy organic apples and apple juice. See the Personal Action Guide at the end of this book for some really excellent mail-order suppliers of organic apples if you cannot find them in a local market.

Apricots. Apricots had residues of azinphos-methyl, captan, carbaryl, diazinon, fenthion, and phosalone.

Artichokes. Artichokes had residues of endosulfan.

Blackberries. Blackberries had residues of captan, rovral, dichlofluanid, and vinclozolin. Buy frozen organic blackberries from Cascadian Farm for a treat without pesticides.

Blueberries. Blueberries tend to be contaminated most often with captan, then chemicals such as botran, rovral, and DDT. Buy organic berries. For a nontoxic taste treat, try Cascadian Farm fresh frozen organic blueberries on nonfat yogurt.

Broccoli. Some broccoli crops can be quite low in pesticide saturation while other farms bomb them with chemicals. Overall, broccoli had forty-five pesticide residues in sixteen samples, representing about twelve different pesticides or their metabolites, which are environmental breakdown products of the pesticides. Most frequently detected pesticides, in at least one-fourth of the samples, included DCPA, DDT, endosulfan, and dieldrin. Less frequently detected pesticides and metabolites included BHC, carbofuran, chlorpyrifos, diazinon, dicofol, dimethoate, endrin, and 3-hydroxycarbofuran.

Cantaloupe. Because so many people love them, I wish I had better news to report on cantaloupes. Unfortunately, however, cantaloupes had fifty-eight pesticide residues detected in sixteen samples, representing some seventeen different pesticides or their metabolites. The pesticides detected most frequently were carbaryl, DCPA, dicofol, dieldrin, dimethoate, endosulfan, and toxaphene. Less frequently detected were BHC, chlordane, dimethoate, endrin, ethion, lindane, methamidophos, methomyl, omethoate, and pentachloroaniline. In my study of Mexican cantaloupes, I found that dieldrin residues were quite prevalent. Mexican cantaloupes arrive from October through June and our consumption of them is heaviest through the winter. Eating an average of slightly less than 2 ounces of cantaloupe a day over a lifetime would result in a risk of as many as seventeen excess cancers* in one million persons. That is simply too high. Substitute pineapple, watermelon, or grapefruit for chemically grown cantaloupe, or buy organically grown cantaloupe.

Celery. Celery had seventy-eight residues representing thirteen pesticide formulations or their metabolites. Acephate, DDT, diazinon, dicloran, endosulfan, methamidophos, permethrin, and 2,4-dichloro-6-nitrobenzenamine were detected in at least one-fourth of the samples. Less frequently detected pesticides included chlorothalonil, chlorpropham, disulfoton sulfone, methomyl, and parathion. Buy organic celery instead; it makes a wonderful day-long snack food. It's reasonably priced, and you need not be concerned about pesticide residues.

Cherries. Cherries had sixty-one pesticide residues in sixteen samples, representing some sixteen different pesticide formulations or environmental metabolites. Most frequently detected pesticides, in at least one-fourth of the samples, included captan, dicloran, endosulfan, malathion, and 2,4-dichloro-6-nitrobenzenamine. Less frequently detected pesticides included acephate, BHC, carbaryl, chlorpyrifos, DDT, diazinon, ethion, parathion, perthane, phosalone, and phosmet. These chemicals represent some potent cancer-causing and neurotoxic chemicals.

Cherry tomatoes. Cherry tomatoes had residues of chlorothalonil, chlorpyrifos, endosulfan, and methamidophos.

Chili peppers. Chili peppers had residues of EBDCs and parathion. The group of dangerous cancer-causing fungicides known as EBDCs (ethylene bis-dithiocarbamates) may cause liver, lung, and thyroid tumors, according to studies, as well as birth defects and mutations. They are among the most widely used fungicides in the world; yet our own government has very poor laboratory methods for their detection.

Choysum. Choysum, which is actually Chinese chard or bok choy heart

* The term "excess cancers" means that beyond the number of cancer incidences we would expect in a normal unexposed population of one million persons, there could be additional cancers as a result of the pesticides that contaminate a certain food, the air, or our water. Cancer risks are determined by using the best available laboratory animal data and translating these data to humans. They are probably reasonably accurate. I consider any cancer risk below four or five excess cancers in one million to be relatively insignificant, especially when compared with the cancer risks posed by some of our more toxic foods. Mind you, I do not condone even one excess cancer in an age where cancer has become so profoundly common. But in a comparative sense, that number is relatively insignificant.

  Excess cancer assessments take into account the total concentration of carcinogens in a food, not just the number of residues. You may notice occasionally that foods with relatively low numbers of residues have high excess cancer assessments, and vice versa. This is because a food with a few residues could have traces of particularly carcinogenic substances, while one with many residues could have low concentrations of relatively mild pesticides.

and available year-round from California, sometimes had extremely high levels of malathion.

Collard greens. Collards are rich in A and B vitamins, but unfortunately they are pesticide-saturated. They had eighty-seven residues in sixteen samples, representing approximately twenty-three different pesticide formulations or their metabolites. DCPA, DDT, dicloran, dieldrin, endosulfan, and permethrin were detected most frequently. BHC, chlordane, chlorpyrifos, demeton-s sulfone, diazinon, dimethoate, endrin, HCB, lindane, linuron, methamidophos, methomyl, mevinphos, nonachlor, omethoate, parathion, and pentachloroaniline were found less often. Eating an average of slightly less than 2 ounces of collards a day over a lifetime would result in a risk of as many as twenty-one excess cancers in one million persons. Collard greens are a high-toxin food. Your solution is organic substitution.

Cranberries. Cranberries had residues of captafol, chlorothalonil, chlorpyrifos, diazinon, malathion, and parathion.

Crenshaw melons. Crenshaw melons had residues of endosulfan and methamidophos.

Cucumbers. Even pared cucumbers contain plenty of pesticide contamination. Some sixty-seven pesticide residues were detected in sixteen samples, representing approximately twenty-two different pesticide formulations or environmental metabolites. Most frequently detected pesticides included chlordane, dieldrin, endosulfan, endrin, heptachlor, and methamidophos. Less frequently detected pesticides included acephate, BHC, carbaryl, chlorpyrifos, DCPA, dicloran, endrin, lindane, methamidophos, methomyl, nonachlor, octachlor, omethoate, oxamyl, tecnazene, and toxaphene. All these pesticides are either carcinogens or neurotoxins. Eating an average of slightly less than 2 ounces of cucumbers a day over a lifetime would result in a risk of as many as thirty-four excess cancers in one million persons. Organic cucumbers alleviate all concern; they can be eaten with their nutritional peel, too, without concern.

Eggplant. Eggplant had residues of dimethoate, ethion, methamidophos, and permethrin.

Escarole. Escarole had residues of dimethoate and omethoate.

Grapefruit juice. Grapefruit juice had thirty-two pesticide residues in sixteen samples, representing three different pesticide formulations. Most frequently detected pesticides, in at least one-fourth of the samples, included chlorobenzilate, dicofol, and ethion.

Grapes. The 1989 cyanide-in-Chilean-grapes scare was ironic. Because cyanide-tainted grapes posed an immediate threat, the decision to stop shipments from Chile probably was wise—provided that the scare was real and not manufactured by a beleaguered agency trying to divert public attention from the pesticide problem. But many more consumers are likely to suffer premature cancers and even death as a result of the pesticide contamination of domestically grown and imported grapes than from a few cyanide-tainted grapes. Unfortunately, grapes from Mexico and Chile, the two largest exporters, often contain the fungicide captan. Among its breakdown products, one closely resembles the severe birth defect–causing chemical thalidomide. Captan is suspected of being a cause of birth defects among the babies of women farm workers. Captan is also a potent carcinogen. It is not the kind of chemical to which sensible people want their children exposed. Furthermore, Mexican grapes are sprayed with omethoate, a pesticide that U.S. farmers are not even allowed to use on food crops. Omethoate is an acute neurotoxic pesticide to which neither consumers nor Mexican farm workers should be exposed. The FDA has done little to stop omethoate-tainted grapes from entering the market from Mexico.

No matter where your grapes are from, unless they've been grown organically, you should expect low-level pesticide contamination. In the FDA Total Diet Study, grapes had sixty-three residues of some fifteen different pesticide formulations or environmental metabolites. Most frequently detected pesticides, in at least one-fourth of the samples, included captan, DDT, dicloran, dimethoate, endosulfan, and omethoate. Less frequently detected pesticides included BHC, carbaryl, chlorpyrifos, diazinon, dicofol, iprodione, methomyl, parathion, and 2,4-dichloro-6-nitrobenzenamine. Fortunately for consumers, California table-grape growers are moving quickly toward totally organic agriculture. Already, organic grapes are widely available at mainstream supermarkets. Also, look for NutriClean-certified grapes, which have no detectable residues.

Green bell peppers. Green peppers had eighty-three residues in sixteen samples, representing some twenty-two different formulations. Most frequently detected pesticides were acephate, chlorpropham, chlorpyrifos, diazinon, dicloran, dieldrin, endosulfan, methamidophos, and omethoate. Less frequently detected chemicals included carbaryl, dimethoate, diphenyl 2-ethylhexyl phosphate, heptachlor, methomyl, nonachlor, oxamyl, parathion, pentachloroaniline, penta, tecnazene, tributyl phosphate, and 2,4-dichloro-6-nitrobenzenamine. The sheer number of pesticides on each bell pepper is amazing. In one study of the FDA crop records, out of 233 samples that were tested, 419 pesticide residues were detected, meaning most samples had two or more residues.

Honeydew melon. Honeydew had residues of chlorothalonil, chlorpyrifos, dieldrin, dimethoate, endosulfan, methamidophos, and omethoate.

Jalapeño peppers. Jalapeño peppers had residues of acephate, BHC, carbaryl, chlorpyrifos, DDT, diazinon, endosulfan, ethion, fenvalerate, lindane, malathion, monocrotophos, methamidophos, and omethoate.

Kale. Kale had residues of DCPA, DDT, diazinon, endosulfan, and permethrin.

Kiwi fruit. Kiwi had residues of diazinon, phosmet, and vinclozolin.

Leeks. Leeks had residues of DCPA and quintozene.

Lettuce. Lettuce had thirty-six pesticide residues detected in sixteen samples, representing some nine pesticide formulations. The most frequently detected pesticides were acephate, endosulfan, and methamidophos. Less frequently detected pesticides were demeton-s sulfone, diazinon, dimethoate, disulfoton sulfone, methomyl, and mevinphos. Be sure to discard the outer leaves of chemically grown lettuce; those leaves have the greatest pesticide saturation.

Lima beans (immature). Immature lima beans had forty-one residues of ten different pesticide formulations or their metabolites. Most frequently detected were acephate, dicofol, and methamidophos. Less frequently detected pesticides included DCPA, DDT, dimethoate, lindane, malathion, omethoate, and toxaphene.

Mung beans. Mung beans had residues of lindane, malathion, pirimiphos-methyl, and quintozene.

Nectarines. Nectarines had residues of chlorpyrifos, diazinon, dicloran, endosulfan, and phosmet.

Okra. Okra had residues of EBDCs, malathion, mevinphos, and parathion. Mexican okra is especially pesticide-saturated.

Orange juice. Orange juice had forty-three pesticide residues in sixteen samples, representing five different pesticide formulations. Most frequently detected pesticides were chlorobenzilate, dicofol, and ethion. EDA and methidathion were detected less frequently.

Parsley. Parsley had residues of chlorpyrifos, DCPA, DDT, diazinon, and disulfoton sulfone.

Parsnips. Parsnips had residues of DDT, diazinon, dieldrin, heptachlor, and tecnazene.

Peaches. Peaches are dangerous. They're right up there with apples. Tests detected ninety-seven industrial chemical and pesticide residues in sixteen samples of peaches, representing some twenty pesticide formulations or their metabolites. Most frequently detected pesticides included azinphos-methyl, carbaryl, diazinon, dicloran, endosulfan, parathion, phosmet, and 2,4-dichloro-6-nitrobenzenamine. Less frequently detected chemicals included BHC, captan, chlorpyrifos, DDT, diphenyl 2-ethylhexyl phosphate, ethion, methamidophos, penta, pentachloroaniline, phosalone, sulfur, and tris-(beta-chloroethyl) phosphate. Virtually all of these heavy-duty toxic substances remain in the food after cooking and preparation.

That peaches have captan residues is troubling. I predict that in this decade captan, with its thalidomidelike metabolite, will be banned. Americans should not be forced to tolerate a highly risky chemical like captan at levels above one part per million on their peaches and strawberries. That is not healthy eating any way you cut the pie. The use of parathion is also quite disturbing. The connection between bird kills and parathion use is quite clear: where parathion is used, bird populations decline. One farmer told me she hates to see the dying birds, but parathion is cheap, so her family uses it. She said she herself experiences parathion-induced toxicity whenever a piece of equipment is left in the orchard and she has to retrieve it. The farmers I know say they wish they did not have to use parathion. For your family, here's my advice: buy organic peaches—they offer maximum protection, and they are a taste treat.

Pears. There were seventy-nine pesticide residues in sixteen samples of pears, representing thirteen different pesticide formulations. Most frequently detected pesticides, in at least one-fourth of the samples, included azinphos methyl, DDT, diazinon, dicloran, dicofol, endosulfan, and ethion. BHC, chlorpyrifos, HCB, methamidophos, parathion, penta, and phosalone were detected less frequently. Buy organic pears. My favorites are *Asian pears,* the oldest cultivated pear known. They are a fairly easy fruit to grow without chemicals, and they're sweet and crunchy. You can recognize these pears by their apple-like shape and green, yellow, or russet skin. Asian pears are available from July to late October. Asian pears are also known as apple pear, Japanese pear, chalea, and shali.

Persimmons. Persimmons had residues of dicloran.

Plums. Plums had sixty-eight industrial chemical and pesticide residues representing seventeen different formulations or their metabolites. DDT, dicloran, endosulfan, and 2,4-dichloro-6-nitrobenzenamine were detected in at least one-fourth of the samples. Chemicals less frequently detected included azinphos-methyl, chlorpyrifos, diazinon, dicofol, dimethoate, diphenyl 2-ethylhexyl phosphate, ethion, methoxychlor, parathion, penta, phosalone, phosmet, and tri (beta-chloroethyl) phosphate. Fortunately, organic plums are reasonably priced. I always wait till the middle of summer when the organic plums flood the shelves, shining and enticing.

Poblano peppers. Poblano peppers had residues of acephate, chlorpyrifos, endosulfan, ethion, malathion, and methamidophos.

Pomegranates. Pomegranates had residues of dicloran.

Potatoes. Boiled peeled potatoes had less pesticide saturation than potatoes baked in their skins. Sixty residues were detected in sixteen samples of boiled potatoes, representing approximately fifteen different formulations or metabolites. The most frequently detected residues were chlorpropham, tecnazene, and tetrachloro (methylthio) benzene. Less frequently detected were aldicarb, chlordane, DDT, demeton-s sulfone, dieldrin, disulfoton sulfone, endosulfan, heptachlor, octachlor, penta, and quintozene. Peeling did not eliminate aldicarb, which indicates that it permeates potatoes.

Aldicarb at extremely low exposure levels has been shown to promote changes in the human immune system. It has become a common and dangerous drinking-water contaminant in potato-growing regions of New York, Rhode Island, Wisconsin, and other states. Aldicarb is so dangerous that California's Department of Health Services has proposed to ban the use of this chemical, but the federal government unwisely continues to allow its use throughout the rest of America on much of the potato crop. The effects of aldicarb may be particularly acute for children; indeed, some children probably are going through bouts of flulike illnesses, the real cause of which could be low-level pesticide poisoning. This just does not need to happen. Organically grown potatoes are the best solution.

Potatoes baked in their skins had ninety-six residues of twenty-one different pesticide formulations. Residues detected in at least one-fourth of the samples were chlorpropham, which is used as a post-harvest pesticide to prevent potatoes from sprouting (it is a possible mutagen), DDT, dieldrin, endosulfan, tecnazene, tetrachloro (methylthio) benzene, and 2,3,5,6-tetrachloroaniline. Less frequently detected pesticides included chlordane, demeton-s sulfone, diazinon, dicloran, disulfoton sulfone, HCB, isopropyl 1-3-chloro-4-methoxy-phenylcarb, octachlor, pentachlorobenzene, phorate sulfone, quintozene, and tecnazene. These are chemically hot potatoes. Eating an average of slightly less than 2 ounces of baked potatoes a day over a lifetime would result in a conservative risk of as many as eleven excess cancers in one million persons. If you must eat chemically grown potatoes, it is best to peel them.

Prunes. Prunes were saturated. They had sixty-two industrial-pollutant and pesticide residues detected in sixteen samples, representing thirteen different industrial-pollutant and pesticide formulations and their metabolites. Most frequently detected pesticides included DDT, dicofol, endosulfan, malathion, penta, and phosalone. Less frequently detected were carbaryl, chlorpyrifos, diphenyl 2-ethylhexyl phosphate, ethion, PCBs, tri (2-ethylhexyl) phosphate, and tributyl phosphate.

Radishes. Radishes had residues of chlorpyrifos.

Raspberries. Raspberries most often were coated with residues of captan (sometimes at concentrations above one part per million, which is a significantly elevated concentration), carbaryl, procymidone, and dichlofluanid.

Rutabagas. Rutabagas had residues of chlorpyrifos.

Serrano chilies. The hottest of all chili peppers, serrano peppers had residues of azinphos-methyl, chlorpyrifos, diazinon, fenvalerate, methamidophos, and omethoate.

Spinach. Popeye's meal of strength had ninety-five pesticide residues in sixteen samples, representing nineteen different pesticide formulations or their metabolites. Most frequently detected pesticides included chlordane, chlorpyrifos, DCPA, DDT, dieldrin, endosulfan, pentachloroaniline, and permethrin. Less frequently detected residues included BHC, dicloran, dimethoate, heptachlor, HCB, methamidophos, nonachlor, omethoate, parathion, penta, and toxaphene. Eating an average of slightly less than 2 ounces of spinach a day over a lifetime would result in a risk of as many as twenty-eight excess cancers in one million persons. That simply is too high.

Canned spinach undergoes processing that significantly cuts down pesticide saturation. There were thirty-five pesticide residues in sixteen samples of canned spinach, representing twelve pesticide formulations and environmental metabolites. DDT and permethrin were found in at least one-fourth of the samples. BHC, chlordane, chlorpropham, DCPA, dicloran, heptachlor, HCB, methamidophos, parathion, and pentachloroaniline were found less frequently. This is an improvement over fresh spinach, but it's still pretty bad. Stay away from chemically grown spinach. Buy organically grown spinach for its purity.

Strawberries. I love strawberries, but I won't eat chemically grown ones anymore. Strawberries had eighty-six pesticide residues in sixteen samples, representing sixteen different pesticide formulations. Most frequently detected pesticides, in at least one-fourth of the samples, included captan, carbaryl, DDT, dicofol, endosulfan, methomyl, mevinphos, and vinclozolin. Less frequently detected pesticides included BHC, diazinon, dieldrin, malathion, methamidophos, methoxychlor, parathion, and toxaphene. The captan and carbaryl residues are especially troubling because of their neurotoxic and teratogenic properties.* Taste treats children love should not pose the threat of cancer or neurotoxicity. Strawberries from Canada and Mexico are equally pesticide-saturated, frequently showing residues of captan. The only realistic solution is to buy organic strawberries. Too many pesticides and fungicides are found in chemically grown samples to make them even closely approximate a safe food.

String beans. String beans had residues of acephate, chlorpyrifos, dimethoate, ethion, methamidophos, and omethoate.

Summer squash. The pesticide residues in summer squash are dangerous to your health. I highly recommend organic squash. In the Total Diet Study, summer squash had eighty-one pesticide residues representing seventeen pesticide formulations or their metabolites. The most frequently detected pesticides were chlordane, DDT, dieldrin, endosulfan, endrin, heptachlor, HCB, and toxaphene. Less frequently detected residues included DCPA, diazinon, dicloran, methamidophos, octachlor, parathion, pentachloroaniline, pentachloro-phenyl methyl sulfide, and quintozene. Eating an average of slightly less than 2 ounces of summer squash a day over a lifetime would result in a risk of as many as eighty-nine excess cancers in one million persons. I have had organic squashes lab-tested at extremely minute detection limits, and the organically grown produce has been completely free of detectable residues.

Sweet potatoes. Sweet potatoes baked in their skins were another moderately pesticide-saturated vegetable, with forty-three pesticide residues detected in sixteen samples, representing ten different pesticide formulations or metabolites. Most frequently detected residues, in at least one-fourth of the samples, included DDT, dicloran, dieldrin, and 2,4-dichloro-6-nitrobenzenamine. Less frequently detected pesticides included chlorpropham, chlorpyrifos, endosulfan, phosmet, tecnazene, and 2,3,5,6-tetrachloroaniline.

Swiss chard. Swiss chard had residues of DCPA and permethrin.

Tomatillos. Tomatillos had residues of BHC, chlorothalonil, DDT, lindane, and methamidophos.

---

* Teratogens are chemicals that cause birth defects. They may be subtle neurological birth defects or apparent defects such as deformed limbs.

Tomatoes. Tomatoes are quite saturated. Tomatoes in the Total Diet Study had fifty industrial pollutant and pesticide residues in sixteen samples, representing some thirteen industrial-pollutant and pesticide formulations or metabolites. Chlorpyrifos, dicloran, endosulfan, methamidophos, and permethrin were found in at least one-fourth of the samples. Less frequently detected were acephate, DDT, diazinon, EPN, lindane, phosphamidon, PCBs, and tri (2-butoxyethyl) phosphate. On the other hand, vine-ripened organic tomatoes quiet the pesticide concern, and they are a taste treat.

Tomato juice. Tomato juice had thirty-five residues representing eight formulations. Most frequently detected were carbaryl, endosulfan, and methamidophos. BHC, DDT, dicofol, parathion, and pentachlorobenzene were less frequently detected.

Tomato sauce. Canned tomato sauce had thirty-six pesticide residues representing eight different pesticide formulations. Most frequently detected pesticides, in at least one-fourth of the samples, included DDT, endosulfan, and methamidophos. Less frequently detected pesticides included DCPA, dicofol, dieldrin, malathion, and toxaphene.

Turnip greens. Turnip greens had residues of DCPA, DDT, EBDCs, mevinphos, and permethrin.

Turnips. Turnips had residues of chlorpyrifos, DDT, and dieldrin.

Winter squash. Winter squash had forty-eight residues representing some eighteen different formulations or their environmental metabolites. Most frequently detected pesticides, in at least one-fourth of the samples, included chlordane, dieldrin, endosulfan, and nonachlor. Less frequently detected were BHC, DCPA, diazinon, endrin, heptachlor, HCB, methamidophos, parathion, pentachloroaniline, pentachlorobenzene, PCBs, quintozene, tecnazene, and 2,3,5,6-tetrachloroaniline. Eating an average of slightly less than 2 ounces of winter squash a day over a lifetime would result in a whopping risk of as many as sixty-two excess cancers in one million persons. Buy organic.

RED LIGHT

The two red light foods are far more pesticide-saturated than other plant foods. Avoid them! Substitute organic varieties.

Peanuts. Peanuts take the grand prize for the most pesticide-saturated food in the American diet based on results from the Total Diet Study. Peanuts had 183 residues in sixteen samples, representing seventeen different formulations or their environmental metabolites. Most frequently detected pesticides were chlorpyrifos, diazinon, dicloran, dieldrin, fonofos, HCB, malathion, pentachloroaniline, penta, quintozene, tecnazene, and toxaphene. Less frequently detected were BHC, chlorpropham, DDT, heptachlor, and tetrachlorobenzenes. Eating an average of slightly less than 2 ounces of dry-roasted peanuts a day over a lifetime would result in a risk of as many as twenty excess cancers in one million persons. A naturally occurring carcinogenic mold, aflatoxin, grows on peanuts, adding to the potential risk of this food. Look for organic brands that are sun-dried in the field to prevent aflatoxin growth. Arrowhead Mills organic peanut butter is made with peanuts dried this way.

Raisins. Raisins had 110 industrial chemical and pesticide residues in sixteen samples, representing seventeen different formulations or metabolites. Isn't that tragic? The most frequently detected residues included carbaryl, DDT, dicofol dimethoate, endosulfan, ethion, omethoate, and penta. Less frequently detected were captan, chlordane, chlorpyrifos, diazinon, malathion, nonachlor, phosalone, sulfur, and tributyl phosphate. Eating an average of slightly less than 2 ounces of raisins a day over a lifetime would result in a risk of as many as twenty-one excess cancers in one million persons. That is a heavy cancer price to pay for eating raisins.

There are solutions. Dole—one of the major suppliers of produce in the nation—has bought an organic raisin-packing house, so organic raisins will become mainstream. Buying organic is the way to go for raisins. Organically grown raisins have significantly fewer, if any, residues, and their price is similar to that of their chemical cousins. Despite the cute raisin singers who now appear on television, raisins are a highly pesticide-saturated food, and consumers would be better off finding organic varieties.

Shopping Tips

Buy locally grown produce whenever possible. Find the nearest farmers' market and go there regularly. You will more than likely find a wide variety of organically grown fruits and vegetables. At your supermarket you can buy locally grown produce by buying in season. Although this produce will have varying degrees of pesticide contamination, it is more likely to have retained its full nutritional value, and we need the nutrients in fresh produce to fight off the ravaging effects of pollution and toxic chemicals.

Out-of-season produce is likely to have been imported. Imported produce is often more pesticide saturated, and it may have lost much of its nutrient value. One study of out-of-season Brussels sprouts and cabbages —both of which are usually good sources of vitamin C—found absolutely no vitamin C. Mishandling of produce during long trips from foreign nations or from the farm fields to the market can also result in loss of the B vitamin complex and other vitamins.

Out-of-season produce is likely to have been imported from Mexico, where many dangerous chemicals that are not used in the United States are routinely used. Roughly 40 to 60 percent of the fresh produce sold in the United States in winter is imported, much of it from south of the border.

When you want to eat out-of-season produce, frozen fruits and vegetables are preferable to imported. Frozen produce is more likely to retain its nutrient contents. To make sure your body gets all the pollution-fighting nutrients it needs, when you buy frozen fruits or vegetables shake the boxes and make sure you hear them loosely clatter. If they've been thawed and refrozen, they will stick in a clump and will be silent when you shake the box. Frozen produce should never be thawed and then refrozen. High freezer temperatures also result in nutrient loss. And that means we're not getting the nutrients we need to survive and flourish in a toxic world.

Canned fruits and vegetables tend to have low pesticide levels but may have slightly elevated lead concentrations as a result of their containers. Consider these higher lead levels when choosing between fresh or canned fruits and vegetables. The lead concentration of fresh produce may be one-thirtieth of that in the canned product. The nutritional benefits of canned fruits and vegetables, however, are nearly equal to those of fresh produce, except for some vitamin loss. Obviously, eating canned fruits and vegetables once in a while will not hurt and many people do. Take comfort; you have reduced your pesticide exposure. But if you eat a great many canned fruits and vegetables when organically grown fresh produce and frozen produce are available, you may be needlessly adding to your lead exposure.

Be wary of precut fresh fruits and vegetables. Oxidation occurs after cutting and will result in significant loss of nutrients, including the B vitamins and vitamin C. Buy your watermelons whole, in other words, if you value optimum nutrient content.

Once vitamin C–rich foods are cut or sliced they undergo oxidation, which destroys significant amounts of vitamin C. So try not to cut or slice fruits and vegetables until just before you eat them. If you must slice them ahead of time, squeeze a little lemon juice on the cut or sliced surfaces; the acidity of the lemon juice will reduce oxidation and prevent vitamin C loss. With antioxidation in mind, add lemon wedges or tomatoes to sliced zucchini and other summer squashes to preserve vitamins. Add lemon juice dressing to homemade coleslaw to prevent vitamin C loss.

Waxing

Wax is applied to many fruits and vegetables to preserve them and enhance color. If you were covered with carnauba wax you might look pretty well preserved, too.

Consumers should be aware that many fresh produce items are coated with a layer of wax or shellac, which may contain fungicides and pesticides, including suspected carcinogens and neurotoxins.

Federal law requires supermarkets to disclose the presence of wax on fresh produce at the point of sale. But when was the last time you saw a notice to that effect? Most supermarkets are in violation of federal law in failing to tell customers which produce items are waxed.

Among the fungicides used with waxes:

- Benomyl is believed to be possible human carcinogen and is known to increase skull and central nervous system anomalies in offspring of rats.

- Dicloran has not been sufficiently tested for carcinogenicity, birth defects, and mutagenic effects.

- Imazalil has not been sufficiently tested for carcinogenicity, birth defects, and mutagenic effects.

- Ortho-phenylphenol has been shown to suppress the immune system.

- Sodium ortho-phenyl phenate has been classified by the International Agency for Research on Cancer as a possible human carcinogen and has been demonstrated to produce urinary bladder cancer in rats and liver cancer in mice.

Unfortunately, you cannot always tell just by looking which produce items have been waxed. The federal law that requires waxed food to be labeled was intended to make this guessing game unnecessary. The law does not require disclosure of the fungicides and pesticides in the waxes, but if consumers were aware that certain produce items were coated with wax, they would also be alerted to the likely presence of chemicals such as fungicides.

Waxes cannot be removed with just water. You will need a mild detergent. Special nontoxic produce washes have been developed that remove most of the waxes and even nonsystemic pesticides. These products are often sold near the produce section in supermarkets. Removing waxes is worthwhile because they so frequently are laced with carcinogens and neurotoxins.

By the way, the criminal penalty for not complying with this labeling law can be up to a year in prison and/or up to a $1,000 fine. Tell the produce manager at your market that you want to know which fruits and vegetables have been waxed. Let your grocers know that they are breaking the law by not labeling waxed produce. You can report violators to:

Sonia I. Delgado
Assistant to the Director
Division of Regulatory Guidance

Center for Food Safety and Applied Nutrition
Department of Health and Human Services
Food and Drug Administration
200 C Street SW
Washington, DC 20204

Send a copy of your letter to the president of your supermarket company.

These fruits are likely to be waxed:

Apples	Lemons	Passion fruit
Avocados	Limes	Peaches
Cantaloupes	Melons	Pineapples
Grapefruits	Oranges	

These vegetables are likely to be waxed:

Cucumbers	Peppers	Squashes
Eggplants	Pumpkins	Sweet potatoes
Parsnips	Rutabagas	

Often, even if wax is not applied, fungicides are. The little white paper pads on the bottom of citrus boxes often have been impregnated with pesticides. More than 90 percent of the California citrus crop is fumigated after the harvest! Pesticides are applied to oranges, tangerines, mandarins, tangelos, grapefruits, lemons, and limes to prevent green and blue mold decay. One post-harvest pesticide, benomyl, is an animal carcinogen, and another, ortho-phenylphenol, is known to depress the immune system; ortho-phenylphenol is probably a carcinogen. Dried fruits and nuts are fumigated to control beetles, flies, moths, and worms. Methyl bromide, which may be a carcinogen, is applied to almost all chemically grown nuts and dried fruits including walnuts, almonds, chestnuts, raisins, prunes, figs, dates, and apricots. More good reasons to buy organic!

Radiation

Some wild European mushrooms have excess radiation as a result of the 1986 Chernobyl nuclear disaster. You should be especially careful of boletes and chanterelles. They will remain hot for years from absorbing radioactive cesium 137, which is present in decaying leaves and which the mushrooms cannot distinguish from potassium. Pregnant and nursing women especially should avoid these mushrooms. These mushrooms are usually found in gourmet food sections.

Apple juice is often made from imported apple juice concentrate. These concentrates may well be contaminated with low levels of radiation from the Chernobyl accident. Using sophisticated sampling techniques at the FDA radiation laboratory in Winchester, Massachusetts, scientists have identified isotopes of cesium 137 in imported apple juice concentrate and have confirmed that they stem from the accident.

About one-third of the apple juice concentrate from Austria, Hungary, West Germany, and Yugoslavia that is presently being sold here and used in American products is radioactive. Much apple juice sold in the United States is made with European concentrate. Austrian apples are the most radioactive, but the FDA has not prevented any Austrian apple juice concentrate from entering the United States. The action level for total cesium is 10,000 picocuries per liter (pCi/L). Detected levels have come to nearly half that.

New research into the health effects of radiation has revealed how little scientists actually know about low-level responses. Most experts say there is no threshold of safety for radiation and that even a single exposure can initiate or promote cancer. Others believe repeated exposures are required to initiate or promote cancer and other diseases. New technology is beginning to shed light on this issue. Scientists studying radiation effects are beginning to see chromosomal aberrations at doses five to ten times lower than before. Unfortunately, Chernobyl's legacy of radiation will persist for many years, thanks to the extended half-life of cesium 137. Some consumers in Finland, Hungary, Rumania, Poland, and Switzerland are getting regularly dosed.

It is not wise for anybody to regularly drink apple juice laced with up to 4,600 pCi/L of radiation when the solution to the problem is near: Drink apple juice made from organically grown U.S. apples, since the FDA has not found any abnormal radiation in American apples. Be sure the label says that the juice is made from organically grown U.S. apples.

Cooking Tips

To peel or not to peel? The peels of fruits and vegetables are sometimes waxed, and often have high levels of pesticides. But the peel is often a good source of essential nutrients and fiber. I avoid this problem by buying organic and eating the skin. If you must eat chemically grown produce, I recommend that you wash green light foods thoroughly and eat the skin; for yellow light foods, I recommend that you peel them if possible.

Remove and discard the outer leaves of leafy vegetables such as lettuce; they have higher pesticide residues than the inner leaves. Also, the leaves at the top of some vegetables, such as celery, actually act like a sponge and soak up the pesticide residues. By removing the leaves, you will lower your exposure.

Use minimal amounts of water when boiling vegetables. Vitamin C and other nutrients dissolve in the water. Better yet, steam vegetables in a stainless-steel steamer. One-third of the potassium in carrots will be lost during boiling but virtually none will be lost in steaming. If you boil vegetables, first let the water come to a rolling boil, then put in vegetables. Leaving vegetables in the water as it comes to a boil results in higher nutrient loss.

One key for maximum nutrient retention when steaming or boiling is to use as little water as possible and to cook in as short a time as possible.

If you own a microwave and wonder whether to use it for cooking vegetables, you should know that microwave cooking results in excellent nutrient retention. Researchers report microwaving can result in 100 percent retention of a food's vitamin C content and 70 percent of its B vitamins. Flavor and color also tend to be well preserved with microwave cooking.

Leafy vegetables like spinach or cabbage tend to lose the most nutrients when cooked. Short cooking times are preferred. Cook vegetables whole to preserve nutrients and cut them up after cooking.

Safe Shopping List: Vegetables and Fruits

For your convenience I've summarized all this information into lists showing how safe or dangerous different foods are. You can have these copied and take them shopping with you until you remember which foods are safe.

Some foods appear in these lists that I have not discussed in the preceding pages simply because there isn't room in this book to spell out what chemicals are in all foods.

I have listed the foods in order of the number of residues found in the Total Diet Study, starting with the safest. (Again, this is because foods with the fewest total number of residues usually have the lowest average concentrations and are your safest choices in the supermarket.) Within each green light, yellow light, and red light section, I also sometimes list foods without giving an exact number of residues. These foods have been analyzed in ways that tell me how safe they are, but they were not covered by the Total Diet Study, so I don't have an exact number of residues to report.

FRUITS

Green Light	Number of Residues
Bananas	0
Pears (canned)	1
Avocados	2
Watermelons	10
Fruit cocktail	11
Applesauce	13
Peaches (canned)	14
Grapefruit	16
Oranges	23

OTHER GREEN LIGHT FRUITS

Bitter melon	Limes
Coconut	Papayas
Dates	Passion fruit
Figs	Pineapples
Guavas	Plantains
Lemons	Tangerines

Yellow Light	Number of Residues
Cantaloupe	58
Cherries	61
Prunes	62
Grapes	63
Plums	68
Pears	79
Apples	80
Strawberries	86
Peaches	97

OTHER YELLOW LIGHT FRUITS

Apricots	Feiojas
Blackberries	Honeydew
Blueberries	Kiwi fruit
Casaba	Kumquats
Cranberries	Nectarines
Crenshaw melons	Persimmons
Currants	Pomegranates

Red Light	Number of Residues
Raisins	110

VEGETABLES

Green Light	Number of Residues
Onions	0
Peas (canned)	1
Corn (canned)	1
Corn (fresh)	2
Navy beans	2
Pinto beans	2
Cauliflower	3
Beets (canned)	4
Cabbage	7
Red beans	7
Asparagus	8
Peas (fresh)	12
Snap green beans (canned)	12
Tomatoes (canned)	13
Black-eyed peas (cowpeas)	18
Lima beans (mature)	19
Mixed vegetables (canned)	20
Mushrooms (canned)	31
Radishes	32
Carrots	32
Snap green beans (fresh)	34

OTHER GREEN LIGHT VEGETABLES

Alfalfa sprouts	Garlic
Asparagus	Jicama
Adzuki beans	Kidney beans
Bamboo shoots (canned)	Leeks
Bean sprouts	Mushrooms (fresh)
Beets (fresh)	Radicchio
Brussels sprouts	Rapini
Cassava	Red chard
Chives	Rhubarb
Cilantro	Shallots
Daikon	Snow peas
Fava beans	Watercress
Fennel root	Yams

VEGETABLES (*continued*)

Yellow Light	Number of Residues
Spinach (canned)	35
Lettuce	36
Tomato sauce (canned)	36
Lima beans (immature)	41
Sweet potatoes	43
Broccoli	45
Winter squash	48
Tomatoes (fresh)	50
Potatoes (peeled)	60
Cucumbers	67
Celery	78
Summer squash	81
Green bell peppers	83
Collards	87
Spinach (fresh)	95
Potatoes (with peel)	96

OTHER YELLOW LIGHT VEGETABLES

Artichokes
Bok choy
Cherry tomatoes
Chili peppers
Choysum
Dandelion greens
Dill
Eggplant
Endive
Escarole
Green peppers
Jalapeño peppers
Kale
Kohlrabi
Lentils
Mung beans
Mustard greens

Okra
Parsley
Parsnips
Poblano peppers
Pumpkin
Purslane
Radishes
Red peppers
Rutabagas
Serrano chilies
Soybeans
String beans
Swiss chard
Tomatillos
Turnip greens
Turnips

NUTS AND SEEDS

Green Light	Number of Residues
Pecans	14

OTHER GREEN LIGHT NUTS AND SEEDS

Almonds	Sesame seeds
Chinese pine nuts	Sunflower seeds
Flax	Walnuts
Hazelnuts	Water chestnuts
Pistachios	Watermelon seeds
Pumpkin seeds	

Yellow Light	Number of Residues
Lychee nuts	
Radish seed	

Red Light	Number of Residues
Peanuts	183

JUICES

Green Light	Number of Residues
Pineapple	0
Lemonade	8
Grape	16

OTHER GREEN LIGHT JUICES

Apricot nectar	Lime
Carrot	Mixed vegetable
Cranberry	Prune

Yellow Light	Number of Residues
Apple	15
Grapefruit	32
Tomato	35
Orange	43

OTHER YELLOW LIGHT JUICES

Boysenberry

JAMS, JELLIES, AND SPREADS

YELLOW LIGHT

Blackberry spread   Strawberry jam
Raspberry spread   Boysenberry spread

MISCELLANEOUS PRODUCE ITEMS

GREEN LIGHT

Aloe vera   Langon
Arrowroot   Lotus root
Burdock root   Pai kon
Cactus   Rombuton
Cardoni   Seaweed seasoning
Cole   Shredded bamboo
Durian   Taro

4. GRAINS

Grains are extremely important in the low-toxin high-energy diet. I want you to learn to love whole grains. Together with fruits and vegetables, grains should form the mainstay of your diet. Remember the two-thirds rule: plant foods, including grains, should make up two-thirds of your diet. Plant foods, especially grains, will play a very important role as you cleanse your body of a lifetime's accumulation of toxic chemicals. As you learn what grains can do for your body, you will want to eat them as often as you once wanted to eat pesticide-laced foods such as ice cream, milk shakes, french fries, hot dogs, hamburgers, and pizza.

The great news is that even chemically grown grains have among the lowest levels of pesticides and industrial chemicals. Overall you can feel relatively safe with grains.

And we all need to eat grains. They are essential for feeling great. They're an important source of vitamins and trace minerals, and the fiber in whole grains can aid in weight loss. Many people should give up counting calories and instead just replace meat and dairy foods with whole grains, fruits, and vegetables. Animal fats contain nine calories per gram, twice the calories per gram of high-fiber foods. You get more clout per calorie with plant foods such as whole grains.

That's because whole grains provide dietary satiety: they help you feel full with fewer calories. A breakfast of fiber-rich oat bran or another whole grain cereal with skim milk or soy milk, fresh fruit, and whole grain toast will provide an excellent fuel source of complex carbohydrates to keep you going strong until lunch as well as a fabulous complete-protein meal. Whole grain pasta; whole wheat tortillas, bagels, macaroni, and muffins; rice; oatmeal with organic peanuts, raisins, and dates; whole wheat graham crackers; amaranth cookies; and puffed corn, wheat, and millet all make tasty, relatively low-calorie dishes for breakfast, lunch, dinner, and snacks.

Eating grains is good for the planet, too. When you eat grains you maximize our planet's resources. As Frances Moore Lappé tells us in *Diet for a Small Planet,* grain crops are used much more efficiently when they're fed to people than when they're fed to livestock. If all the grain and soybeans fed to U.S. livestock were used to feed humans instead, they could feed at least 1.3 billion citizens of the planet—far, far more than could be fed by the livestock raised with that grain.

Whole grains are also wonderful for people who must control their blood sugar. Whole grain, high-fiber complex carbohydrate foods such as grains, vegetables, and pasta smooth out blood sugar fluctuations. "If I were to give my mother a white [enriched flour] bagel in the morning, her blood sugar would be about 385 milligrams per deciliter by noontime," says nutrition expert Elaine Grossman, of Nutrition Network, Los Angeles. "However, if I give her a whole grain or pumpernickel bagel in the morning, her blood sugar will only be about 185 milligrams per deciliter at noontime. The difference is simply that the body had to work to separate the sugar molecules from the fiber, and that slow process is the key to stabilizing blood sugar, feeling full longer, and obtaining the most nutrients from your food. This also applies to whole wheat pasta and whole grain brown rice. In fact, all of my patients with diabetes who eat white rice find that it jumps their blood sugar level up over 450 milligrams per deciliter while brown rice keeps their blood sugar at a nice, even pace. For those of us who have problems with sugar, such as hypoglycemia, or just too many sugar highs and lows, the use of whole grains will help to solve this problem."

The most important benefits of grains from our point of view is their extraordinary cancer-preventing and detoxifying qualities. A grain-rich diet is your surest way of minimizing the effects of toxins in your food and water. And it's your best way of undoing the toxic exposures of a lifetime.

Toxic chemicals will penetrate the body despite the strictest low-toxin diet. It is what happens to these toxic chemicals once they get into the body that counts, and that is where whole grains are so valuable. All plant foods, and especially whole grains, contain fiber, nature's miracle pollution-fighter. Yes, the same fiber that helps us combat cholesterol is valuable in neutralizing the effects of toxic chemicals.

Once toxic invaders have entered your body, the fiber in whole grains can prevent them from infiltrating very far. They can actually route toxic molecules from the body before they can pass through the thin, porous wall of the gastrointestinal tract. They accomplish this by absorbing toxic chemicals. One reason fiber seems to attract many toxic chemicals is that both are composed of carbon, and on a chemical level, like attracts like.

After absorbing and binding them, fiber transports these villains from your body before they can leave a trace behind.

Fiber protects us against damage from industrial pollutants and pesticides by helping to break the circular route of the entero-hepatic pathway. In this particular bodily pathway, many toxic chemicals pass from the digestive tract into the bloodstream and move on to the liver, which produces substances called bile salts. Unfortunately, the liver cannot detoxify many of these complex chemically engineered toxic chemicals, and so these toxic compounds go into the bile salts. The liver then sends these bile salts— now contaminated with impurities such as carcinogens and neurotoxins, which it cannot detoxify—on to the gallbladder. The gallbladder secretes them back into the digestive tract, where the bile salts can be eliminated. In people who eat a low-fiber diet, these bile salts remain for a very long time in the colon, where they have a great chance to pass through the gastrointestinal wall's thin membrane, become reabsorbed by the body, and reenter the bloodstream. Thus these contaminated substances can cause carcinogenic and mutagenic harm to cells in the colon and other nearby organs. The key concept here is that the longer these bile salts remain in the digestive tract, the more time there is for carcinogenic impurities to permeate the gastrointestinal membrane and pass into the bloodstream. And once these noxious substances pass into the bloodstream they are circulated throughout the body and can cause widespread cellular damage.

Many pesticides are engineered to be fat-soluble or they are dissolved in inert ingredients or mixed with detergents that are fat-soluble, so that they will permeate the tough exoskeletons of insects; this allows them to slip through your body's cell membranes, which are made up of basic fatty materials called lipids. Once the pesticide has penetrated a cell, its toxic chemicals may kill the cell—which would be the preferable outcome, for then the cell's legacy would be at an end—or, worse, the chemical could harm the cell by causing a genetic mutation. This could create a damaged and potentially cancerous cell that would be vulnerable to further toxic exposure.

But when fiber is present in large amounts in the colon, it attracts and traps carbon-based toxic compounds just like an activated granular carbon water filter. With adequate fiber, bile salts that contain carcinogenic and mutagenic impurities can be moved out of the body quickly, because fiber, unlike animal foods, passes very quickly through the body. It is precisely their lack of fiber that makes pesticide-contaminated flesh foods such as hamburger and salami so dangerous. The body absorbs toxic chemicals in animal foods very efficiently, because those poisons are bound up not in fiber but in lipids, which take longer to excrete and are much more easily absorbed through the gastrointestinal membrane. And as we shall see when we discuss meat and poultry, saturated fats may in themselves potentiate the effects of toxic chemicals.

If you know ahead of time that you are going to eat a meal that is rich in animal foods—dairy products, meat, or poultry, which have absolutely no fiber—you should eat fresh high-fiber produce and grains all day and during the animal-food meal. Make it a point to eat whole grain bread and a salad of fresh vegetables or fruits every day. These high-fiber foods will help your body transport and eliminate potent carcinogens that find their way into your diet.

Many studies have shown that eating grains helps reduce our cancer risk. Wheat bran, for example, appears consistently to reduce the frequency of colon tumors in animals. In the past decade, a number of other studies have been conducted in which laboratory rats were fed fiber-rich diets and were also exposed to certain known colonic carcinogens. When wheat bran was used as a source of dietary fiber, a protective effect was seen in the majority of rats. Wheat bran, scientists definitely believe, is protective. Studies of corn bran, rice bran, oat bran, pectin, and guar have shown that these also may have a protective effect.

Several epidemiologic studies show that whole grains are important in our fight against disease. Comparison of rural and urban Finns shows that the intake of calories and fat is similar in both groups, but the rural Finns eat more fiber. Not surprisingly, rural Finns have lower rates of colon cancer. In Denmark a decrease in dietary fiber consumption from 1927 to 1977 has been closely correlated with a rise in prevalence of colon cancer. In seven other countries, changes in flour milling practices during World War II led to increased consumption of total fiber, which correlated with a reduced mortality from colon cancer in those countries fifteen years later.

All grains contain different kinds of fiber, and these different kinds of fiber help your body in different ways to fight toxic chemicals. Since grains differ in their ability to adsorb and expel carcinogens from your digestive tract, the smart, tasty choice is to enjoy a wide variety of cereals and grains, including recently rediscovered exotics such as amaranth and quinoa from Central and South America, and North American crops such as barley, buckwheat, millet, and rye. Eat them all and help reduce the pollution level in your body.

Remember that it's *whole* grains that you want to eat. Many grains are processed in such a way that only the innermost portion, known as the endosperm, is used. This is how white bread and most pastas and other white-flour products are made. This part of the grain has little fiber and virtually no nutrients. That's why the labels on these products always say they're made with enriched flour—federal regulations require the manufacturers to add nutrients to give the flour some nutritional value. Even with nutrients added, however, these products have little fiber.

Whole grain foods contain the endosperm and also the two outer layers, called the germ and the bran. Bran, which surrounds the endosperm, is the fibrous portion. The germ is the outer nutrient-dense cover of the kernel. It is high in protein, essential nutrients such as the B vitamin complex, and micronutrients, including chromium, copper, magnesium, manganese, molybdenum, phosphorus, selenium, and zinc. The bran and germ are sifted out of refined, enriched grains. So if you've been eating white bread and enriched-flour pasta all your life, you should make the switch now to whole grain breads and pastas. It doesn't have to be just whole wheat, either. Many people cannot tolerate wheat. If you're among those who cannot, choose from many other whole grains. The point is to eat a variety of delicious whole grains. You can eat all the white bread, enriched-flour pasta, and processed rice in the world, but you won't get any of the benefits I've been discussing. And believe me, you need them!

The bran and the germ are also removed from white rice, and with them go the protein, fiber, calcium, phosphorus, iron, vitamin E, and B vitamins. What's worse, converted rice, which lacks the bran and germ, often has behavior-altering preservatives such as BHT (a chemical that has been shown conclusively to alter the behavior of experimental animals and has been associated with similar changes in children and adults). Seasoned rices may have additional additives including irradiated herbs and spices. Fortunately, most progressive supermarkets and organic and natural food stores sell brown rice. Brown rice and all the many varieties of whole grains are easy to find in the bulk bin of any health food market.

So reduce your exposure to chemical carcinogens, and let your love affair with grains flourish all day every day. Instead of sneaking into the kitchen late at night to eat ice cream, take out the whole grain graham crackers. By choosing low-calorie whole grain graham crackers over ice cream, you can cut your exposure to industrial chemicals and pesticides by as much as 60 percent—not to mention the calories you will save!

I know you are thinking that transforming your craving for ice cream into a desire for graham crackers is quite a switch. But try it some night. Listen the following morning to your body. It will tell you all you need to know about feeling good after a midnight snack. On another night air-pop some organic popcorn (but leave off salt and butter). That's another midnight snack that will be kind and gentle with your body! Popcorn is a great whole grain food, high in nutrients and virtually fat free.

This I promise: make the switch to whole grains and other plant foods for snacking and you will soon find your body feels great and very pure.

Breads, cereals, crackers, muffins, and mixes made with organically grown grains should become new treats in your low-toxin high-energy diet. Puffed corn, puffed millet, rice cakes, and buckwheat cakes provide excellent low-calorie snacks. Arrowhead Mills apple spice muffin mix is simply delicious. Nature's Path makes a superb organic raisin bran cereal. Amy's Kitchen offers frozen macaroni and soy cheese dinners made from virtually all organic ingredients. Many major supermarkets and virtually all health-food and natural-food stores carry organic whole grain pastas, cookies, and crackers, often in special sections. The Personal Action Guide at the end of this book has information on ordering breads and other organic grain foods by mail.

I encourage you to seek out *organic* grains and *organic* grain products. Good as grains are for you, there have been many disturbing findings about chemically grown grains. They have been found to contain very dangerous residues of cancer-causing chemicals such as carbon tetrachloride, ethylene dibromide, and methyl bromide. Compared to many other foods, grains are relatively safe, but they're not perfectly safe. Based on my analyses of FDA Total Diet Study results, all chemically grown grains had *some* pesticide traces.

In the 1980s as much as 70 percent of the nation's stockpiled grain was found to contain traces of ethylene dibromide (EDB). Now, if you knew what an all-around nasty chemical EDB is you would be plenty concerned. This chemical (now banned) was used as a post-harvest fumigant. It causes low sperm counts and is suspected of causing cancer, birth defects, and central nervous system disorders and has caused cancer and other diseases in virtually every laboratory animal studied. In the Los Angeles area a man stored EDB near his rabbit hutch. His doe gave birth to three bunnies: one had three legs, another had three ears, and the third had only one ear. Residues of this extremely toxic chemical saturated the American grain supply throughout the early 1980s until its residues were found in grain products on supermarket shelves in Massachusetts, Florida, and elsewhere in the country. The EDB contamination hit even the big cereal and bread companies. One major producer of children's cereals found EDB residues in its products even after they were put on supermarket shelves and sold to innocent families. And EDB was detected in virtually all bread sampled for use in school lunch programs.

There is a moral to this story to which we should pay careful attention. Savvy consumers who bought organically grown grains were safe from EDB throughout the heaviest contamination period in the early 1980s. Organically grown grains are your best protection against exposure to chemicals in the grain supply. No doubt there will be future lapses in government and industry's safety programs for chemical grains. Organically grown grains provide maximum protection, since absolutely no toxic chemicals are used in their post-harvest treatment.

The chemical threat to the consumer is smaller than the threat faced by workers who are directly exposed to toxic pesticides, but that does not mean we should ignore the effects of chemically grown foods. By buying organic foods you can help lessen the suffering of others. I say that if we have any sense of decency we cannot turn our backs on the dangerous exposures faced by workers who grow and fumigate grains, especially since the key to lessening the burden of our fellow Americans is as simple as being an informed shopper. Buy organic grains and grain foods when you can. If you can't find organic grains, don't let that stop you from eating those grains that are available. Grains are low in pesticide saturation relative to all other foods, and it is vital that you eat a generous amount of whole grain daily to maintain the pollution-fighting low-toxin high-energy diet.

Grains Survival Guide

Some fruits and vegetables, such as apples, peaches, and summer squash, contained 80 or more pesticide residues. And peanuts had nearly 185 residues in sixteen samples. As you will learn when we discuss flesh foods, a fast-food quarter-pound hamburger has more than 100 residues, whereas the grain with the greatest pesticide saturation, rye, contained fewer than 50 pesticide residues.

This survival guide takes a close look at chemically grown grains and grain-based products available in any supermarket anywhere in the United States. It is based on results from the FDA Total Diet Study and considers grains and grain-based foods from throughout the nation. The number of residues cited is the number found in sixteen samples of that food. This survival guide will show you the least toxic of the chemical grains so you can tell which foods have relatively high pesticide saturation and which foods have the fewest residues. By purchasing low-residue foods you encourage farmers to plant crops that need fewer pesticide applications. That will help save our nation's land, the purity of our precious freshwater resources, and wildlife. Unfortunately, many grains have residues of diazinon and malathion, both of which are highly toxic to wildlife and responsible for decimation of our migratory bird populations. Although you would be better off buying organic grains and grain-based products, by buying low-pesticide chemically grown grains you still cast a vote for a cleaner America.

Use this survival list when shopping in supermarkets that sell only chemically grown food. When you cannot find organic foods, green light grains and grain-based foods are the safest and most healthful foods American chemical agriculture has to offer. Yellow light grains are a little less safe but can be eaten fairly often. There are no red light grains. Make green light grains your first choice for day-to-day eating. Supplement moderately with yellow light foods. Do this consistently and let your body tell you the good news.

GREEN LIGHT

Biscuits. Who doesn't love biscuits? Fortunately, they are not too badly contaminated. Biscuits made with enriched flour and found in the refrigerator section of your supermarket had twenty-eight pesticide residues in sixteen samples, representing six different pesticide formulations. The pesticide detected most frequently was malathion. Pesticides detected less frequently were chlorpyrifos, DDT, diazinon, dieldrin, lindane, and penta. These are heavy-duty pesticides. Your best choice is to use an organic biscuit mix, which can be found at health food markets. One biscuit contains .8 grams of saturated fat and traces of cholesterol.

Corn bread. Southern-style corn bread was not so bad. The FDA Total Diet Study found thirty-two pesticide residues in sixteen samples, representing five different pesticide formulations. The pesticides detected most frequently were diazinon and malathion. Pesticides detected less frequently were chlorpyrifos, DDT, and penta. One slice of southern-style corn bread contains .2 grams of saturated fat, no cholesterol.

Cornflakes. The great American cereal, cornflakes with skim milk, even if from nonorganic crops, makes a great breakfast choice. Cornflakes had ten pesticide and industrial chemical residues representing five formulations. Tributyl phosphate (possibly from packaging) was detected most frequently, and diazinon, diphenyl 2-ethylhexyl phosphate (also from packaging), malathion, and penta were also found. Some of these are heavy-duty chemicals; that cannot be denied. But compared with other more pesticide-saturated foods such as beef, cheese, butter, and bacon, cornflakes stack up well. A bowl of conflakes with low-fat or nonfat milk is a whole lot better than a sausage-and-eggs breakfast or a cheese omelet with fried potatoes. Cornflakes, with fresh low-residue fruits and juices and other grain foods such as whole wheat toast, can make a powerfully good low-toxin breakfast at home or on the road.

Crisped rice cereal. An American favorite, crisped rice cereals such as Rice Krispies are the least contaminated of any grain product in the Total Diet Study. So enjoy! You can find crisped rice cereals on any supermarket shelf from San Diego, California, to Woods Hole, Massachusetts. Crisped rice cereal had only five low-level pesticide and industrial chemical residues in sixteen samples representing four formulations. The pesticides and industrial chemicals detected were diazinon, malathion, tributyl phosphate, and methoxychlor. Weight watchers should note that one cup of crisped rice cereal contains just traces of saturated fat and no cholesterol. Add skim milk, and you still get great pesticide exposure reduction, since skim milk is virtually free from pesticides.

Egg noodles. Enriched egg noodles made with enriched white flour had thirty pesticide residues representing six different pesticides: chlorpyrifos, diazinon, malathion, BHC, chlorpropham, and DDT. One cup of enriched noodles contains .5 grams of saturated fat and 50 milligrams of cholesterol.

Farina. Farina is a relatively safe choice when made from chemically grown corn, and it's a great choice when made from organic corn. That is because corn is well protected from residue contamination by its husk; the pesticides most often biodegrade before they reach the kernels, so they do not show up in your diet at high levels.

Farina had twenty-one residues of four pesticide and industrial chemical formulations: malathion, tributyl phosphate, diazinon, and EDB. I am concerned about the frequent appearance of malathion and diazinon as well as EDB in grains. The EDB was detected before it was banned. It should not be detected in farina or any other foods anymore. Buying organic farina would help you be certain to avoid neurotoxic chemicals altogether.

By federal regulation, farina has had its bran, which contains its fiber, removed. Be sure to purchase farina that still has the nutrient-dense germ portion of the grain kernel. Unless the label specifically states that the germ is included, assume that it has been removed.

Fruit-flavored sweetened cereal. Here's an interesting case. As far as pesticides are concerned, fruit-flavored sweetened cereals such as Froot Loops are by no means as pure as the driven snow, but they are not nearly as bad as many other foods. They had twenty-six pesticide and industrial chemical residues representing eight formulations. Pesticides detected most frequently —in at least one-fourth of the samples—were malathion and methoxychlor. Pesticides and industrial chemicals detected less frequently were chlorobenzilate, diazinon, dicofol, ethion, heptachlor, and tributyl phosphate. Several of these pesticides bioaccumulate in the body and probably cause cancer. However, these pesticides are much more dangerous for children, who eat these cereals most frequently, because pound for pound children get a more concentrated dose. One ounce of fruit-flavored sweetened cereal contains .2 grams of saturated fat, no cholesterol. In addition, such cereals often contain behavior-altering preservatives such as BHA or BHT. As we shall see when we discuss food additives—and from what we know about the greater effects pesticides have on children—these chemical concoctions make sweetened fruit cereals a poor breakfast food choice.

Granola. Plain granola is a tricky food. The supermarket brands often contain loads of sugar and hydrogenated or tropical oils, both of which are rich in saturated fat and may be tainted with pesticides. Look for plain, unsweetened granola with just natural grains, nuts, and perhaps bits of fruit. It is much better for reducing your body's toxic exposures. Plain granola had only twenty-seven pesticide and industrial chemical residues in sixteen samples, representing six different formulations. Pesticides detected most frequently were chlorpyrifos, diazinon, and malathion. Pesticides and industrial chemicals detected less frequently were chlordane, diphenyl 2-ethylhexyl phosphate, and heptachlor.

Grits. Corn (hominy) grits are a southern favorite. And they also do well from the pesticide saturation standpoint. In the FDA Total Diet Study, fifteen residues were detected representing three pesticide and industrial chemical formulations. Malathion and tributyl phosphate were detected in at least one-fourth of the samples, diazinon less frequently.

Oatmeal. This winter favorite had twenty-four pesticide and industrial chemical residues in sixteen samples, representing three formulations. Pesticides and industrial chemicals detected most frequently were malathion and tributyl phosphate; diazinon was found less frequently.

The Quaker Oats Company, which produces Quaker Oats oatmeal, ought to produce organic oatmeal, which would come to consumers without dangerous pesticides such as diazinon and malathion. But do not let this slightly gloomy picture keep you away from oatmeal. It is among the best cereals you can choose if you want to fashion a low-toxin diet out of the mainstream chemically grown food supply. Compared with many other breakfast choices, oatmeal with a banana, whole grain toast, and pineapple juice will keep your toxic exposure relatively low.

Oat rings. These very popular breakfast cereals, which include Cheerios, are easy to find anywhere in the United States, at markets, coffee shops, hotel restaurants, and workplace cafeterias. Only four industrial chemicals and pesticides were found in unsweetened oat rings with a total of nine residues. Malathion was in more than one-fourth of the samples, and diphenyl 2-ethylhexyl phosphate, penta, and tributyl phosphate appeared less frequently. An ounce of unsweetened oat ring cereal contains .3 grams of saturated fat and no cholesterol. So it is a good all-around cereal that provides you with a relatively nontoxic breakfast even in coffee shops and restaurants.

Pancakes. Pancakes are not bad, chemically speaking. I ate some recently at a restaurant in Louisiana where everybody else was eating omelets and sausages. The best breakfast food I could find on the menu was the pancakes, which have far fewer pesticide residues than either omelets or sausages. I cut my exposure to at least one-fifth that of the diners who chowed on eggs, cheese, and sausages.

The Total Diet Study found that pancakes made from commercial mix (enriched flour, egg, milk, and oil) contained thirty-five pesticide residues in sixteen samples, representing six different pesticide formulations. Pesticides detected in at least one-fourth of the samples included chlorpyrifos, diazinon, and malathion. Pesticides detected less frequently were DDT, dieldrin, and penta. One pancake has .5 grams of saturated fat and 16 milligrams of cholesterol.

Pasta. Love pasta. But watch out for the butter sauces the gourmet chefs pitch at you. They can make any trip to the plate a toxic strike-out. Butter is loaded with pesticides. Prefer tomato-based sauces. Spaghetti made with enriched flour and served with tomato sauce has been carefully analyzed for toxic chemicals and found to be a fairly low toxin food, with about ten residues in sixteen samples. Spaghetti with meat sauce had only thirty-three residues. The pesticides detected most frequently in pasta alone, without sauce, are malathion, diazinon, and chlorpyrifos.

Remember to buy whole grain pastas for use at home. Enriched-flour pastas lack fiber. Whole grain pastas are widely available.

One cup of pasta contains .1 gram of saturated fat, no cholesterol, so it is a wonderful diet food, too, especially when served with a light tomato sauce instead of a butter-based sauce or a meat sauce.

Popcorn. Corn popped in oil is fairly high in pesticides, but don't blame the corn, which was probably fairly pure. The oil in which the corn was popped probably was loaded with pesticides. That is why popcorn had thirty-seven pesticide residues representing eight pesticide formulations. Diazinon, malathion, and methoxychlor were detected most frequently. Pesticides detected less frequently were carbofuran, chlorpyrifos, dieldrin, EDB, and penta. One cup of popcorn contains .5 grams of saturated fat, no cholesterol.

You can buy a hot-air popcorn maker and have oil-free popcorn. And organically grown popcorn is reasonably priced and widely available. Eat as much air-popped organic popcorn as you please. It makes a wonderfully satisfying nontoxic, low-calorie midnight snack. Hold the butter and salt, please.

Rice. Any kind of rice is likely to be low in pesticide saturation. As long as you have no allergies to this food, you can dine freely on rice. Rice will help you keep your exposure to toxic chemicals down to very minimal amounts when you dine out because you can always order low-toxin rice instead of highly toxic baked potatoes and sour cream. Prefer brown rice, which is made with the whole grain, for its additional fiber content.

Rice examined in the FDA Total Diet Study had eighteen residues in sixteen samples, representing seven different pesticide and industrial chemical formulations. The pesticide detected most frequently was malathion. Pesticides and industrial chemicals detected less frequently included chlorpropham, diazinon, diphenyl 2-ethylhexyl phosphate, methoxychlor, penta, and tributyl phosphate.

White rice is sometimes coated with talc, which may contain asbestos impurities. Such white rice is sold in many Latin and Asian food stores. There is no safe level of exposure to asbestos. Stay away.

Saltine crackers. Saltines had twenty-eight pesticide residues representing four pesticide formulations. Pesticides detected most frequently included diazinon and malathion. Pesticides detected less frequently included chlorpyrifos and penta. Four saltines have .5 grams of saturated fat and 4 milligrams of cholesterol. That may not sound like a lot of fat. But who eats just four saltines? It is not a great idea to eat saltines all the time. They contain quite a load of salt, but fortunately, unsalted crackers are widely available now.

Shredded wheat cereal. Shredded wheat had thirty-one residues representing six pesticide and industrial chemical formulations. Detected most frequently were diazinon, malathion, and tributyl phosphate. Chlorpyrifos, methoxychlor, and penta appeared less frequently. One ounce of shredded wheat contains .1 gram of saturated fat, no cholesterol. Shredded wheat with non-fat milk is one of your better choices among chemically grown foods. It is a fairly rich fiber source; as a result, the shredded wheat itself, despite its contamination, helps prevent significant exposure to the same pesticides that contaminate the product.

Tortillas. Tortillas made with enriched white flour were found to contain quite a few pesticides. Pure corn tortillas would have fewer pesticides, because corn is protected by its thick husk, it is sprayed less than wheat, and the pesticides with which corn is sprayed tend to degrade rather quickly in the environment. Tortillas made with organically grown grain are widely available at reasonable prices at health food markets, so you can always have organic corn or flour tortillas on hand. For a quick nontoxic snack or meal, pile shredded organic lettuce and peppers, vegetarian refried beans, and soy cheese on a crisp tortilla. What an excellent, satiating meal! Tortillas are indeed a versatile snack food; heat them in the oven and dip them in organic salsa for a wonderful spicy snack. Unfortunately, tortillas from supermarkets did contain pesticides; thirty-four industrial pollutant and pesticide residues were detected in sixteen samples, representing eleven different formulations. Pesticides detected most frequently included chlorpyrifos, diazinon, and malathion. Pesticides and industrial pollutants detected less frequently included DDT, dibutyl phthalate, dieldrin, diphenyl 2-ethylhexyl phosphate, lindane, methoxychlor, penta, and PCBs. One tortilla has about .1 gram of saturated fat and no cholesterol. Since chemical-free tortillas are so competitively priced, they are definitely the solution.

YELLOW LIGHT

Even the grains with the heaviest pesticide saturation have only about half the pesticide saturation of the worst dairy, meat, fruit, and vegetable foods. Eat yellow light grains less often than the green light group, but prefer them always over meats and high-fat dairy foods. Seek organic varieties of these yellow light grains whenever possible.

Dinner rolls. Soft white enriched dinner rolls had forty-four pesticide residues representing nine pesticide formulations. Chlorpyrifos, diazinon, and malathion were detected most frequently. Pesticides detected less frequently were DDT, dicloran, EDB, fenitrothion, penta, and pirimiphos-methyl. One soft white enriched dinner roll contains .5 grams of saturated fat, no cholesterol. It is easy to find organic whole grain dinner rolls. Try to replace chemically-saturated dinner rolls with their organic cousins.

Muffins. Muffins with fruit filling had forty-six residues in sixteen samples, representing eleven different pesticide and industrial chemical formulations. Pesticides detected most frequently—in at least one-fourth of the samples—included chlorpyrifos, DDT, diazinon, malathion, and penta. Pesticides and industrial chemicals detected less frequently included dicofol, dieldrin, fenitrothion, tecnazene, tri (2-ethylhexyl) phosphate, and methoxychlor. One muffin contains 1.5 grams of saturated fat, 19 milligrams of cholesterol. Muffin mixes made from chemically grown grains without fruit will have fewer pesticides.

Raisin bran cereal. Raisin bran had forty-two pesticide and industrial chemical residues representing thirteen formulations. Pesticides detected most frequently were DDT, dicofol, and malathion. Less frequently detected toxic chemicals were captan, diazinon, dicloran, dimethoate, diphenyl 2-ethylhexyl phosphate, endosulfan, ethion, penta, phosalone, and tributyl phosphate. Many of the pesticides in this cereal, such as dicofol and dimethoate, are present because of the pesticides sprayed on the fruit. Fortunately, several excellent brands of raisin bran with organic bran flakes and organic raisins are sold nationwide. One ounce of raisin bran cereal contains .1 gram of saturated fat, no cholesterol.

Rye bread. Rye bread had forty-nine residues representing thirteen pesticide and industrial chemical formulations. Pesticides detected in at least one-fourth of the samples were chlorpyrifos, diazinon, fenitrothion, and malathion. Pesticides and industrial chemicals detected less frequently were BHC, bromophos-ethyl, dicloran, lindane, parathion, penta, pirimiphos-methyl, tri (2-ethylhexyl) phosphate, and tributyl phosphate. One slice of rye bread contains .2 grams of saturated fat, no cholesterol. Most so-called rye bread contains very little rye flour. However, 100 percent organic rye bread is now widely available at health food markets and by mail. One excellent organic rye, available nationwide, is baked at Mill City Bakery in Minneapolis and is 100 percent organic—an excellent, tasty sandwich bread.

White bread. White bread was not tested. However, it is safe to assume that its pesticide concentrations are similar to those in dinner rolls, in which the same enriched flour is used.

Whole wheat bread. Wheat is heavily sprayed both before and after harvest. Although many of the most dangerous post-harvest chemicals that we have previously discussed were not detected in the FDA Total Diet Study, an array of pesticides were detected in whole wheat sandwich bread. This bread had forty-nine residues in sixteen samples, representing ten different formulations. Pesticides and industrial chemicals detected in at least one-fourth of the samples included chlorpyrifos, diazinon, fenitrothion, malathion, and tributyl phosphate. Pesticides and industrial chemicals detected less frequently were diphenyl 2-ethylhexyl phosphate, lindane, parathion, pirimiphos-methyl, and tri (2-ethylhexyl) phosphate. One slice of whole wheat bread contains .4 grams of saturated fat, no cholesterol. So many excellent, reasonably priced organic breads are available by mail order and at health food markets that you should really try to bring them into your home. These breads really offer satiety because their ingredients are pure and wholesome. And of course they allow you to avoid toxic exposure. I have seen many laboratory reports that attest to the purity of organic grains. See the Personal Action Guide in this book for the names of bakeries that produce wholesome, pure organic breads.

Shopping Tips

If your market does not sell organic whole grains, I recommend that you seek a health food store that carries them. If you cannot find one in your community, there are plenty of distributors that sell organic whole grain products by mail. Organic grains, cereals, and even breads keep well enough so that delivery is absolutely no problem.

Baldwin Hill Bakery in Massachusetts, for example, produces wonderful whole grain raisin bread, which can be shipped to your home. Mill City Bakery of Minneapolis produces pure and tasty sandwich breads, which are sold by mail order and in many major Minnesota markets. Sunrise Sourdough Bakery in Oregon was recently founded by bakers who learned their skills at Baldwin Hill Bakery. Breads from all these bakeries can be ordered by mail. Organic breads are crunchy, filling foods full of pure ingredients with wonderful taste. See the Personal Action Guide to find out where you can find organic breads and other grains and grain products.

Fortunately for all of us and our land and rivers and seas, the market for organically grown grains and grain-based products is expanding! This is great! I can go almost anywhere now and find organic whole grain foods. I recently visited supermarkets in Washington, D.C.; Takoma Park, Maryland; Seattle; New York City; Phoenix; Los Angeles; San Francisco; and Thibodaux, Louisiana, and found that organic whole grain products, from cookies and crackers to pasta, were widely available. The whole nation is catching on. But we need to keep bringing forward this great message that is so good for America.

Organically grown raw whole grains are sold packaged and in bulk at health food markets. You can find organically grown wheat berry, millet, rye, rice, wild rice, amaranth, triticale, barley, oats, quinoa, and many other grains for sale in health food stores. Be sure to keep plenty of organic whole wheat pasta on hand at home from your favorite good-foods market.

Be wary of some grain products' ingredients. Some breads and other grain foods such as cereals contain hydrogenated or partially hydrogenated vegetable oils. These oils make grains and cereals tender. They most often include hydrogenated corn, cottonseed, and soybean oils. The hydrogenation process adds hydrogen atoms to the liquid vegetable oils under high pressure, which provides longer shelf life. But the hydrogenation of vegetable oils turns them to semisolid saturated fats. Some researchers believe trans-fatty acids, created in the hydrogenation process, can interact with your body's cells and alter cell membranes, which are made up of layers of fat, so that they will allow carcinogens, which are fat soluble, to pass through even more easily. Hydrogenated fats are also suspected of playing a role in the increased incidence of bladder and breast cancers; certainly, the increased trend of using hydrogenated oils parallels the rising incidences of these cancers and it is possible that they might play a contributing cumulative role. You should drop foods with these oils from your diet.

Potassium bromate is an oxidizer (other oxidizers include potassium iodate, calcium bromate, and calcium iodate) added in relatively large amounts to flour to help make bakery foods fluffy and soft. Potassium bromate has been shown to be a mutagen. Many breads contain potassium bromate, which is usually listed on the label. Avoid them.

Some muffin mixes could be dangerous to your health. Most mixes are made with nutritionally deficient enriched flour lacking in fiber, and they introduce aluminum baking powder—also known as SAS or sodium aluminum phosphate—to your body. Baked goods containing sodium aluminum phosphate may introduce as much as 5 to 15 milligrams of aluminum into your body with each serving. That, my friend, is a lot of aluminum to be eating. After all, we are talking about a toxic metal! Aluminum has no nutritional value and is believed to play a role in Alzheimer's disease and related disorders. We're not sure of the exact role, but nobody can say it plays no role, and there is good evidence that aluminum is an especially dangerous metal, one to which we are chronically exposed. So why take a chance when the use of aluminum compounds is such an absolutely needless additive and risk?

Baked goods with sodium aluminum silicate or sodium silicoaluminate also introduce aluminum into your body. Sodium tartrate powders that have no aluminum are better choices. Labels are not required to specify when aluminum baking powder is used. So you should assume an aluminum baking powder is used unless the label specifically states that none is in the mix.

Have you ever noticed how many "country" breads are sold today? Well, "country" breads are often baked with inferior enriched flour, hydrogenated oils, additives, and preservatives. Don't be fooled!

Sweeteners such as sugar, corn syrup, fructose, dextrose, honey, and molasses are used to feed the yeast in bread, and they may add some flavor. But there are better, tastier breads made without sweeteners. Seek them out.

If any of these ingredients or processing practices are listed on the label of a grain product you can consider it suspect. And any one of these suspect chemicals should sound a clear and strong warning that you are looking at a product made with inferior ingredients or one that has undergone less than top quality processing. Regard any inferior ingredient or processing method as a red flag, and keep that product out of your cart.

Follow these tips for storing whole grains, flour, cereals, and other grain-based foods:

• **Grains.** All grains contain enzymes that produce rancidity under improper storage conditions. Store in a cool place or in a refrigerator or freezer, out of direct sunlight, to keep them fresher for a longer time. Remember, organic grains have no preservatives. So use them! And proper storage, in a cool dark place, will help preserve their freshness longer.

• **Brown Rice.** Store brown rice in an airtight container, as it can produce an odor. In hot weather, store brown rice in the refrigerator. Use in three to six months.

• **Flour.** Store flour in the freezer in an airtight, moisture-free container. Always store soy flour, with its high fat content, in the refrigerator.

Safe Shopping List: Grains

Green Light	Number of Residues
Crisped rice cereal	5
Oat ring cereal	9
Corn flakes	10
Pasta (with tomato sauce)	10
Grits	15
Rice	18
Farina	21
Oatmeal	24
Fruit-flavored sweetened cereal	26
Granola	27
Saltines	28
Biscuits	28
Egg noodles	30
Shredded wheat cereal	31

Corn bread	32
Pasta (with meat sauce)	33
Tortillas	34
Pancakes	35
Popcorn (popped in oil)	37

Yellow Light

Raisin bran cereal	42
Dinner rolls	44
Blueberry muffins	46
Whole wheat bread	49
Rye bread	49
White bread	—

5. ANIMAL FOODS

Most Americans eat far more of them than they need. I eat animal foods including seafood no more than twice a week, and red meat no more than once every couple of weeks. I truly relish these foods when I have them. But knowing what I do of their toxic dangers, of the burden that raising cattle places on the environment, and of the inhumane conditions under which many animals are raised, I feel it's vital to eat these foods seldom and to eat only the safest cuts.

In the low-toxin high-energy diet, I recommend that absolutely no more than one-third of all food come from animal sources including meat, poultry, seafood, dairy foods, and eggs. Many experts believe that even this is too high. Go for plant foods—they're much better for you for reducing your exposure to the most dangerous pesticides and to cholesterol and saturated fat, as well. Always remember the two-thirds rule. Fruits, vegetables, and grains are far more healthful in many ways and should make up at least two-thirds of your diet. But, selected with care and an understanding of safe eating guidelines, animal foods can be nutritious and can provide a life-enhancing variety of flavors.

Eating the wrong animal foods can place a huge toxic burden on your body. Farm animals are high on the food web; in their flesh they bioconcentrate toxins from the thousands of pesticide-sprayed grasses and grains they've consumed or, in the case of some fish and game meats, from thousands of other animals. The most potent toxins routinely found in the American diet are in meat, seafood, poultry, and dairy products.

There are fewer residues in some animal foods than in some plant foods, but those found in the animal foods are often more dangerous. This is because the residues that bioaccumulate in animal flesh are likely also to bioaccumulate in human flesh. Some of the residues on plant foods are less

72

likely to bioaccumulate. Toxins in animal flesh are absorbed into the human body more easily than toxins in plant foods, and the toxins may be activated to become more potent carcinogens by the fats in which they are stored.

The pesticides and industrial pollutants in animal flesh are not its only danger. Modern animal raising methods, like modern farming methods, rely far too heavily on chemical intervention. Cattle and hogs are given hormone implants to increase their growth, and these chemicals, when improperly used (as they have been by American ranchers), can affect humans. The European common market recently banned the import of U.S.-grown beef that has been treated with hormones. And there is a serious problem with routine use of antibiotics and sulfa medicines in animal feed to combat diseases caused by overcrowding. These drugs can harm consumers, and they have helped create many superstrains of antibiotic-resistant bacteria, which are affecting our health and even causing some deaths.

Most of the toxins in animal foods come from the same source as the toxins in plant foods: farmers' overuse of chemicals. Pesticides are in the feed given to cows, pigs, and chickens, and they pollute rivers and lakes, infesting the flesh of freshwater fish and many saltwater species.

The dangerous long-term carcinogens and neurotoxins found in meat, poultry, dairy foods, and seafood include BHC, chlordane, DDT, dieldrin, dioxin, heptachlor, HCB, and lindane, according to records obtained from the FDA and the U.S. Department of Agriculture (USDA). A 1987 USDA report indicated that among a sampling of 278 cows, 74 had DDT; 24 had dieldrin; 22 had heptachlor; 10 had BHC; 7 had HCB; and 2 had chlordane. These potent cancer-causing chemicals are among the most dangerous long-term poisons in the American diet. The pesticide contamination of the worst cuts of meat, seafood, and even some dairy products poses a risk that is 30 to more than 1,000 times above the government's negligible-risk standard for cancer caused by toxic chemicals in our food and water, according to risk assessments I have performed for both the *Arizona Republic* newspaper and the National Academy of Sciences.

When looking at pesticide profiles of individual blood samples, it is easy to tell which people eat a lot of animal foods, particularly beef, and which ones have supplanted many of their meat and dairy dishes with plant foods. Invariably, the flesh and dairy food eaters will have easily detectable compounds of these potent pesticides circulating in their blood, whereas those who eat a largely vegetarian diet will have a little bit of DDT—often less than one part per billion—and that is all. Since these powerful chemicals are probable cancer-causing agents in the human body in addition to having neurotoxic properties, it would seem prudent to reduce exposure to them. We can find out how to reduce our toxic exposures significantly by learning which animal foods are the purest and which are the most contaminated. And by cutting down our exposure, we can give our bodies the chance they need to detox a lifetime's accumulation of toxic chemicals.

Since animals store toxins in their fatty tissues, an important rule to remember is that the fattier the food, the more dangerous it is. This applies across the board. Ground meats, fatty meats, processed meats, the skin of poultry, the dark fatty portions of fish, whole milk, cheese, and ice cream are all high in toxins. Since the fats in these foods also contribute to high cholesterol levels and heart disease, avoiding them is doubly beneficial to your health.

Fatty foods may even potentiate the toxic chemicals that are lodged in them. In one animal study, chemical carcinogens given to rats were more likely to produce tumors in a group that was fed fatty foods than in a group fed low-fat foods. Thus, a high-fat diet of animal foods is double trouble: the most potent pesticides are concentrated in fat, and the chemical properties of fat itself may actually enhance their carcinogenicity.

Worldwide, a clear association consistently appears between the highest rates of cancer of the breast, colon, and prostate and nations that have the fattiest diets. I believe that the link results from a combination of the fat itself and to some extent the toxic chemicals, such as industrial pollutants and pesticides, lodged in fatty tissues.

The link between cancer and meat eaters' exposure to toxic chemicals goes even deeper. All fried and broiled foods contain mutagens, chemicals that can damage cellular reproductive material. But fried and broiled meats have far more mutagens than similarly prepared plant foods. One study indicates that some 20 percent of American meat eaters may have toxic mutagens in their digestive tract that can be absorbed into the bloodstream and can attack cells. The same study indicated that vegetarians are unlikely to have *any* mutagens in their digestive tract.

My research indicates that thousands of Americans are likely to develop premature cancer—and possibly symptoms of neurotoxicity—simply as a result of the industrial chemical and pesticide residues in their favorite cuts of meat, poultry, and seafood. Heavy meat eaters who eat high-fat meats such as frankfurters and hamburgers will have higher body burdens of cancer-causing pesticides and are at higher risk of serious illness than persons who eat little meat, choose lean cuts, trim the fat from red meat, and remove the skin from poultry.

My goal is to inform Americans that the risk from pesticides ingested in their favorite foods is much higher than they know and certainly higher than the government concedes. Consumers have been made the unwitting victims of low-level pesticide exposures. I estimate that 50 percent of animal foods could easily be contaminated with carcinogenic pesticides, based on my review of USDA meat inspection reports. Yet less than 1 percent of the meat eaten in this country is sampled for contamination. And the routine tests used by federal inspectors often are not designed to detect many dangerous pesticides and chemicals. Federal officials (whose numbers were greatly reduced during the 1980s) regularly inspect for no more than a tenth of all possible chemical contaminants in poultry and meat, many of which are known or suspected health hazards, according to a recent statement by Public Voice for Food and Health Policy, a Washington-based advocacy group promoting safer food.

Despite these knowledge gaps, we know enough to make us passionately concerned about the safety of our animal foods. In 1989, some 400,000 chickens belonging to Townsend Poultry Products of Batesville, Arkansas, had to be destroyed because of contamination by the pesticide heptachlor. In 1986, Banquet Foods destroyed 200,000 chickens in Arkansas as a result of chlordane contamination. A few years earlier, Washington turkeys were found to be contaminated with PCBs. After the inadvertent contamination of Michigan cattle with a cancer-causing fire retardant made with polybrominated biphenyls (PBBs) in 1973–74, more than 5 million pounds of PBB-tainted hamburger was consumed by the state's residents. Smoked chubs from the Great Lakes, catfish, bluefish, striped bass, and many other seafood favorites are regularly sold even though they contain dangerously high amounts of PCBs, dieldrin, dioxin, and other toxic chemicals.

An internal audit by the inspector general's office of the U.S. Department of Agriculture in 1988 discovered that tainted meat had been allowed to pass on to American kitchens even after federal inspectors found that it was chemically contaminated. The federal auditors discovered that the Agriculture Department's Food Safety and Inspection Service was unable to successfully investigate pesticide violations in 79 percent of the cases reviewed. All too often, by the time lab results were complete the product was already sold—and consumed. The General Accounting Office reported that the Food and Drug Administration has a similarly dismal record for protecting consumers from contaminated seafood. Despite government officials' constant reassurances, they cannot protect us all from eating harmful amounts of toxic chemicals.

You must be responsible, ultimately, for the safety of your food. Government isn't. You must seek the safest meat, poultry, and seafood, or buy from ranchers who feed their animals organically grown grains.

Fortunately, many ranchers are bringing safe, pesticide-free meat and poultry to market, and there is plenty of pristine seafood. Shopping savvy is the key to safe eating, but you can shop smart only if you know which pesticides are in your foods and at what concentrations. When you know the facts, you can take action and protect yourself.

6. MEAT AND POULTRY

Ask children where their meat or chicken comes from and they will tell you it comes from the supermarket. A cute answer—for a child. But we're not children. We should be aware of where our foods come from, the conditions under which the animals are raised, and especially what chemicals used in raising the animals may affect the health of those consuming them.

The Factory Farm

In addition to the pesticide residues concentrated in the flesh of food animals, a huge array of chemicals is fed to cattle, pigs, and poultry by farmers hoping to increase their yield. In a way, these chemicals are the animal equivalents of chemical fertilizers and pesticides used on plants. Not content with nature's way, meat and poultry farmers try to speed the animals' weight gain, "improve" the appearance of their flesh, and achieve other desirable marketing qualities by feeding them various chemicals. They also try to increase their profit by raising animals in the smallest space possible and by giving them measurable, controllable feed instead of allowing them to forage. The result, of course, is increased disease and mortality among the animals. Farmers try to solve this problem with—you guessed it—more chemicals. Their drugs of choice include antibiotics and sulfa drugs. Antibiotics are used to kill bacteria. Sulfa drugs usually prevent bacteria from reproducing.

The routine use of antibiotics in the diets of pigs, cattle, and fowl is a serious problem in the factory farmyard. Today at least half of all antibiotics produced yearly in the United States are fed to farm animals to prevent disease. About 30 to 90 percent of the chickens, 80 percent of veal calves and pigs, and 60 percent of the beef cattle raised for food in the United States are routinely given antibiotic medications mixed directly with their feed.

For more than a decade the government has watched as the pork industry has consistently brought to market products with elevated residues of sulfamethazine and other sulfa drugs. The most popular of these drugs, sulfamethazine, is suspected to be a human carcinogen. Why are they used? Steve Marbery, editor of the trade publication *Hog Farm Management,* has noted, "For the majority of producers, sulfa is a low-cost crutch that can mask poor management practices or bad environment—maybe both." According to the magazine, 97 percent of hog producers rely on feed-grade medication. "As farm size [grows] among the operations surveyed, so [does] the tendency to use feed additives," he says. A 12.6 percent violation rate for sulfa residues was found among thirty-four Indiana swine herds in one survey. In Illinois, nearly 20 percent of the hogs sampled in a year-long residue-monitoring program contained sulfa residues above the violation rate. One Illinois farm had a 50 percent violation rate.

The factory farm setting is directly responsible for the sulfamethazine-tainted cuts of pork consumers purchase. "Reduce overcrowding and you reduce the need for sulfa," says British swine scientist Tom Alexander. "Instead of enlarging accommodations, the average producer will increase the number of pigs per pen. This overcrowding works its way through the growing and finishing, resulting in a gradual slowing of growth rate and, throughout, a rise in disease levels and reliance on medication."

If you have ever been inside a modern hog barn, one of the first things you will notice is an ammonia stench. The smell is hard to ignore. The reason for the stench is that hog barns are often built with slatted floors over large pits so that feces and urine can fall through to be collected and hauled away, often to the fields. Still other hog farmers have installed flush gutters that transport the feces and urine into holding lagoons; however, these huge pits of toxic animal waste have become a major pollution problem in the Midwest, in some areas severely contaminating shallow groundwater. In the traditional hog barn, all this feces and urine interact with the environment and form a witches' brew of toxic gases that includes ammonia, methane, and hydrogen sulfide. First-time visitors to Midwest hog barns frequently report feeling light-headed and feeble even hours after their visit has ended.

Hogs, confined to tiny stalls, inhale these fumes twenty-four hours a day. Around 20 percent of the largest hog farms in America now raise hogs in total confinement, allowing them absolutely no time outside from birth to slaughter. The threat of pneumonia is omnipresent. Sometimes hogs become sick and lose weight. Others may contract contagious rhinitis, a disease that causes the bones and tissues of the pig's snout to degenerate. The hog farmer lives in fear of rhinitis because it spreads through a barn like fire.

Unlike the consumer, who must have a physician's prescription to obtain antibiotics and other medications, ranchers simply go to the local feed store and purchase enormous sacks of antibiotics, which they then mix with the animals' feed. But how careful can the farmers be? Not too careful, sometimes. The result often is an excess amount of residue in the animals' tissues after they are slaughtered. Yet there is little chance that the government, which has an embarrassingly small sampling program, will detect those animals with excessive antibiotics or sulfamethazine in their tissues. The ranchers know this. So sickly animals are loaded with antibiotics and sulfa drugs.

Sulfamethazine has been used since the 1940s to prevent respiratory disease among market hogs. It is known to cause toxic effects on the thyroid gland of humans, including nodules that could be cancerous. Recent tests on mice and rats also indicate sulfamethazine could be a carcinogen. In both laboratory animals and humans, the effects seem to be centered on the thyroid gland. There is a good chance that sulfamethazine use may be restricted further by the government and that sulfa drugs will even be pulled completely from the market for use with animals intended for human consumption because of concerns over putting another carcinogenic substance into the food supply and the excessively high levels found in pork.

The presence of residues of antibiotics and sulfa drugs in meat and poultry can cause severe allergic reactions in people sensitive to these drugs. People sensitive to penicillin, for instance, have been known to have serious reactions after eating veal because of the penicillin residues in the meat.

Government regulations restrict use of antibiotics and sulfa drugs. But government watchdogs are hard pressed to stop the unlawful and widespread antibiotic and sulfa drug contamination of pork. More than 80 million hogs are slaughtered annually. At most, a fraction of 1 percent of these are inspected for chemical residues. There is little reason to believe that the Department of Agriculture's sampling program has any statistical significance. Ranchers, like freeway drivers exceeding the speed limit, have little fear that they will be caught.

Thus the figures presented here, from USDA meat inspection reports, are probably low-end estimates of the extent of the sulfamethazine contamination of pork products. Nevertheless, these very conservative figures are disturbing. In 1987, for example, more than 10 percent of market hogs that were tested at slaughtering plants and intended for the dining tables of Americans had residues of sulfamethazine, and more than 5 percent of those residues were high enough to warrant violation notices and warnings. The sulfa problem will be difficult to eliminate; most ranchers who use sulfamethazine do not even think of the medication as a toxic chemical.

When consumers eat bacon and eggs, they are not counting on exposure to a suspected tumor-inducing chemical such as sulfamethazine. But that is the reality that has been spawned by the modern factory farm.

It's sad. Hogs are among the most intelligent of our farmyard animals. Turning them into biomachines and confining them in overcrowded pens is something you may not want to take part in. In the Personal Action Guide at the end of this book you will find the names of pork producers whose animals are raised under humane conditions without massive doses of antibiotics and sulfamethazine.

Ranchers' reliance on hormones in raising cattle is another result of the factory farm system. Hormones are given to between 65 and 99 percent of the cattle raised for slaughter in the United States. Farmers find that the hormones speed growth and produce leaner meat. Industry experts claim there is no danger to humans from these hormones when they are used properly. But, like antibiotics, growth hormones are sold to ranchers over the counter without a veterinary prescription, and there is no adequate system of inspection for hormone levels in meat and poultry—despite the fact that added estrogenic and androgenic burdens on our bodies can cause cancer, and hormones implanted in cattle may contain both estrogens and androgens.

And there have been horror stories. In Puerto Rico in the early 1980s, premature puberty—menstruation and the development of breasts and pubic hair in children under the age of eight—reached epidemic levels. Physicians studying the problem found that removing chicken and milk from the children's diets significantly reduced symptoms. An independent investigation of supermarket meats in Puerto Rico by a university researcher indicated extremely high estrogen levels in some samples of pork and chicken. Other researchers found synthetic hormones circulating in the bloodstream of the children.

In Italy in 1980, some children age two and three experienced puberty. The culprit proved to be the synthetic hormone DES (diethylstilbestrol), which was being used illegally. DES was banned in the United States and Europe in the late 1970s because of its ability to interact directly with DNA and cause cancer. In West Germany in August 1988, some 14,000 veal calves sold to a U.S. military base were found to have been given a mixed hormone cocktail; many of the calves had to be destroyed. Both of these debacles made the use of hormones a red-hot health and political issue in Europe.

Then, in January 1989, the European Economic Community prohibited the import of American cattle treated with growth hormones. The ban affected $100 million worth of U.S. beef and beef by-products.

Now, what was all the fuss about? The American beef industry has been telling us that hormones pose absolutely no threat to the health of the American consumer. After all, we are told, the amounts added to meat are absolutely minuscule.

Let's look at the use of hormones from the European point of view. There are three primary reasons for European opposition to the use of hormones in raising farm animals. First, several significant human health tragedies involving indiscriminate use of hormones have been reported in Europe in recent years. Second, much of the American meat sold in Europe consists of organ cuts, which *do* accumulate toxic chemicals such as antibiotics and possibly hormones. Third, Europeans have not been brainwashed into believing that factory farming is the only way to raise animals intended for human consumption. Indeed, European public opinion is soundly opposed to the factory farm. In 1985 European farmers were prohibited from using hormones in raising livestock. Earlier, England prohibited the regular subtherapeutic use of antibiotics in animal feed.

When used properly, hormones *may* be safe. However, when used improperly, as they have been by American and European ranchers, some hormones—such as those that contain estrogen—can cause cancer as well as ovarian cysts and premature sexual development, according to medical experts.

Meanwhile, the American consumer has good reason to be concerned about the prolific use of hormones in raising beef. The sale of DES was outlawed in July 1979, but government documents indicate that forty-nine drug distributors illegally sold DES after the ban. That DES was eventually used in 318 feedlots in twenty states. A total of 427,275 cattle were illegally implanted with DES after the deadline. Another 245,000 were illegally implanted with DES and already had been slaughtered before their carcasses could be recovered.

In 1983, DES was illegally used again by American cattle ranchers, this time in nearly 1,500 veal calves from five different farms in upstate New York. And, as the National Academy of Sciences has clearly stated, because of poorly designed government monitoring programs for hormones, nobody knows today the extent to which abuse of hormones occurs among American livestock ranchers. Historic evidence clearly points to the fact that American ranchers have no problem flouting the regulations that restrict the use of hormones. After all, who's there to catch them?

Other questionably safe drugs have been regularly used in livestock. They include dimetridazole, ipronidazole, and carbadox, all of which are potential human carcinogens that leave residues in meat and poultry. Up to

90 percent of the nearly 30,000 animal drugs now in use have not been approved by the government.

The beef industry, of course, says there is no health threat. But why, then, did the Puerto Rican children's symptoms regress when they were taken off chicken and milk? If estrogenic hormones are not directly carcinogenic at low levels, why was DES banned?

My position on the use of hormones runs counter to the beef industry's. One theory on the link between estrogen and the onset of cancer asserts that the body's endogenous production of estrogen and the exogenous intake of estrogenic substances work together upon estrogenic-sensitive tissues and promote or directly cause cancer. Therefore, chronic elevation of estrogenic activity, above that which would be considered normal, may well put the human body at risk for estrogen-linked cancer. In women, cervical or uterine cancer could be the end result of ingesting meat from livestock treated with hormones. Since chemical poisons often leave no traces, the link with synthetic hormones in beef will never be known. The contribution of estrogen from implanted beef to our diets may *appear* trivial, but our bodies are extremely responsive to minuscule doses of hormones. In a perfect world, perhaps with proper use, estrogenic hormones could be safe. But the livestock industry has shown little regard for the safe, sanctioned use of hormone implants, and there have been abuses of safe food regulations.

That is why there is no reason, from the consumer viewpoint, to add any more of a burden to our bodies, especially with regard to some hormones—particularly estrogen—which are already suspected of being a natural cancer burden on the body.

Another objection consumers have to hormones and other chemicals such as antibiotics is that their use is symptomatic of the factory farm mentality of American ranching. The meat many people eat today comes from animals that have spent their entire lives crowded like prisoners in cells, implanted with hormones, and fed antibiotics. This isn't the America we want.

The raising of veal calves as it is practiced today is the most extreme example of factory farm techniques. In order to get especially pale, tender meat, veal farmers raise the calves under extraordinary conditions that produce extensive toxic contamination.

More than one million calves are raised for veal annually in the United States, many of them in the Midwest, California, and Pennsylvania. Although the calves are slaughtered at four months of age, mortality rates before slaughter range from 10 percent to as high as 30 percent. Milk-fed calves slaughtered for veal are kept chained in tiny stalls about 22 inches wide—too small for the calves even to turn around in. To prevent muscle development and speed weight gain, the calves are allowed absolutely no exercise. Chained in tiny crates, veal calves cannot groom themselves, stretch their legs, or lie down in a natural position.

The light meat sold as "premium" or "milk-fed" veal is from calves that have been made anemic by withholding iron. The veal industry may claim their calves are given adequate iron. But watch what they do, not what they say. And what they do is spend their money on water-conditioning systems meant to remove every trace of naturally occurring iron from the water given their veal calves. One advertisement for a water conditioning system for veal calf ranching specifically admonishes the industry: "Attention veal farmers! It's a fact. Iron in your water supply will hurt you on money day at the market."

Veal calves are kept in total darkness to make them less restless. Serious leg injuries are caused by the complete lack of straw covering the wood-slatted floors. Respiratory and intestinal diseases run rampant among veal calves, so they are given frequent doses of antibiotics and sulfa drugs. Veal calves are denied virtually all solid food and even pure, plain drinking water. In a futile attempt to quench their thirst, calves drink milky feed that causes them to gain weight quickly. The calves then suffer chronic diarrhea from being fed a liquid diet of growth stimulators, antibiotics, powdered skim milk, and mold inhibitors.

These conditions are considered simply the industry standard. In Sonoma County, California, veal rancher Michael Cambra, of Santa Rosa, was found guilty in 1987 of animal cruelty and neglect after law enforcement authorities discovered 159 calves under his care chained in small crates inside a stifling hot barn. More than 90 other calves were dead, their decomposing bodies piled outside. Cambra was fined a paltry $250—because he was simply doing his job. Veal ranching is a high-mortality profession—for the calves!

The conditions required for production of milk-fed veal promote the widespread use of antibiotics and sulfa drugs that can help keep sickly animals alive long enough to be slaughtered. By depriving veal calves of their mothers' milk, fresh air, exercise, adequate nutrition, and proper veterinary care, veal farmers create a breeding ground for countless infectious diseases.

I undertook an extensive review of government reports on the antibiotic and sulfa drug residues in veal calves. My review indicates that an array of drugs do, in fact, contaminate veal raised on factory farms. Liver, kidney, and muscle tissues were tainted with a variety of antibiotics and sulfa drugs: penicillin, streptomycin, tetracycline, neomycin, oxytetracycline, gentamycin, sulfamethazine, sulfathiazole, and sulfaquinoxaline. Residues of sulfamethazine—a possible human carcinogen—in veal calves were as high as five parts per million, the absolute limit allowed by the government.

In one recent USDA survey, 20 of 881 calf tissue samples were in clear violation of government standards for drug residues. That rate of 2.3 percent is quite high by regulatory standards. And that is just what we know.

Dr. Kenneth Stoller, of the Department of Pediatrics at UCLA Medical Center and Cedars-Sinai Medical Hospital, points out that calves raised humanely, in a healthy environment with proper nutrition and exercise, do not need continual doses of antibiotics and other drugs. It's that simple.

Hearings were held recently in the California State Assembly upon introduction of humane farming legislation. As I write this passage, the bill, against all odds and great opposition from the state's powerful agribusiness lobbies, has made it through the full assembly. The bill awaits a full state senate vote and approval of the governor. If it passes, it will be the first bill in the United States to protect victims of factory farming. Since introduction of the California legislation, similar humane farming bills have been introduced on the federal level as well as in the New York and Massachusetts legislatures. The California bill is closest to passage. Let's hope it makes it.

We can learn from other nations' actions. Sweden passed an animal bill of rights in 1988, the world's most sweeping, stringent set of protection laws pertaining to farm animals. "Cattle, pigs, and chickens are being freed from the restrictions of intensive or factory-farming methods, in which animals are kept in crowded conditions and antibiotics and hormones are often administered," reports the *New York Times*. In Sweden cattle must now be allowed to graze, and pigs no longer may be confined and tied down. In addition, pigs must be allowed to bed and feed in separate places. Both cattle and pigs must have access to straw and litter. The Swedish legislation stipulates that chickens be given the opportunity to roam and peck for grub and that they not be kept confined all their lives in cages. Veal calves may roam their pastures. The use of subtherapeutic doses of antibiotics and hormones is strictly forbidden.

We Americans who eat flesh and dairy foods must wake up to institutionalized cruelty to animals on the factory farm, for unless we awaken, we as a nation will lose a precious portion of our own humanity. Perhaps we cannot do away with the factory farm entirely. But if enough of us use our consumer dollars to vote by buying free-range animal foods we can certainly alleviate the suffering of some farm animals. That's because free-range animals are given the opportunity to graze in pastures or move about the farmyard. They aren't cooped or penned their entire lives.

Contamination by salmonella bacteria, a major cause of food poisoning in this country, is another result of factory farm methods. Many experts contend that the contamination of our favorite cuts with microorganisms such as salmonella is of more immediate concern than the long-term threat of cancer from industrial pollution and pesticides.

Each year at least 1 to 2 percent of the American population suffers salmonellosis; that means there are at least two million and perhaps as many as four million cases of salmonellosis annually. Some experts believe many more Americans go through at least one case of food poisoning a year. Healthy people may not recognize a bout of salmonellosis for what it is, and so they will not report it to a doctor. Often mild salmonellosis is shrugged off as an upset stomach or flu with cramps and diarrhea.

No wonder many scientists assert that salmonellosis poses a health problem of large proportions in the United States. With more than 40,000 reported cases (the vast majority of cases are never reported) and 500 deaths annually, salmonella contamination of our meat and poultry is, indeed, a significant problem. And the problem just keeps growing. In the early 1940s only about 4 in 100,000 persons suffered from nontyphoid salmonellosis, the kind of salmonellosis that often results from eating the contaminated flesh of warm-blooded animals. By 1983, that number had increased nearly five times. Today 20 out of 100,000 persons will be afflicted by nontyphoid salmonellosis, according to data compiled by the Centers for Disease Control. And that figure includes only reported cases. You can conduct your own poll. Ask your own friends if they've gotten sick this year as a result of something they ate. Most will tell you that they have. Food poisoning is very common.

This increase in animal-related salmonellosis parallels the rise of the factory farm, increased antibiotic use in livestock ranching, and increasingly filthy slaughterhouse conditions. As factory farming methods have become more commonplace, the bacteria in our nation's food have become far more deadly. The result of widespread use of antibiotic medications in livestock feed has been the inadvertent breeding of antibiotic-resistant salmonella. These bacteria are not only deadly; they are rendering our antibiotics useless.

In one FDA study, salmonella from healthy chickens, beef cattle, and swine from 1978 to 1981 were analyzed to see what percent were resistant to antimicrobial drugs. The results: 61 percent of salmonella were found to be resistant to sulfadiazine; 56 percent were resistant to streptomycin; 33 percent were resistant to tetracycline; 5 percent were resistant to kanamycin and carbenicillin; 3 percent were resistant to ampicillin.

Ten salmonella serotypes account for more than 70 percent of the food poisoning cases reported in the United States annually. The most common is *Salmonella typhimurium*. Fifteen percent of various isolates of this family are now resistant to antimicrobial drugs. Overall, 24 percent of common serotypes are resistant to antimicrobials. It is estimated that as many as

200 salmonella-linked deaths annually result from the use of subtherapeutic antibiotics in animal feeds.

For decades, chloramphenicol has been the drug of choice for treating complications associated with salmonellosis. However, throughout the mid-1980s, the drug was widely used on cattle and hogs. Its widespread use could very well have been the reason why, when 1,000 persons were infected with *Salmonella newport* in California in 1985, this strain was resistant to chloramphenicol. Exposure to chloramphenicol has also been associated with the onset of a rare form of human bone marrow disease, aplastic anemia, which is almost always fatal.

It is also now known that antibiotic-resistant bacterial strains are passed from animals to humans. A recent FDA study of food poisoning in the Seattle area suggests that poultry is a major path by which resistant bacteria reach humans. The FDA reports, for example, that 22 percent of chicken and turkey samples from local Seattle markets showed campylobacter bacteria contamination, and about one-third of these samples contained antibiotic-resistant bacteria. Studies suggest that the antimicrobial drugs to which food animals are exposed eventually lead to the appearance and persistence of resistant strains in humans; only a small proportion of resistant salmonella outbreaks can be attributed to transmission from other humans.

Although food poisoning is not a very serious illness for most people, infants under two years are at high risk, as are elderly and immune-weakened persons. Death results for one in every 1,000 persons infected by salmonella, and it is usually individuals at the extremes of age who die.

Salmonellosis begins as diarrhea and abdominal cramps one to three days after eating contaminated food. Do not suspect the meal you just ate. Only in rare cases will the infecting dose of salmonellae be so large as to cause illness immediately after your meal. For healthy adults, the episode will last one day to one week.

Unfortunately the bacterial contamination problem of our food supply is not likely to improve. The number of chickens in a typical flock with salmonella may number as few as three or four percent, but as a result of slaughterhouse conditions during the processing of the animals, salmonella and other bacterial contamination could spread to as many as 38 percent of the carcasses.

Your best protection against bacterial infections is to heed the shopping and cooking tips that follow the Meat and Poultry Survival Guide in this chapter.

There are other reasons to cut down on animal foods, especially beef. Cattle raising takes a tremendous toll on our land and is contributing substantially to the desertification of the West. Dairy cows drink as much as

50 gallons of water a day, and they compact the soil on which they graze until it becomes so hard that the soil's ability to absorb rainfall is impaired. In South America the equatorial rain forests are being destroyed at a phenomenal rate to provide temporary pasture for cattle, much of it to provide beef for export to the United States and Europe. This destruction of the rain forests is one of the great ecological threats to our future. All because of our appetite for meat! So we can help save our planet—and our rain forests—by cutting way down on the amount of beef we eat.

Meat and Poultry Survival Guide

The following analyses of popular cuts of meat and poultry are based, for the most part, on the FDA Total Diet Study in which sixteen samples of each food were tested between 1982 and 1986. The samples were taken from markets in four major regions of the United States, and all analyses were done *after* foods were prepared and cooked. So there can be no overestimation of the chemical residue concentrations. These are very accurate findings. Quite possibly, they are understated.

The Total Diet Study did not take into account the presence of hormones and antibiotics. Since these chemicals are commonly used on factory farms, there is a good chance that a slightly increased concentration of hormones will be present in some meats. Poultry is not given hormones, except capons. You should, however, expect the presence of antibiotics or sulfa drugs in some cuts of beef, veal, pork, and poultry. The only way you can be certain these foods do not contain hormones, antibiotics, or sulfa drugs is if they are certified organic (fed organically grown grains) or certified to have been raised hormone- or chemical-free. Such groups include crop growing organizations such as the international Organic Crop Improvement Association and the Oregon Tilth, both of which also certify livestock practices. The government also has a special program with a few select ranchers to ensure that they take extra precautions to prevent traces of antibiotic or hormone residues in their products. Sources of certified organic as well as hormone- and chemical-free meats and poultry are listed in the Personal Action Guide.

As before, I've used the number of pesticide residues as the most accurate indicator of a food's relative safety or danger. In some foods, however, the number of residues may be high while the concentration of each residue is unusually low, or a small number of residues may have unusually high concentrations. In such cases I've taken the concentration level into account when assigning the food to the green, yellow, or red light food group, and I have mentioned the variation in the discussion of the food.

Green light meats and poultry have the lowest pesticide saturation, present the smallest cancer risk, and are the richest source of nutrients while being lowest in cholesterol and saturated fat. Eat these cuts of meat and poultry as often as you like, but remember that animal foods—meat, poultry, fish, eggs, and dairy products—should make up not more than one-third of your total diet.

Chicken (oven-roasted). Americans eat chicken often. Over a third of the population eats chicken at least once every three days, and one person in fifteen eats it at least twice in three days. Oven-roasted chicken had forty-two pesticide residues representing nine pesticide formulations. Pesticides detected most frequently were DDT, dieldrin, heptachlor, HCB, and penta; those detected less frequently were BHC, diazinon, lindane, and pentachlorobenzene.

Forty-two residues is a lot of residues for a green light food. But there are very low concentrations of most of these. Chickens (except for capons) are not raised with hormones, and major brands including Holly Farms and Foster Farms are raised without antibiotics. The pesticide dieldrin is the greatest source of risk for oven-roasted chicken. To lower your pesticide exposure when eating roast chicken, eat only the white meat, which is less fatty than dark meat, and always remove the skin, since that's where most of the fat is. One 3-ounce serving of oven-roasted chicken without skin contains only .9 grams of saturated fat and 73 milligrams of cholesterol.

Game. Many game foods are quite pure. Turtle meat, alligator meat, frogs' legs, and escargot (snails) present virtually no cancer risk. Buffalo meat may be slightly contaminated with residues of chlordane and DDT, but it is free of the antibiotics and sulfa drugs routinely used in raising beef. Duck, rabbit, and goose all had some residues but the levels were low enough to be considered safe. Alligator from some areas of Florida may contain high levels of methylmercury; pregnant women should avoid alligator just in case.

Lamb chops. Although lamb chops had forty-nine pesticide residues representing eight different pesticide formulations—a relatively high number—most of the concentrations were very, very low, so I have classified this as a green-light food. Pesticides detected most frequently were BHC, DDT, HCB, and octachlor. Less frequently found were dieldrin, heptachlor, pentachlorobenzene, and penta. Trimming the fat from your chops will help. One 2-ounce lamb chop, untrimmed, contains 7.3 grams of saturated fat and 78 milligrams of cholesterol. A lean 2-ounce broiled lamb chop contains 2.6 grams of saturated fat and 60 milligrams of cholesterol.

Pork roast. Oven-roasted pork loin is surprisingly low in pesticides. It had nineteen pesticide residues representing three pesticides: DDT, penta, and

HCB. The cancer risk as a result of pesticides in pork roast was insignificant. One 3-ounce serving of pork rib roast, untrimmed, contains 7.2 grams of saturated fat and 69 milligrams of cholesterol. The same 3-ounce serving, trimmed, contains 3.4 grams of saturated fat and 56 milligrams of cholesterol. Pork roast is safer than ham, because nitrates are not used to preserve pork roast. It is the safest cut of pork.

Be careful of pork, however, because of sulfa drugs. Sulfa medication is commonly administered by hog farmers.

Turkey. Turkey is the safest of all meat and poultry commonly eaten. Oven-roasted turkey breast had only nine pesticide residues representing five formulations. DDT was found in one-fourth of the samples; dieldrin, HCB, octachlor, and penta were found less frequently. The cancer risk as a result of pesticides in turkey breast is negligible. Turkey white meat has fewer pesticide residues and less cholesterol and saturated fat than dark meat. Remove the skin from turkey and all poultry; it is the fattiest and most pesticide-laden portion.

Three ounces of boneless roast turkey contains 1.6 grams of saturated fat and 45 milligrams of cholesterol.

YELLOW LIGHT

With a few exceptions, these yellow light cuts have about twice the pesticide saturation of the green light group and about half the total pesticide saturation of the red light group. These foods should be eaten in moderation.

Beef round steak. Beef round steak had thirty-nine pesticide residues in sixteen samples, representing eight pesticide formulations. Pesticides detected most frequently were BHC, DDT, HCB, and octachlor. Pesticides detected less frequently were dieldrin, heptachlor, lindane, and penta. By trimming away the fatty portions, you can significantly reduce your pesticide exposure. A 3-ounce serving, untrimmed, will have 4.8 grams of saturated fat and 81 milligrams of cholesterol; 3 ounces of trimmed round steak will contain 2.7 grams of saturated fat and 75 milligrams of cholesterol.

Be warned that cuts of beef may be contaminated with antibiotics and hormone residues.

Chicken (fried). I have placed fried chicken in the yellow light category because it is breaded and fried in fat and because people are much more likely to eat the skin of fried chicken. In the FDA Total Diet Study, breaded and fried chicken had forty-four residues representing eleven formulations. Pesticides detected most frequently were DDT, dieldrin, heptachlor, HCB, malathion, and penta. Detected less frequently were BHC, chlorpyrifos, diazinon, lindane, and pentachlorobenzene. One 4.9-ounce serving of a fried chicken breast with skin contains 4.9 grams of saturated fat and 119 milligrams of cholesterol.

Ham. Cured ham had only twenty-one residues representing six formulations. Pesticides and industrial chemicals detected most frequently were penta and lindane; diphenyl 2-ethylhexyl phosphate, HCB, lindane, and toxaphene were detected less frequently. This is a low level of pesticide saturation; the cancer risk for eating ham, as a result of pesticide contamination alone, is insignificant. However, ham is cured with nitrites to preserve the reddish color of the meat and to prevent botulism, and nitrites form dangerous cancer-causing nitrosamines in the human body. The combination of pesticides and nitrites makes this a yellow light food. The use of nitrates and nitrites dates back to ancient China and India; it became a firmly established practice in Europe during the Middle Ages. There is strong evidence that excess exposure to these chemicals in food constitutes a significant cancer threat. In southern China, where they are found in high concentrations in salted fish, nasopharyngeal cancer is very common; some experts believe the causative agent is this family of chemicals. Because vitamin C blocks the formation of nitrosamines, it is wise to eat vitamin C–rich foods when eating meats cured with nitrites.

Be sure to trim the fat from ham. A 3-ounce portion of untrimmed ham has 6.4 grams of saturated fat and 79 milligrams of cholesterol. The same portion, trimmed, has only 2.7 grams of saturated fat and 68 milligrams of cholesterol. See the shopping tips that follow for important safety information concerning Chernobyl cesium radiation in hams imported from Europe.

Pork chops. A well-trimmed pork chop is a surprisingly nontoxic food. Pork chops pan-fried in fat had twenty-eight pesticide residues representing nine pesticide formulations. Pesticides found in at least one-fourth of the samples (at very low concentrations) were penta and octachlor; pesticides detected less frequently (at very low concentrations) included BHC, DDT, diazinon, dieldrin, HCB, lindane, and malathion. The cancer risk as a result of the pesticide residues in pork chops is insignificant.

Trim as much fat as possible from your chops. An untrimmed 3-ounce serving of pan-fried pork chops contains 9.8 grams of saturated fat and 92 milligrams of cholesterol. The same serving, trimmed, contains 3.7 grams of saturated fat and 72 milligrams of cholesterol.

Be warned that cuts of pork may be contaminated with sulfamethazine.

RED LIGHT

You should eat these foods very seldom. They are saturated with high concentrations of powerful cancer-causing pesticides, and they are very likely to contain residues of antibiotics and sulfa medications. If you are concerned with reducing toxic exposures, you should strike them completely from your diet.

Bacon. The FDA Total Diet Study found that oven-cooked bacon had forty-eight different pesticide residues representing twelve different pesticide formulations. Pesticides detected most frequently were DDT, dieldrin, lindane, octachlor, and penta. Pesticides detected less frequently were aldrin, BHC, chlorpyrifos, heptachlor, HCB, methoxychlor, and toxaphene. Pork bacon is cured with cancer-causing nitrites, and some cuts of bacon are also likely to contain high levels of cancer-causing sulfamethazine and other sulfa drugs. In addition, three slices of bacon had 3.3 grams of saturated fat and 16 milligrams of cholesterol.

Bologna. Some American children are given bologna sandwiches nearly every day for lunch by parents who probably believe that this luncheon meat is wholesome and healthful. If only they knew the truth. Bologna is obscenely saturated with pesticides, as are other high-fat cold cuts. The bologna samples analyzed in the FDA Total Diet Study contained 102 different industrial pollutant and pesticide residues representing nine pesticide formulations. That means roughly six industrial chemical and pesticide residues were detected in each sample. BHC, DDT, dieldrin, heptachlor, HCB, lindane, octachlor, and penta were detected in at least one-fourth of the samples. PCBs were found less often. Two slices of bologna will have 6.1 grams of saturated fat and 31 milligrams of cholesterol. Concerned parents should not give their children bologna on a regular basis. There simply is too much pesticide contamination. If you do, be sure to purchase the least fatty brands of chicken or turkey bologna.

Fast-food hamburgers. When was the last time a fast-food corporation warned you that the pesticides in your burger could be harmful to your health? Smart shoppers have known for years that these red light foods are high in cholesterol and saturated fat. But those aren't the only problems. The FDA Total Diet Study found that fast-food hamburgers—the analyses included the buns, condiments, lettuce, and tomatoes—had 113 different pesticide residues, representing fourteen different pesticide formulations. That means each burger contained roughly seven pesticide residues. The pesticides detected were BHC, chlorpyrifos, DDT, diazinon, dieldrin, heptachlor, HCB, lindane, octachlor, parathion, chlorpropham, endosulfan, fenitrothion, and penta. One hamburger has 7.1 grams of saturated fat and 71 milligrams of cholesterol. You would be well advised to strictly limit your consumption of this pesticide-saturated food.

Frankfurters. Beef frankfurters and beef and pork frankfurters had 123 different pesticide residues representing 13 different pesticide formulations. That means that each sample in the FDA study had nearly eight pesticides. This is a very dangerous food for consumers. Pesticides detected in at least

one-fourth of the samples were BHC, DDT, dieldrin, heptachlor, HCB, lindane, octachlor, and penta. Pesticides detected less frequently were chlorpyrifos, diazinon, malathion, tecnazene, and toxaphene. Among the 43 million
Americans who regularly eat hot dogs, there could be as many as twenty-four
excess cancers in one million persons. That means we should expect as many
as 1,032 persons alive today to develop cancer just from eating pesticides in
hot dogs every three days. That is too high a risk. If the producers of hot dogs
truly cared about the public, they would tell consumers what pesticides are in
their products and at what concentrations. But because the government is not
forcing them to provide this information, millions of Americans are playing
cancer roulette every time they eat a hot dog. The actual risk could well be
higher, because frankfurters are often preserved with nitrites, which form
cancer-causing chemicals in the human body. I advise you to keep your consumption of frankfurters way down. Almost all other foods are much safer.
One frankfurter has 4.8 grams of saturated fat and 23 milligrams of cholesterol.
Stay away!

Ground beef. Ground beef has a very high fat content and is saturated
with pesticides. In the FDA Total Diet Study, eighty-two industrial chemical
and pesticide residues were detected, representing eleven formulations. Pesticides detected in at least one-fourth of the samples were BHC, DDT, dieldrin, heptachlor, HCB, and octachlor. Pesticides and industrial chemicals
detected less frequently included chlorpyrifos, diazinon, diphenyl 2-ethylhexyl
phosphate, lindane, and penta. The average ground beef–eating American eats
nearly 2 ounces of ground beef daily—the equivalent of a quarter-pound hamburger every other day. The cancer risk is relatively significant. One regular
3-ounce patty of ground beef has 6.9 grams of saturated fat and 76 milligrams
of cholesterol.

There are sources of very pure, virtully pesticide-free ground beef. See the
Personal Action Guide in this book, and buy your beef from these sources.

Liver. The FDA Total Diet Study revealed that pan-fried beef and calf liver
had forty-nine different pesticide residues representing eight pesticide formulations. BHC, DDT, dieldrin, heptachlor, HCB, octachlor, and penta were
found in at least a quarter of the samples; ronnel was detected less frequently.
Eating an average of about 1½ ounces of liver daily over a lifetime could cause
as many as nine excess cancers in one million persons.

Liver and other organ meats such as kidneys tend to accumulate toxic
metals and antibiotics. My review of USDA 1986 toxic chemical monitoring
data for cuts of beef showed that many cuts of liver tended to be tainted with
residues of antibiotics such as streptomycin, tetracycline, and oxytetracycline.
In addition, extremely high residues of sulfamethazine, above five parts per
million, were found in liver and kidney cuts. A review of the 1986 monitoring
data specifically for calf liver also revealed that residues of antibiotics were
detected in many organ cuts. Antibiotics found in the kidneys or livers of
calves included penicillin, streptomycin, tetracycline, neomycin, oxytetracy-

cline, and gentamycin. The sulfa drugs sulfamethazine, sulfadimethoxine, sulfa-quinoxaline, and sulfathiazole also were found in kidney and liver tissues. One 3-ounce serving of fried beef or calf liver contains 2.5 grams of saturated fat and 410 milligrams of cholesterol.

Pork sausage. The FDA Total Diet Study revealed that pork sausage had seventy-one pesticide residues in sixteen samples representing eleven pesticide formulations. That means the study found that each sample had about four pesticide residues. Pesticides detected in at least one-fourth of the samples were BHC, DDT, dieldrin, heptachlor, HCB, lindane, octachlor, and penta. Detected less frequently were chlorpropham, nonachlor, and pentachlorobenzene. The cancer risk from eating pork sausage regularly is relatively significant—at least as many as eight excess cancers in a million persons. And that number actually could be higher because pork sausage may also contain nitrites and residues of sulfamethazine. Each 1-ounce pork sausage is loaded with 11 milligrams of cholesterol and 1.4 grams of saturated fat.

Roast beef. About one in five Americans eats beef chuck roast at least once every three days. The average amount eaten daily is almost 2 ounces. Based on this average and chuck roast's pesticide content, there will be as many as 15 excess cancers in one million persons, or as many as 684 excess cancers in our lifetime, simply as a result of average American consumption of pesticides in roast beef.

The most dangerous residue in beef chuck roast is the pesticide dieldrin. The FDA Total Diet Study showed that beef chuck roast had fifty-two pesticide and industrial chemical residues representing ten formulations. Pesticides detected most frequently were BHC, DDT, dieldrin, heptachlor, HCB, and octachlor. Detected less frequently were chlorpyrifos, diphenyl 2-ethylhexyl phosphate, penta, and tri (2-ethylhexyl) phosphate. One 3-ounce serving of untrimmed chuck roast contains 10.8 grams of saturated fat and 87 milligrams of cholesterol. The same serving, trimmed, contains 3.9 grams of saturated fat and 66 milligrams of cholesterol. Trimming fat from your chuck roast will significantly reduce pesticide exposure.

Salami. Salami is loaded with pesticides. (Whether it is kosher or non-kosher makes no difference.) The FDA Total Diet Study revealed that this luncheon meat had ninety-eight pesticide residues representing eight pesticide formulations: BHC, DDT, dieldrin, heptachlor, HCB, lindane, octachlor, and penta. Among average salami-eating Americans (who eat slightly less than one ounce daily), there will be as many as thirty-one excess cancers in one million persons. Two slices of salami have 4.6 grams of saturated fat and 37 milligrams of cholesterol.

Sirloin steak. The FDA Total Diet Study found that beef sirloin and loin steak had forty-nine pesticide residues representing nine different pesticide formulations. BHC, DDT, dieldrin, heptachlor, HCB, and octachlor were detected in at least one-fourth of the samples. Less frequently detected pesticides included diazinon, malathion, and penta. Although the number of pesticide residues detected was relatively moderate, the concentrations at which they were found were significantly elevated. Consumers can significantly lower their ingestion of pesticides simply by trimming all visible fat from steak. Whereas a 3-ounce serving of untrimmed sirloin has 6.4 grams of saturated fat and 77 milligrams of cholesterol, the same serving, trimmed, contains 2.6 grams of saturated fat and 64 milligrams of cholesterol.

Veal. Although the apparent cancer risk as a result of ingesting pesticides in veal is relatively small, veal must be placed in the red light group because of its extensive antibiotic and sulfa drug residues and the nightmarish conditions under which most veal calves are raised.

The FDA Total Diet Study showed that breaded and pan-fried veal cutlets had forty-seven industrial pollutant and pesticide residues representing fourteen different formulations. The pesticides detected most frequently included DDT, diazinon, malathion, and penta. Industrial chemicals and pesticides detected less frequently included BHC, chlorpyrifos, dieldrin, diphenyl 2-ethylhexyl phosphate, heptachlor, HCB, lindane, octachlor, PCBs, and toxaphene.

The industrial pollutants and pesticides in veal could result in as many as six excess cancers in one million persons. That is probably a low estimate, since sulfamethazine residues may add to the cancer risk. One 3-ounce serving of braised or broiled veal cutlet contains 4.1 grams of saturated fat and 109 milligrams of cholesterol.

When buying veal, avoid light-colored, pale veal, which tends to be more expensive and indicates that calves were raised in stalls and intentionally kept anemic. Stay away from products with labels that proclaim the veal was *milk-fed, formula-fed, premium,* or *fancy.* In the Northeast, factory-farmed veal is called *nature veal.* Seek products simply called *veal;* these cuts are the same red color as other beef products; they are the least expensive cuts. See the Personal Action Guide for sources of safe veal from humanely raised, free-range animals.

Venison. The major problem with venison, which many people purchase by mail and from specialty meat shops, is that European reindeer herds were severely affected by the Chernobyl nuclear disaster. Particularly hard hit were reindeer herds in Finland and Sweden, nations that export reindeer meat. The full impact of Chernobyl is discussed in the Shopping Tips section that follows. U.S. venison is relatively safe.

Shopping and Cooking Tips

One of the best ways to reduce your exposure to toxic chemicals is to use meat and poultry as condiments and side dishes instead of as the main dish. When you serve homemade stew, chicken casserole, Chinese chicken salad, or pork chow mein, you cut down pesticide exposure by combining meat and poultry with low-residue vegetables and grains.

Always buy the leanest cuts of meat, and choose the leanest ground beef available. Cuts of beef with the lowest pesticide saturation include top round (6 percent fat), eye of round (6 percent fat), and top loin (9 percent fat).

Cuts of poultry with the least pesticide saturation include breast of chicken or turkey (3 percent fat) and drumsticks (5 percent fat). Buy skinless chicken parts or skin the chicken yourself before you cook it. You can cut your chemical exposure by 50 percent or more by trimming the fatty portions from all meat and poultry.

Do not be misled by deceptive labeling on meat and poultry products claiming that the product is "natural." Government regulations allow beef and poultry to be labeled "natural" as long as it has undergone minimal processing after slaughter. However, the "natural" claim does not preclude use of antibiotics and hormones. Make sure the label specifically states that no antibiotics or hormones were used. For your best protection, buy meat and poultry from producers and distributors listed in the Personal Action Guide later in this book. They provide the purest, safest meat and poultry in the country, and their farm animals are raised humanely.

Buffalo meat is an excellent choice if you must avoid exposure to antibiotics and hormones. Buffalo ranchers rarely use antibiotics or hormones.

Limit ingestion of meats cured with nitrites. They form nitrosamines in the gastrointestinal tract and can cause cancer. Foods cured with nitrites include bacon, corned beef, frankfurters, hams, luncheon meats, pork sausages, salami, precooked meats, and preserved and smoked meats, including smoked salmon.

If you insist on buying ground meat, bologna, or frankfurters, buy those made with turkey or chicken, not beef or pork. Seek brands without nitrites. Better yet, try tofu frankfurters, which are made of soybeans. These excellent hot dog substitutes are available throughout the nation at health food markets. They taste wonderful. Children love them, and they are far less toxic than hot dogs. And try tofu burgers instead of ground beef. They taste wonderful.

Avoid charcoal-broiling meats until they are black. That goes for steaks, hamburgers, roasts, poultry, pork, and seafood. Slight grill marks are fine. However, heavy charring of meats produces high concentrations of benzopyrene, a carcinogen that belongs to a family of potent carcinogens known as PAHs (polycyclic aromatic hydrocarbons). Unfortunately, benzopyrene isn't the only PAH in grilled meats with which we need to be concerned, although it is among the most potent carcinogens among the PAHs; some eighteen different PAHs have thus far been found in our food. Although the data are not entirely conclusive, researchers believe that at least five and perhaps as many as twelve of these eighteen PAHs cause cancer. PAHs form when fat from grilled meats falls down on flames or hot coals. The PAHs that are formed in this reaction rise with the smoke and permeate the meat.

There are ways to minimize formation of these cancer-causing chemicals in grilled meats:

• Be sure to buy the leanest foods for grilling. The leanest choices for grilling include chicken breast, lobster, scallops, yellowfin tuna, flounder, sole, grouper, monkfish, halibut, and shrimp. Trim all meats well before cooking.

• By broiling meat in the oven, where heat comes from above, you can eliminate cancer-causing PAHs; the fat does not drip onto the flame.

• Before grilling, allow meat to completely defrost; otherwise the outside of the meat heavily chars while the inside takes longer to cook.

• When purchasing fuel for your barbecue, prefer regular hardwood charcoal to mesquite. Researchers have discovered that cooking with mesquite produces far more numbers and far higher concentrations of PAHs than cooking with regular hardwood charcoal.

• When grilling, raise the grill higher than usual from the charcoal and place the charcoal on one side of the barbecue and the meat on the other side.

• If you like smoked flavoring, rather than trying to burn in that smoky wood flavoring on your home grill, prefer liquid smoke products. Such products are filtered; tars, resins, and most PAHs are removed. Supermarkets carry liquid smoke in the condiment section.

• You might want to try a Swedish innovation called the Vertikal Grill, which allows you to barbecue meat without allowing its fat to drip into the flames. See the Personal Action Guide for more information.

• When dining out, prefer the least fatty cuts; ask that they be well trimmed or skinned before cooking.

• Although the formation of PAHs appears limited primarily to barbecuing and grilling, you must be careful when broiling and pan frying meats to prevent formation of another group of cancer-causing chemicals known as heterocyclic amines (HAs), which are created when amino acids and other substances in all meats are burned. Use lower temperatures. Of course, because of bacterial contamination, you should not eat meat, poultry, or seafood raw. But do not overcook. Another technique for reducing HA formation: before broiling or frying, precook meat in the microwave on high for 30 to 90 seconds and toss out the juice.

Many supermarkets sell brands of meat and poultry that are specially raised to have no antibiotic residues and even, in some cases, few pesticides. The companies that make these products take extra precautions to eliminate residues. They've signed memorandums of understanding (MOUs) with the Department of Agriculture. These are legal agreements between the USDA and the company concerning drugs and residues in feed and water. They are upholding standards that are far more strict than regular USDA guidelines. These producers strictly monitor their animals to make sure they have eliminated many pesticides, antibiotics, hormones, and other drugs.

These companies, among others, have signed MOUs with the USDA:

Beef
Bradley 3R, Childress, Texas
Harris Ranch, Selma, California
Hitch Enterprises, Guymon, Oklahoma
Nebraska Beef, Osmond, Nebraska
Chicken
Foster Farms, Turlock, California
Holly Farms, Wilkesboro, North Carolina
Turkey
Foster Farms, Livingston, California
Norbest, Salt Lake City, Utah
Louis Rich, Davenport, Iowa
Swift-Eckrich, South Chicago, Illinois

Chernobyl Radiation

The explosion of a nuclear reactor at the power plant in Chernobyl in the U.S.S.R. in late April 1986 released the largest quantity of nuclear material ever freed in one technological accident. If you eat imported European meats, such as Polish hams or reindeer meat from Finland, you should be wary of low-level radiation exposure due to the Chernobyl disaster.

Shortly after the Chernobyl accident, the U.S. Department of Agriculture Food Safety and Inspection Service began to monitor the radiation levels of European meat and poultry to assess the extent of radioactive contamination in products that would enter the U.S. food supply. Very few of the samples exceeded the guidelines developed by the Food and Drug Administration for accidental radioactive contamination of human food and animal feed. However, by October 1986, approximately 50 percent of the 1,000 samples taken contained cesium residues exceeding normal background levels. The country with the highest levels in its food products was Rumania, followed by Brazil, which imports meats from Poland for processing at its plants. Four countries that export significant amounts of meat and poultry to the United States had samples with significantly high total cesium levels: Hungary, Poland, Yugoslavia, and Brazil. The half-life of cesium ranges from 2.1 to 30 years; thus the problem will remain with us for quite some time.

Poland is one of the biggest exporters of canned ham and pork shoulders to the United States (78.3 million pounds in 1986). A sampling of Polish products indicated that some had total cesium levels as high as one-third of the allowable levels for foods.

In 1986, Hungary exported 24.7 million pounds of canned ham and pork shoulders to the United States. Total cesium levels of Hungarian meats were as high as one-fifth of the allowable level.

In 1986, Yugoslavia exported 18.5 million pounds of canned ham and shoulders into the United States. Total cesium levels of Yugoslavian meats were as high as one-fourth of the allowable level.

Brazil is a principal exporter of canned beef into the United States (46.1 million pounds in 1986). Be wary of Brazilian beef and beef extract. Brazilian beef extract recently has had total cesium levels that were nearly twice the allowable level. Other Brazilian beef had cesium levels as high as one-tenth of the federal response level.

These European nations' meat and poultry were least affected by the Chernobyl disaster: France, Germany, Italy, and the Netherlands.

Meat and poultry from the following nations were moderately affected by the Chernobyl disaster: Belgium, Czechoslovakia, Denmark, Hungary, Sweden, and Yugoslavia. Eat meat and poultry from these nations no more than once every few months.

Meat and poultry products from these nations were significantly contaminated by the Chernobyl accident: Brazil, Finland, Poland, Rumania, and Switzerland. Avoid eating meat and poultry products imported from these countries.

Protecting Yourself Against Food Poisoning

Cook meat, pork, and poultry thoroughly to kill salmonella. These bacteria are heat-sensitive and are destroyed at cooking temperatures of 140°F. or higher. To be completely safe, cook poultry until the meat reaches 180°F. to ensure the destruction of any salmonella that may be present. Boneless parts should be cooked to an internal temperature of 160°F. When poultry is cooked thoroughly, juices will be clear, not pink.

To make sure that meat and poultry are cooked all the way through, use a meat thermometer to measure internal temperature. Insert the tip into the thickest part of the meat, avoiding fat and bone. For poultry, insert the thermometer tip into the thick part of the thigh next to the body.

Meat and poultry dishes are safe to eat when they are cooked to the temperatures listed below. Rare beef is popular, but you should know that cooking it to only 140°F. means some food poisoning organisms may survive. Remember, use a meat thermometer to record the internal temperature.

SAFE MEAT AND POULTRY COOKING TEMPERATURES

	Fahrenheit	Centigrade
Fresh Beef		
Rare	140	60
Medium	160	71
Well-Done	170	77
Ground Beef	170	77
Fresh Veal	170	77
Fresh Lamb		
Medium	170	77
Well-Done	180	82
Fresh Pork	170	77
Poultry		
Chicken	180–185	82–85
Turkey (boneless)	180–185	82–85
Turkey roast	170–175	77–80
Stuffing (inside or outside the bird)	165	74
Cured Pork		
Ham (raw)	160	71
Ham (fully cooked)	140	60
Shoulder	170	77
Game		
Venison	160–170	71–77
Rabbit	180–185	82–85
Duck	180–185	82–85
Goose	180–185	82–85

Reprinted from *The Safe Food Book,* published by the USDA Food Safety and Inspection Service, 1985.

Always wash your hands before handling meats and poultry. Do not use the same knife for meat, pork, or poultry and for produce. Wash knives well with hot water and soap before using on produce. Do not chop produce on the same surface where you cut meat, pork, and poultry. Thoroughly wash all surfaces where meat juices have dripped.

Your refrigerator temperature should be below 40°F., and your freezer should be set at 0°F. Always allow frozen food more time to cook— generally 1½ times longer than food that has been thawed. Always thaw meats in the refrigerator or microwave, never on the kitchen counter. The warmth of the kitchen and exposure to other foods creates ideal conditions for growth and spread of bacteria. Meat and poultry thaw from outside to inside, so thawing your meat and poultry in the refrigerator will keep bacteria from growing on the outside while the inside thaws.

Don't carry cooked meat to the table on the same platter you used to transport the raw meat to the grill.

Cooked poultry that is not eaten immediately should be kept hot (between 140°F. and 185°F.) or refrigerated at 40°F. or below. Slice the meat or poultry before refrigerating so it will cool quickly. Store casseroles and stews in shallow pans so they will cool quickly in the refrigerator.

Reheat leftovers to at least 165°F. before eating. Cover the pot to retain as much moisture and flavor as possible and to make sure the food will heat evenly all the way through. Bring leftover gravy to a rolling boil before serving.

Store chicken for picnics or luncheons in an insulated container or ice chest. Keep all cooked poultry refrigerated until you are ready to eat it.

Do not leave any food unrefrigerated for more than two hours. Never leave foods—particularly meats—in the oven overnight; microorganisms find the oven environment a perfect hatchery.

If you are preparing a brisket for the Seder, or any time you prepare food long before eating it, you should take special steps before serving to prevent contamination from the cafeteria germ *Clostridium perfringens*. These microscopic organisms are present in the soil, in the intestines of animals and humans, and in sewage. Perfringens are one of the leading causes of food poisoning in the United States. You should hold cooked meat dishes at no less than 140°F. Better still, cook your dish ahead of time and refrigerate it. Then reheat it in the microwave, or reheat it in a warming oven at 200°F. for about one hour before serving. Wrapping the meat in foil and reheating it in its own gravy will keep it moist.

Should any meat or product have an off odor or an unusual color or texture, return it to the store. Do not taste it. The microorganisms responsible for food poisoning cannot be tasted, anyway.

Safe Shopping List: Meat and Poultry

Photocopy this list and use it when you shop for meat or poultry. Always prefer green light cuts of meat and poultry. They are the safest cuts and significantly reduce your toxic exposures. They may not be pesticide and chemical free, but these cuts have far fewer residues than the most dangerous cuts.

Within each group I've listed the foods with the fewest pesticide residues at the top.

Green Light	Number of Residues
Turkey	9
Pork roast	19
Roast chicken	42
Lamb chops	49

OTHER GREEN LIGHT MEAT AND POULTRY

Alligator meat	Goose
Buffalo steak	Rabbit
Duck	Turkey breast luncheon meat
Escargot	Turtle meat
Frogs' legs	Venison (U.S.)

Yellow Light	Number of Residues
Ham	21
Pork chops	28
Beef round steak	39
Fried chicken	44

OTHER YELLOW LIGHT MEAT AND POULTRY

Chicken hot dogs and hamburgers
Chicken cold cuts
Turkey hot dogs and hamburgers

Red Light	Number of Residues
Veal	47
Bacon	48
Beef and calf liver	49
Beef sirloin and loin steak	49
Beef chuck roast	52
Pork sausage	71
Meat loaf	80
Ground beef	82
Salami	98
Bologna	102
Fast-food quarter-pound hamburger	113
Frankfurters (beef and pork)	123

OTHER RED LIGHT MEAT

Venison (imported)

7. SEAFOOD

I mentioned in the Introduction that fish eaters in Los Angeles who were exposed to DDT- and PCB-contaminated seafood were found to have levels of DDT up to nineteen times higher than people who ate little or no fish. The fish-eating subjects in our study regularly had DDT and PCB levels six to ten times higher than would be expected in a "normal" unexposed population.

That was pretty bad. Most people have two to seven parts per billion (ppb) DDT in their blood and about two to five ppb PCBs. They probably have a few other pesticides, too—just from eating the food, drinking the water, and breathing the air of the late twentieth century. These L.A. fish eaters had it even worse. But something else we discovered was even more disturbing. A few of the people with the highest levels had been eating fish caught many miles offshore, in a region where commercial fishermen throw their nets. That finding suggested a much more dangerous and widespread threat.

In 1986 I began buying fish from markets throughout Los Angeles, from Koreatown to Long Beach. We used a laboratory technique called electron-capture gas chromatography to detect pesticides in the seafood. We hoped we would find none. But we found that even commercially sold fish straight from supermarket freezers were polluted. The white croaker—a very popular species that is fished commercially with more than 100,000 pounds landed annually and sold locally—were grossly polluted. This fish, cheap and plentiful, would contaminate the bodies of thousands of persons. Other local seafood, including mackerel, ocean perch, and swordfish, had industrial pollution and pesticide traces, too. The contamination seemed to be centered in fish caught off the Los Angeles coastline and gradually diminished north and south, away from the dump sites. I reported this site-specific contamination in my articles, and commercial fishermen have since been able to steer clear of the most contaminated sites. They are now bringing in fish with significantly less pollution.

I demanded to see U.S. Food and Drug Administration pesticide monitoring files for the entire nation, and that's how I discovered that it was not just L.A. whose fish were contaminated. Not by a long shot. Some popular fish from all across the nation were, in fact, significantly polluted. Were seafood lovers shocked? Were women of childbearing age shocked? Were public officials? Absolutely.

At the request of elected state and federal officials, I testified before environmental committees of both the state legislature and the federal government. I believed I had to speak out. I was one of only a few people who actually knew innocent men and women who had become poisoned with DDT and PCBs from the fish they were catching and eating.

People needed to get smart to protect themselves, and they needed to know that government's mandate to protect the public health had been compromised. Part of my task was to explain that they could no longer count on the government to protect their health.

That was why I testified as an expert witness before the U.S. Congressional Subcommittee on Health and the Environment in February 1986 at the request of Representative Henry Waxman of Los Angeles. I testified that despite the efforts of Food and Drug Administration pesticide watchdogs, a tremendous amount of poisoned seafood was being sold in markets throughout the nation. I presented evidence from the FDA's own files. The next day my findings were printed on the front pages of newspapers in Los Angeles and became the subject of stories throughout the nation.

Almost overnight people responded. No longer were they simply buying fish. They were asking grocers where their fish came from. Restaurant patrons questioned chefs about where their catfish was caught. Was swordfish all right? What about snapper? Halibut? Farm-raised trout? Lobster? Shrimp? We needed answers.

I have since studied the entire supply of U.S. and imported fish and shellfish. I will tell you the relative risks of eating each species. There are significant differences. Some species of fish present cancer risks thousands of times greater than other species. There are fish to be avoided, but there is plenty of delicious seafood that is safe, too.

Ironically, all this information about toxins in seafood has come at a time when an increasing number of Americans are switching from meat to fish because studies have shown that eating fish and shellfish may help prevent heart disease.

You *should* include seafood in your diet. In the low-toxin high-energy diet I recommend that you eat two or three servings of fish a week. But beware! Fish is one of the primary sources of pollutants such as mercury, dioxin, DDT, and PCBs. So you must take care to eat fish and shellfish that are pure.

Seafood is high in protein and low in fat, and studies report that eating an average of one ounce a day (roughly a half-pound a week) of fatty cold-water fish, rich in beneficial fatty acids known as omega-3 fatty acids, can help prevent heart disease, the nation's leading cause of death. Compared with meat and poultry, seafood is extremely rich in these beneficial fatty acids. A 4-ounce serving of chinook salmon has a whopping 2.4 grams of omega-3 fatty acids, whereas that same amount of chicken breast has only 0.03 grams, and round steak and ground beef have bare traces of omega-3 fatty acids.

Interest in omega-3 fatty acids was first sparked when scientists discovered that Eskimos in Greenland who ate large quantities of fish had a low incidence of coronary heart disease despite a high fat and cholesterol intake. A more recent study of Dutch men showed that mortality from coronary heart disease was reduced by 50 percent among those persons who consumed at least an ounce of fish a day.

Don't give up seafood and start buying omega-3 fatty acid supplements just yet. Although fish oils may be effective in reducing serum cholesterol levels, experts really are not quite positive yet whether benefits conferred upon fish eaters are a result of omega-3 fatty acids or some other benefits associated with fish consumption. I recommend eating fish, not simply taking fish oil capsules.

Seafood is also a valuable source of low-calorie protein, fat-soluble vitamins, vitamin B_{12}, calcium, chromium, and phosphorous.

At its best, seafood is as safe as any organic fruit or vegetable. But a few seafood dishes should never be set on your family's table because they are a primary source of harmful industrial pollutants and pesticides. At its worst, seafood is the most dangerous source of powerful carcinogens in our diet. The broad range of pollution to which fish are exposed means that concentrations of some industrial pollutants will be extremely elevated. The tragedy is best illustrated, perhaps, by one fact: more than two thousand advisory warnings against eating certain seafoods have been issued by coastal and Great Lakes states.

Seafood Survival Guide

So how safe is your seafood? The truth is that safety levels for seafood pollution represent a compromise between the government and the fishing industry at the expense of our health. The government says that the risk from industrial pollution and pesticides in food and water should be so low that, at worst, no more than one person in one million should get cancer from toxins in that food or water. But, as usual, the law was written with a loophole that allows regulators to balance consumer risks against economic harm. Many Great Lakes and other freshwater fish, for instance, are extremely toxic and far exceed this one-in-a-million cancer risk. But public officials in state and federal government have decided that banning Great Lakes and other freshwater fish would impose too great an economic burden on the commercial freshwater fisheries, particularly of the Great Lakes. In this case (and many others), government says that its one-cancer-out-of-a-million standard is too stringent and will hurt the seafood industry; so it allows the sale of poisoned seafood throughout the nation.

Knowing where your seafood was caught will tell you a lot about how safe it is. This survival guide discusses fish caught in specific regions. (At the end of the chapter is a safe shopping list you can use even if you don't know where a particular fish was caught.) In researching seafood safety I have analyzed thousands of fish and reviewed the results of tests of many U.S. and foreign waters for industrial pollution and pesticides. You will be surprised at how many safe fish there are.

It is important to keep in mind that this list includes only commercially marketed fish. Sport fish, which are often caught closer to shore, nearer polluted regions, are not included in this list. Thus, halibut caught from Santa Monica Bay and flounder caught from Boston Harbor may be quite contaminated whereas commercially caught halibut and flounder from deeper offshore waters in most cases will be less polluted. We are interested in the effects of overall lifetime doses, so occasionally eating seafood dishes from relatively polluted inshore regions is unlikely to affect the overall dose.

The modern supermarket is filled with seafood imported from around the world. Some 60 percent of seafood sold in the United States is imported. You should know that seafood from Mexico, Argentina, Chile, and New Zealand is the purest the seven seas can give. Central and South American deep ocean fish should be coveted for their purity.

I have been reviewing analyses of food safety for years now, and what follows is based on the best information available. It does not cover every fish or every region, and in some cases the number of samples taken may not have been large. But I believe that every bit of information we can gather is important when it comes to cutting back on toxins in our food. These lists may help you cut a toxin source out of your diet or introduce some safe, new seafood dishes.

GREEN LIGHT

These fish have the smallest concentrations of industrial pollutants and pesticides, and should be the mainstays of your seafood menu. I have listed the major sources of each seafood item as well. Eat them often!

Abalone is virtually pollution free.

Arctic char from Canada is virtually pollution free.

Blue crab from Puerto Rico is virtually pollution free.

Catfish from Brazil and Thailand is virtually pollution free.

Caviar from Canada is relatively pollution free.

Cod from Canada, Denmark, Iceland, and New Zealand is virtually pollution free.

Crab from California, Georgia, Argentina, China, and Korea is virtually pollution free. **Dungeness crab** from Alaska and Washington is virtually pollution free. **Imitation crab** (surimi) from Korea is virtually pollution free. Beware of additives in surimi.

Crawfish from Louisiana is virtually pollution free, but crawfish from Arkansas is slightly polluted.

Croaker from Uruguay is virtually pollution free.

Dace from Hong Kong and China is virtually pollution free.

Dover sole from California, Washington, France, Korea, and the Netherlands is virtually pollution free. There are a few localized pollution hot spots in California and Washington that affect recreational fishing more than the commercial fishery.

English sole from California is virtually pollution free.

Fish sticks have very low levels of industrial pollutant and pesticide contamination. They do, however, often have MSG and other additives that may not be good for some people.

Flounder (including East Coast yellowtail flounder) from Massachusetts, Rhode Island, New York, New Jersey, Virginia, North Carolina, Texas, California, Argentina, Iceland, Japan, Mexico, and the Netherlands is virtually pollution free. There are some local pollution hot spots in Massachusetts, so if possible stay away from flounder caught from Boston Harbor.

Freshwater bass from Mexico is relatively clean for a freshwater fish.

Grouper from Texas, Argentina, Chile, Mexico, and Uruguay is virtually pollution free.

Haddock from Canada, Iceland, and the United Kingdom is virtually pollution free.

Halibut from Alaska, California, and Iceland is virtually pollution free, although your best bet is Alaskan or Icelandic halibut. Halibut is a moderate mercury accumulator. Some Los Angeles–area halibut may be tainted with PCBs.

Mahimahi from Florida and China is virtually pollution free. It is a low-level mercury accumulator.

Marlin from California is virtually pollution free. It is a mercury accumulator.

Menpachi from Hawaii is virtually pollution free.

Milkfish from the Philippines is virtually pollution free.

Monkfish from New Zealand and Thailand is virtually pollution free.

Mud fish (dried) from Thailand is virtually pollution free.

Mullet from Puerto Rico, Mexico, and Thailand is virtually pollution free.

Octopus is virtually pollution free.

Orange roughy is virtually pollution free.

Palani from Hawaii is virtually pollution free.

Pollock from Canada is virtually pollution free.

Pomfret from Hong Kong, China, and Thailand is virtually pollution free.

Red mullet from Mexico and Thailand is virtually pollution free.

Red snapper is virtually pollution free, no matter where it's from.

Rock bass from Florida is virtually pollution free.

Salmon from Ireland and the United Kingdom is virtually pollution free.

Pacific salmon (chum, king, silver, sockeye) from Alaska, California, Oregon, and Washington is virtually pollution free.

Sand dabs from California are virtually pollution free.

Sand goby from Thailand is virtually pollution free.

Scallops, domestic and imported, are virtually pollution free.

Sculpin from northern California is virtually pollution free.

Sea bass, domestic and imported, is virtually pollution free.

Sea urchin roe is virtually pollution free.

Shrimp, domestic and imported, is virtually pollution free. Because of the possible use of banned antibiotics in foreign farm-raised shrimp, prefer U.S.-harvested shrimp.

Sole from California, Washington, and the Netherlands is virtually pollution free.

Spiny lobster from Australia, New Zealand, and California is virtually pollution free. Spiny lobsters differ from common lobsters in that they have no claws.

Squid is virtually pollution free.

Striped bass from North Carolina is relatively pollution free. It is a mercury accumulator.

Talapia from California, Puerto Rico, Hong Kong, China, Singapore, and Thailand is virtually pollution free.

Tarpon from Puerto Rico is virtually pollution free. It is a mercury accumulator.

Trout from California, Georgia, Louisiana, Argentina, Canada, Chile, and Uruguay is virtually pollution free. Farm-raised trout may contain antibiotic residues. Trout from alpine lakes and streams are fine.

Tuna, domestic and imported, is virtually pollution free. It is a moderate mercury accumulator.

Wahoo from Mexico and Singapore is virtually pollution free.

Whiting, domestic and imported, from Chile, Japan, and Uruguay is virtually pollution free.

Yellowtail from the Pacific Coast is virtually pollution free.

YELLOW LIGHT

Seafood under the yellow light heading tends to concentrate significantly lower levels of industrial pollutant and pesticides than the red light items. Yellow light seafood still warrants a cautionary approach, however. Eat it seldom.

Angel shark is moderately saturated with DDT. It is a mercury accumulator.

Belt fish from Hong Kong is moderately saturated with BHC, DDT, and lindane.

Bonito from California is moderately saturated with DDT and PCBs.

Bream from Arkansas is moderately saturated with DDT and nonachlor.

Butterfish from Virginia is moderately saturated with BHC and DDT.

Catfish from Iceland and Mexico is moderately saturated with DDT.

Caviar from Iran is moderately saturated with DDT.

Crab from the Chesapeake Bay is moderately saturated with chlordane and PCBs.

Croaker from China is moderately saturated with BHC and DDT.

Drum from Arkansas is moderately saturated with DCPA, DDT, and dieldrin.

Northern pike from Canada is moderately saturated with BHC, DDT, and dieldrin. It is a mercury accumulator.

Norwegian salmon is moderately saturated with BHC, lindane, PCBs, and tecnazene.

Ocean perch from California is moderately saturated with DDT and PCBs.

Pacific barracuda is moderately saturated with DDT and PCBs.

Rainbow trout from Colorado and Missouri is moderately saturated with chlordane, DDT, PCBs, and toxaphene.

Ribbonfish from Japan is moderately saturated with BHC and DDT.

Rock cod from California is moderately saturated with DDT.

Rockfish is moderately saturated with DDT and PCBs.

Sea trout from New Jersey is moderately saturated with BHC, DDT, dieldrin, and PCBs.

Smelt from Oregon and Canada is moderately saturated with DDT, dieldrin, and PCBs.

Spot from New Jersey is moderately saturated with DDT, dieldrin, and PCBs.

Thresher shark from California is moderately saturated with DDT and PCBs. It is a mercury accumulator.

Walleye from Canada is moderately saturated with BHC, DDT, and dieldrin. It is a mercury accumulator.

Whitefish from Canada is moderately saturated with BHC, DDT, dieldrin, and HCB.

RED LIGHT

These red light fish concentrate in their flesh the greatest amounts of industrial pollutants and pesticides such as BHC, chlordane, DDT, dieldrin, heptachlor, PCBs, and dioxin. These include some of the most dangerous foods in the American food supply. I have cut them out completely.

Black cod (also sold as California black cod, butterfish, and sablefish) is highly saturated with DDT.

Bluefish is quite saturated with PCBs, chlordane, DDT, DCPA, dieldrin, HCB, nonachlor, and octachlor. Smaller bluefish are not as polluted as larger ones.

Buffalo fish from Alabama, Arkansas, Illinois, Louisiana, Minnesota, Missouri, Ohio, Tennessee, and Wisconsin is saturated with chlordane, DDT, diazinon, dioxin, HCB, heptachlor, nonachlor, PCBs, penta, and toxaphene. Buffalo fish is also a mercury accumulator.

Carp from Arkansas, Maryland, Michigan, Minnesota, Ohio, Wisconsin, and Virginia is saturated with PCBs, BHC, chlordane, DDT, dieldrin, dioxin, HCB, heptachlor, nonachlor, octachlor, and penta. Gefilte fish is made with carp. Manischewitz gefilte fish is made with carp from the lakes of northern Manitoba in Canada. It is probably less polluted than gefilte fish made with domestic carp.

Catfish from the rivers of Alabama, Arkansas, Georgia, Kansas, Illinois, Louisiana, Michigan, Missouri, Minnesota, North Carolina, Ohio, Tennessee, and Wisconsin is saturated with BHC, chlordane, DCPA, DDT, dieldrin, dioxin, HCB, heptachlor, nonachlor, octachlor, PCBs, penta, and toxaphene. It is so absolutely polluted that it should be banned *now* from the market. Farm-raised catfish is also polluted, though slightly less; however, its contamination with chlordane and dieldrin is quite significant. The southern breeders of farm-raised catfish must take stronger measures to prevent contamination of their product with these two pesticides and with DDT and lindane.

Caviar from Michigan and China is saturated with chlordane, DDT, and PCBs. If you eat it often, you should be concerned. If you buy it only once or twice a year, go ahead and enjoy it.

Chub from Illinois, Michigan, Ohio, and Wisconsin is saturated with BHC, chlordane, DCPA, DDT, dieldrin, dioxin, endrin, HCB, heptachlor, lindane, nonachlor, and octachlor. Smoked chub is very popular, but it is also extremely polluted. This one fish will expose you to more pollution in one meal than a careful shopper might be exposed to in a lifetime.

Cod from California and the Pacific Northwest is saturated with DDT and PCBs. Imported cod is very pure, however; it is listed in the green light category.

Coho salmon from the Great Lakes is saturated with BHC, chlordane, DCPA, DDT, dieldrin, dioxin, HCB, heptachlor, nonachlor, octachlor, PCBs, penta, and toxaphene. Any large coho salmon from the Great Lakes is extremely dangerous to eat. Smaller coho are safer but still quite dangerous. Stay with Pacific Coast salmon for your purest choices.

Croaker caught along the Atlantic seaboard has low to moderate levels of chlordane, DDT, dioxin, PCB, and toxaphene contamination. Imported croaker is slightly purer than the domestic catch.

Dace, often imported from China, is saturated with BHC, DDT, and lindane.

Eels from Massachusetts, New Jersey, New York, Delaware, Canada, and Japan are saturated with BHC, chlordane, DDT, dieldrin, dioxin, HCB, heptachlor, nonachlor, lindane, octachlor, and PCBs. Eels accumulate mercury.

Lake trout from Minnesota and the other Great Lakes states is saturated with BHC, chlordane, DDT, dieldrin, heptachlor, HCB, nonachlor, octachlor, and PCBs.

Lobster from Maine and Massachusetts is saturated with PCBs. The worst of the pollution is concentrated in that portion of the lobster called the tomalley, which is popular in ethnic markets in Massachusetts as a delicacy and sauce; not eating the tomalley will somewhat reduce your exposure. Be wary of lobster sauces, which are sometimes made with tomalley and which will be contaminated with PCBs. Even edible portions of Maine and Massachusetts lobsters are extremely contaminated with PCBs. Lobster from California and imported lobster are listed under the green light category.

Mackerel from New York is saturated with PCBs, BHC, chlordane, DDT, HCB, nonachlor, and octachlor. Pacific mackerel from California is slightly cleaner and therefore relatively safer but not pure by any means.

Mullet from California and North Carolina is saturated with PCBs, DCPA, DDT, dieldrin, and traces of dioxin. However, imported mullet is quite clean and is listed as a green light fish.

Northern pike from Minnesota and other Midwestern waters is a tremendous accumulator of mercury and often other pesticides and industrial chemicals.

Sea herring from the United States, Canada, the Netherlands, and New Zealand is saturated with BHC, chlordane, DDT, dieldrin, endrin, HCB, heptachlor, lindane, nonachlor, and PCBs.

Shark, domestic and imported, is saturated with DDT and PCBs. Shark is a mercury accumulator.

Sheepshead from Minnesota and Wisconsin is saturated with BHC, chlordane, DCPA, DDT, dieldrin, HCB, heptachlor, nonachlor, octachlor, and PCBs.

Smallmouth bass from Minnesota is contaminated with dioxin.

Striped bass from New York, New Jersey, and other northeastern states and from San Francisco Bay and the Sacramento Delta in California is saturated with PCBs, BHC, chlordane, DDT, dieldrin, HCB, nonachlor, and octachlor. It is also a mercury accumulator. Stay away!

Sturgeon from Illinois and Minnesota is saturated with BHC, chlordane, DDT, dieldrin, dioxin, HCB, heptachlor, lindane, nonachlor, octachlor, penta, and other pesticides such as DCPA and trifluralin.

Swordfish, domestic and imported, is moderately saturated with DDT and PCBs, and it is a prime mercury accumulator.

Trout from New York, New Jersey, Maryland, Virginia, Florida, Missouri, and Michigan is contaminated with BHC, chlordane, DDT, dieldrin, nonachlor, and octachlor.

Walleye from Illinois, New York, Minnesota, Michigan, and Wisconsin is saturated with DDT, dioxin, and PCBs. Walleye is a mercury accumulator.

Weakfish from New York and Pennsylvania is saturated with BHC, chlordane, DDT, dieldrin, HCB, nonachlor, and octachlor.

White bass from Ohio and many other areas is saturated with BHC, chlordane, DCPA, DDT, dieldrin, HCB, nonachlor, octachlor, and PCBs. Be wary of all white bass.

White croaker from California is saturated with DDT and PCBs.

Whitefish from Pennsylvania and many other areas is contaminated with dioxin.

White perch from New York and Pennsylvania is saturated with DDT, dieldrin, dioxin, and PCBs.

Yellow eel from China is saturated with BHC, DDT, and lindane.

Yellow perch from Pennsylvania has traces of dieldrin. Be wary of all freshwater perch.

Natural Toxins

Other perils of both shellfish and fish include certain completely natural toxins that can be deadly to the unwary consumer, and viruses and other microorganisms that are found in shellfish, often as a result of coastal sewage pollution.

The three most common naturally occurring perils—aside from the dangers of eating sushi, which I will discuss below—include ciguatera, scombroid fish poisoning, and paralytic shellfish poisoning. None can be prevented through cooking.

Let's take ciguatera first. Ciguatera is an illness caused by a tiny, naturally toxic microscopic creature known as a dinoflagellate that lives in tropical areas such as the Caribbean and Hawaii. These dinoflagellates bioconcentrate up the food web into some of our favorite game fish, causing thousands of cases of ciguatera each year. In the continental United States, the only real threat from ciguatera is along the southern tip of Florida, and even there the threat often comes from fish caught in other areas of the Caribbean. Other areas likely to produce ciguatoxic fish include Australia, the Bahamas, Cuba, Hawaii, Puerto Rico, and the U.S. Virgin Islands.

Where it is prevalent, ciguatera strikes hard and frequently. In Queensland, Australia, ciguatera appears to strike as many as 1,828 out of every 100,000 individuals, roughly 2 percent of the population. In the Virgin Islands there are about 730 cases for every 100,000 people. In Miami the incidence is about 5 in 100,000. Outbreaks in Maryland and Vermont have been the result of fish shipped from Florida. In the United States our main problem with ciguatoxic fish is mainly in Hawaii and the Caribbean with recreationally caught species. Restaurants do very well at protecting their customers.

Ciguatera symptoms may be felt from a few minutes to thirty hours after the offending meal. Most symptoms begin to appear one to six hours after the meal. They include abdominal pain, diarrhea, and vomiting. Other symptoms could include a metallic taste in the mouth and severe tooth pain. There are also reversals in nerve sensation: hot coffee may feel cold; ice cream may feel hot; cold water may seem to burn the skin. And ciguatera can be a fatal disease.

The ciguatoxin chemicals are powerful neurotoxins, and their effects may linger twenty years or longer. It is possible that people build up concentrations of the ciguatoxin in their bodies, becoming sick once the levels reach a break point.

I have spoken with persons who have been hit with ciguatera. For some it is mild. But for others, ciguatera can cause extreme nerve damage whose effects linger painfully for years. I have a friend who was afflicted with ciguatoxin. He finds that even several years later his nerve endings are still extremely sensitive. Long periods of sitting or of athletic activity cause him pain.

Restaurants in areas where ciguatera is a problem are very careful not to serve fish that might be contaminated with ciguatoxin. And imports of fish that could harbor the toxin rarely come into the United States. The real problem lies with sport fishermen in areas such as Hawaii who eat their catch. They are at much higher risk.

What should you do when visiting areas likely to have fish infected with the ciguatoxin? I would avoid eating these species of fish that might harbor the ciguatoxin:

> Barracuda
> Forktailed snapper
> Grouper
> Mahimahi
> Royal sea bass
> Snapper

Large fish, weighing more than four pounds, are more likely to harbor ciguatoxin than are smaller fish.

Because of Hawaii's tremendous popularity as a tourist destination and because a large amount of sport fishing is done there, I have also included a list of Hawaiian fish implicated in ciguatera poisoning. I have given the common English names with the Hawaiian names in parentheses. As I noted, restaurants tend to be extremely careful to avoid serving any fish that could harbor ciguatoxin. However, just to be on the safe side, you might want to copy this list for your next trip to Hawaii. These fish from Hawaiian waters may harbor ciguatoxin:

> Amberjack (kahala)
> Barracuda (kaku)
> Black snapper (wahanui)
> Blue spotted grouper (roi)
> Eel (puhialo)
> Goatfish (weke)
> Jack (ulua)
> Milkfish (awa)
> Thread-fin fish (moi)
> Mullet (uouoa)
> Skipjack (aku)
> Snapper (opakapaka)
> Surgeonfish (manini or palani)
> Wrasse (po'ou)

Researchers are on the verge of developing a "stick test," which anyone can use to detect harmful ciguatoxin concentrations in their sport catch.

Scombroid fish poisoning, another naturally occurring illness, is caused by poor handling aboard fishing vessels, and it occurs worldwide. Cooking cannot destroy the infecting agent in scombroid poisoning. Symptoms include nausea, abdominal cramps, tingling and burning sensations around the mouth, oral blistering or burning, rashes and itching, redness, headaches, dizziness, and vomiting. If your fish tastes peppery, it could be infected with scombroid poisoning. The actual agent that makes you sick is a form of histamine toxin that multiplies rapidly if fish are allowed to remain at high temperatures for several hours. The preventative step for sport fishermen is immediate icing and chilled storage. The fish that most commonly cause scombroid poisoning are tuna, mackerel, bonito, bluefish, and mahimahi. Also sometimes involved are herring, sardines, amberjack, anchovy, jack mackerel, and skipjack.

Paralytic shellfish poisoning (PSP) results when naturally occurring dinoflagellates, which build up in red tides, concentrate in mussels, oysters, scallops, and clams. Paralytic shellfish poisoning was a tremendous problem earlier in the century, but is largely contained today by vigilant public monitoring although it may sometimes occur in the United States as well as Chile and Japan. In the United States, a freak red tide off the North Carolina coast in 1987 resulted in forty-eight cases of paralytic shellfish poisoning.

Your own knowledge of the environment can help you steer clear of paralytic shellfish poisoning. Recreational shellfish harvesters should get to know their tidelands and when the red tides occur. Red tides in the United States usually occur between May and October. If you harvest clams recreationally, note whether there is discoloration of the water, bird or fish deaths, or if there are eye, respiratory, and skin irritations in humans. A red tide bloom may be occurring. You should stop harvesting at the first sign of a red tide and wait however many weeks are needed until the tide has completely gone. Once red tide recedes, shellfish quickly excrete the toxic dinoflagellate—except Alaska butter clams, which store the dinoflagellate toxin for months.

Symptoms of PSP occur within thirty minutes and include nausea and vomiting; paralysis may set in. Paralytic shellfish poisoning is lifethreatening and makes you feel as though you have had a stroke. *Cooking will not destroy the toxin responsible for paralytic shellfish poisoning.* Paralytic shellfish poisoning can occur during clambakes and barbecues; recognize its symptoms. Victims should get help immediately from a doctor or a poison control center.

Shopping Tips

Patronize fish markets and supermarkets that provide accurate information about where your seafood was harvested. You cannot put this information about the safety of fish from different places to use if your retailer won't tell you or doesn't know where the stock is from. Certainly now that even government officials admit that some of our favorite seafoods are contaminated with industrial and pesticide pollution, shops have an ethical obligation to tell patrons where their seafood was caught. Unfortunately, they have no legal obligation to do so.

Many markets now offer this information, however. One California supermarket provides fliers noting where the day's fish was caught. Other markets announce on the P.A. system that they have just gotten in a supply of a particular fish. These are responsible attempts to provide consumers with invaluable information.

If you and others like you buy seafood from retailers who post the origins of their seafood, other retailers will follow suit. Remember, the way you spend your food dollars has an effect on retailers and ultimately on the environment. Every fish market and supermarket manager should know where the seafood was harvested. Stay with those retailers who know. Vague or delayed answers to your questions should tip you off that this manager does not know where the seafood was caught.

Market workers *should* know where shellfish were harvested. Federal law requires that all shellfish moving in interstate traffic be tagged with the site where they were harvested. If the people who work in your market do not know where the shellfish were caught, find another store where the staff does have such information. You should do this to protect yourself. Shellfish that are tagged are from harvest areas that are strictly monitored for bacterial contamination. Untagged shellfish could be from illegal harvest grounds. Illegal harvesting of shellfish is particularly prevalent in the Narragansett Bay area and the Louisiana Delta.

Unfortunately it is still hard in many places to find out where a seafood catch is from. To help you find safe fish anyway, I have devised a chart that identifies safe and dangerous fish by species, without regard to the geographic location where they were caught. These lists are at the end of this chapter.

Buy fish that has been well chilled. All fresh fish sold in fish markets and supermarkets should be kept on ice at about 33°F. Be wary of fresh fish kept in unenclosed areas that are unshielded from customers. This can lead to the spread of disease. Eyes of whole fish should be bright and shiny, never sunken or watery. Eyes that bulge are a sign of freshness. Skin should be moist, scales shiny. Flesh should be moist and firm and spring back when touched. If your finger leaves an indentation, the fish has gone bad. Gills should be red on the inside, not black, brown, or gray. Use your nose. Fish that smells fishy has gone bad. Beware of an ammonia scent, especially in shark, another indication of mishandling.

The claims by some markets that fish are "fresh frozen" is oxymoronic. "Fresh frozen" simply means that the fish was frozen quickly after harvest. In the opinion of most fish lovers, "fresh frozen" fish is never as tasty as fresh fish. Never buy fish that has been frozen and thawed if you value taste and quality.

Lobsters and crabs should fight back when they are being handled. Make sure clam, mussel, and oyster shells are shut tightly; this indicates that they are alive. The shells of dead clams will gape open.

Beware of an iodine smell or off odor in shellfish. Beware of any fishy smell in scallops; this indicates that they are bad. Good fresh squid should smell sweet. Shellfish that smells fishy has gone bad.

Buy these fish and shellfish that are high in omega-3 fatty acids. Grams of omega-3 fatty acids in a 4-ounce cut are given in parentheses.

Chinook salmon, canned (3.3)	Shrimp (0.5)
Chinook salmon (2.4)	Tuna, white, in water (0.5)
Pink salmon (2.2)	Halibut (0.4)
Coho salmon, canned (1.8)	Red snapper (0.4)
Sockeye salmon, canned (1.8)	Scallops (0.4)
Rainbow trout (1.2)	Flounder (0.3)
Pacific oysters (1.0)	Lobster (0.3)
Squid (1.0)	Sole (0.3)
Mussels (0.8)	Turbot (0.3)
Pollock (0.6)	Clams (0.2)
Crabs (0.5)	Haddock (0.2)
Eastern oysters (0.5)	Tuna, light, in water (0.2)

Adapted from *Nutrition Action,* September 1984.

Raw Shellfish

By far the greatest immediate toxic risk in eating seafood lies in raw shellfish. If it were not for raw shellfish, very few people would get sick from bacterial contamination as a result of seafood. Thousands of Americans who have suffered through an excruciating bout of gastroenteritis attribute their illness to eating raw shellfish. In New York State in 1982 shellfish were identified as the cause of more than 100 reported outbreaks of viral gastroenteritis that involved more than 1,000 people. Almost invariably people report that they've eaten raw clams. Since 1982, the New York Department of Health has recorded 33 outbreaks of illness caused by eating clams, involving more than 250 cases of gastroenteritis and 20 cases of hepatitis.

Between July 22 and July 29, 1982, the New York State Health Department evaluated 908 establishments that sold clams and found that 125 of them stocked clams that were untagged or improperly certified to identify their waters of origin.

Louisiana Delta shellfish were responsible for an outbreak of cholera that was the first indigenous outbreak in the nation since 1911. During the summer and fall of 1982 twelve cases of cholera were linked with eating crabs and shrimp caught along the Gulf of Mexico. Cholera from seafood can be largely prevented by proper refrigeration and thorough cooking.

Ordinarily one would not think of fish or shellfish as harboring listeria and salmonella bacteria, which are normally associated with meat from warm-blooded animals. Some imported shellfish such as shrimp, however, appear to be contaminated with salmonella and listeria microorganisms. Avoid eating imported shellfish raw. Thoroughly boil shrimp before serving.

People with AIDS, cancer, and liver disease and other immune-weakened persons should forgo eating raw shellfish and possibly even steamed shellfish.

When I cook shellfish, I bring the water to a boil and then steam the clams or other shellfish seven to eight minutes. Some chefs recommend steaming just until the shells open, but for maximum safety, steam shellfish seven to eight minutes. I never have gotten sick; even at seven minutes, the shellfish taste fine.

If you love raw oysters and clams and are unwilling to give them up, at least be aware of the risks. Be sure the shellfish you're eating were very fresh when you opened them; ideally you should eat at a raw bar where you can watch them being opened. If there is the slightest hint of an off odor don't eat them.

Sushi

We have heard a lot in recent years about bacteria and parasites entering people's systems from sushi and other raw fish. As Japanese restaurants have become increasingly popular this has become a matter of serious concern for many people. Parasites can cause extreme pain similar to that of appendicitis. They are not deadly, however.

The species most likely to harbor parasites are raw or undercooked freshwater fish such as pike or perch as well as anadromous species that spend their lives in both fresh water and salt water, such as salmon. Saltwater fish that might have parasites include European herring, mackerel, rockfish, salmon, raw squid, and members of the cod family including whiting and haddock. Be especially careful of parasites in raw Pacific salmon. In Hawaii, raw Pacific salmon has been the cause of a number of cases of anisakis parasitic infections. Parasites can also survive in ceviche (raw fish marinated in lime juice).

Some sushi favorites are much more likely than others to harbor parasites. Many sushi restaurants serve raw salmon (sake) as well as freshwater fish, such as carp and trout, soaked in vinegar or salted and fermented. These fish may harbor parasites. Neither soaking in vinegar nor salting destroys the anisakis parasite.

The most commonly consumed types of sushi include bluefin tuna, yellowfin tuna, shiro maguro, which is also known as albacore, and hamachi, which is known as Japanese yellowtail. These fish, when raw, may occasionally harbor parasites. But this is truly rare.

Other uncooked seafood commonly served in sushi restaurants—fish roe, clams, abalone, and octopus—are not known to be sources of parasitic infections in humans, according to Michael Ruttenberg, M.D., an expert on medical problems associated with sushi.

The best solution for making sushi at home is to heat the fish fillets to 140°F. for 30 seconds. You can also freeze sushi or sashimi to kill bacteria and parasites and stop spoiling.

Symptoms of parasitic infection can be mild or severe and might be mistaken for ulceration or inflammation. In severe cases, the symptoms include extreme abdominal pain. Physicians can detect embedded parasites with a gastrofiberscope and remove them.

These are your best picks (with American names in parentheses) for safe sushi:

> Amaebi (sweet shrimp)
> Ebi (shrimp)
> Kani (crab)
> Hamachi (Japanese yellowtail)
> Hotategai (scallop)
> Maguro (albacore)
> Tako (octopus)
> Tai (red snapper)
> Toro (fatty tuna)
> Uni (sea urchin roe)

These are some of the *least safe* sushi choices:

> Kazunoki (herring roe)
> Saba (mackerel)
> Sake (salmon)
> Most freshwater fish species.

Be careful when you eat some sushi delicacies. This is particularly important now that fugu, a sashimi made with blowfish (puffers), is served in this country. Fugu must be properly prepared to remove the deadly tetrodotoxin found in the liver, entrails, and ovaries. As many as 50 to 100 Japanese die each year after the thrill of eating this delicacy. I do mean thrill, too. A mild dose of the poison found in puffer fish apparently provides a mild high. So when traveling in Japan you might want to be careful of puffer dishes. If you are going to eat puffer in Japan, make sure the restaurant employs a trained, licensed chef. How will you know if you have been poisoned? A tingling and numbness of the lips, tongue, and fingertips will become quite evident, followed by progressive paralysis of the arms and legs and difficulty in breathing. Death could result in two to twenty-four hours. Survival beyond twenty-four hours means that you just might live. Artificial respiration is the only known treatment. No antidotes to the poison exist.

Cooking Tips

Always store fresh fish in the coldest part of your refrigerator. Use fresh fish the day it is bought. Frozen fish should be cooked while frozen. Thawing leads to rapid deterioration of taste and quality. Cook shellfish within twenty-four hours.

To destroy any harmful bacteria on fish, follow this rule of thumb for cooking temperatures. For every inch of thickness of the fillet, cook the fish at 450°F. for thirteen minutes. Use an internal thermometer to make sure that the temperature of the flesh is at least 145°F. for a minimum of five minutes.

Broil fillets on an open rack and let the juices drip out. Research shows that by discarding the oil before serving pan-fried fish you can reduce industrial pollution and pesticide concentrations by as much as 65 percent. That's because many toxic chemicals are lipid soluble and leach into the oil. Unfortunately it will not reduce levels of mercury.

Remember that pesticides accumulate in fatty tissue. Avoid fat whenever you eat fish (or any other food) whose purity you suspect. Trim and discard the skin and the fatty portions from the top, side, and belly of pike, walleye, Greak Lakes coho salmon and lake trout, and other Great Lakes fish if you must eat fish from those waters.

Safe Shopping List: Seafood

These lists show you the relative safety of many different kinds of fish, *regardless of where they were caught.* These charts are based on samples of particular species of fish from sites around the nation.

Use these charts when you shop for fish and can't determine the fish's origin. They will also provide a guide for ordering seafood in restaurants.

Green Light

Abalone	Imitation crab (surimi)	Sea urchin roe
Arctic char	Mahimahi	Shrimp
Crawfish	Marlin	Sole
Dover sole	Menpachi	Spiny lobster
English sole	Monkfish	Squid
Dungeness crab	Octopus	Talapia
Fish sticks	Orange roughy	Tuna
Flounder	Pacific salmon	Wahoo
Grouper	Red snapper	Whiting
Haddock	Scallops	Yellowtail
Halibut	Sea bass	

Yellow Light

Belt fish	Ocean perch	Rockfish
Bonito	Pacific barracuda	Sea trout
Bream	Pacific mackerel	Smelt
Butterfish	Porgy	Spot
Drum	Rock cod	Thresher shark
Norwegian salmon		

Red Light

Bass (freshwater)	Great Lakes salmon	Sturgeon
Black cod	Lake trout	Swordfish
Bluefish	Lobster	Trout
Buffalo fish	Mackerel	Walleye
Carp	Mullet	Weakfish
Catfish	Northern pike	White bass
Caviar	Sablefish	White croaker
Chub	Sea herring	Whitefish (freshwater)
Cod	Shark	White perch
Croaker	Sheepshead	Yellow eel
Dace	Striped bass	Yellow perch
Eel		

8. DAIRY FOODS

Milk and other dairy foods are extremely nutritious, and they contribute generous amounts of protein, calcium, phosphorus, riboflavin, and vitamin A to our diet. In our low-toxin high-energy diet, adults can enjoy two servings of dairy products a day, if they want—but not just any dairy products. As you will see, some dairy foods are very bad for you. I'll point out which products to eat and which to avoid.

Dairy products are an excellent source of amino acids, which are the building blocks of protein synthesis. The amino acid cystine, plentiful in dairy foods, helps our bodies fight the ravages of toxic chemical pollution by working with vitamins A, C, and E and selenium to protect the body from a host of industrial pollutants, radiation, heavy metals, and pesticides. In addition, cystine helps the body process vitamin B_6, which is involved in some fifty chemical reactions with other amino acids.

Other amino acids in milk—glutamine, phenylalanine, and tyrosine—increase our mental alertness and clarity of thought and help us overcome depression. These three amino acids have also been shown to help in weight loss and weight maintenance by acting as natural appetite suppressants.

Despite these benefits, many health experts recommend that adults eliminate dairy products from their diet. They point out that humans are the only species who drink milk beyond infancy. Many people lack the enzymes necessary to digest dairy products when they grow older. And the nutrients in milk *are* available in many plant foods. Peaches, for example, are an excellent source of vitamin A and riboflavin. Raspberries provide generous amounts of riboflavin. (Peaches and raspberries are high in pesticides, though, so choose organic varieties if you eat them for their vitamin content.) Plantains are another excellent source of vitamin A.

Some vegetarians are under the impression that they must eat dairy foods in order to get enough protein, calcium, and B vitamins. But in fact people can live completely healthy lives without any dairy products.

We need to be extra careful to choose safe dairy products because children eat so many of them and because we know that some dairy foods contain dangerous pesticides, veterinary medicines, and industrial chemicals. Unfortunately there is real cause for concern. Some dairy products present a clear, significant, measurable, and avoidable cancer risk. As we know, toxins are concentrated in animals' fatty tissues, and dairy products can be high in fats. So before you lift that cold, inviting glass of whole milk to your lips, consider that you just might be about to drink a chemical cocktail spiked with dioxin, pesticides, antibiotics, and sulfa drugs.

Fortunately, the nonfat dairy products that are safest for your heart (and your waist) are also the lowest in toxins.

Unwisely chosen dairy foods can be a primary source of heavy doses of a wide variety of dangerous cancer-causing and neurotoxic chemicals. Some dairy foods have among the highest levels in our diet of the banned pesticides BHC, chlordane, DDT, dieldrin, heptachlor, and HCB. These are long-term toxins that pollute the soil for decades after their last application and continue to contaminate grains fed to dairy cattle. In fact, pesticide contamination of dairy foods is every bit as serious as the contamination in meat, poultry, and seafood—possibly even more dangerous. Some seafood is highly contaminated, but relatively few people eat large quantities of the worst seafood dishes, whereas huge numbers of people eat milk, butter, cheese, and ice cream regularly.

I am particularly concerned about the low-level poisoning of our children. Babies who are fed whole milk or evaporated milk are at risk, and so are breast-fed babies. Mothers who eat a lot of dairy foods and other high-toxin foods accumulate the toxins in their breast milk and pass on industrial pollutants and pesticides to their infants. And what about all the pesticide-contaminated ice cream our children eat?

The simple fact is that pesticide contamination of dairy products is pervasive. Government dairy monitoring files reveal that contaminated products are sold throughout the country. Food and Drug Administration records indicate, for example, that virtually 100 percent of the cheese produced and sold in the United States has detectable pesticide residues. As we discuss the myriad industrial pollution and pesticide problems in dairy foods, you will see how much cleaning up of our food supply needs to be accomplished.

Dairy products are also linked, together with raw-egg dishes, to at least one-tenth of the food-poisoning cases in this country every year. Most of these cases are listeria or salmonella poisoning, which can be deadly to fetuses, babies, elderly people, and those with weakened immune systems.

The listeria bacteria favor moist, soft cheeses such as Brie, blue-veined cheeses, and Mexican cheeses. Harder cheeses have less moisture and higher acidity, which prevents bacteria from multiplying. Persons with strong immune systems can subdue the listeria bacteria without discomfort. But among children, the elderly, and immune-weakened people, the death rate in reported listeriosis cases is 19 percent. Listeriosis can also lead to meningitis and encephalitis, which have a 70 percent fatality rate in reported cases.

To avoid this danger, pregnant and nursing women, the elderly, and people who are ill or institutionalized should be very cautious about unpasteurized dairy products and soft cheeses such as Brie, Camembert, and blue-veined cheeses.

Dairy Foods Survival Guide

GREEN LIGHT

These are the least toxic dairy foods available. Choose your two servings of dairy foods a day from this list.

Buttermilk. The FDA Total Diet Study found only three pesticide residues in sixteen samples of buttermilk, representing two pesticide formulations, DDT and penta. One cup of buttermilk has only 1.3 grams of saturated fat and 9 milligrams of cholesterol. Buttermilk is an excellent, relatively safe food choice.

Chocolate milk. Chocolate milk made with low-fat milk has a fairly low chocolate content, and therefore it poses little risk. Only twelve industrial pollutant and pesticide residues were detected in sixteen samples of chocolate milk, representing seven industrial pollutant and pesticide formulations. Pesticides and pollutants detected were BHC, chlorpyrifos, DDT, dieldrin, heptachlor, octachlor, and PCBs. The cancer risk as a result of industrial pollutant and pesticide contamination in chocolate milk is relatively insignificant. One cup of low-fat chocolate milk has 3.1 grams of saturated fat and 17 milligrams of cholesterol.

Low-fat milk (1 percent or 2 percent fat). Only nineteen pesticide residues were found in sixteen samples of low-fat milk, representing seven pesticide formulations. DDT and dieldrin were detected in at least one-fourth of the samples. BHC, chlorpyrifos, heptachlor, HCB, and octachlor occurred less frequently. The cancer risk as a result of pesticide contamination of low-fat milk is insignificant. One cup of low-fat milk has 2.9 grams of saturated fat and 18 milligrams of cholesterol.

Low-fat and nonfat yogurt. Only six pesticides representing two pesticide formulations, DDT and penta, were detected in sixteen samples of plain low-fat yogurt. The concentrations at which these pesticides were detected presented an insignificant cancer risk. One 8-ounce container of plain low-fat yogurt provides 125 calories, .3 grams of saturated fat, and only 4 milligrams of cholesterol. Obviously, nonfat yogurt, because of its very low milk fat content, is an even safer choice. Substitute low-fat or nonfat yogurt for butter in baked potatoes and other dishes calling for butter, mayonnaise, or sour cream. It's also perfect as a salad dressing.

Skim milk (nonfat milk). This is one of the safest dairy choices of all. Skim milk had only three pesticide residues representing two pesticide formulations, octachlor and penta. One cup of skim milk has only .3 grams of saturated fat and four milligrams of cholesterol.

YELLOW LIGHT

Only three dairy foods fit in the yellow light grouping. Limit your consumption of these foods. They contain pesticides combined with saturated fat and cholesterol.

Ice milk. There were thirty-five pesticide residues in vanilla ice milk, representing seven different pesticide formulations. The FDA found BHC, DDT, dieldrin, and HCB in at least one-fourth of the samples and heptachlor, octachlor, and penta less frequently. Eating slightly less than 2 ounces daily of vanilla ice milk would result in at least five excess cancers in one million persons, which is on the border between a significant and less significant risk. One cup of vanilla ice milk (4 percent milk fat) contains 3.5 grams of saturated fat and 18 milligrams of cholesterol. You should assume that other flavors of ice milk have similar levels of pesticides.

Margarine. Nineteen industrial pollutant and pesticide residues were found in sixteen samples of partially hydrogenated margarine, representing five pesticide formulations. Detected in at least one-fourth of the samples were diphenyl 2-ethylhexyl phosphate and penta. Pesticides and industrial pollutants detected less frequently included HCB, pentachlorobenzene, and PCBs.

Although margarine is much safer than butter in terms of pesticide saturation, cholesterol, and saturated fat, you should nevertheless limit your margarine consumption. Be wary of misleading ads claiming that margarine is free from cholesterol. The oils used in margarine are usually hydrogenated, and any vegetable oils that are even partially hydrogenated contain saturated fats, which dramatically increase serum cholesterol levels. Even though margarines may contain no cholesterol, their oils can still help our bodies make cholesterol. One tablespoon of margarine (80 percent fat) has 2.2 grams of saturated fat. One tablespoon of imitation margarine (40 percent fat) has 1.1 grams of saturated fat. For cooking, substitute unsaturated vegetable oils such as avocado, canola, corn, olive, and sesame.

Milk shakes. Twenty-three pesticide residues were detected in chocolate milk shakes, representing nine pesticide formulations. BHC and DDT were detected in at least one-fourth of the samples, and chlorpyrifos, diazinon, dieldrin, heptachlor, HCB, malathion, and penta were found less frequently. Chocolate milk shakes provide a relatively significant source of calories, saturated fat, and cholesterol. One thick 10-ounce chocolate shake provides 335 calories, 4.8 grams of saturated fat, and 30 milligrams of cholesterol. Although only chocolate milk shakes were tested, you should assume that other flavors have similar levels of pesticides.

Yogurt with fruit. Thirty-two pesticide residues representing five different pesticide formulations were detected in sixteen samples of yogurt with fruit. DDT, endosulfan, and vinclozolin were found in at least one-fourth of the samples, dicofol and dieldrin in fewer. The cancer risk from eating fruit yogurt is relatively insignificant. Most of the pesticides found (dicofol, vinclozolin, and endosulfan) resulted not from dairy contamination but from the application of chemical pesticides to the strawberries used in the samples that were tested.

You have a much safer option. Buy plain nonfat yogurt, which is very pure, and mix it with low-toxin or organically grown berries or other fruits.

RED LIGHT

The foods in this red light section are the most dangerous dairy products. I have cut them completely out of my diet. You should eat them as seldom as possible, or seek out organic dairy products made with milk from cows fed a pesticide-free diet. Good products are available; see the Personal Action Guide in this book.

Butter. If you thought that high cholesterol and saturated fat levels were the only problems in butter, well, here's the sad truth: pesticides are another serious danger. Butter and some cheeses have the highest pesticide concentrations of any dairy foods. This should completely convince you that butter is bad news. Now, don't get me wrong. The pesticide levels in dairy products such as butter and cheese all meet government standards. But government standards are so pro-industry that they are, in effect, a license for the wholesale poisoning of America. You have to take responsibility for the safety of your food. Government hasn't.

In the FDA's study of sixteen butter samples from around the nation 101 residues of pesticides and industrial pollutants were found, representing twelve pesticides and pollutants. BHC, DDT, dieldrin, heptachlor, HCB, octachlor, and penta appeared in at least a quarter of the samples; diphenyl 2-ethylhexyl phosphate, lindane, methoxychlor, nonachlor, and PCBs appeared less frequently.

Butter is one of the most frequently eaten foods in the American diet. Given the large amounts of butter we eat and the high concentrations of pesticides and pollutants in it, butter alone will cause at least several thousand excess cancer cases among people living today. According to a major food consumption study by the U.S. Department of Agriculture, the average butter-eating American eats about one-half tablespoon of butter daily. Among the approximately 76 million Americans who eat butter regularly, the risk of cancer—which I worked out using a standard cancer risk assessment formula—translated into as many as seventy-one excess cancer cases a year in one million persons; we should expect roughly 5,400 Americans alive today to get cancer from the pesticides lodged in butter.

In addition, one tablespoon of butter has 7.1 grams of saturated fat and 31 milligrams of cholesterol. Even one pat of butter has a whopping 2.5 grams of saturated fat and 11 milligrams of cholesterol.

So learn not to use butter on your toast; use jam or jelly alone. Enjoy low-fat yogurt or salsa on your baked potato instead of butter or sour cream. Cook with unsaturated vegetable oils, not with butter or margarine. At restaurants, ask that your vegetables be served without butter. Learn to do without it in general, or save it as a once-a-month treat if there's some food you feel cries out for it.

Cheese. Like butter, most cheese is bad news. The FDA tested sixteen samples of cheddar cheese from around the nation. There were one hundred pesticide and industrial chemical residues in the samples, representing eleven formulations. BHC, DDT, dieldrin, heptachlor, HCB, octachlor and penta were found in at least a quarter of the samples. Pesticides and industrial chemicals detected less frequently were diphenyl 2-ethylhexyl phosphate, lindane, methoxychlor, and tri (2-ethylhexyl) phosphate. This is serious contamination, the result of years of pesticide use, which has laced our soil with poisons. These poisons taint crops and are then concentrated in the milk of dairy cows that feed on those crops. The high fat content of cheddar and other cheeses concentrates the toxins even more. One ounce of cheddar cheese has a whopping 6 grams of saturated fat and 10 milligrams of cholesterol as well, making it a multiple health hazard. The average cheese-eating American eats a little less than an ounce of cheddar cheese daily. Based on this consumption pattern we can expect as many as thirty-six excess cancers in one million persons. That makes cheddar—and any other high-fat nonorganic cheese—a high-risk food. Learn to look for low-fat cheeses or to substitute other foods. Excellent organic tofu cheese substitutes are available at health food markets.

Limit yourself to a small helping of cheese as a treat every couple of weeks, or buy organic cheeses.

Cottage cheese. Six pesticide formulations were found in creamed cottage cheese (4 percent milk fat) with forty-nine total residues. The pesticides detected were BHC, DDT, dieldrin, heptachlor, HCB, and penta. Eating around 2 ounces daily would result in a cancer risk of thirteen excess cancers in one million persons. One cup of large-curd cottage cheese has 6.4 grams of saturated fat and 34 milligrams of cholesterol. When you shop for cottage cheese, purchase the product with the lowest percentage of milk fat, preferably 1 or 2 percent. That will significantly reduce your intake of saturated fat and your exposure to pesticides.

Evaporated milk. Forty-nine residues representing nine formulations were found in sixteen samples of canned evaporated milk. Pesticides detected in at least one-fourth of the samples were BHC, DDT, dieldrin, heptachlor, HCB, and penta. Pesticides and other toxic chemicals detected less frequently were malathion, octachlor, and trichlorobenzenes. One cup of canned evaporated whole milk has 11.6 grams of saturated fat and 74 milligrams of cholesterol.

Half-and-half. There were sixty-six industrial pollutants and pesticide residues representing nine formulations in sixteen samples of half-and-half. Pesticides detected most frequently—in at least one-fourth of the samples—were BHC, DDT, dieldrin, heptachlor, HCB, and octachlor. Pesticides and industrial pollutants detected less frequently were lindane, penta, and PCBs. In addition, one tablespoon of cream, the amount used in one cup of coffee, provides 1.8 grams of saturated fat and 10 milligrams of cholesterol. That may not seem like a lot. But after a few cups of coffee and a few tablespoons of cream, the pesticides contained in saturated fat add up. The industrial pollutants and pesticides you unwittingly ingest in half-and-half should offer another reason for eliminating it from your diet. Powdered cream substitutes made with vegetable oils are a better choice if you want to avoid industrial pollutant and pesticide residues. One tablespoon of cream substitute has no cholesterol and only .7 grams of saturated fat. And powdered cream substitutes are far purer. They have only one-ninth the number of pesticides, at significantly lower concentrations; the three pesticides detected in powdered cream substitutes (chlorpyrifos, malathion, and penta) are far less potent and easier for our bodies to metabolize than the pesticides found in cream.

Of course, heavy whipping cream is much more pesticide laden than half-and-half. Sour cream is also likely to be pesticide saturated.

Ice cream. The FDA tested ice cream sandwiches and chocolate ice cream. The ice cream sandwiches had eighty-one different pesticide residues in sixteen samples, representing thirteen pesticides. The pesticides BHC, DDT, dieldrin, heptachlor, HCB, malathion, and octachlor were found in at least one-fourth of the samples. Virtually all of them cause cancer. Detected less frequently were chlorpyrifos, diazinon, fenitrothion, lindane, parathion, and penta. Eating an average of about 2 ounces a day of ice cream sandwiches over a lifetime would result in at least 9.4 excess cancers in one million persons. That is a fairly high risk for doing something as innocent as eating an ice cream sandwich.

You should assume that similar packaged ice cream desserts use the same kinds of ice cream and are equally dangerous. Always look for ice milk products and nonfat dairy desserts, which contain much less fat and are less dangerous.

In chocolate ice cream there were seventy residues in sixteen samples, representing fourteen formulations: BHC, DDT, dieldrin, heptachlor, HCB, lindane, and octachlor in a quarter of the samples; chlorpyrifos, diazinon, malathion, parathion, penta, pirimiphos-methyl, and tri (2-ethylhexyl) phosphate less often. Eating about 2 ounces of chocolate ice cream daily would result in as many as ten excess cancers in one million persons. So, in addition to the high content of saturated fat and cholesterol, dangerous cancer-causing pesticides are another reason to strictly limit ice cream.

You should assume that other flavors of ice cream are as bad for you as chocolate. The pesticides lodged in milk fat are far more dangerous than whatever toxins may exist in the flavorings.

Processed cheese. In sixteen samples of American processed cheese there were ninety-eight pesticide and industrial chemical residues representing ten different pesticides. BHC, DDT, dieldrin, heptachlor, HCB, octachlor, and penta were found in a quarter of the samples; lindane, pentachlorobenzene, and tri (2-ethylhexyl) phosphate appeared less frequently. One ounce of American processed cheese has 5.6 grams of saturated fat and 27 milligrams of cholesterol. Processed cheese is as dangerous as butter and hard cheese.

Soft cheeses. Soft, processed Mexican-style cheese products can be extremely dangerous. In 1985, more than 48 deaths (including stillbirths) and 150 illnesses in the West were linked with eating listeria-contaminated cheese manufactured by Jalisco Mexican Products, of Artesia, California, a Mexican food company, which has since closed.

Unfortunately, many producers of Mexican-style soft cheeses are mom-and-pop operations in which cheeses are produced in poor sanitary conditions. Some soft cheese producers operate out of their garages. In 1989 the Los Angeles district attorney shut down seven California soft cheese producers, some of whom reportedly used rusty pipes and toilet bowl brushes to stir the milk that was being processed into cheese. These soft cheeses were then sold from door to door and by street vendors throughout southern California and as far north as San Francisco.

Avoid purchasing unlabeled soft cheeses, and don't buy soft cheeses from street vendors or door-to-door vendors. In supermarkets and neighborhood grocery stores, avoid Mexican soft cheeses sold in large blocks without labels. Products that are most likely to be poisoned with dangerous listeria bacteria are queso fresco, queso añejo (also called cotija cheese), panela cheeses, manchego, queso enchilado, queso jalapeño, requeson, and adobera cheeses.

Beware of these brands of Mexican-style soft cheese—distributed through-out the West—which have had products recalled due to listeria contamination: Ariza Cheese Company, Cacique Fine Foods, and Rodeo brand cheese. Rodeo, whose products are distributed in Arizona, California, Oregon, and Texas, also produces cheese under two private labels: Jimenez queso fresco and Jimenez adobera (distributed in Texas).

Brie and other imported soft cheeses can also have bacterial infestations. British Chief Medical Officer Donald Acheson warned consumers in February 1989 that pregnant women should not eat soft cheeses such as Camembert, Brie, and blue-veined cheeses because infection from the listeria bacteria could cause miscarriage or stillbirth. Belgium recently banned, temporarily, French Camembert because of listeria contamination. In 1987, twenty-four persons died during one European outbreak of listeriosis, which was traced to a Swiss soft cheese.

The French rate of listeriosis is about 11.3 cases in one million persons; the U.S. rate is about 3.6 per million. I suspect that the higher rate in France can be attributed in part to significantly higher consumption of soft cheeses such as Brie.

Do not misunderstand my message: I'm not saying that no one should eat Brie or other soft cheeses. I'm saying that the elderly, people who are immune-weakened, children, and women who are pregnant or nursing are especially at risk for listeriosis and should avoid these foods.

Imported soft cheeses from Italy have, in the past, posed listeria problems as well. Cheeses made by Mauri, a northern Italian producer, were taken off the American market more than three years ago because of listeria contamination. However, the government has allowed Mauri to once again begin selling cheeses in the United States. Other Italian cheeses that have had listeria contamination include Taleggio, Tortalpina, D'Aravaggio, and Gorgonzola.

I have some good news: America's favorite soft cheese—cream cheese—has a clean bill of health and appears to be free from listeria or salmonella contamination. However, it is probably high in pesticides and should be eaten very seldom for that reason.

Whole milk. The FDA food study found twenty-nine pesticide residues in sixteen samples of whole milk representing seven pesticide formulations. BHC, DDT, and dieldrin were found in at least a quarter of the samples; heptachlor, HCB, lindane, and octachlor occurred less frequently. This is only about one-third the level of saturation of butter and cheddar cheese. But two other families of synthetic chemicals found in milk are of tremendous concern, warranting the inclusion of whole milk in this red light section.

The regulatory history of milk is a prime example of an industry that has been guilty of severe lapses of safety. I must pose two questions: Why should we trust the dairy industry? Have they earned our trust? The answer is an unequivocal no. In 1982, Hawaiian dairy farmers on Oahu fed dairy cows heptachlor-contaminated sugarcane, which contaminated the herds. The heptachlor-tainted milk was then sold without restriction and allowed to invade and contaminate the bodies of thousands of men, women, and children. Heptachlor is a very strong carcinogen and causes birth defects. Mothers in Hawaii must stop breast-feeding their children or breast-feed their newborns heptachlor-tainted milk. Hawaiian children have suffered significantly elevated instances of illness. But the contamination threat wasn't limited to Hawaii. Several years later, heptachlor-contaminated milk invaded the bodies of men, women, and children in Arkansas. During this same period—in the early 1980s —the industry was also forced to recall heptachlor-contaminated milk distributed in Texas, Louisiana, Kansas, Missouri, and Oklahoma. Again, innocent newborns will be victimized for years to come. In Arkansas, 70 percent of nursing mothers examined during the early 1980s had heptachlor-contaminated breast milk. This contamination was so severe that they were advised not to breast-feed children because of high levels of this pesticide in their breast milk. Our children should not be exposed to a carcinogen thirteen to twenty-six times more powerful than DDT. Pesticides like heptachlor represent a very dangerous toxic exposure for both unborn children and babies.

These unsettling heptachlor contamination episodes are occasional dramatic tragedies. However, the historic use of sulfamethazine in dairy cows represents a chronic and far more disturbing and flagrant violation of safe food laws. Serious violations of federal health standards have occurred throughout the 1980s for the drug sulfamethazine in dairy products. I predict that further studies will reveal that our milk supply is contaminated also with traces of penicillin, tetracycline, and other antibiotics and that we will be hearing disturbing reports about drug residues in milk for a long time. When you add cream to your coffee do you really want to ingest low-level residues of sulfamethazine? When you drink milk at night do you really want another dose of sulfamethazine? Of course not! But that's what you get, thanks to the American dairy industry!

In a 1987 FDA study, milk samples collected from supermarkets in ten American cities were analyzed for sulfamethazine. Residues were detected so frequently in milk samples that the regulation against use of sulfamethazine in dairy cows was found to be a joke—a sick joke. But who was sick? The overcrowded dairy cows? Sulfa-sensitive persons? Or the dairy industry, which flouted the regulations banning the use of sulfamethazine in milk? And where was the government that we trusted to enforce safe food laws? Who was minding the store? And how long had this flagrant violation gone on before being discovered? Overall, 41 percent of the samples in this ten-city survey were contaminated with sulfamethazine. Carcinogenicity studies of rats and mice indicate that sulfamethazine may well be a human carcinogen, affecting the human thyroid gland.

According to the FDA survey, these producers were selling milk with illegal residues of sulfamethazine:

Atlanta: Kinnett
Baltimore: Lueis, Lucerne, Embassy, High's, and Giant
Boston: Cumberland Farms, Hood Star, Stop & Shop, and West Lynn
Brooklyn: Food Club, Crowley, and Byrne
Chicago: Muller, South Valley, Dean Food, and Kraml
Dallas: Kroger
Denver: Sinton's, Oak Farms, and Lucerne
Kansas City, Missouri: Price Choppers, Lucerne, Zarda, Anderson Erickson, and Fairmont
San Francisco: Berkeley Farms, Carnation, and Lady Lee
Seattle: Carnation, My-T-Fine, Darigold, Lucerne, and Vita-Milk

Some dairy producers came out with a clean bill of health. These are the dairy producers whom you should patronize. They're the ones who care about your family's health.

Atlanta: Flav-O-Rich, Kroger, and Mathis Dairy
Brooklyn: Dairylea and Meadow Brook
Chicago: Heritage House
Dallas: Borden, Cabell's, and Schepps
Denver: Cream O'Weber

Government officials claim the sulfamethazine problem is under control. They say that the industry has voluntarily curbed its use of this chemical. However, the problem is more widespread than the government concedes. The limits currently being used to detect sulfamethazine in milk are almost twice as high as the levels at which sulfamethazine is usually found. Thus it is possible that the problem is not being controlled as carefully as the government claims. In addition, dairy producers have switched from sulfamethazine to other drugs that the government cannot detect. It is well known that many drugs not registered for use with dairy cows are, in fact, in widespread use. For example, the *Wall Street Journal* reported in 1989 that 38 percent of milk tested from New York, Philadelphia, Minneapolis–St. Paul, and Boston was tainted with residues of sulfa drugs and streptomycin at levels from 5 to 100 parts per billion. The Center for Science in the Public Interest found sulfa residues in 20 percent of the milk sampled from the Washington-Baltimore area.

Dioxin residues also taint our milk. The Health Protection Branch of Canada has reported extremely low levels of dioxin (in the parts per trillion range) in several samples of milk and cream that were packaged in bleached milk cartons manufactured in the United States. Dioxin, which is a by-product of the process used to bleach paper products, had migrated from the cartons to the milk. Very likely U.S. milk products are similarly tainted.

Scientists quibble over minor aspects of the dioxin threat, but there is no question that we should reduce our exposures to environmental contaminants such as dioxin whenever possible. The 2,3,7,8-TCDD form of dioxin in our milk is at least 470,000 times more potent as a carcinogen than DDT. One expert noted that the EPA has compared the chronic toxicity of dioxin with that of plutonium! The EPA's carcinogen assessment group found unacceptable human cancer risk at chronic dietary exposure to one part per trillion dioxin, the lowest dose tested in mammals, and concluded that dioxin is among the most potent carcinogens known, with no safe dose. Dioxin is a cancer promoter and a co-carcinogen, a kind of all-purpose carcinogen that not only may cause cancer but enhances and speeds up cancers triggered by other carcinogens.

Government regulators and the paper industry have tried to quell public concern, saying that low-level dioxin exposure is not likely to result in human health problems. The real truth is that cancer incidence rates keep increasing, and much of the cause will eventually be seen to be cumulative toxic exposures as a result of pervasive industrial and chemical pollution. Here we have one of the most carcinogenic compounds known appearing in our milk! The dioxin problem—prevalent in some fish as well as milk—is plainly out of control. Regulating the pulp paper mills that produce milk cartons and enacting a zero-tolerance policy for dioxin in milk would be logical places to start gaining the upper hand with this problem, which is as urgent today as the chlordane, DDT, dieldrin, and heptachlor problems were two decades ago. A law calling for labeling of products containing dioxin would also help. The paper industry says its products are safe and that the amount of dioxin that migrates into food is so low that nobody will be harmed. But with labeling, consumers could decide for themselves what is safe.

In Sweden, manufacturers of toilet paper, tampons, paper towels, food containers, disposable diapers, and other paper products have begun to use unbleached pulp, which is free of dioxin. England and Germany market a wide range of unbleached food cartons. The marketing of unbleached paper products in America has just begun.

For now, the best way to protect yourself from traces of dioxin is to buy milk in glass containers. Plastic containers are part of an enormous waste problem in America and there may be some migration of plasticizers into the milk product. Glass, which can be easily recycled, is the sensible choice.

Because of low-level residues of antibiotics, sulfa drugs, pesticides, and dioxin, parents may be concerned about feeding whole milk to their children. I know two doctors, one of them a pediatrician, who will not feed their children whole milk. Unfortunately, I don't know of any suppliers of organic whole milk that is guaranteed to be free of pesticides, antibiotics, and sulfa drugs. Remember, children need a lot of dairy fats up to age two, so don't risk switching from whole milk to skim without finding a substitute source of dairy fat. Until organic milk becomes available, you may want to give your child low-fat or skim milk packaged in glass bottles (to avoid possible dioxin exposure) as soon as your pediatrician deems the switch acceptable. Other options are available. Organic cheeses are available, which you can give your child daily to make sure he or she is getting essential dairy fats. Organic yogurt could be another source. You can also make yogurt cheese. See the shopping tips section and the Personal Action Guide for information on the yogurt cheese funnel.

Shopping Tips

Always buy low-fat or nonfat milk and yogurt, and look for the coldest, freshest products in the store. Skim milk has only one-tenth as many pesticide residues as whole milk and one-eighth as many as low-fat milk.

Bacteria such as salmonella or listeria can grow in any dairy product, not just cheese. To cut down the risk of contamination, always buy U.S. Extra Grade milk from government-inspected plants, and do not buy unpasteurized milk. Choose milk from the lower refrigerator shelves. Hot air rises, and temperatures on the higher storage shelves may not be cold enough to prevent the growth of listeria and salmonella (40°F. is minimal for safe storage), so finding the coldest product is important. Find the freshest milk by checking the date on the carton. Buy milk and other dairy products last and store them first when you get home. Don't pour unused milk from the table back into the bottle or carton. Throw it out or store it in a separate glass jar. Milk that has been out at room temperature for even a few minutes has already begun to be invaded by multiplying bacteria, so you're pouring additional bacteria back into your milk, speeding up the spoilage. If you save table milk in a separate jar, use it for cooking, which destroys bacteria, not for drinking.

When buying cheese, be aware that cheeses labeled "natural" could contain chemicals such as hydrogen peroxide, a potential carcinogen that is used to sterilize milk, and benzoyl peroxide, used to bleach milk. Bulk cheese may well have preservatives, mold inhibitors, and antimycotics. Grated cheeses may contain mold inhibitors, anticaking agents, and natural or artificial flavoring. These must be listed on the label.

Buying raw (unpasteurized) milk cheese is no guarantee that the cheese will be without additives, artificial coloring, and preservatives or that it will be free from pesticides. At least make sure the label stipulates that nothing artificial has been added.

Brie, Camembert, and Limburger cheese is free of coloring and preservatives. Any ammonia smell means these cheeses are past their prime. Be wary of smoked cheese. Like smoked fish and meats, smoked cheese contains carcinogenic compounds that are produced in the smoking process. All smoked cheeses, except provolone, are labeled as such.

Try sapsago, a safe, dry grating cheese made with all skim milk, which is perfect for the low-toxin high-energy diet. Some people love sapsago; others are not so fond of it. Cheese producers should note that more cheeses made with skim milk are very much needed. They would help to reduce our exposure to pesticides as well as our consumption of cholesterol and saturated fat.

An excellent nontoxic cheese that you can make at home is yogurt cheese. Yogurt cheese made with nonfat yogurt gives you the rich taste of whole milk cheese without dangerous pesticides. And it is easy to make with cheesecloth or a yogurt cheese funnel, which you can order by mail. This simple plastic funnel has a microsized mesh that removes whey from yogurt. You simply fill the funnel with yogurt, place the funnel over a coffee mug or drinking glass, and six to twenty-four hours later you will have yogurt cheese in the funnel. It takes thirty-two ounces of yogurt to make about two cups of yogurt cheese. I defy you to tell the difference between cheesecake made with nonfat yogurt and cheesecake made with fatty dairy products! Yogurt cheese makes a great substitute for cream cheese, mayonnaise, margarine, butter, and sour cream. It can even replace butter at the dinner table and the sour cream served with baked potatoes. Try yogurt cheese for cheesecake, for layering lasagne, and for dips and spreads. See the Personal Action Guide for ordering information for a yogurt cheese funnel.

Buy organic cheeses. There are presently only a handful of dairies producing chemical-free and low-fat cheeses. North Farm cheeses are made with organic milk; no herbicides, pesticides, chemical fertilizers, antibiotics, or hormones are used. This Madison, Wisconsin, company's organic cheeses are certified by the Organic Crop Improvement Association. Dairy farmers working with North Farm must have practiced an organic program for a minimum of three years. Cheese varieties include mild and aged cheddar, low-fat/low-sodium cheddar, Colby, Monterey Jack, Muenster, mozzarella, provolone, string, pepperjack, and lacy Swiss. I have tested North Farm cheeses and found them free of pesticides at relatively low detection limits. See the Personal Action Guide for more information about other mail-order organic dairy food suppliers.

Many people wonder whether they should substitute goat's milk for cow's milk. Although goat's milk seems to be tolerated better by persons sensitive to cow's milk, you should keep in mind that goat's milk may be as contaminated with pesticides as cow's milk, since it has a higher fat content. Goat's milk also lacks folic acid and vitamin B_{12}, which are valuable in fighting the effects of stress. On the other hand, goat's milk also has a slightly higher calcium content and tends to have less antibiotic contamination than cow's milk.

Be wary of imported powdered milk. In Mexico City, some 7,000 tons of imported powdered milk were allowed to be consumed even though the milk was contaminated with cesium 137 and strontium 90 as a result of fallout from the Chernobyl nuclear accident.

Dairy Substitutes

At our home we rarely eat cheese anymore, because of the calories, saturated fat, and cholesterol in addition to the pesticide contamination. However, we have found excellent dairy substitutes for sandwiches and for grating.

Soya Kaas produces an excellent line of cheese substitutes available nationwide at health and natural food stores. They're tasty. They're convenient. They're made with organic tofu without chemical additives or preservatives. Varieties include Monterey Jack and cheddar. Nu Tofu, available nationwide, is also made with organic tofu without chemical additives or preservatives. Use these tofu cheeses as you would dairy cheese.

Soy milk is a fine milk substitute for older children and adults and can be substituted for most milk uses. It has no cholesterol or lactose, and the fat in it is mainly unsaturated. Nutritionally, soy milk has as much as thirty times more iron than cow's milk, as well as lecithin and vitamin E. It lacks appreciable amounts of vitamin A, vitamin D, and calcium, but these nutrients are found in other staples of the high-energy low-toxin diet such as fruits, vegetables, grains, pure seafood, and some mineral waters. There are several excellent, tasty soy milks available, including Edensoy, Health Valley Soy Moo, which I love, Soy Powder, Vitasoy, and Westbrae. Always buy soy milk made with organically grown soybeans to be sure you're not getting pesticides in your milk. Nut and grain milks can also be used in place of cow's milk. They are made with an almond blend or with cultured rice known as amazake. An unrefined sweetener may be added. They also have less protein, calcium, and vitamins A and D than dairy milk.

When shopping for desserts, buy nonfat yogurt to satisfy your desire for a rich dessert while still following low-toxin guidelines. Nancy's brand nonfat yogurt is one of the best yogurts marketed today. Its ingredients are nothing but skim milk, nonfat dry milk, and beneficial acidophilus and bifidum bacterial cultures.

Nonfat frozen yogurt also makes an excellent dessert. Bring home a family pack of nonfat frozen yogurt and use organic fresh fruits for your topping. Honey Hills Farms nonfat frozen yogurt, available throughout the nation, is an excellent product for reducing your exposure to pesticides and cutting down your intake of calories, cholesterol, and saturated fat.

Other good dairy substitutes include Gise, from France, very low in fat; Vitari, a frozen fruit dessert, virtually nonfat; and Tofutti Lite, a nondairy frozen dessert made from tofu, also very low in fat. Regular Tofutti, however, has 200 to 275 calories in a 4-ounce serving, making it far from a low-calorie alternative dessert. None of these desserts are organic, but because of their ingredients, they are sure to be very low in pesticide saturation.

Sherbet, with only 1 or 2 percent milk fat, is a good choice for dessert or snacks. Avoid brands with artificial flavor and color, which should tip you off to inferior production methods. Sherbet is a great dessert choice when dining out. At home, if a craving for something sweet hits you with full gale force and you find yourself headed for the supermarket, look for sherbet.

Dole fruit sorbet is an excellent dessert that is much better for your body than any dairy dessert. Its ingredients are water, raspberry puree, sugar, corn syrup, locust bean gum, pectin, guar gum, grape skin extract (for color), natural flavors, and citric acid. Sure, sugar and corn syrup are not the very best ingredients for your body. But we are talking about trade-offs. Compared with ice cream, Dole fruit sorbet is excellent. The really big difference comes in the area of pesticide saturation; the sorbet will have far fewer pesticide residues. Cascadian Farm also makes an organic fruit sorbet.

Water ice is another great dessert alternative. Water ices are really gems! They have absolutely no milk ingredients. Instead, egg whites are used. They have very low, if any, pesticide saturation.

Best of all, when you crave a sweet frozen dessert, you can use a blender to create delicious frozen desserts that fit in with the low-toxin high-energy diet. One of my favorites is a banana–fruit juice dessert: slice a banana and freeze it; put the frozen banana slices in the blender; add a handful of ice, and pour in enough of your favorite organic fruit juice to give the dessert a fruit-juice flavor but not so much as to make it runny. Blend at moderate speed until thick and creamy. You have made a sinfully delicious dessert that is absolutely healthy and tastes as delicious as an ice cream milk shake. Enjoy!

Safe Shopping List: Dairy Foods

Green Light	Number of Residues
Buttermilk	3
Cream substitute	3
Skim milk	3
Low-fat and nonfat yogurt	6
Low-fat chocolate milk	12
Low-fat milk	19

OTHER GREEN LIGHT DAIRY FOODS

Cottage cheese (low-fat)   Soy cheese
Low-fat and nonfat frozen   Soy milk
  yogurt
Sherbet

Yellow Light	Number of Residues
Milk shake	23
Yogurt with fruit	32
Ice milk	35

Red Light	Number of Residues
Whole milk	29
Canned evaporated milk	49
Cottage cheese (4% milk fat)	49
Half-and-half	66
Ice cream	81
Processed cheese	98
Cheese	100
Butter	101

9. EGGS

Eggs, like meat, are a great protein source that most Americans eat far too much of. They have exceptionally high amounts of cholesterol, and there is a serious problem with salmonella contamination of eggs in this country. But from the toxic standpoint, eggs are better to eat than the worst pesticide-accumulating meats, such as bologna, frankfurters, ground beef, and salami. I consider eggs overall a yellow light food and try to eat them seldom.

Eggs are the most cholesterol-saturated food Americans routinely consume. There are 213 milligrams of cholesterol in a single egg; by comparison, a single frankfurter has only 23, and a cup of ice cream has 59.

Bad as they are, eggs are *not* the worst food for your heart, because they are relatively low in saturated fats. And studies show that dietary saturated fat is more closely linked than dietary cholesterol with elevated blood cholesterol. While 6 ounces of lean ground beef would have 12.4 grams of saturated fat, two eggs have only 3.1 grams. A 1-ounce slice of cheddar cheese has only 30 milligrams of cholesterol but 6 grams of saturated fat. One cup of whole milk has only 33 milligrams of cholesterol, but it has a whopping 5.1 grams of saturated fat. Eggs may indeed contribute to an increase in some individuals' cholesterol levels, but other animal foods are much more significant contributors.

Unfortunately, people like to combine eggs with other high-fat foods such as cheese, sausages, bacon, or another fatty meat. And therein lies the problem: the combination of these animal foods can be deadly.

I see eggs as part of the larger animal protein picture. Eggs, dairy foods, and meat are all in the same boat. And study after study has shown a direct and strong correlation between groups of people who consume saturated fat and cholesterol and mortality as a result of coronary heart disease. One study in the 1960s—known as the Seven Countries Study—looked at the cholesterol and saturated fat intake of more than 12,000 men in seven countries—Finland, Greece, Italy, Japan, the Netherlands, the United States, and Yugoslavia. The results were clear: those groups of men who ate the most cholesterol- and saturated-fat-rich foods also suffered the highest rates of deaths from coronary heart disease.

The message is that dietary saturated fat and cholesterol *do* raise total blood cholesterol levels; the higher the total blood cholesterol level, the greater the severity of atherosclerosis; the greater the severity of athero- sclerosis, the greater the risk for coronary heart disease. It is that simple.

And your diet is the key!

Unfortunately, many doctors today know far too little about diet and nutrition and are too eager to initiate drug therapy to lower cholesterol. If Americans knew the close interrelationship between diet and high choles- terol, they could radically limit their intake of dairy foods, eggs, and meat, increase their consumption of plant foods, and significantly lower their cholesterol without drugs, adding years to their lives and reducing their risk of heart disease. The drugs in use today for coronary artery disease often are toxic chemicals with many potential adverse side effects that may not become evident for years.

Remember that eggs, like meat and dairy foods, create a risk of heart disease. So eat them seldom. You'll get plenty of protein elsewhere in the low-toxin high-energy diet. And remember *not* to combine eggs with other high-cholesterol, high-fat foods like cheese, bacon, sausage, milk, and creamy sauces. One day we'll all look back at the bacon-and-eggs breakfast as another relic of the American mentality of excess that also brought us gas-guzzling automobiles, DDT, diets high in fats and red meat, and routine consumption of cigarettes and liquor. It's a legacy we can do without.

Salmonella Contamination

The big problem with eggs is bacterial contamination, particularly sal- monella contamination. Nationwide, the reported number of food poisoning cases linked to eggs grew from 7,325 in 1974 to about 14,000 in 1986. These figures represent only 1 to 10 percent of the number of persons who are actually sickened. For every case that is reported, it is estimated that as many as 100 cases go unreported because they are shrugged off as a bug or intestinal flu.

We used to think that eggs were not major carriers of salmonella. Im- proved sanitary standards and use of disinfectants to wash eggs led us to believe that bacterial diseases linked with eggs had been virtually elimi- nated. However, from 1985 to 1987, eating uncooked eggs accounted for

77 percent of the 2,119 salmonella-poisoning cases researchers were able to trace to their sources. And eggs, we now know, have been the cause of a dramatic increase in food poisoning in the Northeast.

The number of salmonella-poisoning cases linked to Grade A eggs underwent a six- to sevenfold increase in the Northeast from 1976 to 1986. Only about 550 cases a year of *Salmonella enteritidis* occurred in the Northeast in the 1970s; one decade later that number had jumped to more than 4,000 cases. *Salmonella enteritidis* is most closely associated with Grade A eggs, the kind sold in supermarkets. Those at highest risk include children under the age of one, pregnant women, and people who are immune-compromised, including individuals undergoing cancer treatment and those with AIDS.

Until recently, salmonellosis outbreaks had been confined to flocks of chickens in Connecticut, Maine, New Hampshire, New Jersey, New York, Pennsylvania, Rhode Island, and Vermont. Then the infections spread to flocks in Mountain and southern states. And in Utah, South Dakota, Mississippi, and Florida the incidence of *Salmonella enteritidis* has recently jumped dramatically and has caused at least 15 percent of the salmonellosis outbreaks. The source of the disease in many of the outbreaks was Grade A eggs that met all state and federal requirements and that even underwent shell washing with chlorine disinfectants.

In the past, salmonella infection of flocks was thought to result from contamination of eggs by animal feces. But *Salmonella enteritidis* may be infecting chickens in a much more insidious and hard-to-combat way. Investigators who have looked into the causes of Grade A egg–related salmonella outbreaks have discovered that the salmonella bacteria were *inside* the eggs, in their yolks and whites. Researchers killed the egg-producing hens and discovered that their ovaries and oviducts were infested with viable, reproducing colonies of *Salmonella enteritidis*. Thus, some experts theorize that *Salmonella enteritidis* may be reproducing, colonizing in the ovaries of hens, and infecting the egg yolk directly—before the shell is even formed! To make matters worse, farmers and veterinarians may not even know that this type of salmonella has taken hold of a flock. The contamination may go on for generations without any visible symptoms in the flock.

How serious is the problem? Well, let's put it in perspective. Some researchers claim that only one in 10,000 eggs in the supermarket will harbor *Salmonella enteritidis*. On the other hand, one of the nation's leading bacteriological experts has remarked that if he were in the Northeast and someone offered him hollandaise sauce, which is made with raw eggs, he would refuse to eat it. Certainly you must not serve raw egg dishes to frail elderly persons, to persons whose immune systems have been compromised by illness, or to babies and toddlers. Their white blood cells may not be able to subdue this salmonella bacterium.

This does not mean you must refuse raw egg dishes. But at least you should be aware of the risks. For those who possess basically strong immune systems, eating raw eggs presents a slight risk of infection that may result in a few days of nausea, vomiting, diarrhea, and fever.

These dishes are usually made with raw, unpasteurized eggs:

Homemade mayonnaise
Homemade ice cream
Milk shakes
Caesar salad
Hollandaise sauce
Soft omelets
Eggs sunny side up (the yolks are virtually uncooked)
Uncooked batter of cakes and cookies (many kids love uncooked cake and
    cookie batter)
Cake filling
Pasta with raw egg–cheese stuffing (don't nibble before cooking)
Stuffing for seafood dishes
Rice balls and meatballs made with eggs (don't nibble before cooking)
Eggnog
Potato-egg salad

If you are traveling, you should know that eggs from England, Wales, the Balkan countries, and the Iberian peninsula are frequently infected. In December 1988, England's junior health minister, Edwina Currie, remarked on national television that most of England's eggs were infected with the salmonella bacteria. This revelation triggered public hysteria that resulted in severe economic losses for the British egg industry. Sales of eggs slumped 50 percent. More than 20 million eggs went unsold. Currie was eventually forced to resign—as a result of her honesty! Meanwhile, the British government announced that thorough cooking was the best method of self-protection.

I do not want to see any more persons sickened. And I am particularly concerned that so many food-poisoning outbreaks occur in institutions. If you have loved ones in institutions, be careful for them; make sure that they are never served undercooked or raw egg dishes. Immune-compromised persons and individuals recovering from heart surgery, cancer therapy, or other illness also should not eat raw egg dishes.

Fortunately, many foods that are made with raw eggs may be quite safe if commercially sold. Commercial products are made with bulk eggs and should be free from contamination. That's because bulk eggs are pasteurized and sterilized and can be used in any recipes that demand raw or undercooked eggs. Pasteurized bulk eggs should always be used by institutions serving toddlers, the elderly, and immune-weakened persons.

Pesticide Contamination

The evidence is quite clear that pesticides have infiltrated commercial eggs sold in most supermarkets. I looked at both chicken and duck eggs and found residues of chlordane, dieldrin, nonachlor, DDT, diazinon, and pentachlorophenol. The levels are low, however, and the cancer risk as a result of pesticides in eggs is negligible.

Shopping and Cooking Tips

These guidelines will help you find the best eggs from humanely raised chickens and protect yourself against egg-related salmonellosis.

Look for labels that state that the chickens were raised without antibiotics. Although antibiotic residues were not detected in eggs I analyzed, their use is a symptom of the factory farm. Also, be sure to look for fertile eggs, available at health food stores and some supermarkets. Here's why: it is impossible to cram roosters into cages with hens, so you can be certain that fertile eggs come from uncaged hens.

Nest Eggs, a brand of eggs available in many urban supermarkets, are certified to be from hens raised humanely and without antibiotics. See the Personal Action Guide for details.

Do not use artificial, cholesterol-free egg substitutes. One such brand, Morningstar Farms' Scramblers, contains aluminum sulfate, which introduces aluminum into your diet. Check other brand labels. If they contain any aluminum compounds, they deserve no place in the nontoxic kitchen. There is a better alternative to these cholesterol-free chemical-laced egg products. Egg whites have absolutely no saturated fat or cholesterol, and they probably have very few industrial chemicals or pesticides. When cooking dishes that require eggs, separate the whites from the yolks and use only the whites. Give your dog or cat the yolk. True carnivores such as cats and dogs do not suffer problems with cholesterol.

My favorite recipe is the white omelet. Instead of using egg yolks with pesticide-saturated cheese, I simply use egg whites with North Farm organic cheese or a tofu cheese substitute. I cook it just as I would a yellow omelet.

Do not buy unrefrigerated eggs. Temperatures between 40°F. and 140°F. are ideal for salmonella to breed. Never leave eggs unrefrigerated for more than two hours. Use only uncracked eggs. Always wash your hands after working with raw eggs. Do not let raw eggs touch other foods.

Wash utensils and cutting surfaces before and after handling raw eggs. You might even want to use a homemade solution of diluted chlorine wash, made with a half teaspoon of chlorine per cup of water, to sterilize cutting surfaces and utensils.

Observe the hot and cold rules. Egg-rich foods should be served hot immediately after cooking; refrigerate them quickly after use. An egg-rich food to be served cold should be refrigerated right after preparation and kept in the refrigerator until serving time. Do not prepare hollandaise sauce in advance and allow it to sit in a double boiler on the back of the stove.

The especially prudent will cook all eggs thoroughly and avoid runny eggs cooked sunny side up. French toast and scrambled eggs should also be thoroughly cooked. Boiling eggs for seven minutes, poaching five minutes, or frying three minutes on each side will kill all salmonella. These cooking times may be a little long for some, but they are ideal cooking times for your health. Do the best you can.

Once they are boiled, eggs lose the protective outer membrane around their shell, and bacteria can pass into the egg. Always store hard-cooked eggs at as cold a temperature as possible in order to prevent salmonella contamination. Hard-cooked eggs with shells intact will keep one week in the refrigerator. Any that crack should be used the same day. It is safe to leave hard-cooked eggs unrefrigerated for an hour or two for, say, an Easter egg hunt, but refrigerate any that are not immediately eaten.

For best quality use whole eggs within a week of purchase. The fresher the eggs the less likely they are to contain high salmonella concentrations. The outside limit for keeping whole eggs in the refrigerator is five weeks. After that they lose quality. For safety's sake, use leftover separated yolks and whites within two to four days.

10. PREPARED FOODS

A huge part of our diet is made up of prepared foods. These food products are as saturated with pesticides as the whole foods we've already discussed, and many of them are laced with preservatives, taste enhancers, emulsifiers, and other additives as well. Did you know that some of the highest levels of carcinogenic pesticides such as BHC and lindane in any food are found in milk chocolate? Or that some of the highest levels of the carcinogenic pesticide dieldrin are found in pumpkin pie?

The irony is that Americans really do prefer wholesome natural foods without additives and preservatives. Surveys conducted regularly by the Food Marketing Institute indicate most Americans are extremely concerned over the additives and preservatives in their food.

But the major convenience food corporations simply are not responding to consumers. Just take a look at Saturday morning television. On any weekend morning, much of the advertising aimed at our children is hawking breakfast foods of dubious nutritional value loaded with artificial colors, preservatives, additives, and saturated fats. Even the TV network guidelines designed to protect our children backfire. The CBS Television Network Advertising Guidelines require that advertised products be shown for at least three seconds within the context of a well-balanced breakfast. So for a few seconds a child sees a nutritionally suspect cereal in a table setting with milk, orange juice, toast, and fruit. The idea here is to teach our children something about a balanced, nutritional breakfast. But what are the cereal hucksters really teaching our children? No doubt, children get the idea that it is the cereal that provides the bulk of nutritional benefits.

Dr. Michael Jacobson, executive director of the Center for Science in

144

the Public Interest, discussed this situation in a recent letter mailed to CSPI members.

Every once in a while, I force myself to watch Saturday morning television. What a depressing experience! The programming is bad enough, but the commercials make me angry enough to pull the plug. . . .

Week after week, in shameless pursuit of profit, major food corporations spend millions of dollars to persuade children to eat foods that are slowly killing them.

McDonald's alone pours more than $40 million a year into network television ads aimed at children. M&M/Mars spends more than $100 million marketing its candies. General Foods spends $20 million a year just on Kool-Aid commercials. And General Mills backs its junky Ice Cream Cone cereal with $10 million worth of ads.

In dazzling TV commercials, food conglomerates hawk hamburgers and fries loaded with saturated fat and calories . . . candy bars packed with fat and sugar . . . soft drinks that contain ten teaspoons of sugar in every can . . . breakfast cereals that are no more than glorified candy, with as much as 50 percent sugar.

And they target the most vulnerable segment of our society—our children—the ones least able to separate the facts from the commercial hype.

Many children's foods are made from the cheapest ingredients. They contain artificial colorings, flavorings, and preservatives. And few have anything to do with nutritious food—or with building a future generation of healthy Americans. . . .

What's even more intolerable than the massive amounts of money poured into food advertising is that the commercials routinely try to deceive us. And where children are concerned, they succeed far too often.

In Trix ads, for instance, brightly colored pieces of fruit hop into the cereal box while the announcer shouts, "Made with natural flavorings." Fine. But what the ads don't disclose is that Trix *does not* contain any fruit . . . and that it *does* contain artificial coloring! And how many children will understand the brief disclaimer that the pretty-colored cereal is only "part of a balanced breakfast"—the part, in fact, they could most healthfully do without?

Despite a decade of urgent calls for improved diets from the surgeon general, government agencies, and other health authorities, our society has not changed the way it shapes children's eating habits. If anything, thanks to the power of TV advertising combined with the greed of corporate America, things are getting worse.

If eating had no impact on health, no one would care about kids' diets. But the fact is that *right now,* the seeds of disease—ranging from tooth decay and obesity to heart disease—are being planted in our children and grandchildren:

- Saturated fat and cholesterol, which lead to heart attacks, begin to clog youngsters' arteries by their teenage years. Yet the hamburger chains target children in particular. Medical studies show that many teenagers and even younger children already have cholesterol levels over 200!

- Obese children usually become obese adults. Yet children's products—candy bars, hot dogs, hamburgers—are overwhelmingly fatty or fried, and *very fattening!* Obesity among six- to eleven-year-old children has increased 54 percent in the last twenty years.

- Additives cause allergic and hyperactive reactions in a small but significant number of children—yet the junk-food makers load their products with synthetic chemicals.

Worst of all, dietary habits formed in childhood are highly likely to persist into adulthood, where they are harder to change and where effects all too often lead to sickness and death. . . .

The real shame of it is that the institutions that could ensure that children eat a healthful, wholesome diet have simply turned their backs on their responsibility. TV networks have refused to turn away junk-food advertising. Fast-food restaurants will not stop targeting kids with their fattiest foods. Many schools continue to serve meals that are little more than junk food. And doctors and hospitals are so busy treating adult heart attack victims that they have no time to work on preventing heart attacks among the young.

Cynical campaigns aimed at capturing the hearts and minds of our children also have been launched in the print media under the guise of educational journalism. Some 500,000 copies of *Sports Illustrated for Kids,* a monthly child's version of the adult sports magazine, are distributed nationwide without charge to public schools. Although its ostensible purpose is to help promote literacy, this magazine is actually an advertising forum for promoting the great American junk-food mentality! What right does this magazine have to use the credibility of our schools to provide its junk-food advertisers with access to the bodies and minds of our children? Corporate advertisers such as Frito-Lay, Hershey, M&M/Mars, Pepsi-Cola, RJR Nabisco, and General Mills pay $250,000 for ten pages of advertising a year in this magazine. No wonder they're willing to make such costly investments! Advertisers gain credibility, because the magazine becomes part of the educational curriculum.

Let's take the time to teach our children the true facts about food safety. Good nutritional habits can never begin too soon.

Materials used to package convenience foods are a legitimate cause for concern. Unfortunately, federal scientists know little about the toxic chemicals that are released into food from packaging, and there is very lenient regulation concerning migration of toxic chemicals into convenience foods from their containers. The FDA does approve packaging, but the scientists simply do not have a handle on all the different chemicals that could be leaching into your food. This is especially of concern today when so many of us are using microwave ovens to heat foods contained in heat-susceptor packaging. Heat susceptor packaging enables intense microwave cooking temperatures. When temperatures start to exceed 300°F., migration of chemicals such as plasticizers and adhesives in the food packaging occurs. What's in these chemicals? Benzene, toluene, and xylene are among the toxic chemicals found in packaging materials, and all cause cancer.

We have some control over this situation. Foods that are likely to be in heat-susceptor packaging include pizza, french fries, waffles, popcorn, and breaded fish, according to Lisa Lefferts and Stephen Schmidt of the Center for Science in the Public Interest. The best self-protection method is to take convenience foods out of their packaging whenever possible and transfer them to glass cookware or Corning Ware, whether cooking in the microwave or conventional oven.

Microwave radiation itself is probably not dangerous in the amounts leaked from microwave ovens. Although there can be some leakage from a microwave oven, the amount truly appears to be inconsequential. Nevertheless, Lefferts and Schmidt advise, "It's prudent not to allow children to stare into a microwave while it's on."

Plastic wraps in which foods come and which are used for food storage also contain chemicals that can migrate into our food at all temperatures, whether in the oven, at room temperature, or stored in the refrigerator. One chemical that scientists know migrates into food from plastic wrap is di-(2-ethylhexyl) adipate (DEHA). Although it has caused cancer in one experimental species, it has not caused cancer in two, leaving the scientific jury still out to decide whether it should be classified as a potential human carcinogen. DEHA is often found in plastic wrap used for meats. Your best personal solution is to use glass containers or wax paper as a liner for food storage between your food and cling wraps or aluminum foil. Instead of cooking in plastic wraps, it is prudent to transfer foods from plastic wraps to glass cookware.

In this section I'll point you to the many safe convenience foods available in any supermarket. There are thousands of prepared foods; I've tried to look at the most popular ones. Once you see how saturated with pesticides some of these foods are, you will be convinced more than ever that you must go nontoxic!

I'll also look into all the chemical concoctions—such as BHA, BHT, MSG, TBHQ, aspartame, benzoic acid, carrageenan, food and dye colorings, saccharin, and other additives and preservatives—that lace the thousands of brands of prepared foods in all those colorful, enticing, and often misleadingly labeled packages. I'll explain how these additives and preservatives can dramatically affect your health, as well as that of your children. These insights will help you in strengthening your commitment to buy safe, healthful foods and beverages.

CONVENIENCE FOODS

Did you think that the pesticide controversy was strictly limited to raw foods? Unfortunately, pesticides make no distinctions between raw and processed foods. Nor does food processing always destroy them. Some convenience foods are thoroughly saturated with pesticides. Others are not. You need to know the difference.

In this section I've looked at foods commonly bought in supermarkets for use as a main course or side dish. As before, I've used the FDA Total Diet Study's very thorough analysis of chemicals in foods. I assure you that some of these are heavyweight industrial chemicals and pesticides, and pretty packaging cannot make them vanish.

Convenience Foods Survival Guide

GREEN LIGHT

Beef broth. Canned beef broth had only two pesticide residues. Penta was the only pesticide detected. One cup of beef broth has about .3 grams of saturated fat and a trace of cholesterol. There is virtually no cancer risk. Be careful, though, of high salt levels in this and other canned soups.

Chicken noodle soup. Canned chicken noodle soup had only five residues of the pesticides malathion and penta. There is virtually no cancer risk as a result of toxic contamination. One cup of canned chicken noodle soup has only .7 grams of saturated fat and 7 milligrams of cholesterol. Be sure there are no chemical additives such as preservatives or monosodium glutamate (MSG).

Pork and beans. Canned pork and beans had only one pesticide residue, dieldrin. The amount of meat is tiny, so the pesticides usually associated with red meat do not appear.

Spaghetti in tomato sauce. Canned spaghetti in tomato sauce had only ten pesticide residues representing five pesticide formulations. Malathion was detected in at least one-fourth of the samples. Chlorpyrifos, diazinon, dimethoate, and methamidophos were detected less frequently. There is virtually no significant cancer risk as a result of this contamination. One cup of spaghetti in tomato sauce has virtually no saturated fat or cholesterol.

Tomato soup. In the FDA Total Diet Study, canned cream of tomato soup had twenty-three pesticide residues representing six pesticide formulations. Pesticides detected most frequently were DDT and malathion. Detected less frequently were BHC, endosulfan, parathion, and toxaphene. Plain, uncreamed tomato soup is even better; you would probably eliminate half the pesticides including BHC, DDT, and possibly toxaphene. The malathion, endosulfan, and parathion are probably residues from the spray used on the tomatoes. Malathion was found in 75 percent of the sixteen samples. There is virtually no significant cancer risk as a result of the toxic contamination. One cup of canned cream of tomato soup has about 5.1 grams of saturated fat and 20 milligrams of cholesterol.

Vegetable beef soup. Canned vegetable beef soup is astoundingly safe: absolutely no residues were found in it. The vegetables are highly processed and there is so little beef that its pesticide residues were not found. One cup of canned vegetable beef soup has only .9 grams of saturated fat and 5 milligrams of cholesterol. Seek soups that are not cream-based; cream adds significantly to the pesticide saturation. Also, look for soups without additives.

YELLOW LIGHT

Frozen dinners. Frozen dinners are a favorite convenience food. Fried chicken dinners had forty-two pesticide residues representing nine different pesticide formulations. That is not too bad, compared with other foods we've discussed. Pesticides detected most frequently were DDT, diazinon, and malathion; other pesticides detected were chlorpropham, chlorpyrifos, dicloran, dieldrin, octachlor, and penta.

Select the safest frozen dinners by following safe meat and poultry guidelines. Dinners with beef, such as Salisbury steak, or with cheese and beef, such as enchiladas and tacos, will have the greatest pesticide contamination. A better choice would be a frozen turkey dinner, since turkey breast has far less pesticide saturation.

Frozen chicken potpies. A very popular American convenience food, frozen potpies had forty pesticide residues representing ten pesticide formulations. Pesticides detected most frequently included DDT, diazinon, and malathion. Other pesticides detected included BHC, chlorpropham, chlorpyrifos, dieldrin, lindane, penta, and 2,4-dichloro-6-nitrobenzenamine.

Lasagne. Homemade lasagne with meat sauce, in the FDA Total Diet Study, had forty-one pesticide residues representing eleven different pesticide formulations. BHC, DDT, and malathion were detected in at least one-fourth of the samples. Other pesticides detected included chlorpyrifos, diazinon, dicloran, dieldrin, endosulfan, HCB, octachlor, and penta.

Macaroni and cheese. With thirty-five different pesticide and industrial chemical residues in sixteen samples, representing ten different pesticide formulations, macaroni and cheese made from a box mix was not so great and not so bad. Pesticides detected in at least a quarter of the samples included dieldrin, malathion, and penta. Other pesticides and industrial chemicals detected less frequently included BHC, captan, chlorpyrifos, DDT, diphenyl 2-ethylhexyl phosphate, heptachlor, and HCB. Because macaroni and cheese does have a moderately significant contamination problem, I would advise consumers to be on the lookout for new organic varieties of macaroni and cheese, which will significantly cut down pesticide exposure. One such brand, available in health food markets, is Amy's frozen macaroni and soy cheese dinners. You could also buy North Farm organic cheese—which I personally tested without detecting any pesticides—and organic pasta and make your own nontoxic macaroni and cheese. One cup of macaroni and cheese made with margarine has 9.8 grams of saturated fat and 44 milligrams of cholesterol.

Spaghetti with meat sauce. In the FDA Total Diet Study homemade spaghetti with meat sauce had thirty-three pesticide residues representing nine pesticide formulations. DDT and malathion were found most frequently; BHC, chlorpyrifos, diazinon, dicloran, HCB, octachlor, and penta less often. Clearly, the meat sauce in this pasta dish adds a tremendous number of pesticide residues. However, the cancer risk compared with that of many other foods was insignificant. One cup of spaghetti with meat sauce has about 3.9 grams of saturated fat and 89 milligrams of cholesterol.

RED LIGHT

Limit your consumption of these foods.

French fries. In the FDA Total Diet Study, frozen, commercial french fries were found to contain seventy pesticide residues representing twenty different pesticide formulations or metabolites. Chlorpropham, DDT, dieldrin, endosulfan, penta, tecnazene, tetrachlor (methylthio) benzene, 2,3,5,6-tetrachloroaniline, and 2,3,5,6-tetrachloroanisidine were found in at least one-fourth of the samples. Also detected were aldrin, captan, chlorpyrifos, DCPA, diazinon, heptachlor, HCB, isopropyl 3-chloro-4-methoxy-phenylcarb, malathion, pentachloroaniline, and pentachlorobenzene. Wow! Stay away! Ten large french fries cooked in vegetable oil have 2.5 grams of saturated fat, no cholesterol.

Frozen pizza. In the FDA Total Diet Study, frozen cheese pizza had sixty-seven industrial pollutant and pesticide residues representing fourteen formulations. Pesticides detected in at least a quarter of the samples were BHC, DDT, diazinon, dieldrin, heptachlor, malathion, and penta. Other industrial pollutants and pesticides detected were chlorpropham, chlorpyrifos, endosulfan, HCB, octachlor, parathion, and PCBs. A pizza with meat would have even greater pesticide saturation, in addition to nitrites. One slice of cheese pizza has 4.1 grams of saturated fat and 56 milligrams of cholesterol.

DESSERTS AND SWEET SNACKS

Who would expect that eating milk chocolate candy every day could present a cancer risk as a result of toxic contamination that is nearly 100 times greater than government standards recommend? Keep the faith, though. You can satisfy your sweet tooth: many commercial desserts are quite safe, and sources of pesticide-free desserts and snacks are listed in the Personal Action Guide at the back of this book. But you should be outraged that our government allows such heavy-duty carcinogenic pesticide residues in foods as seemingly innocent as plain milk chocolate, ice cream, and pumpkin pie!

Desserts and Sweet Snacks Survival Guide

GREEN LIGHT

These desserts and snacks are your best choices. They had the fewest pesticide residues and presented the lowest toxicity and cancer risk.

Apple pie. In the FDA Total Diet Study, frozen apple pie was found to contain twenty-nine pesticide residues representing ten pesticide formulations. The cancer risk is insignificant. Again, the added processing is great for reducing pesticide residues. Pesticides detected most frequently were malathion and penta. Other pesticides detected were BHC, DDT, diazinon, dieldrin, EDB (which should no longer be found because it has been banned), heptachlor, HCB, and lindane. One slice of apple pie has 4.5 grams of saturated fat, no cholesterol. Hold the ice cream, please!

Chocolate pudding. Instant, powdered chocolate pudding made with whole milk had fourteen pesticide residues representing six pesticide formulations. The cancer risk as a result of these toxic chemicals is virtually nonexistent. Pesticides detected in at least one-fourth of the samples were BHC and DDT. Other pesticides detected were lindane, octachlor, penta, and tecnazene. A half-cup of instant chocolate pudding contains 2.3 grams of saturated fat and 14 milligrams of cholesterol.

Gelatin desserts. Gelatin desserts are quite pure. However, be sure they do not contain dangerous additives and preservatives such as aspartame, BHA, BHT, or TBHQ. Jell-O, for example, doesn't have many pesticides, but it does contain aspartame, BHA, and TBHQ, and that should be a clear warning to keep that product out of your shopping cart. (These chemical concoctions will be discussed fully in the chapter on additives.) The FDA Total Diet Study revealed that gelatin had five pesticide and industrial chemical residues representing two formulations: penta and tributyl phosphate.

Yellow cake. Yellow cake prepared from mix with white icing prepared from mix had thirty-one pesticide residues representing six pesticide formulations. Chlorpyrifos, DDT, and malathion were found most frequently; diazinon, EDB, and penta less often. The cancer risk was insignificant. One slice of yellow cake has no cholesterol and only traces of saturated fat.

YELLOW LIGHT

Caramels. Caramel candy had forty-seven residues in sixteen samples representing some fifteen pesticide and industrial chemical formulations or metabolites, including diphenyl 2-ethylhexyl phosphate, penta, BHC, chlorpyrifos, DDT, diazinon, dieldrin, HCB, lindane, malathion, pentachloroaniline, pentachlorobenzene, quintozene, tri (2-ethylhexyl) phosphate, and triphenyl phosphate. One ounce of caramels has 2.2 grams of saturated fat and 1 milligram of cholesterol.

Chocolate milk mix. In the FDA Total Diet Study, sweetened, powdered chocolate had thirty-nine pesticide and industrial chemical residues representing nine formulations: BHC, chlorpyrifos, lindane, and penta in at least one-fourth of the samples; chlorpropham, diazinon, dieldrin, diphenyl 2-ethylhexyl phosphate, and octachlor less often. Fortunately, most of us do not eat all that much chocolate powder sweetener; the cancer risk is slight. However, dieters should note that one ounce of chocolate powder sweetener has about 9 grams of saturated fat, no cholesterol. Note that this mix was tested without added milk.

Danish pastries. Ready-to-eat frozen Danish pastries had fifty-three pesticide residues representing eight pesticide formulations. The cancer risk as a result of the pesticides in Danish pastries was low, but the sheer number of neurotoxic pesticides detected makes them a yellow light dessert. Pesticides detected most frequently, in at least one-quarter of the samples, included chlorpyrifos, diazinon, and malathion. Other pesticides detected less frequently included BHC, DDT, dieldrin, octachlor, and quintozene. One small Danish pastry has about 3.6 grams of saturated fat and 49 milligrams of cholesterol.

Doughnuts. Ready-to-eat frozen plain cake doughnuts had fifty-two pesticide residues representing eight pesticide formulations: chlorpyrifos, DDT, diazinon, malathion, and octachlor in at least one-fourth of the samples; ethion, EDB, and vinclozolin less often. The actual cancer threat, as a result of toxic contamination in doughnuts, is low. However, many of the chemicals in doughnuts could cause neurotoxicity. Their thorough pesticide saturation makes doughnuts a yellow light food. Dieters should note that one plain cake doughnut has 2.8 grams of saturated fat and 20 milligrams of cholesterol.

Sandwich cookies. Sandwich cookies with white cream filling had forty-nine residues representing eleven pesticides. Pesticides detected most frequently were DDT, diazinon, malathion, and penta. Other pesticides detected were BHC, chlorpyrifos, dieldrin, EDB, HCB, lindane, and methoxychlor. Eating 2 ounces of sandwich cookies daily would produce as many as five excess cancers in one million persons, so be wary. Four sandwich cookies have two grams of saturated fat, no cholesterol.

RED LIGHT

Chocolate cake. In the FDA Total Diet Study, ready-to-eat frozen chocolate cake with chocolate icing had sixty-one pesticide residues in sixteen samples representing eight different pesticide formulations. Pesticides detected in at least one-fourth of the samples were BHC, chlorpyrifos, diazinon, lindane, malathion, and penta. Also detected were DDT and EDB. One slice of chocolate cake has 3.5 grams of saturated fat and 37 milligrams of cholesterol.

Chocolate chip cookies. In the FDA Total Diet Study, chocolate chip cookies had sixty-eight different pesticide residues in sixteen samples, representing twelve pesticide formulations. Pesticides detected most frequently were BHC, chlorpyrifos, DDT, diazinon, lindane, malathion, and penta. Other pesticides detected were dieldrin, EDB, heptachlor, HCB, and methoxychlor. Eating slightly less than 2 ounces of chocolate chip cookies daily would result in as many as eight excess cancers in one million persons. Four chocolate chip cookies have 4 grams of saturated fat and 22 milligrams of cholesterol.

Coffee cake. Ready-to-eat frozen coffee cake had sixty different pesticide residues representing eleven pesticide formulations. Pesticides detected most frequently included chlorpyrifos, diazinon, dieldrin, heptachlor, and malathion.

Pesticides detected less frequently included BHC, DDT, EDB, HCB, octachlor, and penta. One slice of coffee cake has 2 grams of saturated fat and 47 milligrams of cholesterol.

Milk chocolate. Parents and children beware! In the FDA Total Diet Study, plain milk chocolate was found to contain ninety-three industrial pollutant and pesticide residues representing some fourteen different formulations. Eating 2 ounces of chocolate each day would result in as many as ninety-five excess cancers in one million persons. Because many children and adults *do* eat about 2 ounces daily of plain milk chocolate, it is an extremely dangerous feature of our national diet. The major troublemakers in chocolate include BHC and lindane. In fact, plain milk chocolate is laced with among the highest levels of BHC and lindane in the American diet. Part of the problem may be that chocolate is made from crops grown in countries where these cancer-causing pesticides are widely sprayed. Rather than pollute your body with all the pesticides in plain milk chocolate, look for safer substitutions such as carob and organic candy bars. Pesticides and industrial chemicals detected in at least one-fourth of the samples included BHC, chlorpyrifos, DDT, diazinon, dieldrin, heptachlor, lindane, malathion, penta, and tri (2-ethylhexyl) phosphate. Other industrial pollutants and pesticides detected were aldrin, HCB, octachlor, and PCBs. One ounce of plain milk chocolate has 5.4 grams of saturated fat and 6 milligrams of cholesterol.

Pumpkin pie. Frozen pumpkin pie had fifty-four pesticide residues representing thirteen pesticide formulations. And the pesticides in pumpkin pie pack a powerful toxic punch. Pumpkin pie is among the most dangerous desserts in the American diet. Virtually every sample of pumpkin pie had residues of dieldrin. Other pesticides found in at least a quarter of the samples were DDT, heptachlor, and malathion. Pesticides found less often were BHC, chlordane, chlorpyrifos, diazinon, endrin, lindane, nonachlor, octachlor, and penta. Eating pumpkin pie once in a while, at traditional meals such as Thanksgiving dinner, is fine, but nobody should eat it on a regular basis. Although pumpkin pie has fewer residues than other foods, the levels of some pesticides were dangerously high. Eating just one 6-ounce slice of pumpkin pie a week would lead to as many as forty-one excess cancers in one million persons. This disturbing news about pumpkin pie should not be a surprise. Remember that pumpkins belong to the squash family, and chemically grown squash is one of the most thoroughly pesticide saturated favorites in the food supply. One slice of pumpkin pie has 6.4 grams of saturated fat and 109 milligrams of cholesterol.

CONDIMENTS AND SNACKS

Although we do not eat large servings of condiments and snacks, it is important to make the safest possible choices, because we eat them regularly, and some items can introduce toxic substances into our bodies. Remember, there are pesticides in almost all foods, and these poisons are combining in our bodies, so we should reduce exposure whenever we can. Some condiments and snacks, like potato chips and peanut butter, are downright dangerous. Fortunately we can find safe, reasonably priced substitutions for these pesticide-saturated foods.

Condiments and Snacks Survival Guide

GREEN LIGHT

These condiments had the fewest pesticide residues. They are your best choices in any supermarket.

Brown gravy. Brown gravy (from mix) had sixteen pesticide residues representing four pesticide formulations: malathion, penta, BHC, and endosulfan. One cup of brown gravy has .9 grams of saturated fat and 2 milligrams of cholesterol.

Honey. Honey had eight pesticide residues representing three pesticide formulations: penta, BHC, and EDB. Honey has no cholesterol or saturated fat. Seek organically grown brands of honey to make sure you avoid exposure to antibiotics, which some beekeepers do use.

Italian salad dressing. Bottled Italian salad dressing had twelve residues representing three formulations: penta, dieldrin, and tri (2-ethylhexyl) phosphate. One tablespoon of regular Italian salad dressing has 1.3 grams of saturated fat and 8 milligrams of cholesterol. Seeking low-calorie Italian salad dressing will cut your pesticide exposure, and it has only 4 milligrams of cholesterol and a bare trace of saturated fat.

Mayonnaise. Mayonnaise had nine pesticide residues representing four pesticide formulations: penta, dieldrin, EDB, and HCB. One tablespoon of regular mayonnaise has 1.7 grams of saturated fat and eight milligrams of cholesterol. Although the pesticide saturation is not dangerous, the fat content is rather high. However, one tablespoon of imitation mayonnaise will cut your pesticide exposure, and it has only .5 grams of saturated fat and 4 milligrams of cholesterol.

Pancake syrup. Bottled cane syrup for pancakes had only three pesticide residues in sixteen samples, representing one pesticide formulation, penta. Two tablespoons of cane syrup have no cholesterol or saturated fat. Not a bad choice for pancakes and waffles in a coffee shop.

Salt. Table salt was not analyzed for pesticides and industrial chemicals.

You should know, though, that some commercial brands of salt use aluminum-based compounds to prevent caking. Choose brands that do not use these compounds, or use natural sea salt.

White sugar. White sugar had nine residues representing three formulations: tributyl phosphate, diazinon, and penta. One tablespoon of white granulated sugar has no cholesterol or saturated fat.

YELLOW LIGHT

These yellow light foods were rather more saturated with pesticides. Use them sparingly.

Corn chips. Corn chips had twenty-six pesticide and industrial chemical residues representing seven compounds. Pesticides detected most frequently were diazinon, malathion, and penta; chlordane, diphenyl 2-ethylhexyl phosphate, lindane, and toxaphene were detected less frequently. Most health food markets sell several brands of organically grown blue corn chips, which you should seek to significantly cut your pesticide exposure. In the supermarket, choose the lesser of two evils by seeking corn chips rather than potato chips. A 1-ounce package of corn chips has 1.4 grams of saturated fat, no cholesterol.

Fruit jelly. Fruit jelly had twenty pesticides representing six pesticide formulations. Pesticides detected most frequently were carbaryl and dimethoate. Pesticides detected less frequently were dicloran, ethion, malathion, and penta. Although the cancer risk for these pesticides is relatively low, they can be extremely potent neurotoxins, even at low cumulative doses. With reasonably priced, absolutely pure organic fruit conserves available at major health food markets, it just seems foolhardy to eat pesticide-saturated jams and jellies. Fruit jelly has no cholesterol and just a trace of saturated fat.

Ketchup. Ketchup had thirty-eight pesticide residues representing seven pesticide formulations: endosulfan, DDT, DCPA, dicloran, dicofol, penta, and methamidophos. It is surprising that so far no brands of organic ketchup have found their way to the market. But, when they do, buy them! They will significantly cut your pesticide exposure. Ketchup has no cholesterol and just a bare trace of saturated fat.

RED LIGHT

Dill pickles. Dill pickles had sixty-five pesticide residues representing twelve pesticide formulations. Pesticides detected most frequently were dieldrin, endosulfan, and heptachlor. Pickles are actually cucumbers, and you may recall that chemically grown cucumbers are quite liberally laced with dieldrin. Pesticides detected less frequently were BHC, chlordane, DCPA, DDT, endrin, lindane, octachlor, penta, and toxaphene. In addition, pickles often are preserved with aluminum-based compounds, which introduce excess amounts of this potentially toxic industrial metal into your diet. I would advise that you seek organic pickles for maximum protection against toxic exposures. One excellent brand is Cascadian Farm.

Peanut butter. In the FDA Total Diet Study, peanut butter had a whopping 183 pesticide residues representing seventeen different pesticide formulations and metabolites. Pesticides and their metabolites detected most frequently were chlorpyrifos, dicloran, dieldrin, dimethoate, fonofos, HCB, malathion, pentachloroaniline, pentachlorobenzene, penta, quintozene, tecnazene, and toxaphene. Other pesticides detected were DDT, diazinon, heptachlor, and lindane. In addition to the pesticide threat, most commercial peanut butter brands have varying amounts of a potent, natural carcinogenic mold known as aflatoxin. Furthermore, although peanut butter has no cholesterol, one tablespoon has a whopping 1.4 grams of saturated fat. I would stay away from peanut butter or substitute organic brands. Arrowhead Mills field dries its organically grown peanut crop to prevent aflatoxin growth.

Potato chips. Potato chips had fifty-three pesticide residues representing ten pesticide formulations or metabolites. If you are packing potato chips with your child's school lunch, stop! Pesticides detected most frequently were carcinogens and neurotoxins such as chlorpropham, DDT, DEF, dieldrin, penta, and tecnazene. Other pesticides detected included diazinon, isopropyl-3-chloro-4-methoxy-phenylcarb, tetrachloro (methylthio) benzene, and toxaphene. In addition, potato chips are often preserved with BHA or BHT. Just ten chips have 1.8 grams of saturated fat, no cholesterol. The high salt content of potato chips, corn chips, and many other snacks and condiments will be of concern to those watching their sodium intake.

VEGETABLE OILS

That old saying that a little learning is a dangerous thing rings especially true in the case of vegetable oils. When chosen properly for their purity and nutrient content, oils are extremely valuable. They can actually strengthen your resistance to pollution-related disease. Then again, some oils can diminish the body's ability to fight off the effects of toxic chemicals. Unfortunately, some of the major brands of vegetable oil sold today in supermarkets contain antinutrients such as pesticides that actually weaken your body's immunity.

As I describe the pesticide and antinutrient saturation of vegetable oils and vegetable oil–based foods, you will see why the best oils available today are expeller-pressed, unrefined, and made with organically grown crops. These guidelines will help you steer clear of excessive industrial pollution and pesticide exposure.

Selecting Oils

The key to purchasing the best oils for reducing your body's toxin load is in the kinds of fatty acids contained in the oils. All vegetable oils contain fatty acids. And while there are different kinds of fatty acids, the ones your body *needs* to fight damage caused by toxic chemicals are called essential fatty acids (EFAs). Why do we call them essential fatty acids? The answer is quite simple. There are some nutrients that the body cannot make but must obtain from the natural world. Of these essential nutrients, some are minerals, some vitamins, some amino acids, and two are essential fatty acids: omega-3 fatty acids and omega-6 fatty acids.

Most of us have no problem acquiring enough omega-6 fatty acids. They are widely available in corn, safflower, and sunflower oils.

Such is not the case for omega-3 fatty acids, which can help the body combat the effects of industrial pollutants and pesticides. So where do you get omega-3 fatty acids? One of the best sources is fresh flax oil, which contains 57 percent omega-3 fatty acids. Pumpkin seed oil contains 15 percent omega-3 fatty acids; canola oil, 10 percent; soy oil, 8 percent.

The reason we need these good oils in our diet is that omega-3 fatty acids contain linolenic acid (LNA). Your body's enzymes metabolize LNA into another family of substances that resemble hormones, called *prostaglandins*, which regulate white blood cells in the body's immune system, particularly B cells and T cells. B cells produce antibodies to help your body destroy potentially toxic invaders, while T cells alert your body when the invaders have been vanquished. B cells and T cells are able to remember who the toxic invaders are, and they know how to produce antibodies that can zap them. But if your immune system is impaired by lack of LNA, your B cells and T cells will have difficulty remembering the enemies and how to make proper antibodies.

So your body's inability to properly make prostaglandins can mean big problems for your immune system. Any time your immune function is impaired, your body's vulnerability to toxic chemicals rises.

Many people *do* require a supplemental boost of omega-3 fatty acids. Industrial pollutants and pesticides may interfere with the body's use of vitamin B_6 and a vitamin B_6 deficiency will prevent the body from properly using omega-3 fatty acids. In addition, pesticides tend to deplete the body's supply of vitamin C and vitamin E, which the immune system needs to battle toxic chemical invaders and to protect the EFAs in your body. We need the EFAs to strengthen our cells' membranes. Without an adequate supply, toxic chemicals will pass through our cells more easily. Because of the scarcity in the American diet of omega-3 fatty acids, it is likely that millions of American adults and children are deficient in this essential nutrient.

How can you detect an omega-3 fatty acid deficiency? There are many signs. Do you suffer from allergies? Is your hair or skin dry? Are there rashes or tiny lumps on the backs of your arms? Are your nails brittle? Do you have acne, allergies, eczema, or dry skin? Any of these symptoms could be a sign that you are suffering from an omega-3 fatty acid deficiency. To find out whether you should be including more omega-3 fatty acids in your diet, try taking a teaspoon or two daily of pure flaxseed oil, the vegetable oil richest in omega-3 fatty acids, and see if symptoms diminish. Many people find flaxseed oil quite tasty—a little sweet and invigorating.

There are other ways to introduce flaxseed oil into your diet, however. You can mix it with fruit juice if you wish, but be sure to mix well and drink quickly, for the oil will soon separate from the juice. You can use flaxseed oil on cooked vegetables, mixed with freshly cooked pasta, or use it in salad dressings. An excellent dressing can be made by blending flaxseed oil with nonfat yogurt or soft tofu. Or try mixing flaxseed oil with a little yogurt and organic fruit topping. Flaxseed oil can also be used in baking, which fortunately does not destroy EFAs. And a little bit of flaxseed oil will not promote weight gain, either.

However, do not use flaxseed oil when frying or sautéeing. The excessive heat and oxygen will destroy its valuable EFAs.

Another good source for omega-3 fatty acids is English walnuts. When using oil made with English walnuts, substitute two tablespoons for every one tablespoon of flaxseed oil. And some of the best sources of essential omega-3 fatty acids are beans: Great Northern, kidney, navy, and soy beans. Eating these beans regularly will help you make sure that you have an adequate supply of essential omega-3 fatty acids in your diet.

Other oils—even though they contain relatively small amounts of omega-3 fatty acids—should also be in your kitchen. Use them for cooking because they contain valuable monounsaturated fats, are highly stable, and do not form cancer-stimulating free radicals when intensely heated and they do not interfere with your body's utilization of EFAs. One example is olive oil, which does not break down under heat into EFA-destroying substances. Other good oils include avocado oil and canola oil. All are extremely heat stable.

Some health experts, such as Dr. Maurizio Trevisan of the State University of New York at Buffalo, believe that we may gain additional benefits by cooking with canola or olive oil. One reason these oils are so stable is that they are naturally high in stable, monounsaturated fats. These monounsaturated fats may help us reduce cholesterol and blood pressure and offer further protection against heart disease risk factors. Although the evidence is not conclusive, one study published recently in the *Journal of the American Medical Association* looked at 4,900 Italian men and women, whose ages ranged from 20 to 59, and found that those people who had a diet high in olive oil and low in butter and margarine also had lower overall levels of cholesterol and blood pressure than persons whose diets included more butter and margarine. Among those oils high in monounsaturated fats are canola, olive, and peanut. All should be purchased in their organic variety; this is especially true of peanut oil, because of the tremendous pesticide saturation of peanuts and peanut butter.

Also prefer these three oils for cooking over those oils that are higher in less stable polyunsaturated fats, such as corn, cottonseed, sunflower, and safflower oils. If you insist on using safflower or sunflower oil, make sure you purchase high-oleic safflower and sunflower oils. High-oleic varieties contain nearly as much monounsaturated fat as olive oil.

Hydrogenated Oils

One of the major problems with vegetable oils used in the preparation of many foods today is that they are hydrogenated. Hydrogenation is a process by which hydrogen atoms are added to unsaturated fats to make them semisolid saturated fats. The hydrogenation of oils prevents rancidity, which is important, because rancid oils can become carcinogenic. In addition, if the oils were not hydrogenated, many favorite foods would change measurably. Margarine spreads because of hydrogenation. Without hydrogenation we would have to pour margarine. But that is where the benefits of hydrogenation end. And the problems with hydrogenation outweigh these scanty benefits.

The hydrogenation process turns oils into compounds that are essentially no different from saturated animal fats. Hydrogenated oils, like saturated fats, appear to promote arterial plaque. They inhibit the production and efficient use of substances in the body that help the immune system, and they reduce our body's ability to rid itself of carcinogens, drugs, and other toxins. In fact, it is quite possible that hydrogenated oils, like saturated fats, potentiate the effects of toxic chemicals. Furthermore, substances known as *phytosterols,* which help reduce cholesterol and which are present naturally in vegetable oils, are modified during hydrogenation into a compound that no longer possesses such potential. Finally, the nonessential fatty acids created in the hydrogenation process can prevent your body from using essential fatty acids. So when you see the word "hydrogenated," put the product down. And that includes margarine, which is often saturated with hydrogenated oil.

Hydrogenated oil, unfortunately, is used in many products: baked goods, potato chips, peanut butter, frozen dinners, potpies, candy, frozen foods, breads, and margarines—to name a few favorites. Labels often, but not always, tell when hydrogenated oils are being used. Any label declaring that the oil used is hydrogenated should send you a clear warning that you are holding a product that deserves no place in your shopping cart.

Vegetable Oils Survival Guide

GREEN LIGHT

Olive oil. Olives are virtually free from pesticide residues, so olive oil is also very pure. Some Spanish olive oil imported into the United States was recently found to have traces of the industrial solvents PCE and TCE, both carcinogens. But no Italian olive oil has been found to be adulterated with TCE and PCE. Imported olive oils that received a clean bill included Bertolli, Gondola, Pastene, and Colavita.

Sesame oil. Based on my review of FDA pesticide monitoring data, sesame seeds are not very saturated with pesticides. Thus, sesame oil is likely to be free from residues.

YELLOW LIGHT

Corn oil. One of the most popular oils sold today in supermarkets, corn oil had twenty pesticide residues representing eight pesticide formulations and metabolites. The pesticide and wood preservative penta was in half of the samples; malathion was found in six of the sixteen samples. BHC, diazinon, dieldrin, HCB, pentachlorobenzene, and methoxychlor were each found once in sixteen samples. Not too reassuring.

Margarine. In sixteen samples of partially hydrogenated margarine, there were nineteen chemical residues. Diphenyl 2-ethylhexyl phosphate was found in half the samples. Penta was found in half the samples. Other industrial chemicals and pesticides detected included HCB, pentachlorobenzene and PCBs.

RED LIGHT

Cottonseed oil. A popular oil, cottonseed oil had ten pesticide residues, representing two pesticide formulations, DDT and dieldrin. I don't recommend using cottonseed oil, however, because of its high saturated fat content.

Soybean oil. A number of pesticide residues were detected in thirty-eight samples tested in a 1970–76 FDA study. Dieldrin was detected in 45 percent of the samples; BHC was detected in 24 percent of the samples. Also detected: endrin, malathion, DDT, heptachlor, and PCBs. No doubt, with time, these pesticides' concentrations have diminished. But they probably can still be found in soybean oil. Substitute organic oil.

Shopping and Cooking Tips

Buy oils made with organically grown crops. A company called Spectrum markets the greatest variety of oils made with organically grown crops. Five of thirty oils sold by Spectrum are organic and grown with certified organic crops. All their organic oils—safflower, sesame, toasted sesame, olive, and flax—are unrefined.

Look for expeller-pressed oils (also known as cold-pressed). This process insures consumers that no residues of solvents, such as hexane, will be left in the oil. Major brand oils are often extracted using solvents to glean every last bit. Expeller-pressing means that the oil source, such as soybeans or corn, has been mashed for the oil, a process that recovers only about 75 percent of the oil but leaves it much purer than that produced through solvent methods.

Buy oils in glass containers; plastic can leach chemicals into the oil. Keep bottles capped. Oxygen accelerates this chemical transfer and promotes rancidity.

Use oils that are low in saturated fats, and seek products that are made with these oils:

> Canola (also high in valuable monounsaturated fats)
> Olive (also high in valuable monounsaturated fats)
> Safflower
> Sesame
> Sunflower

These oils are very high in saturated fats. They have similar disease-promoting qualities to animal fats. Avoid using them or buying foods made with them:

Coconut (nearly 90 percent saturated fat)
Palm kernel (more than 80 percent saturated fat)
Palm (50 percent saturated fat)
Cottonseed (25 percent saturated fat)

Until we know more about its physiologic effects, beware of sucrose polyester, a synthetic substitute fat. The theory is that the body does not metabolize this product and that it passes straight through. But sucrose polyester could be a colon irritant and could steal nutrients from your body.

Beware of spray-on oils which often contain hydrogenated fats and preservatives.

Prefer virgin and extra-virgin olive oil, which are made from the first pressings of the olives. "Pure" olive oil is anything but pure and is often extracted with chemical solvents.

You may want to use different oils for different types of cooking. For flavor use olive oil. If you want to avoid the distinctive taste of olive oil when cooking, try using avocado, canola, safflower, sunflower, or walnut oil. Safflower, sunflower, and walnut are delicate. For cooking fried foods, avocado and canola oils are best because they can be heated above 400°F.

Rancid oil is dangerous because it is highly reactive and could promote cancer. To reduce the chances of oils becoming rancid, buy only a month's worth of oil at a time and be sure to replace it after about a month. Keep oils refrigerated. Heat, light, and air are destructive, so keep them cool, away from direct sunlight, and with as little exposure to air as possible. Some people add vitamin E to oils to retard oxidation. Vitamin E is a natural antioxidant and helpful to your body in metabolizing unsaturated fats. Add 200 international units of vitamin E to a bottle of oil when you open it. Repeat in a few weeks until oil is consumed. Buy vitamin E capsules, break them open, and let the contents drip into the liquid.

Safe Shopping List: Convenience Foods

Green Light	Number of Residues
Canned vegetable beef soup and other uncreamed soups	0
Canned pork and beans	1
Canned beef broth	2
Canned chicken noodle soup	5
Canned spaghetti in tomato sauce	10
Canned cream of tomato soup	23

Yellow Light	Number of Residues
Spaghetti with meat sauce (homemade)	33
Macaroni and cheese (from box)	35
Frozen potpies	40
Lasagne (homemade)	41
Frozen chicken dinners	42

Red Light	Number of Residues
Frozen pizza	67
Frozen french fries	70

Safe Shopping List: Desserts and Sweet Snacks

Green Light	Number of Residues
Gelatin dessert	5
Instant pudding	14
Apple pie	29
Yellow cake	31

Yellow Light	Number of Residues
Chocolate milk mix	39
Caramels	49
Sandwich cookies	49
Doughnuts	52
Danish pastries	53

Red Light	Number of Residues
Pumpkin pie	54
Coffee cake	60
Chocolate cake	61
Chocolate chip cookies	68
Milk chocolate (plain)	93

Safe Shopping List: Condiments and Snacks

Green Light	Number of Residues
Cane syrup	3
Honey	8
Sugar	9
Mayonnaise	9

| Italian salad dressing | 12 |
| Brown gravy | 16 |

Yellow Light	**Number of Residues**
Fruit jelly	20
Corn chips	26
Ketchup	38

Red Light	**Number of Residues**
Potato chips	53
Dill pickles	65
Peanut butter	183

Safe Shopping List: Vegetable Oils

Green Light
Avocado oil
Extra virgin or virgin olive oil
Organic oils
Sesame oil

Yellow Light	**Number of Residues**
Margarine	19
Corn oil	20

Red Light
Cottonseed oil
Hydrogenated oils
Palm and coconut oil
"Pure" olive oil
Soybean oil

11. BEVERAGES

Do beverages such as coffee, cola, and other soft drinks and alcoholic beverages such as beer, wine, and whiskey have additives, pesticides, or other carcinogens? Absolutely—if unwisely chosen. I found pesticides in significant, disturbing concentrations most notably in wine. Your morning cup of coffee could be tainted with dioxin because bleached coffee filters contain minute traces of dioxin that leach into the liquid as it is filtered. And I found the potent carcinogen urethane in plenty of brands of alcoholic beverages. But there are ways to avoid all these problems and still find plenty of safe drinks.

Urethane in Liquor

Urethane is a very potent cancer-causing chemical. The fact that American liquor merchants are moving slowly to eliminate this powerful carcinogen should be enough to make you think twice before drinking. Fortunately, however, many brands of alcoholic beverages are free from harmful amounts of urethane.

In the late 1970s, it was discovered that beer contained such high concentrations of nitrosamines that drinking it was more dangerous than eating meats cured with nitrites. The industry quickly altered its production methods and eliminated harmful amounts of nitrosamines.

Unfortunately, the industry has been a laggard in its attempts to eliminate harmful concentrations of the powerful carcinogen urethane. Wine producers, for example, claim that removing urethane would be too expensive. And the FDA appears to be more on the side of industry than the consumer. That is not right. The presence of urethane in alcoholic beverages is a significant problem. It is there simply as a by-product of present production methods and serves no purpose whatsoever.

Urethane—also known as diethyl carbamate, urethan, ethyl urethan, ethyl carbamate, and carbamic acid ethyl ester—was once used in the production of pesticides. It is an all-around carcinogen and has caused cancer in laboratory animals at a variety of organ sites. The EPA calls urethane a probable human carcinogen. As with most carcinogens, the greater your exposure to the substance, the greater your risk, overall, of contracting cancer. Reducing exposure is the most prudent course of action.

How is ethyl carbamate or urethane introduced into liquor? High ethyl carbamate levels occur in wine in part because of heavily fertilized vineyards. Fertilizers include a chemical called urea, which remains in high levels in the juice used for wine. The urea in the juice reacts with the ethanol formed during fermentation to form ethyl carbamate. Urea also gets into liquor as a result of the use of some kinds of yeast for fermentation, a basic process used in making wines and liquors; urea is a by-product of yeast metabolism. Diethyl carbamate may also form as a result of baking dessert wines.

In its publication *Tainted Booze,* the Center for Science in the Public Interest made the following harrowing estimates: "Based on studies on rats and mice, [it is estimated] that up to 4,700 of every [one million] people who regularly drink moderate amounts of urethane-contaminated booze—say, two daily shots of bourbon at 150 parts per billion urethane or three daily glasses of wine containing 30 parts per billion (the highest levels Canadian regulations permit but not uncommon ones in the United States)—may contract cancer from urethane. . . . That's nearly one in 200 persons who drink moderate amounts of some alcoholic beverages."

That is by any standard a high cancer risk. And the FDA is doing precious little to protect consumers. The FDA has accepted the industry's proposal of voluntary curbs, aiming for levels under 125 parts per billion in all whiskey. But the program will not affect any alcoholic beverage other than whiskey. And since most whiskey is aged for five to twelve years, the safer liquor will not be available until the mid-1990s or later.

On the wine front, *Tainted Booze* reports that "winemakers have agreed to limit the amount of urethane in table wines to 25 parts per billion and to 90 parts per billion for dessert wines, but not until *1995.* Worst of all, the FDA has still failed to commit itself to take legal action, even if it learns that producers haven't met their merely voluntary targets."

Whose side is the FDA on, anyway?

Consumer action in the form of letters to your senators and representatives will help. Tell them you are concerned that so many alcoholic beverages contain dangerous amounts of the cancer-causing chemical urethane.

Tell them to do everything they can to support efforts to clean up our contaminated booze. In the meantime, you can protect yourself by buying liquor with the lowest urethane levels as reported in the following list.

The kinds of alcoholic beverages most likely to be tainted with very high concentrations of urethane are American bourbon whiskey, European fruit brandies, cream sherry, port wine, Japanese sake, Chinese wine, and European liqueurs.

Rums have moderately low levels of urethane. Tequilas have very low levels. Vodkas have virtually none. Champagne and sparkling wines have low levels. Beers and other malt beverages have very low levels.

Grape table wines in general have low levels of urethane. But there are some exceptions. I have included grape table wines with ethyl carbamate levels above the Canadian standard of 30 ppb in the list below.

I am reproducing here the results for whiskeys, fruit brandies, and some wines of a Bureau of Alcohol, Tobacco and Firearms study of urethane levels in liquor. Domestic brandies had very low urethane levels.

The levels of urethane permitted by the Canadian government for these liquors are 150 ppb for all whiskeys, 400 ppb for liqueurs and brandies, and 30 ppb for grape table wines.

Liquor	Urethane Level (in parts per billion)
Blended American Whiskey	
Kessler American	8
McCormick American	10
Seagram's 7 Crown	11
Royale Club	41
Barton Blended American	42
Old Thompson American	58
Jim Dalton	58
Jenkins	121
Sutton Club	140
S.S. Pierce No. 6	171
Canadian Whiskey	
Lord Calvert	6
Piccadilli Club	18
Allen's Finest	18
Gooderham's Rich & Rare	20
Black Velvet (avg. 3 samples)	21.3
Canadian Label	23

Canadian Club 23
Crown Royal 35

Straight American Bourbon Whiskey

George Dickel Old No. 8 37.16
George Dickel Old No. 12 38
Old Crow 55
Ezra Brooks 125
Jack Daniels Old No. 7 129.26
Jim Beam 143
Hallmark 151
McCormick 160
Bourbon Supreme 184
Barclay's Kentucky 219
Evan Williams 8 Year Old 247
Hiram Walker Ten High 250
Early Times Old Style 268
Kennedy's 273
Virginia Gentlemen 360
Sutton Club 687
Newport 741

Scotch

Old Smuggler Blended 12
Harvey's Blended 23
Glen Mavis Blended 28
Allen's Scotch 32
Grants 35.5
Passport 40
Johnnie Walker Red Label 41
Highlander & Lord 44
Dewars White Label 46
Bulloch Lade's B&L Gold Label 53.67
Chivas Regal 12 Year 57
The Argosy 61
Seagrams 100 Pipers 63
Justerini & Brooks J&B 64
Johnnie Walker Black Label 64
S.S. Pierce 65.5
Scoresby 116.5
Chivas Regal 134

Imported Fruit Brandy

Psenner Williams Pear Brandy (Italy) nondetectable
Roner Williams Pear with Pear (Italy) 10

Liquor	Urethane Level (in parts per billion)
Distillerie Meyblum Albe Poire Williams (France)	41
Jean Danflou Calvados Apple Brandy (France)	42
Trimbach Framboise Alsatian Raspberry (France)	74
Zwack Eau De Vie Pear Brandy (Germany)	82
Trimbach Poire William Alsatian Pear (France)	95
Veuve Roth Framboise Raspberry Brandy (France)	105
Original du Valis Williams Pear Brandy (Switzerland)	107
Pecsetes Barack Palinka Apricot Brandy (Hungary)	128
Jean Danflou Framboise Raspberry Brandy (France)	133
Schladeder Williams Pear Brandy (Germany)	163
Debreceni Allami Gazdasig Pear Brandy (Hungary)	266
Maraska Sljivovica 8 Year Plum Brandy (Yugoslavia)	296
Stara Sljivovica Plum Brandy (Yugoslavia)	341
Debreceni Allami Gazdasig Plum Brandy (Hungary)	388
Zwack Eau De Vie Kirsch Cherry Brandy (Germany)	438
Debreceni Allami Gazdasig Apricot Brandy (Hungary)	450
Distillerie Meyblum Albe Eau Kirsch (France)	677
Slivovitz Plum Brandy (Israel)	680
Veuve Roth Kirsch Cherry Brandy (France)	692
Zwack Eau De Vie Apricot Brandy (Germany)	746
Kedem Servian Kosher 4 Year Slivovitz (Yugoslavia)	951

Jean Danflou Mirabelle Plum Brandy (France)	1,007
Carmel Kosher 6 Year Slivovitz (Israel)	1,039
Slivovitz Plum Brandy (Yugoslavia)	1,188
Slovaska Slivovitz Plum Brandy (Yugoslavia)	1,303
Manastirka Slivovitz 10 Year Plum (Yugoslavia)	1,334
Leon Beyer Mirabelle Eau-de-Vie Plum (France)	1,411
Kirsch Kirschwasser Cherry (France)	1,588
Trimbach Prunelle Sauvage Sloe Brandy (France)	1,619
Leon Beyer Mirabelle (France)	1,621
Slitzvoviz Plum Brandy (Yugoslavia)	1,717
Jean Danflou Kirschwasser Cherry (France)	1,899
Veuve Roth Mirabelle Plum Brandy (France)	2,389
Trimbach Mirabelle Alsatian Plum (France)	3,065
R. Jelinek Kosher 10 Year Slivovitz (Czechoslovakia)	4,146

Wine

Achaia Clauss Demestica (Greece)	33
Achaia Clauss Santa Rosa Rosé (Greece)	34
Almaden Cabernet Sauvignon (California)	77
Almaden Monterey Zinfandel 1977 (California)	70
Callaway Temecula California Sauvignon Blanc	270
Carmel Samson Sauvignon Blanc 85 (Israel)	62
Chateau De La Maltroye Wine (France)	80
Chat Doisy-Vedrines Saut 83 (France)	32
Chat Les Justices Sauternes 83 (France)	32
Chateau Ste. Michelle Washington Fume Blanc Sauvignon Blanc 83	37
Chateau Ste. Michelle Washington Johannisberg Riesling 84	42

Liquor	Urethane Level (in parts per billion)
Christian Brothers Cabernet Sauvignon (U.S.)	34
Côte De Nuits-Villages 1981 (France)	46
Galleano California Burgundy	46
Galleano California Zinfandel	40
Giumarra California Pinot Noir	70
Giumarra Pinot Noir Wine (U.S.)	39
Guenoc Lake County Petite Sirah 1983 (California)	45
Imperial Mavrodaphine Wine (Greece)	72
La Rioja Alta Reserva 904 1970 (Spain)	43
Los Vineros Chardonnay (U.S.)	78
Magyar Cabernet Sauvignon 81 (Hungary)	32
Maison Ginestet Medoc Wine (France)	44
Meredyth Virginia Marechal Foch 1979 (Virginia)	86
Montevina Chardonnay Wine (U.S.)	102
Montevina Santa Barbara County Chardonnay 1981 (California)	40
Paul Masson Rare Premium California Burgundy	35
Rieussec Sauternes 1983 (France)	36
Templeton California White Wine	35
Vina Real Gran Riserva (Spain)	49
Weingartener Trappenberg (Germany)	31

Beverages Survival Guide

Let's look at the industrial pollution and pesticide saturation in sixteen popular beverages. Again, these statistics are from the FDA Total Diet Study.

In this case I have *not* classified liquids into green, yellow, and red light groupings because I don't want to give the impression that some of these alcoholic and even nonalcoholic beverages are safe to drink without limits. The beverages are listed in alphabetical order.

Beer. Beer had absolutely no industrial pollutant or pesticide residues detected in sixteen samples. Beer, generally, has low amounts, if any, of urethane.

Coffee (brewed, regular). One FDA study—independent of the Total Diet Study—found that thirty-five of seventy-four samples of imported coffee had pesticide residues. Another danger is that the white filters often used for making coffee may contain dioxin as a result of the paper bleaching process; this dioxin can migrate from the filters into coffee. Dioxin causes cancer, cell mutations, and many other harmful effects at extraordinarily low concentrations in the human body. A person's daily intake of dioxin as a result of contamination of bleached coffee filters could be increased by at least 10 percent, according to experts. What's more, coffee goes directly into the gut, without any of the protective effects of fiber, meaning that dioxin absorption is quite high.

Fortunately, there are several solutions to the dioxin problem. You can buy brown, unbleached coffee filters marketed by Melitta and other companies. If your market does not have them, ask the manager to order them. My decision was to buy a permanent, finely meshed gold-plated filter made by Krups. The gold is nonreactive at high temperatures. Another solution is to use cotton muslin filters. Any of these alternatives will solve the dioxin problem.

Many people want to know whether coffee is safe to drink. Studies have been extremely equivocal about coffee and its role in the onset of cancer and no hard conclusions can be reached.

Caffeine *is* known to have profound effects on fetal development if ingested in large quantities. Pregnant women were warned as early as 1980 by the FDA that caffeine could cause birth defects and that they should drastically curtail or even stop their intake of foods with caffeine. Besides coffee and some teas, caffeine is often in soft drinks and chocolate as well as some analgesics. One human study found that spontaneous abortions, stillbirths, and premature births are more frequent in families where the father's caffeine consumption was high. Yes, that's right—the father! This suggests that caffeine could have some kind of mutagenic effect. The responsibility for healthy babies falls upon fathers, too, in ways we are only now beginning to see.

In another study, female rats that were given the equivalent of twelve to twenty-four cups of coffee daily gave birth to babies with mild growth retardation, missing digits, and poor skeletal development. A human study of more than two hundred women discovered significantly higher numbers of birth defects among the offspring of heavy coffee drinkers. (The study defined heavy coffee drinking as seven or more cups a day.) And yet another study has found that coffee reduces a woman's chances of becoming pregnant.

Clinical reports indicate what many of us already know: coffee drinkers may also experience poor sleep and fatigue.

What are we to make of the coffee dilemma? Obviously, if you are going to have children, you should not be drinking coffee—an admonishment, I might add, which applies equally to men and women. I would also suggest that you try a coffee substitute. Yannoh is a rich-tasting instant coffee alternative from Lima USA, made with organic barley and available at health and natural food markets. You may also mix hot water with a little fresh lemon. Organic green tea from Japan is also a good hot drink. These simple, natural hot beverages can be quite satisfying.

I am quite concerned about low level pesticide residues in coffee because people drink so much of it. I suggest that you purchase coffees made from organically grown beans. The two most widely available brands of organic coffee include Tierra Fuego, which is made with organically grown coffee beans from plantations in Guatemala, Mexico, and Peru, and Altura Tierra coffee from plantations in Mexico whose practices are certified by the Organic Crop Improvement Association. By buying organic coffee, you will help spread the message in Mexico, Central America, and South America that coffee can be grown profitably organically.

Cola. Cola had absolutely no industrial pollutants or pesticides in sixteen samples. But be sure to drink cola from glass containers. You know enough not to cook with aluminum, because of the absorption of this metal into your food and its suspected link in the onset of Alzheimer's. So why drink products packaged in aluminum?

Decaffeinated coffee. Pesticides may contaminate decaffeinated coffee, too. In addition, coffee often is decaffeinated with a solvent called methylene chloride. Small amounts of this cancer-causing chemical are found in many brands of decaffeinated coffee sold by General Foods, according to government reports. We know that methylene chloride, which has been widely used in the beauty industry in consumer products, is dangerous when inhaled, because several studies have indicated inhalation of methylene chloride causes cancer in laboratory animals. Although methylene chloride residues are found in small amounts in decaffeinated coffee and the industry argues the risk to consumers is minimal, methylene chloride is a known carcinogen that contributes nothing nutritionally. It certainly has no place in coffee when alternative decaffeination methods are widely available.

The process of decaffeination that does not use dangerous chemicals is the Swiss Water Process. That is the process you should choose when you purchase decaffeinated coffee.

Instant coffee. Instant coffee had one chemical residue—tri (2-ethylhexyl) phosphate—detected in sixteen samples.

Low-calorie cola. Low-calorie cola had one pesticide residue (EDB) detected in sixteen samples. Be wary of low-calorie drinks sweetened with aspartame. Pregnant mothers would be better off drinking regular cola with sugar.

Powdered soft drinks. Powdered soft drinks, including Kool-Aid, had absolutely no industrial pollutants or pesticides. They may contain aspartame.

Soda. Various sodas had absolutely no industrial pollutants or pesticides in sixteen samples.

Limit your consumption of soda sweetened with NutraSweet (aspartame), particularly if you are pregnant. Many sodas and soft drinks contain chemical additives. For example, the makers of diet mandarin orange Slice may say their product has 10 percent real fruit juices. But it contains aspartame; yellow number 5, which may affect aspirin-sensitive persons; brominated vegetable oil, whose residues are found in body fat and whose safety is suspect, especially for persons who are chemically sensitive; and BHA, which studies indicate may cause cancer and disrupt normal behavior patterns in children.

Tea. Tea (made with a tea bag) had one pesticide residue (penta) in sixteen samples. You will find organic green teas from Japan available at many health food stores and upscale tea shops. There is no guarantee that the popular brands of herbal teas were grown organically, unless specifically stated on the label.

Whiskey. Whiskey (80 proof) had absolutely no industrial pollutant or pesticide residues. However, whiskey can have extremely high levels of urethane.

Pregnant women should note that although beer and whiskey were pretty clean in terms of pesticide residues, they should strictly limit their intake of alcohol, because of profound birth defects which it might cause. (See the chapter on pregnancy for more information.) For everyone, alcohol is an anesthetic that, in essence, puts your brain to sleep, in addition to contributing to high blood pressure, heart disease, and stroke.

Some studies indicate that moderate consumption of alcohol may actually have some benefits, however. As early as 1926 studies indicated that moderate drinkers—people who had one or two drinks a day on average—lived longer than people who did not drink or drank very lightly. Now, if this were the only study that indicated such a finding, we would be skeptical indeed. But, in fact, additional studies have reached the same conclusions. What accounts for the benefits of alcohol? For some reason, moderate drinkers have higher levels in their bloodstream of a beneficial substance called high-density lipoproteins (HDL). These coveted HDLs apparently reduce the buildup of arterial plaque, thereby offering some additional protection against heart attacks. Of course, any benefits derived from alcohol require moderation, for excessive drinking increases levels of triglycerides (which block the arteries) and can cause damage to heart muscle cells, as well as heart and liver disease. Heart patients must be very careful about drinking any alcohol; they should consult their doctor about just how much, if any, alcohol they can safely drink.

Wine. Nonorganic wine has too many pesticides to qualify as a top-quality product. Wine had forty-four pesticide residues in sixteen samples, representing four pesticide formulations or metabolites: carbaryl, dimethoate, omethoate, and dicloran. The concentrations of pesticides in wine were extremely elevated and should send a clear signal to the consumer and to the wine industry that the product needs to be cleaned up! When consumers find out their favorite wines are loaded with pesticides, they will not want to drink them any longer! Would you? Nobody wants to feel like a victim because he or she drank wine that was laced with acute neurotoxins such as carbaryl, dimethoate, and omethoate.

Further, working in vineyards that use pesticides is dangerous for farm workers. Many deaths have been caused by acutely neurotoxic pesticides used in growing grapes, including dinoseb, malathion, methomyl, methyl bromide, parathion, paraquat, phosdrin, and phostoxin.

Have you wondered why you get bad headaches after drinking wine? The pesticides or sulfites could be to blame. Many wine aficionados report that they no longer get headaches when they switch to organic wines. The fact that there are no residues of neurotoxic pesticides certainly could be the reason, as could the significantly lower levels of sulfites in organic wines.

Fortunately for wine lovers, organic wines are easily obtained. They will become more prevalent as more wineries make the switch to organic methods. One of California's major wineries, Fetzer, changed its 155-acre home vineyard in Mendocino County to organic cultivation in 1987. Another excellent, nonsulfite organic wine is produced by Frey vineyards of California, and in New York State Four Chimneys Farm makes great organic wines. In France, there are some 250 certified organic wine producers, many of whom export to the United States. In the United States at present, there are about a dozen organic wine producers. The Personal Action Guide at the end of this book lists wineries producing organic wines and distributors from whom you can obtain them. Chemically sensitive persons will be glad to know many also contain absolutely no added sulfites.

12. ADDITIVES

Pesticides and industrial pollutants aren't the only chemicals added to your food that can damage your health. Thousands of chemicals are added *intentionally* to foods, especially to convenience foods, and these additives can have severe detrimental effects on both physical and mental health, acting alone or in combination with the many other chemicals in the food supply. Nearly three thousand additives and preservatives are used in food today. Many are completely safe, but there are plenty of bad actors, too.

Additives and preservatives perform a number of tasks. Some enhance flavor; about 1,700 natural and artificial flavoring agents are used in food today. Some additives heighten color. Others are used as artificial sweeteners. Some additives help in the processing and preparation of foods. Some help baked goods rise evenly. Others are used to prevent the formation of ice crystals in frozen dairy products. Additives may be used in peanut butter to prevent the separation of oil and dry layers. All these chemicals help manufacturers bring prepared foods to people without enough time to cook.

But how often have you looked at the list of ingredients on a package and wondered what all those chemicals were? Don't you wonder whether there is anything even remotely resembling wholesome, natural food in some of these products?

There comes a point when convenience foods no longer are food. Instead, they become chemical cocktails that supply our bodies with additives, preservatives, pesticides, sugar, and salt. They become sources of wasted calories that make our waistlines bulge and leave us as hungry after we've eaten them as we were before.

Some of the chemicals added to our food are truly dangerous. Earlier in the century eggs and milk were often adulterated with formaldehyde. Borax was used to conceal rancidity in food. None of these chemicals is used in food today.

In the 1950s many children were sickened by eating popcorn with artificial food dyes. Some fifteen food dyes have been banned since 1956. More recently, we have seen cyclamates—which we were once told were safe—removed from the market because of their cancer-causing properties; the use of saccharin was severely curtailed in 1976 because of its potential to cause cancer in experimental animals. Yet, at one time, we were told saccharin was completely safe.

Who knows which of the chemicals being used today will be banned in five, ten, or twenty years, when their carcinogenic or neurotoxic effects are finally conclusively proved? We have an idea which are the dangerous ones—see the red light list later in this chapter—but it's best not to let yourself be a guinea pig for the food industry's experiments. Remember, eating safe, healthful food is your best defense.

It has been clearly demonstrated in many ways that additives to food have a dire effect on behavior. In 1982, students at the Canyon Verde School, a private school in Hermosa Beach, California, performed a study. They kept four groups of rats in four separate cages and fed each group different foods. The rats in the first cage ate natural food and drank clean water. Those in the second cage ate the same natural foods plus frankfurters. The rats in the third cage ate only sugar-coated cereal and drank fruit punch. In the fourth cage, the rats got only sugar doughnuts and cola.

For three months the students—all of whom had behavioral problems, autism, or marginal retardation—watched the rats. The school nutritionist, Pam Mobley, set up the study to show the children why the school had strict nutritional guidelines and how profoundly their behavior could be influenced by their food and beverage decisions.

Throughout the study, the rats in the first cage remained alert, curious, calm, and social. The rats in the rest of the cages exhibited different types of behavior.

The rats that were fed hot dogs became violent. They fought aggressively and bit off their own tails. In some instances, the rats even severed their own tongues.

The rats that ate sugar-coated cereal and fruit punch ran around and around the cage; they were nervous, hyperactive, and aimless. Some hung upside down from the ceilings of their little homes.

The rats that ate sugar doughnuts and drank cola had trouble sleeping. They did not huddle together as rats normally would but chose instead to hunker quivering in corners, unable to function as a social unit. When approached from outside the cage, they became extremely fearful.

Some of the mother rats had pups, and their offspring showed similar behavioral traits. Some of the pups immediately displayed antisocial traits. Others were fearful. Still others experienced constant sleeplessness. Some pups were born without hair; others' coats quickly became greasy, matted, and knotted.

No wonder! Perhaps the pups were genetically damaged, or they may have been imitating their mothers' behavior. Another theory is that the nursing mothers may have passed chemicals from their diet on to their newborns in their milk.

Finally, the rats in cages two, three, and four were switched to the same natural foods and pure water given the cage-one rats. After several weeks, the rest of the animals became sociable and interacted in a more normal manner. They improved in appearance as their bodies became sleek with full, furry coats and gleaming tails. They were rats. Sure. But they were civilized rats.

The experiment provided the students a model for their own behavior. The study was able to demonstrate to the students that, in part, the knot that bound them to unhealthy behaviors was of biological origin—food.

At Canyon Verde School, the students' switch from chemical foods to natural foods without additives produced miracles in some cases, and in other cases it was a certain factor in helping students cope better with life. Badly behaved children underwent profound and positive behavioral changes. After changing their diet, some stopped punching their teachers and throwing chairs.

Canyon Verde children began to assert their own needs for wholesome food and they began to demand good food at home and in restaurants, too. They stood up for their safe food rights!

Here are some comments from the children of the Canyon Verde School, as reported in the Pritikin Foundation newsletter:

"If you fed a sixteen-year-old boy the junk we fed to the rats, it would make him go crazy. I ate sugar a lot, and sometimes I'd act hypnotized, sometimes confused. I was argumentative—not the way I am when I eat healthy food."

"Me and my mom have fewer arguments now that I'm eating healthy food. I'm not so hyper and I'm easier to get along with."

"Some of the additives in the food can cause brain damage. For the rats to go crazy, to bite off their tongues from eating hot dogs, well . . . We should shop at health food stores. I mean, what's a few dollars more if you're healthy instead of like a test rat? Who wants to be like a test rat?"

This school experiment is just one example of the many studies demonstrating very clearly that behavioral problems are indeed linked to our food and beverage decisions. We have accumulated a whole body of scientific and medical evidence—epidemiological and clinical—that demonstrates this incredibly close link between our food and beverage decisions and our behavior.

Authorities at the Tehama County Juvenile Hall in Red Bluff, California, had positive results in curbing antisocial behavior when they used honey in place of sugar and eliminated meats cured with nitrites and other foods with additives.

U.S. Naval Correction Center officials in Seattle discovered that removing white bread and refined sugar from the diet of inmates reduced the incidence of violent behavior.

Removing additives and preservatives actually helps increase children's intelligence. In 1979, the New York City public schools ranked in the 39th percentile on standardized California Achievement Test scores, which means that 61 percent of the nation's public schools scored higher. That same year, the New York City Board of Education ordered a reduction of the sugar content of foods served in the schools and banned two synthetic food colorings. In 1980, New York's achievement test scores went up to the 47th percentile. Next, the schools banned *all* synthetic colorings and flavorings. Test scores increased again, bringing New York City schools up to the 51st percentile. By 1983, when BHA and BHT were removed, New York City schools scored in the 55th percentile. Researchers believe that the removal of additives such as synthetic colorings, flavorings, and preservatives was responsible for the test score improvements.

The most extensively documented effect of food additives is hyperactivity in children. Researchers writing in the *Lancet*, the leading British medical journal, reported that artificial colors and preservatives were definitely able to provoke hyperactivity. Two artificial food chemicals—tartrazine (yellow number 5) and the preservative benzoic acid—provoked the most dramatic reactions when administered to children; in fact, twenty-seven of the thirty-four children tested (79 percent) reacted to these additives.

One vivid example of the dangers of the behavior-modifying chemicals in our foods is the story of Jeffrey, the young son of registered nurse Colleen Smethers of Mira Loma, California.

Jeffrey's diet in 1976 was just like millions of American children's diets, and like thousands of American children, he had severe emotional problems. Waking up the child for school was difficult. His mother had to pull him, shouting and screaming, from the bed, stuff him into his clothes, drag him to the kitchen, and sit with him long enough to calm him down. Then he would eat.

For breakfast Jeffrey ate cereal with sugar, preservatives, and artificial colors and flavorings. Because his mother wanted him to get enough vitamins and minerals, Jeffrey took a chewable vitamin pill containing artificial colors and flavors. Jeffrey brushed his teeth with a toothpaste that had artificial colors and flavors.

His mother would then pick him up physically, put him in the car, and hold him there because sometimes he would try to jump out while she was driving him to school. The principal would be waiting at the curb. The boy's mother would pull Jeffrey out of the car while he bit and screamed, put him in the arms of the principal, and drive away.

For lunch Jeffrey would have soup made with monosodium glutamate and the preservatives BHA and BHT and whole milk, which often has hidden preservatives including BHA or BHT. Jeffrey ate bread made with lard, which is also preserved with BHA or BHT. The cookies he ate were made with artificial flavorings and colors and, once again, lard preserved with BHA and BHT.

Jeffrey was very aggressive, destructive, and belligerent. He threw temper tantrums. He did not sleep well. He displayed signs of schizophrenia and psychotic behavior. Before he was seven, Jeffrey had violently attacked his little brother, causing him to fall through a window.

Colleen Smethers sought medical assistance, but nothing helped. When she took Jeffrey to doctors, he would act fine for them. Some doctors said his problems were the result of his home environment, because Smethers was divorced and her other children lived with their father. One physician told her that she had an unstable personality and considered having her son put in protective custody. Another prescribed tremendous doses of Dexedrine. At age seven, Jeffrey went after his mother with a butcher knife.

Desperate, she read a book called *Why Your Child Is Hyperactive* by the late Dr. Ben Feingold, an allergist at Kaiser-Permanente in San Francisco.

Dr. Feingold asserted that childhood behavior and learning disorders were related to synthetic colors and flavors and to preservatives such as BHA, BHT, and TBHQ in the American diet, in addition to a naturally occurring chemical known as salicylate, which is very close in structure to aspirin and is found naturally in some fruits and vegetables.

Smethers could not believe anything as simple as changing her child's diet could make a difference. But out of desperation she decided to try. She spent time learning about the diet and got in touch with a local chapter of the national Feingold group. (There are now 200,000 families using the Feingold diet, with support groups worldwide; see the Personal Action Guide for more information.)

The first three days, as Jeffrey came off the Dexedrine at the same time that his diet began to change, he was ten times worse. The transition period is often the worst time of all.

And then on the third night it was as if someone had taken Colleen Smethers's child away and given her a new one. On the morning of the fourth day she saw an incredible change.

She got up and went to the kitchen and found Jeff, dressed, sitting at the table with a toy, waiting for his breakfast. She put him on the school bus, and off he went. No fighting. No shouting.

Smethers is certain that her son's behavioral disorders were caused by salicylates and the additives dumped in his food, and that their disappearance was helped along by elimination of the troublesome chemicals. It would be hard to convince Smethers and hundreds of thousands of other parents that synthetic food additives do not influence behavior.

A thirteen-member panel of experts recently assembled by the National Institutes of Health stressed that a diet that eliminates certain preservatives and other food additives should be used as initial treatment for childhood hyperactivity.

Unfortunately, medications such as Ritalin, Dexedrine, and Cylert are too often recommended by the medical profession. Children do not suffer from Ritalin, Dexedrine, or Cylert deficiencies; such medications often mask symptoms without solving problems. Ritalin and other medications should be used as a last resort.

Instead, people concerned about a child's hyperactivity should try adjusting the child's diet, stressing low-toxin wholesome foods. They should eliminate foods with preservatives such as BHA, BHT, and TBHQ; foods with artificial coloring; foods with artificial flavors, even vanillin, and foods with salicylates, including apricots, cucumbers, grapes, oranges, prunes, peaches, plums, raspberries, and tomatoes. These are obviously not foods we would all want to eliminate from our diets; however, people afflicted with salicylate sensitivity must eliminate them or risk suffering as a result of their allergy.

Additives that have such dramatic effects on the behavior of children can have subtle but nonetheless powerful effects on all of us. Some of the most popular processed and prepared foods—including frozen snacks and dinners, instant gelatin and pudding, luncheon meats, and canned foods—contain additives and preservatives, some of which are harmless and some of which are not.

Nearly all convenience foods are laced with chemicals:

• Among the ingredients in Stouffer's Lean Cuisine cheese cannelloni with tomato sauce are modified cornstarch, BHA, and BHT.

• Banquet frozen dinners have sulfites and artificial flavors.

• Tina's Red Hot beef burritos have enriched flour, and the lard is preserved with BHA or BHT.

• Swanson chicken broth contains monosodium glutamate (MSG).

- Bazooka bubble gum has artificial color and BHT.

- M&M's plain chocolate candies contain yellow food coloring number 5.

- PayDay nut bar has mono- and diglycerides, BHA, and TBHQ.

- Twix has TBHQ.

- Zagnut contains yellow number 6 food coloring, BHA, and BHT.

- Shasta Diet drinks contain aspartame and saccharin, which is still used despite its ban in the 1970s because of legal loopholes.

- Diet mandarin orange Slice has a host of artificial ingredients: aspartame, yellow number 5 coloring, brominated vegetable oil, BHA, and artificial colors.

And I have just barely scratched the surface! Even labels that claim the product has no "added" preservatives can be misleading. Federal laws do not require processors to tell whether ingredients they use were already preserved with BHA or BHT before being processed in the final product. Almost all lard is treated with BHA or BHT. Most milk is fortified with vitamin A palmitate, which contains small amounts of BHA or BHT.

These chemicals in the food supply are clearly dangerous. The Surgeon General estimates as many as eight thousand cancer deaths annually could result from artificial chemicals in food.

The bottom line is that we are all different. Some people have more sensitivity to additives than other people. The human body is an exquisitely delicate system that can be thrown off kilter with even the smallest amounts of toxic and behavior-altering chemicals.

And it's not just the dangers of individual chemicals we have to be concerned about. We must also be concerned with the addition to our food of *many* chemicals, combined, and their sum effect upon people throughout the population with different sensitivities and allergies. Once again we are talking about the chemical cocktail syndrome.

Scientists cannot possibly test the combined effects of all the additives, preservatives, industrial pollutants, and pesticides that might be present in prepared meals. They do not have the faintest idea of their impact. Yet all these chemicals are poured into your food.

Again, the insights of Dr. Michael Jacobson, executive director at the Center for Science in the Public Interest, are relevant: "Additives are tested on animals protected from cigarette smoke, alcohol, drugs of any sort, pollutants, and other additives. The cloistered existence of a lab rat or mouse scarcely suggests the life-style of most Americans. While it would be impossible to test every additive combination, FDA [should] require companies to treat additives both in isolation and against a 'cocktail' of aspirin, BHT, nitrite, oral contraceptives, caffeine, and other chemicals millions of people regularly consume. [Unfortunately] the law does not require this kind of testing, so it is never done."

As usual, you have to take responsibility yourself for the safety of your food. Take the time to read labels. Learn about your foods, and learn to judge for yourself the effects foods have on you. How do you *feel* after eating certain foods? Try eliminating foods with loads of additives and eating simpler foods and see how you feel. I speak with many people about food. I ask them what they eat and what makes them feel really healthy. I find that many people are discovering for themselves that they do not feel all right after ingesting foods with additives. They feel tired, disoriented— any of a hundred symptoms. Let your body do the talking.

Try keeping a food diary for two weeks in which you record what you have eaten and your physical and emotional feelings after certain meals. Did you feel deflated and logy after eating a frozen egg and sausage breakfast? You might notice that after eating food with preservatives such as BHA or BHT you feel irritable and suffer headaches. Other foods could make you feel dreamy or angry. Some foods might make you hyperactive. Asthma sufferers might find that their condition worsens after they eat certain foods.

After two weeks, try eating only foods that have no preservatives or additives. Again, record how you feel after meals. See if you find yourself in a good mood, relaxed, at ease with yourself, and positively motivated in your work more often when you have eaten meals without additives, preservatives, or contaminants.

Although results vary with individuals, you should know within a few weeks whether these dietary changes are helping you. As a rule, young children respond most quickly.

I know that it's unrealistic to expect people to cut out fast foods, prepared foods, and convenience foods completely from their diet. These foods are important because we all need quick meals sometimes. But there are fast, healthful alternatives to assembly-line hamburgers and additive-laced packaged foods. Let me show you how you can find the best, purest convenience foods sold today, the ones without dangerous additives, the products that are made with the purest ingredients. That way you can avoid harmful additives, industrial pollutants, and pesticides.

Additives Survival Guide

When shopping you should know which food additives are safest and which are the most dangerous. This survival guide will help you find your way through the supermarket jungle of food additives and preservatives.

These additives and preservatives are the safest, according to our best knowledge.

Alginates and propylene glycol alginate. Obtained from seaweed, alginates are found in ice cream, frozen custard, chocolate milk, cheese spreads, and salad dressing. They are completely safe.

Alpha tocopherol (vitamin E). Obtained from vegetable oils through a form of vacuum distillation and used as an antioxidant in oils and animal fats, alpha tocopherol is a completely safe and necessary nutrient. It is, in fact, a beneficial, nutritious food additive.

Ascorbic acid (vitamin C). Used as an antioxidant in many products such as apple juice, canned fruits, dry milk, and beer, ascorbic acid is a valuable, essential nutrient that can prevent formation of cancer-causing nitrosamines.

Beta carotene. A precursor of vitamin A that is used to color foods, beta carotene is a valuable, nutritious additive that will help you fight off various forms of cancer.

Calcium propionate and sodium propionate. Calcium propionate and sodium propionate are relatively safe preservatives that are used in breads and rolls to inhibit mold. Although most experts consider sodium propionate a safe preservative, I have received at least one report that it may be a cause of migraine headaches in some chemically sensitive persons. Also, for persons on low-sodium diets, any preservative with sodium should be considered a warning flag.

Calcium stearyl lactylate and sodium stearyl lactylate. Used in bread dough to strengthen the product and prevent the dough from gumming and in egg whites, these additives are safe. Again, be wary of additives with added sodium.

Casein and sodium caseinate. An excellent, complete protein containing all the essential amino acids, casein and sodium caseinate are used as a texturizer in ice cream and many other dairy products. Some persons may be allergic to this compound.

Citric acid and sodium citrate. Used as a fruit flavoring and to brighten colors in a variety of prepared foods, citric acid is a completely safe and even beneficial food additive. Sodium citrate is used as an emulsifier in ice cream and other dairy products and used to control acidity in fruit products. Sodium citrate may interact with other drugs and make them either more toxic or not quite as effective. Despite this caveat, most experts consider sodium citrate among the safest food additives.

Erythorbic acid. An antioxidant used in much the same way as ascorbic acid in products such as pickling brine, meat products, baked goods, and beverages. One major difference between ascorbic acid and erythorbic acid is that erythorbic acid has no vitamin value.

Ferrous gluconate. Used as a food coloring and flavoring, ferrous gluconate, in the small amounts found in food, is relatively safe. It can, in fact, help correct anemia and is also used to treat iron deficiencies.

Fumaric acid. Obtained from plant tissues, fumaric acid is used as an antioxidant in baked goods and to impart a tart flavor in food products. It has no known toxicity.

Furcelleran. A stabilizer and emulsifier, furcelleran is derived from a northern European red seaweed. Furcelleran appears to be safe.

Gelatin. Obtained from animal tissues, gelatin is a protein used as a food thickener and stabilizer. Gelatin is completely safe, although strict vegetarians will want to avoid this compound.

Ghatti. An emulsifier derived from the stems of plants grown in India and Sri Lanka, ghatti is used in beverages. It may cause allergic reactions in some people, but it is generally considered safe.

Glycerin (glycerol). An important ingredient in candies and used in the edible coatings of meats, glycerin appears to be completely safe.

Guar gum. Obtained from plants grown in India, guar gum is often used as a stabilizer and thickener in hot and cold drinks. Guar gum has also been used as an appetite suppressant and for treatment of peptic ulcers. At levels used in foods, guar gum should pose no human hazard.

Gum arabic. Although gum arabic is basically safe when used as a stabilizer and to prevent sugar crystallization, some people may suffer skin rashes and asthmatic attacks after ingesting it.

Gum tragacanth. Derived from plants grown in Iran, Turkey, and Syria, gum tragacanth is used as a thickener and stabilizer. It has been used with virtually complete safety in America since at least the 1820s.

Invert sugar. A combination of glucose and fructose, invert sugar is extremely sweet. It has no known toxicity.

Karaya. From trees grown in India, karaya is used as a flavoring in a variety of foods in virtually all food groups. It appears to be completely safe.

Lactic acid. A product of fermentation produced from natural plant tissues and dairy whey, lactic acid is used as an acidulant in a variety of products from candy to butter to make foods more acidic, enhance taste, remove undesirable aftertastes, add color to meats, and to act as a preservative. There is no known toxicity for lactic acid when used in food products.

Lactose. Used in the food industry as a culture medium and nutrient, lactose is considered safe by most experts.

Lecithin. Common to all living plants and animals, lecithin is an important antioxidant in cereals, pastries, and other foods. Lecithin is used as an emulsifier in dairy products and in products that combine animal and vegetable fats to ensure their consistency and stabilize the mixture, preventing different ingredients from separation. Lecithin, which contains the B vitamin choline, is generally safe.

Locust bean. Also known as carob bean and Saint John's Bread (the "locusts" eaten by John the Baptist in the wilderness were probably carob beans), locust bean is extracted from the carob tree seed. It is used for flavoring in a variety of products from beverages to ice cream and gelatin desserts. Locust bean may help to lower cholesterol, according to one study.

Mannitol. Used as a texturizer in chewing gum and as a sweetener in sugar-free products, mannitol is relatively safe, although it may cause complications and worsen illness in persons who suffer from kidney disease. Further, mannitol can cause diarrhea if large amounts are ingested.

Potassium sorbate. A mold inhibitor, potassium sorbate is used in bakery products, supermarket salads, cheeses, cheesecake, pie fillings, and many other products. Potassium sorbate is safe.

Sodium benzoate. One of the earliest preservatives, used to prevent the growth of microorganisms, sodium benzoate can cause allergic reactions, but it is safe for most people.

Sorbic acid. Also known as acetic acid, hexadienic acid, hexadienoic acid, and sorbistat, sorbic acid is derived from mountain ash berries or made artificially in factories. It is a mold and yeast inhibitor that is safe the way it is presently used in foods.

Sorbitan monostearate. Used as an emulsifier and as a defoaming and flavor-dispersing agent, sorbitan monostearate is relatively safe.

Sorbitol. Used as a sweetener in candy, chewing gum, and dietetic drinks and foods, sorbitol is very closely related to other fruit sugars. For diabetics, one advantage of sorbitol is that it is absorbed very slowly and does not cause rapid blood sugar increases. However, most of the products in which sorbitol is used are nutritionally poor foods.

Vanillin and ethyl vanillin. Used as a substitute for vanilla, vanillin and ethyl vanillin are safe for most persons. They have, however, been implicated in behavioral disturbances.

YELLOW LIGHT

Products with yellow light additives and preservatives should be kept to a minimum.

Artificial flavoring. These are flavorings that are not found in nature but which may comprise all natural ingredients. Artificial flavorings are usually used in junk food and their presence often indicates nutritionally poor products. Artificial flavoring may have an adverse impact on hyperactive children and should be eliminated from their diets.

Carrageenan. A stabilizer and emulsifier, carrageenan is used in a variety of products from chocolate to cheese spread, sherbets, and dressings. It is considered relatively safe and may even help in lowering cholesterol, although reports also indicate that carrageenan could contribute to ulcerative colitis and colon cancer.

Corn syrup (dextrose). Corn syrup is a simple sugar used as a flavoring. It promotes tooth decay.

Ethylene diamine tetraacetate (EDTA). This preservative is found in mayonnaise, salad dressings, sandwich spreads, margarine, fruit drinks, canned fruits, vegetables, cooked and canned crabmeat, beer, and other foods. Technically, EDTA is known as ethylene diamine tetraacetic acid and sometimes as calcium disodium EDTA or disodium EDTA. EDTA has been used in detoxifying from lead contamination. But in your food—away from the therapeutic setting—it is a binding agent that can rob your body of needed mineral elements such as copper, iron, and zinc. EDTA is used in food processing because sometimes metal ions enter food from mixing vats and produce off flavors, off colors, and changes in food texture. By binding with these minerals, EDTA takes them out of the food. But you end up eating EDTA, and it robs your body, too.

Also consider the implications of the use of EDTA. Such an additive is a cover-up of something undesirable in your food. EDTA helps disguise metallic tastes and hide off colors. EDTA is often listed on the label.

Green number 3. Used in baked products, cereals, and candy, green number 3 is probably one of the safest food colorings. Nevertheless, it may cause or promote bladder tumors, and it has been banned in many European nations.

Heptyl paraben. Used as a preservative to prevent growth of molds and yeast, heptyl paraben is used in jams, jellies, and many frozen dairy desserts. It is generally safe, except for pregnant women; heptyl paraben has been found to cause birth defects at high doses fed to laboratory animals. Pregnant women should avoid or strictly limit their consumption of products with heptyl paraben.

Hydrolyzed vegetable protein. Although safe for adults when used to enhance flavor in soups, beef, and other products, hydrolyzed vegetable protein may be harmful for children. It has nevertheless been used in junior baby foods at levels known to interfere with growth. It also contains monosodium glutamate and may have an effect similar to MSG on some chemically sensitive persons.

Modified food starch. Because starch will not dissolve in cold water, chemists use other chemicals to make starch dissolve; this starch is said to be *modified*. Most chemicals used to modify starch—including propylene oxide, succinic anhydride, 1-octenyl succinic anhydride, and sodium hydroxide—appear to be completely safe. However, one chemical that raises concern is aluminum sulfate (also used in pesticides and detergents) because of the aluminum traces it could introduce into the diet. Since we, as consumers, have no way of knowing which chemicals are used to modify the starch, our safest policy is to avoid modified food starch altogether.

Monoglycerides and diglycerides. Although these compounds do occur naturally, the mono- and diglycerides that are used as food additives are usually prepared synthetically. They belong to a family of chemicals known as glycerides. Many different compounds can be used to synthesize them. One form of monoglyceride fed to mice resulted in poor growth and high mortality; the compound apparently decreased the body's ability to absorb essential fatty acids. Other chemicals in this family fed to laboratory rats have resulted in enlarged kidneys and livers as well as significantly smaller testes and uterine discoloration among females. Other studies have verified that low levels of mono- and diglycerides prevent the body from absorbing other essential fatty acids. And some studies have found that other members of the glyceride family cause testicular growths. Despite this evidence, they continue to be used. I urge a cautious approach. Eating foods with mono- and diglycerides once in a while will probably not cause any substantial damage, but regularly eating foods with this common chemical could harm your body.

Phosphates. A family of nutrients that are essential for proper parathyroid functioning, phosphates are found in evaporated milk and bakery products. Many products contain phosphate compounds with added aluminum. Phosphates at high levels in your diet may create a dietary imbalance and prevent absorption of calcium, which can lead to osteoporosis.

Phosphoric acid. Used for flavoring cola beverages, phosphoric acid appears to be safe. However, it is most useful for removing rust from chrome and for cleaning automobile battery connectors. In other words, it is not really suited for the human body.

Sodium carboxymethylcellulose (CMC). Derived from cotton by-products and used as a thickening and stabilizing compound and to prevent sugar crystallization, sodium carboxymethylcellulose is slightly controversial. While some experts claim CMC is safe, other experts point out that it has caused cancer in animals. It is probably best to avoid CMC.

Yellow number 5. Found in many foods popular among children, yellow number 5 has been implicated in behavioral disturbances among children. Aspirin-sensitive persons may also have allergic reactions to yellow number 5. Federal label laws require complete disclosure of the use of this coloring agent, and it should be eliminated from the diet of hyperactive children.

RED LIGHT

Simply avoid products with red light additives. All of the food dyes and colorings should definitely be eliminated from the diet of any child who is sensitive to food additives and preservatives. From the nutritional standpoint, also keep in mind that food dyes and colorings and other red light additives are usually found in nutritionally inferior junk-food products and in other products that are made with inferior ingredients.

Aspartame. This chemical sweetener rates the longest list of complaints —more than three thousand—that the FDA has ever received. Aspartame is also sold under such brand names as NutraSweet and Equal. Aspartame replaced saccharin, which was shown to cause bladder cancer in laboratory animals and was widely restricted for use in 1977.

Aspartame was discovered by a scientist who was trying to make an ulcer medication. The compound ran over the top of the beaker. The scientist absentmindedly licked his finger and found the substance tasted sweet. No wonder! Aspartame is 180 to 200 times sweeter than sugar.

This is a synthetic compound consisting of two amino acids—aspartate and phenylalanine—that are held in chemical bond by methanol—also known as wood alcohol. Aspartame is a very tiny molecule that the body cannot metabolize slowly; it goes directly into the bloodstream. When the aspartame molecule enters the bloodstream, the chemicals in aspartame break down into their constituents. Methanol is poisonous when found alone, as it is after aspartame enters the bloodstream and breaks down. Although we eat many foods that contain methanol, it usually is found with ethyl alcohol, which neutralizes the methanol. In aspartame the ethyl alcohol is absent. Signs of methanol poisoning include headaches, numbness of the extremities, vertigo (dizziness), depression, blurred vision, nausea, and abdominal pain.

Methanol specifically seeks out the blood vessels of the optic nerve, binding to them and, at high enough levels, destroying the blood supply to the retina, causing blindness. In pregnant women, high methanol levels during certain periods of pregnancy have resulted in lack of formation of their child's eyes.

If aspartame is heated to a temperature of over 85°F., a chemical decomposition occurs in the product itself in which freestanding methanol is created. There is a good chance of products being exposed to 85°F., especially on a hot summer day when the foods are stored in a warehouse, delivery truck, garage, or cupboard.

Many doctors now warn pregnant women not to eat *any* products containing aspartame. They should at least drastically cut their intake to no more than one serving daily of products containing aspartame. Dr. William Pardridge of the University of California Medical School says that he believes that women with an intolerance for phenylalanine, one of aspartame's major components, may give birth to infants with a 10 to 15 percent drop in IQ levels if the mother has consumed large amounts of aspartame-containing products. Other scientists have gone further and have said that mothers who consume large amounts of aspartame during pregnancy could give birth to mentally retarded babies.

Persons who *must* restrict their intake of aspartame include individuals who cannot metabolize the amino acid phenylalanine. These people suffer from phenylketonuria (PKU). As many as 20 million Americans may be carriers of the PKU gene, although they themselves are not phenylketonuric. This means that parents can pass on the PKU genes to their child, who will have an intolerance for aspartame. The test for PKU carriers, however, is not done unless requested. You could be a carrier without knowing. If both parents have the gene, the child will be PKU. But how will they know? Surely, if you or your child suffer from symptoms of aspartame intoxication, avoidance is the best policy.

What are the symptoms of aspartame intoxication? There are many diverse symptoms, including severe headaches, nausea, vertigo, insomnia, loss of control of arms, legs, and hands, blurred vision, blindness and other visual problems, memory loss, slurred speech, mild depression to severe suicidal depression, hyperactivity, gastrointestinal disorders, seizures, skin lesions, rashes, anxiety attacks, muscular and joint pain, numbness, subtle mood changes, loss of energy, menstrual cramps, irregularity or loss of menstrual cycle, symptoms mimicking heart attacks, hearing loss, ringing ears, and loss or change of taste.

Do not use aspartame products to lose weight. Many dieticians and physicians today believe that aspartame products *do not* aid in weight loss, because they prevent satiety. Usually, when you eat a meal rich in carbohydrates, your brain produces serotonin. Serotonin is responsible for the happy, relaxed feeling after a healthful, natural meal containing complex carbohydrates derived from plant foods. When aspartame is served in combination with carbohydrates, the aspartame causes the brain to cease producing serotonin. That means you will never feel full after you eat foods with aspartame. The result is that you keep eating. And you may eat more and more diet foods sweetened with aspartame, increasing your chance of suffering from aspartame intoxication.

Of the thousands of consumer complaints about adverse reactions to aspartame products, diet soft drinks accounted for the vast majority—40.4 percent. Tabletop sweeteners accounted for 20.9 percent of the complaints. Puddings, lemonade, Kool-Aid, hot chocolate, canned iced tea, chewing gum, cereal, punch mix, sugar substitute tablets, breath mints, nondairy toppings, chewable multiple vitamins, and fruit drinks accounted for virtually all of the rest of the complaints.

Headaches are the reaction most commonly complained of. Others report —in order of frequency of occurrence—dizziness, problems with balance, changes in moods, vomiting and nausea, abdominal pain and cramps, seizures and convulsions, and changes in vision.

A team of physicians from the Cleveland Clinic Foundation writing in the *New England Journal of Medicine* noted, "For the past few years in our headache clinic, we have systematically inquired about aspartame use. We have been impressed by the number of cases in which an observer (not necessarily the patient) detected a clear aggravation of symptoms at the time of introduction of aspartame into the diet. . . . Persons susceptible to migraine and other vascular headaches should continue to be warned of the possible aggravating role of aspartame, and this substance should remain on the list of items to be excluded from the diets of these patients until further studies are complete."

And what about cancer?

"I do not concur that aspartame has been shown safe with respect to the induction of brain tumors," argued FDA scientist Dr. Robert Condon in an internal government document in 1981. A crucial two-year rat study produced results that some experts assert showed aspartame could cause brain tumors when ingested in huge quantities, but the sweetener's manufacturer argued that although there were in fact tumors they did not appear to be caused by aspartame. Yet another study showed a significant incidence of uterine polyps in rats fed at the two highest dose levels. FDA said the polyps were not linked with aspartame. Another indication that a compound has carcinogenic potential is early occurrence of tumors. Two aspartame-fed rats in the two-year rat study died from tumors early on in the study.

Aspartame was approved for marketing in dry foods by the FDA in 1981 only after the FDA commissioner overturned a federally appointed public board of inquiry's recommendation that aspartame's approval be denied based on the need for more studies to determine whether aspartame causes brain tumors or not.

Personally, I would be careful of excess aspartame consumption, especially in the form of diet drinks containing NutraSweet, which are consumed in large quantities by millions of people.

BHA (butylated hydroxyanisole). Found in many products including Jell-O, BHA is an antioxidant that prevents food from changing color, changing flavor, or becoming rancid. Researchers report that BHA in the diet of pregnant mice resulted in brain enzyme changes in the newborn offspring including a 50 percent decreased activity in brain cholinesterase, which is responsible for the transmission of nerve impulses. In addition, the behavior of animals receiving either BHA or BHT in the diet differed from control animals with respect to sleep, aggression, and their ability to engage in instinctive freezing behavior, and they exhibited a marked decrease in the exploratory reflex and a reduction in weight.

The study's authors speculated that BHA could affect the normal sequence of neurological development in young animals. The final report to the FDA on BHA in 1980 stated that no evidence in the available information demonstrates a hazard to the public at current use levels. But you should know better. The behavioral responses caused by BHA in the laboratory animals are remarkably similar to the profound behavioral effects BHA may have on children. And children do get dosed with quite a large amount of BHA, which has been used in convenience foods since 1947. Per capita use of BHA increased by three times between 1960 and 1970. Unwary consumers eat an average of 13 milligrams or more of BHA every day. Babies are estimated to ingest as much as 8 milligrams, according to the National Research Council. BHA is a preservative that could have a profound impact on childhood behavior. Its presence in our food is widespread. Foods with BHA include potato chips, chewing gum, kids' presweetened breakfast cereals, frozen pork sausages, enriched rice, lard, shortening, candy, and, of course, Jell-O.

BHT (butylated hydroxytoluene). BHT, which is similar to BHA, should be eliminated from the diet because of its potential to cause cancer and alter behavior.

Blue number 1. Used in candy and soft drinks, blue number 1 is a potential carcinogen. Although it is not always listed on the label, you should know that junk foods are the usual carriers of this dangerous compound. Eat wholesome natural foods to stay away from blue number 1 and other food dyes and colorings. Banned in Finland and France, blue number 1 may also cause chromosomal damage.

Blue number 2. At present we have very little information about blue number 2, which is used in baked products, candy, and soft drinks. However, it is now believed that blue number 2 may cause brain tumors in laboratory animals. Unfortunately for your pet, this compound is often found in pet foods. It is banned in Norway.

Brominated vegetable oil (BVO). A potentially very dangerous additive for some persons, BVO is used as an emulsifier in some foods and as a clouding agent in many popular soft drinks. Bromate, the main ingredient of BVO, is a poison. Just 2 to 4 ounces of a 2 percent solution of BVO can seriously poison a child. Soft drinks with BVO can inhibit the body's natural defenses because BVO is an instant reducer of the body's histamines, which are needed to fight infections and allergies. If the body's ability to fight infections and allergies is inhibited, a person can undergo a severe allergic reaction. One woman nearly died as a result of an acute allergic reaction after she took the antibiotic tetracycline together with BVO-tainted soft drinks. Traces of BVO have been found in human fat tissue.

Citrus red number 2. Used to color orange skins, citrus red number 2 is a probable carcinogen and may cause chromosomal damage. Experts contend that this compound does not migrate from the orange skin into the pulp. But its use should be one more reason to seek organically grown oranges. The FDA has recommended a ban.

Monosodium glutamate. Also known as MSG, monosodium glutamate is a flavor enhancer that does not affect the food but the person ingesting the food. MSG is not only found in Chinese food; its use has spread across the whole spectrum of canned and processed foods, including soups, flavored potato chips, frozen dinners, and processed lunch meats. Many people have an allergic reaction to MSG, which is also known as Chinese restaurant syndrome since MSG is so frequently used in preparing Chinese food. Whatever it is called, the symptoms are real, and they include headaches, flushing of the skin, tightness of the chest, heart palpitations, and nausea. An MSG reaction can trigger asthma attacks and difficulties in balancing in the elderly. Sensitivity seems to be dependent on the dose, although some persons who regularly ingest MSG can become hypersensitive to it and develop reactions at extremely low doses. MSG is also found in two other additives, hydrolyzed vegetable (or plant) protein and autolyzed yeast, and can make up 6 to 40 percent of these compounds.

Nitrite. See sodium nitrite.

Propyl gallate. An antioxidant used in food fats and oils, often in combination with BHA or BHT, propyl gallate may be a carcinogen. Avoid it.

Quinine. Used in tonic water and as a flavoring in some beverages, quinine may cause birth defects. Pregnant women should avoid products with quinine.

Red dye number 3. After eight years of debate, red dye number 3 was banned in 1990 from use in many foods and cosmetics. Unfortunately, products containing red dye number 3 may remain on the market until supplies are used up. So beware: Yes, maraschino cherries are dyed. Yes, the dye is dangerous. Be kind to your body and do not eat the maraschino cherry atop your sundae. (Better yet, forget the sundae! It'll be loaded with pesticides.) Used in canned fruit cocktail, cherry pie mix, maraschino cherries, ice cream, candy, bakery products, and many other dessert products, red dye number 3 has induced thyroid cancer and chromosomal damage in laboratory animals; it may also interfere with brain-nerve transmission. Although FDA experts recommended that this coloring agent be banned, high-ranking officials during the Reagan presidency pressured the FDA to keep it on the market. Definitely avoid it.

Red number 40. One of the most recently developed colorings, red number 40 is suspected of being a carcinogen.

Saccharin. Ten years after the FDA proposed banning it, saccharin is still widely used in artificial sweeteners. This use continues despite the determination that saccharin is a probable human carcinogen. A series of studies conducted under the auspices of the Canadian government confirms what earlier American studies have suggested: that saccharin poses a significant risk of cancer for humans. The risk is real, and as usual, the risk is related to the size of the dose. Every packet of Sweet 'n Low has 40 milligrams of saccharin. Saccharin is also used as a sweetener in soft drinks. Avoid regular use of saccharin-tainted foods and beverages.

Salt (sodium chloride). Salt, which is added to a huge number of processed foods, can cause high blood pressure and increase the risk of heart attack and stroke. Avoid foods with high levels of salt; seek those foods with negligible amounts. Many foods now list their sodium content on the label, and many food producers are now beginning to market low-sodium products, which you should seek.

Sodium nitrite. Nitrites are used as a preservative in cured meats such as bacon, ham, and smoked fish to prevent spoilage that could lead to botulism poisoning and to help the meats retain their fresh color. Nitrites can form cancer-causing compounds in the gastrointestinal tract. They should be avoided; food with nitrites should always be eaten with vitamin C–rich foods. Food companies often add vitamin C to nitrite-cured products.

Sugar (sucrose). Used as a sweetener in a huge number of foods, sucrose has no nutritional value. Because sucrose is immediately released into the bloodstream, products high in sugar often do not provide satiety. This means you are likely to keep eating, thus increasing your caloric intake.

Sulfur dioxide, sodium bisulfite, and sulfites. These compounds are used to preserve foods. They prevent dried fruits from drying out and stiffening. They are also used on shrimp and may still be used on frozen potatoes. Their use on shrimp must be declared on the label. However, there are many violations of this label disclosure law. Sulfites are dangerous for some asthmatics. The FDA has received more than three hundred letters reporting adverse reactions in asthma sufferers after their having consumed foods with sulfiting agents. At least four deaths caused by acute reactions to sulfites have been reported to the FDA. In one 1983 sulfite-caused mortality case, FDA investigators reported that samples of lettuce served with one meal contained as much as 409 ppm sulfite and the guacamole served at the same meal had 272 ppm sulfite. In another death caused by sulfites the following year, analysis of shredded potatoes served to the victim indicated that the product had 96 ppm sulfite.

The use of sulfites on fresh produce in food service establishments is being discouraged by the National Restaurant Association and the Produce Marketing Association, and use has decreased over the past two years. Such voluntary curtailment of sulfite use is an important step in reducing opportunities for unsuspecting sulfite-sensitive individuals to be exposed.

TBHQ (Tertiary butylhydroquinone). This chemical is often used along with BHA or BHT. TBHQ, which is toxic at extremely low doses, has been implicated in childhood behavioral problems.

Yellow number 6. Used in candy and carbonated beverages, yellow number 6 dye appears to increase the number of kidney and adrenal gland tumors in rats. It may also cause chromosomal damage. It has been banned in Norway and Sweden.

13. IRRADIATION

Food irradiation is the process of exposing food to high doses of gamma radiation. Proponents of this process claim that it kills pests, eggs, and larvae, controls sprouting and ripening, and extends the shelf life of foods—which would be wonderful *if* it really worked, *if* it were safe for the people consuming the irradiated foods, and *if* it were safe for workers. But it *doesn't* work, and it *isn't* safe.

Food irradiation is a technology that a small cadre of nuclear energy proponents, in concert with the U.S. Department of Energy, is trying to foist upon the American public. Why? The DOE and the nuclear weapons and energy industries are stuck with some of the most toxic chemicals ever created. Some 20,000 tons of highly radioactive waste, with an estimated life span of a quarter-million years, are buried at temporary sites throughout the country. Much of this highly radioactive waste was produced in the manufacture of plutonium for nuclear weapons.

The DOE believes that the solution to this toxic waste problem lies in the creation of a food irradiation industry. Proponents of irradiation have been trying to implement this processing of food for more than thirty years. The original idea was tied in with President Dwight D. Eisenhower's Atoms for Peace program, launched in the 1950s.

Proponents would like to see small, portable irradiation units used on farmlands where highly perishable crops could be quickly irradiated. The Energy Department's plans have called for one thousand food irradiation plants to be established across the country as part of a larger waste-disposal recycling scheme.

At the moment, very little food irradiation is done, and that mainly for spices used in prepared foods. A citrus irradiation plant is close to being built in Florida, however, and another may be built in Washington State, possibly for irradiating apples. Irradiation is used in other industries—to sterilize medical equipment, for example.

In the irradiation process, foods are placed on a conveyor belt and pass through a long, biologically shielded irradiation chamber, past a cobalt 60 or cesium 137 irradiator source plaque. The foods are then exposed for one to two minutes to high-dose beams of radiation. One chest X ray is the equivalent of one RAD (Roentgen absorbed dose). Exposure to 300 RADs would kill half the people directly exposed and sterilize the rest of them. In food irradiation, fruits and vegetables can receive up to 100,000 RADs. The exposure limit for herbs and spices is 3 million RADs. The food itself does not become radioactive—unless there is an equipment malfunction or radiation leak.

Over the long history of food irradiation, its effect on human health has been much studied. In 1968, the FDA reported that irradiated food fed to laboratory animals caused a significant increase in testicular tumors, pituitary cancer, weight loss, cataracts, shortened life span, and reduced fertility. In 1982 in its own internal food irradiation audit, the FDA further concluded that only 1 percent of 413 studies of food irradiation in a period of more than thirty years supported the claim that irradiated food was completely safe.

Soviet studies indicate that rats fed irradiated food suffered higher rates of kidney and testicular damage. Canadian studies indicate that laboratory animals fed irradiated food developed an extra set of chromosomes. In Hungary, 1,223 studies on food irradiation safety have been conducted, and not one of them supports the safety of irradiated food. And in West Germany food irradiation is banned because of studies indicating the possibility of mutations, reduced fertility, metabolic disturbances, decreased growth rate, reduced resistance to diseases, changes in organ weight, and cancer.

The cells in the human body appear to be very sensitive to gamma radiation–altered by-products in irradiated food. Carbohydrates in irradiated food may impair cell division. Fats and fatty acids in irradiated foods are changed into peroxides and other toxic chemicals. Other completely new compounds, created during irradiation, have not been tested for carcinogenicity, mutagenicity, or teratogenicity. These new compounds are called unique radiolytic products (URPs). The FDA says the URPs are "probably" safe because the levels are so low. But one could expect a concentration of URPs within a range of three to thirty parts per million. In the world of toxic chemicals, three to thirty parts per million can be a significant concentration.

Food irradiation also creates many times more free radicals. In foods, these free radicals can cause human cancer as well as premature aging of the skin and body. Australian physicists at Melbourne University found that exposure to gamma irradiation increased the levels of free radicals in all food between three and fifty times, depending on the specific food that was irradiated, according to a 1989 report from the International Organization of Consumer Unions.

This danger to consumers is only one of the drawbacks to food irradiation. Worldwide there is a history of significant contamination of our environment and of workers due to accidents, leaks, and spills of nuclear substances. Setting up miniature nuclear plants and transporting nuclear materials to all these sites in our neighborhoods is bound to lead to exposure.

At the Isomedix, Inc., irradiation plant, in Parsippany, New Jersey, fire broke out during a welding operation. The fire was extinguished with a chemical that is believed to have caused the cobalt 60 energy source to corrode and leak. The water was filtered and released into the public sewer system. In a subsequent cleanup of the facility, the toilet, toilet pipe, and concrete were found to be radioactive and had to be removed and buried as radioactive waste.

In Dover, New Jersey, in 1974, a cobalt 60 source at the International Neutronics, Inc., irradiation facility was damaged. During the cleanup a discharge line was left unattended overnight. By morning, some 5,700 liters of contaminated water had leaked onto the floor of the facility and migrated outside. The INI management instructed employees to dump the spilled water down bathroom drains into the *public* sewer system. Employees working on the cleanup were instructed to wear their radiation film badges in a way that would give false low readings to the Nuclear Regulatory Commission. The INI officials were later indicted and convicted by a New Jersey grand jury on six counts of fraud and conspiracy against the Nuclear Regulatory Commission in connection with the event. The cleanup cost was two million dollars.

Many other accidents have occurred and will continue to occur as long as irradiation of food is permitted.

The release of all this additional radiation cannot be good for the planet. Earth has always been inundated with radiation, from below ground and from the atmosphere. Naturally occurring background radiation has always played a role in the onset of illness. There does not appear to be a threshold limit for radiation; this means that the smallest dose can initiate cancer. The radiation releases from nuclear explosions between the 1950s and the 1980s have all become part of an increasing radiation belt, and fallout from nuclear testing has had a very real and damaging effect upon human populations in Utah and other southwestern regions. In *Radiation and Human Health*, radiation expert Dr. John Gofman, discoverer of uranium 233, wrote:

No one seriously doubts the overwhelming evidence that ionizing radiation causes a wide variety of injuries to the health of human beings. Many of these injuries either are fatal or guarantee a life of misery.

Every new use of the atoms adds, imperceptibly and inexorably, to ambient radiation levels throughout the world. Each year's "permissible releases" of radiation become part of the next year's background level. The toxic radiation environment that surrounds us all is thickening. The inevitable consequences of these cumulative additions, following the expiration of latency periods, will be borne by generations to come. It is they who will pay the terrible cost of our failure to halt releases of radioactivity to our air, land, and water.

And all this is happening when the benefits of irradiating food are suspect. "There is utterly no possibility that gamma radiation, as we now use it, could possibly replace fungicides," says Dr. Noel Sommer, lecturer and post-harvest pathologist at the University of California at Davis. "Instead there is considerable evidence to indicate that certain diseases of harvested citrus fruits would be more active after irradiation. Radiation-induced cellular injury . . . causes a reduction in the normal level of the commodity's disease resistance."

Sommer and the late Dr. Edward Maxie performed studies on the use of gamma radiation to control post-harvest diseases of fruits and vegetables for ten years (1963–73) with support from the Atomic Energy Commission. They found that diseases were often worse in irradiated than in nonirradiated citrus.

The researchers concluded that irradiated strawberries "weep" from irradiation-caused injury when they are cut, citrus fruits are more sensitive to disease and chilling injury after being irradiated, and changes occur in the color, odor, flavor, and texture of irradiated produce, which may then require the addition of synthetic chemical flavoring additives. Finally, it is doubtful that any fresh commodity's shelf life would be increased by more than a few days by using irradiation to control rot organisms. Irradiation is simply not needed—unless you want to eat a seven-year-old hamburger!

In 1989, New York Governor Mario Cuomo signed into law legislation that prohibits the sale of irradiated food (except spices) for two years, dealing the food irradiation industry a devastating blow. And he had huge consumer support! The statehouse was flooded with letters. Since New York is one of the main consumer markets in the nation, its ban on irradiated foods is certain to stymie the industry's growth.

In 1987, Maine banned the sale of virtually all irradiated foods. The New Jersey legislature overwhelmingly approved a measure similar to the Maine legislation only to have Governor Thomas Kean veto the bill. Alaska, Vermont, New Hampshire, Pennsylvania, Oregon, Minnesota, and other states have been considering legislative prohibitions on irradiated food.

In Florida, where the state legislature is dominated by agribusinesses, residents are seeking a referendum to amend the state constitution to make irradiation illegal. Florida will be a tough state for activists. A company known as Vindicator of Florida plans to build an irradiation facility in Polk County near Mulberry. Vindicator would use the plant for cobalt 60 application of fruit and might even expand to seafood.

In Santa Cruz, California, the city and county enacted the nation's first food irradiation labeling ordinance. This decree requires food retailers to post shelf signs designating all irradiated whole foods and all foods that contain irradiated ingredients.

Alaskan Governor Steve Cowper announced that his state would refuse federal funds for an irradiation demonstration plant in Kodiak. He said he was convinced that the association of Alaska with food irradiation would have a detrimental effect on the Alaska seafood industry. The Copper River Fishermen's Cooperative and the United Fishermen of Alaska said they were worried about potential health risks. In addition, many of Alaska's important worldwide seafood markets, such as Great Britain, West Germany, Sweden, and New Zealand, have banned food irradiation.

In Congress, Representative Douglas Bosco, a California Democrat, and Senate Majority Leader George Mitchell, a Maine Democrat, have introduced similar bills to ban the sale and distribution of radiation-exposed foods until the National Academy of Sciences can conduct a study to determine the human health and ecological consequences of irradiation on communities, groundwater, air, workers, roads, transportation, and potential nuclear accidents.

Around the planet, food irradiation is meeting stiff opposition. In December 1988, New Zealand banned food irradiation, following extensive review after a gamma irradiation plant was proposed for the city of Auckland. In banning food irradiation, New Zealand joins twelve other nations: Austria, West Germany, Rumania, Switzerland, the United Kingdom, Sweden, Abu Dhabi, the Dominican Republic, Botswana, Ethiopia, Kenya, and Tanzania.

We must ask whether we want to tie in our food supply to toxic wastes from nuclear radiation. Why introduce yet another potential danger into a food supply that is already contaminated?

Shopping Tips

The FDA requires that whole foods be labeled with the internationally recognized food irradiation symbol known as the "radura" as well as the statement, "Treated with ionizing radiation." The radura looks like a stylized flower:

Unlabeled irradiated spices are already being used in sausages, tomato sauces, and frozen pizzas.

The FDA recently approved the use of gamma radiation on poultry products because of the high rate of disease and bacterial contamination of poultry. Instead of forcing ranchers to correct the factory farm conditions that lead to contamination, irradiation would allow them to "correct" the problem by endangering your health in a different way. We must not let this happen! Write to your representatives. Let's stop irradiation of poultry before it begins. You can also inform the top poultry companies in the United States of your concern about food treated with radiation. Poultry producers should clearly understand that the use or endorsement of this technology will hurt them at the marketplace. Toll-free numbers for these companies are in the Personal Action Guide.

Herbs and spices are authorized for irradiation, but so far only those herbs and spices used in processed foods appear to be undergoing irradiation. Be sure you buy spices whose labels specifically state they are not irradiated. These herbs and spices may be irradiated:

Allspice	Fennel seed	Pepper, black
Anise	Fenugreek	Pepper, white
Basil	Garlic powder	Pepper, red
Bay leaves	Ginger	Peppermint
Caraway seed	Grains of paradise	Poppy seed
Black cumin	Horseradish	Rosemary
Cardamom	Mace	Saffron
Celery seed	Marjoram	Sage
Chamomile	Mustard flour	Savory
Chervil	Mustard seed	Sesame seed
Chives	Nutmeg	Spearmint
Cinnamon	Onion powder	Star anise
Cloves	Orange petals	Tarragon
Coriander	Oregano	Thyme
Cumin seed	Paprika	Turmeric
Dill seed	Parsley	
Dill weed		

14. DRINKING WATER

There's really nothing more delicious when you're thirsty than a glass of cold, pure water. Hydrate thy body! Work out hard and then hydrate with water instead of coffee. Buy a fine bottle of pure water and give yourself a treat. The body needs good water. A glass of bottled water is *très chic*, ladies and gentlemen. When you're out, you need not always order beer, wine, mixed drinks, or coffee. Don't worry; nobody will think any less of you for ordering bottled water instead.

On the low-toxin high-energy diet we need good, pure water because we're trying to lower our toxic burden. Water is a natural diuretic and essential to detoxing because, along with fiber, it speeds toxins out of the body. Drink four to eight glasses of water daily, depending on your size and activity level. But make sure you've got a good source of pure, contaminant-free water.

It is astonishing, on a planet whose surface is composed mostly of water, how extraordinarily little of it is safe to drink—less than 1 percent. The vast majority is salt water and much too saline for human consumption. And much of our fresh water is unavailable, hidden in underground seas, streams, and rivers.

Fresh water is the most precious and *finite* resource of our planet. All water is recycled. Earth is not in the business of creating more water; it recycles existing water, which evaporates from the ground and oceans, creeks, rivers, and lakes and then falls as snow or rain and sinks into the underground network of ebbing rivers and still seas. From water underground comes life. Groundwater provides drinking water for 53 percent of our nation's population, including virtually all of our rural population.

Finding pure water is becoming increasingly difficult. The accumulated wastes of our society, particularly in the form of pesticide runoff and industrial pollutants, have fouled huge portions of our fresh water supply. And many modern chemicals synthesized in the laboratory do not break down quickly as a result of natural processes. These persistent chemicals poison our water. By the time the Grand Calumet River in Illinois empties into Lake Michigan, 90 percent of its volume is industrial runoff. Large parts of its riverbed are incapable of supporting any kind of life. And the Great Lakes supply drinking water to 30 percent of the United States. This is what we're doing to ourselves! Not only have we allowed contamination of vast numbers of freshwater fish, not only is pollution destroying forests far and wide through acid rain, but we are also poisoning ourselves, slowly and surely, by permitting the buildup of toxins in our drinking water supplies.

The magnitude of this catastrophe has become increasingly apparent to the nation with each passing year. In farm areas, drinking water supplies have been thoroughly polluted with pesticides. In 1988, the EPA found more than sixty pesticides contaminating portions of groundwater in thirty states. Government estimates are that 28 percent of all public water supplies may now contain toxic or bacterial contaminants. The National Wildlife Association puts the estimate as high as 37 percent. One government report identified 2,110 chemicals in drinking water. Another documents the closure of over 10,000 public and private wells across America. And only a handful of the nation's 59,000 water companies actually test for a wide spectrum of chemicals. These facts have profound implications for our health.

The pollution of our water, we are discovering, is vast. But our drinking water supply will shrink as greenhouse effects increase. Already portions of the West and Midwest have faced drought conditions for several years. Rivers, lakes, and underground seas are like funnels. More pollution goes into them every year, but they are shrinking in size. And the nation's wetlands, natural filters that clean toxic chemicals from fresh water, are being destroyed, too. As our water supply diminishes, pesticide overkill coupled with industrial pollution becomes biological suicide; as people in drought- and cancer-plagued Kansas have learned, with less water, the chemical carcinogens in the supply become more concentrated and their effects more pronounced.

Our exposure to contaminants in drinking water is constant. We wake up in the morning and drink a glass of water or make a pot of coffee or tea; we drink water all day—as much as six to eight glasses. We shower and bathe in water. We wash our dishes and bathe our children in water. Our contamination is not just the result of what we drink; we also absorb some of the most toxic chemicals through our skin and inhale them in significant concentrations when we shower, wash dishes, or flush the toilet.

People wonder whether minuscule amounts of toxins in their water can harm them; after all, the government in many cases permits low levels of toxins in public water supplies. The government says its allowable levels are safe levels. I cannot emphasize how strongly I disagree with government policies on drinking water safety and on what constitutes a safe level of exposure to carcinogens in our water supplies. There is *no safe level* of cancer-causing substances in our water supplies.

Congress, in the Safe Drinking Water Act as amended in 1989, requires that drinking water supplies be made economically available. When there is a carcinogen in the drinking water, standards are to be set that take into account technology available to reduce the poisons to the lowest levels possible, taking cost into consideration. These standards are known as Maximum Contaminant Levels (MCLs). There are also health goals required under the law when the poisons are known or suspected human carcinogens. These are the Maximum Contaminant Level Goals (MCLGs). For carcinogens the MCLG is *zero*.

It is not that the government is lying to the public. Congress has written the rule and the bureaucrats are implementing the intent of Congress. The argument should be with Congress and the imperfect laws it passes, not with the people whose job it is to implement those laws.

The real public policy question to be addressed is whether the American people should demand that Congress change its laws and appropriate funds to clean up our drinking water sources and prevent their further contamination. In the entire United States there are only eleven or so sole source aquifers. The EPA is powerless to prevent their contamination if state and local governments approve development on top of them. In Maryland, a housing project is going to be built that will severely affect the recharge zones necessary to maintain an aquifer. The EPA simply refuses to get involved because it has no authority. Yet the asphalt paving is made up of toxic chemicals, and its runoff will most certainly poison the Piedmont Sole Source Aquifer.

If we are to conserve and improve our groundwater supplies, easily enforceable public policy needs to be legislated and set into play.

Furthermore, the Safe Drinking Water Act specifically excludes privately owned wells and nonpublic water supplies from government regulation. Thus, the EPA is powerless to protect persons whose private water wells are contaminated with bacteria and nitrates.

Effects of toxins can no longer be measured accurately by the government with traditional cancer-risk assessments that do not take into account the cumulative effects of toxins in water, food, and air. The effects of low-level poisoning are myriad, including an array of common chronic illnesses ranging from flulike symptoms, to inability to concentrate and decreased IQ to decreased immunity to disease and Epstein-Barr syndrome. Unfortunately, government risk paradigms are far behind the times.

Although there has been very little research into the noncancerous, low-level cumulative effects of the most common toxic chemicals found in drinking water, such as solvents, observations of the noncancerous effects of such toxins are well supported by case studies. According to the authors of the article "Lymphocyte Subpopulations in Solvent-Exposed Workers," published in 1986 in the *International Archives of Occupational and Environmental Health,* scientists do know that exposure to solvents can alter immune system responses and suppress lymphocyte function among workers. The common drinking water contaminant trichloroethylene was once used as an anesthetic gas that acts on the central nervous system. Often, symptoms of CNS depression that occur on either a short-term high level or a chronic low-level basis result in nonspecific, vague symptoms. According to researchers writing in the *American Journal of Industrial Medicine,* symptoms arising from chronic solvent exposure include memory loss, decreased problem solving ability, decreased attention, impaired dexterity and hand-eye coordination, altered reaction time, reduced psychomotor functions, and altered personality or mood.

It's not only low-level poisoning we have to worry about, either. *People are dying* because of poisons in their water. As someone who has been involved in analyzing the government's weighing of risks and benefits, I am telling you straight out that the government is deceiving us about the safety of drinking water each time its bureaucrats set a safe level for a cancer-causing or birth defect–causing chemical or neurotoxin in our drinking water. There is no safe level of a cancer-causing chemical or of a chemical that causes cell mutations, birth defects, or illnesses. The government is simply hiding the effects of toxic chemicals on the population.

Government health agencies have turned into departments of public reassurance. In 1985, days before I testified before a California state legislative committee on toxic chemicals and human health and revealed that consumers of locally caught sport fish in southern California were being poisoned by DDT, I received a politely menacing phone call from three of the highest officials in the state of California's Department of Health Services. Speaking on a conference line, these three officials warned me in very strong language that I should never mention that DDT might cause human cancer when I testified about fish eaters who had excessive DDT contamination—despite strong evidence in animal studies that DDT may well cause human cancer. They stressed that they feared public hysteria, that the public could not handle the truth. These bureaucrats want to keep the poisoning of America quiet. You'd think they worked for the pesticide industry or agribusiness instead of for us taxpayers.

If the government ever did a truly fair, honest risk-benefit analysis of the presence of cancer-causing and birth defect–causing chemicals in drinking water, an analysis that took the medical costs of those illnesses and birth defects into account, the total social cost of these toxins would clearly be prohibitive, and the benefit to industry of permitting pollution would appear slight in contrast. But the government leaves out these costs of cancer and birth defects and other toxic effects from risk-benefit analyses. It is my belief that if the public knew the true cost of many of the toxic chemicals used in industry and farming, Americans would not tolerate policies that allow them in our drinking water.

TAP WATER

People who care about their health but regularly drink tap water, believing that local governments are looking out for their health, may be making a deadly mistake. You must find out for yourself whether your tap water has a significant concentration of cancer-causing chemicals.

Despite the use of various water-treatment systems, bacterial contamination is a problem in many places. Chlorination, a much-used water treatment for many decades, turns out to cause problems of its own including cancer. Industrial pollution is a danger in areas where manufacturing takes place. Lead in water is a serious danger, especially in urban areas, and I believe lead poisoning is the number one preventable pediatric disease in America today. Naturally occurring radiation in water supplies causes birth defects and childhood cancers. Nitrates and pesticides lace the water in many of our farm states.

I don't mean to sound discouraging. Many cities and counties have wonderfully pure water supplies. But it makes me furious that across our nation people may be daily drinking water that could harm them, and health officials are not informing them of the dangers.

Bacteria, Protozoa, and Viruses in Water

Public water supplies can contain bacteria and viruses as well as man-made chemicals. Some bacteria are opportunistic and can cause sickness in persons with weakened immune systems.

Throughout America, a simple little protozoan, *Giardia lamblia,* has become well-known for its appearance in water supplies. Usually, only surface water, as opposed to well water, is affected by *Giardia lamblia.* These protozoa seem to be resistant to the usual amounts of chlorine added to drinking water to kill bacteria. The only practical method for their removal is sand filtration, a technology that has been available since the turn of the century. *Giardia lamblia* like to live in our intestines, where conditions are ideal for them to colonize, and they cause problems such as cramps and chronic diarrhea. Other symptoms of giardiasis include bloating, fatigue, and weight loss. In some cases beavers infected with giardiasis pass on the protozoa, in concentrated form, to humans through the water supply.

At home, a water filter with a five-micron or smaller screen can help protect you from *Giardia lamblia*. (I'll discuss water filters in detail at the end of this chapter.) When you are in the wilderness, you should use a small portable water filter as protection against this and other organisms. Or you can boil your water at high temperature and use chlorine tablets. Remember: chlorine alone may not kill protozoa. Using both methods together will help purify your drinking water and kill any naturally occurring toxins that might be present. See the Personal Action Guide for information about ordering a portable water filter.

Viruses can also contaminate drinking water. They occur naturally or as a result of sewage mingling with the drinking supply. Viruses were the cause of a severe outbreak of sickness among nearly 80 percent of the 13,000 residents of Georgetown, Texas, in 1980. Among these cases, more than 35 cases of hepatitis A were recorded after heavy contamination of the town's water supply with a variety of viruses that were immune to the disinfection properties of chlorination.

These biological infestations can happen anywhere. A good home filter system can ensure that you will not get sick from drinking your tap water. If you have reason to suspect water contamination where you live, it's best to invest in one.

Chlorination

Chlorination of community water supplies throughout America has been invaluable in preventing widespread occurrences of once-common infectious waterborne diseases such as typhoid. At least 80 percent of the nation's population now drinks water that has been chlorinated.

But we have learned in the last twenty years that chlorination of our water supplies is not without its downside. For one thing, bacteria seem to be gaining resistance to chlorination, based on evidence from the water supplies of Lexington, Kentucky; Marion, Ohio; and Kokomo, Terre Haute, Muncie, and Seymour, Indiana. In these cities, bacteria counts have recently begun to remain high even when megadoses of chlorine are added to the water.

More serious still, chlorination introduces a group of cancer-causing chemicals called trihalomethanes to our water. These chemicals—THMs, as they are known—form when chlorine interacts with tiny particles of decayed organic matter in the water, from insects, soil, and anything else that is or was living. Studies by scientists throughout the country show that THMs have probably caused thousands of human cancers. A strong link has been found in many communities between drinking chlorinated tap water with elevated THM concentrations and bladder, gastrointestinal, and urinary tract cancer.

The most significant studies of the effects of chlorination on humans concentrated on surface water supplies from rivers such as the Mississippi and Ohio. Surface water is exposed to the environment and contains more particulates and other organic matter than well water. So higher concentrations of the cancer-causing trihalomethanes are formed during chlorination. The pioneering Environmental Defense Fund study of 1974 in the New Orleans area linked tap water from the Mississippi River with increased cancer mortality, particularly involving cancers of the bladder, kidney, and stomach—bodily organs that come into direct contact with organic chemicals, such as THMs, in drinking water.

This study was done after the government reported a much higher cancer incidence in the immediate New Orleans area than anywhere else in Louisiana. The Bayou State has sixty-four parishes, but only eleven parishes—about one million persons, all in the New Orleans area—drink water from the Mississippi River. There is truth, then, to a longtime Louisiana saying that along the Mississippi's chemical corridor the rich buy bottled water and the poor get cancer.

In Ohio, researchers found that cancers of the stomach and bladder were significantly more common among persons whose water supplies were from surface sources—in this case, the Ohio River—with higher amounts of organic chemicals such as THMs.

Another seven-state study, conducted by a researcher from the University of North Carolina, took place in the Ohio River Valley. It covered portions of Illinois, Indiana, Kentucky, Ohio, Pennsylvania, Tennessee, and West Virginia and involved nineteen million persons, roughly one-twelfth of the entire U.S. population. Once again, Hodgkin's disease and cancers of the bladder, esophagus, rectum, breast, and larynx occurred in significantly higher numbers among persons whose water was from chlorinated surface sources.

In the upstate New York counties of Erie, Schenectady, and Rensselaer, drinking chlorinated water has been linked with increased incidences of cancer of the bladder, gastrointestinal tract, kidney, large intestine, liver, pancreas, stomach, and urinary tract.

An Illinois study found that women who drank chlorinated water had an increased incidence of gastrointestinal, large intestine, and urinary tract cancers.

In Wisconsin, colon and brain cancers have been linked with chlorinated water supplies. Other researchers have specifically linked high levels of chloroform—the most common substance in the THM family—with an increase in bladder and rectum cancer. And a Florida study of women drinking water known to have THMs found that they had twice as much chloroform in their blood as women who drank nonchlorinated water.

Many studies, conducted by many different research teams using many different methods, have all come to the same conclusion. That should make it quite evident that these common contaminants in water *do* cause cancer. The higher your exposure to these contaminants in water the higher your risk of contracting cancer.

How high is the risk? If your water supply has as much chloroform (one of the THMs) as is allowed by government safety standards (100 parts per billion) and you drink a normal amount of tap water—six or seven glasses a day—your chances of contracting cancer as a result of this contamination would be about one to four in ten thousand, according to EPA experts. Many water systems, such as Washington, D.C.'s, do have THM levels that approach this standard or exceed it. And chloroform is only one of the many cancer-causing THMs that might be in your drinking water!

Because chlorination of water has prevented countless epidemics of waterborne disease, we do not want to give it up unless we have adequate, safer substitutions. One is ozonation, which has been shown to be highly effective in killing bacteria. This method works well because ozone is a powerful oxidant that can actually strip electrons from an organic compound, making it an effective disinfectant. Ozonation has been used throughout Europe and in Paris to treat water from the Seine, but it has been used only infrequently thus far in the United States.

Unfortunately, ozonation has its own set of problems. As with food irradiation, new and unique chemicals are formed during the ozonation process. Ozonation is a powerful oxidizing process that, at times, forms more potent chemicals than present originally. In addition, there is no residual disinfection potential that remains to kill any bacteria that may be in the pipes or infiltrate the water distribution system.

For your own safety, you can begin by writing your supplier to ask for information on THM levels in your water. (Later in this chapter I have included a sample letter asking for this and other information.) Generally, water should have no more than ten parts per billion THMs; the federal standard is set at one hundred parts per billion but soon may be reduced to fifty and should be halved again. You can also drink bottled or filtered water. A high-quality water filter, whether it is portable, fitted underneath the sink, or attached to the faucet, will reduce the THM level in your drinking water to virtually nondetectable concentrations.

Industrial Pollution

In cities and towns across America—places like Richton Park, Illinois; Pecos, Texas; and San Gabriel, California—people drink tap water laced with industrial chemicals. Vinyl chloride, a known human carcinogen, has been found in a drinking well in South Chicago Heights. PCBs poisoned drinking water wells in Wauconda, Illinois. Wells in Burbank, near Los Angeles, had to be shut down after industrial wastes contaminated groundwater. At Fort Sam Houston in San Antonio, men and women have drunk from a water supply tainted with the industrial pollutant tetrahydrofuran, which can cause nausea, dizziness, headaches, dry throat, and dermatitis.

I do not believe anyone should regularly drink water with any industrial pollutants, even if levels are minuscule. Most people will not be affected by low-level doses of a single chemical carcinogen. But some will be affected and many will suffer low-level effects that are difficult to measure epidemiologically. Still others will be strongly sickened. I say let us protect everyone; each of us is different, and some people—those with weakened immunity, for example—may be sickened by an industrial chemical at a concentration that might not bother others.

Many of the industrial pollutants present in our drinking water are solvents belonging to a family of chemicals known as volatile organic chemicals (VOCs). Solvents are liquid chemicals capable of dissolving or dispersing other chemical substances. They are widely used in industry to ensure smooth, even delivery of chemical mixtures, as well as for cleaning and degreasing metals. Exposure to VOCs can cause significant depression of the central nervous system. Some of the neurobehavioral symptoms of low-level solvent or VOC poisoning include memory loss, decreased ability to solve problems, decreased concentration, impaired dexterity and hand-eye coordination, altered reaction time, reduced psychomotor functions, and altered personality or mood. Exposure to solvents can alter the immune system and even cause kidney damage. Experts believe low-level exposure to industrial solvents is making a significant contribution to rising cancer incidence in this country.

Volatile organic chemicals quickly become airborne when exposed to air. If you live in an area where tap water is contaminated with VOCs, you inhale VOCs and absorb them through your skin whenever you shower, bathe, use your dishwasher or washing machine, flush your toilet, or boil water. In fact, public health officials assert that inhalation of these pollutants in tap water and, to some extent, even skin absorption are routes of significant exposure. While taking a fifteen- to thirty-minute shower you could inhale double the quantity of VOCs that you get from drinking a day's supply of water.

In surface water, VOCs quickly decrease in concentration as they escape in the form of gases into the atmosphere. But in groundwater, which about half of all Americans drink, VOCs remain virtually undisturbed and can be found at high concentrations. Health effects, of course, depend on the size of the dose. And some levels that the government says are safe are actually safe only for most people. A woman in Los Angeles was poisoned by low-level solvent contamination of her drinking water, even though the chemical concentrations were within legal limits. She had contracted mononucleosis when she was twenty-one; the disease had compromised her immune system, the added stress of the contaminants in her bloodstream was enough to break down her immunity, and she was constantly sick with fatigue, elevated temperatures, and chronic low-grade infections. She eventually developed Epstein-Barr syndrome with full-blown symptoms.

One major cause of our water pollution is that many businesses violate the clean-water ordinances that are meant to protect us from industrial pollution. Much contamination in urban areas stems from leaking underground storage tanks filled with fuel and chemical solvents. Nationwide, the EPA has reported, only just over half of some 30,000 potential company polluters had filed toxic dumping reports by the July 1988 deadline.

In Arizona, the number of groundwater sites poisoned by VOCs dramatically increased between 1983 and 1986, rising from seventeen to thirty. Ten of those thirty sites were drinking-water wells. Officials have said they have no idea how badly the shallow groundwater has been polluted by dangerous chemicals from old leaking storage tanks that were buried and forgotten years ago. In the eighteen months between January 1987 and June 1988, nearly sixty companies violated the Phoenix dumping ordinance five hundred times. Yet only one company was ever closed by the city for repeated toxic dumping. I believe these polluting corporate criminals belong in a county jail or a state prison in the same cells with drug dealers, for both deal poison to the citizens of our nation's cities.

In California, fewer than 60 percent of the 142,000 tanks covered by state law had been tested for leaks three years after a state deadline for such tests. At most, 42 percent of buried tanks meet state and local laws for permanent leak monitoring.

In California's sprawling Riverside County, of 4,000 tanks only 700 were monitored—and 400 of them were leaking.

In Contra Costa County, in the San Francisco Bay area, more than 10 percent of underground tanks leak. None has been cleaned up. In Alameda County, in the Bay area, 6,043 underground tanks were examined, and 733 of them leaked.

These are just a few examples of the scofflaw attitude that is choking this nation's freshwater resources and threatening our health. I have seen hundreds of reports on the devastation of our freshwater lakes, rivers, and underground seas. That devastation is not nearly complete. But it will be completed in the time it takes for slow-moving plumes of industrial solvents, leaking from underground tanks, to reach aquifers that supply this nation with drinking water. And our nationwide plume of industrial pollution is certainly spreading. In one survey of drinking water served in New York, Philadelphia, Cincinnati, Seattle, and Miami as well as Terrebonne Parish, Louisiana; Tucson, Arizona; Grand Forks, North Dakota; Ottumwa, Iowa; and Lawrence, Massachusetts, 129 toxins were found, including 22 potential carcinogens.

The sickness caused by industrial chemicals is also widespread. Kidney diseases plagued the New Jersey town of Jackson. A nine-month-old baby died of kidney cancer, and one of her father's kidneys atrophied. Mothers reported their children suffered for weeks with rashes, attacks of dizziness, and severe headaches. And only after they were sickened did residents learn that nearly forty toxic chemicals had leached into the town's water from a toxic landfill. Public officials had blandly assured the anxious citizens that nothing was wrong with their drinking water.

We've got a lot of public officials telling innocent American citizens that their poisoned water is all right to drink. Meanwhile, babies are born with birth defects, children develop cancer and leukemia, and adults become sickened with cancer and ill with constant headaches and flu symptoms. But despite government assurances that America's water is safe to drink, our own scientists say they have no idea how badly the nation's groundwater has been poisoned by dangerous chemicals that leach from waste sites and leak from decaying underground tanks. No one knows how widespread the problem has become or how long it may be until the shallow contamination seeps into the deeper groundwater pools, where it could create a major threat to public health.

In 1979 abandoned toxic waste dumps were discovered during excavation for a new industrial park in the city of Woburn, Massachusetts. In these dumps were industrial chemicals used in the manufacture of pesticides, paper, explosives, and glue. This discovery led to another discovery —that a variety of common and deadly industrial pollutants from these and other industries had leached into two of the town's wells.

Angered and outraged, concerned citizens organized. They formed FACE (For A Cleaner Environment) and began to investigate; their findings proved quite disturbing. More than twenty children in the city had contracted leukemia—and many had died—in the 1970s and 1980s. Six of those children lived in one six-block area. The tainted wells were shut down in 1979, but the state investigators, as usual, announced that this increased leukemia incidence was in no way linked with the town's water.

Anne Anderson of Woburn undertook a crusade to prove that the children had contracted leukemia from drinking water contaminated with hazardous chemical wastes. The victims included her twelve-year-old son, Jimmy, who died in 1981. Anderson testified before the U.S. Senate in 1984 and told the lawmakers, "We do not think that what has happened in Woburn happened by chance. While we carried our children in our wombs, nursed them, and weaned them to drink from a cup, we unknowingly offered them the poisons that their bodies could not withstand. I won't, nor should I be expected to, quietly accept it."

Another Woburn child who succumbed to leukemia in 1983 was nine-year-old Robbie Robbins. Robbie's mother, thirty-nine-year-old Donna Robbins, said that her son had been chronically ill with bronchitis, ear infections, strep throat, and skin rashes since he was eight months old. Those symptoms were compounded by severe pains that began in his groin when he was four years old. The leukemia was diagnosed shortly afterward. Donna Robbins recalls feeling compelled to boil the yellowish, foul-smelling water that poured from the tap before she gave it to Robbie as an infant.

Today Donna Robbins says she was extremely naive in the early months of Robbie's illness about the intentions of the companies involved and the government agencies. "I'd like to tell people in this country a couple of things," she says. "First, to keep a watchful eye on their neighbors' health because it could be related to them. Then I'd say, don't be so naive. It's time for Americans everywhere to wake up and begin protecting themselves, to find the sources of pollution and go after those responsible. It's the only way to stop it. The government agencies aren't going to protect you."

In 1984, Harvard researchers came to Woburn and conducted a thorough study that included more than five thousand interviews. The Harvard research team found that the tainted water was linked with childhood leukemia, kidney disease, prenatal deaths, and several other illnesses. Pregnant women were at increased risk for giving birth to children with eye and ear birth defects.

Since the wells were shut down, incidences of illness and birth defects have returned to normal patterns. Indeed, the residents in one area of town, who had been drinking well water with the highest pollution concentrations, experienced none of the birth defects or miscarriages previously associated with the tainted wells, once they switched to an untainted water supply.

In the community of Brookhurst, Wyoming, pollution from an oil refinery led to severe contamination of the neighborhood groundwater. Linda Burkhart and her family moved to the community and soon discovered that the water they drew from their tap was smelly, and she began to develop severe headaches. At the nearby oil refinery were open, reeking pits of toxic waste, cluttered with dead birds. After forming the Brookhurst Citizens Committee and calling for well testing, Burkhart was met by representatives of the EPA, who assured Burkhart and her group that the wells were free from pollution. The citizens committee insisted on deciding which wells the government should test. Not surprisingly, all the wells tested were found to be contaminated. Now citizens of Brookhurst are working on a fair agreement from the company that did the polluting to purchase the polluted land so that they can move.

What can you do about industrial pollution? First, use common sense. Do you know where the water in your tap comes from? Is it groundwater or from a river? What do you know about the purity of your source? Are there manufacturing plants in the vicinity of your water supply? Knowing these basic facts can help you decide whether to test for industrial pollutants in your water.

Lead Contamination

Lead makes no contribution at all to human health, but it has a long history of causing sickness. Lead was used by the Roman ruling class in cooking vessels, eating utensils, wine and beverage containers, and water pipes. Lead causes infertility, loss of mental acuity, and hypertension. These lead-induced afflictions of Roman nobility probably were instrumental in Rome's eventual downfall. And the historian Ramazzini noted in 1740 that "grievous maladies" afflicted persons who had to grind lead or breathe the vapor of molten lead used to glaze pots. "First their hands become palsied, then they become paralytic, splenetic, lethargic, cachectic and toothless, so that one rarely sees a potter whose face is not cadaverous and the color of lead."

Lead is used today in storage batteries, as a gasoline additive, and in plumbing and solder. It is found in nature, and sometimes appears in water supplies at very low levels.

Lead is probably a human carcinogen and a cancer promoter. Its noncancer effects include lowered physical and mental development capacity for growing children, slowed nerve conduction velocity in adults, a loss of hearing, high blood pressure, and stroke. Lead can have a tremendous effect on your blood pressure. One epidemiological study in an area of Scotland where water lead levels were high noted a significant association in males between high serum lead levels and high blood pressure. Another study in 1984 found a direct and significant relationship between lead and blood pressure for men and women, white and black, young and old. The relationship was found in people whose blood levels ranged from four to thirty parts per billion of lead.

Lead affects male fertility as well. Mildly elevated lead concentration in the bloodstream has resulted in male gonadal impairment.

The average blood lead level today in children is six to eight parts per billion. Many children have blood lead level concentrations as high as ten to sixteen parts per billion. And some children have levels as high as twenty to twenty-five parts per billion. The U.S. Centers for Disease Control has set twenty-five parts per billion of lead in blood as an intervention level for therapy. But that level is far too high. Recent reports indicate lead is associated with increased blood pressure at levels as low as four to eight parts per billion. Permanent neurological effects—in terms of IQ loss and a decrease in nerve conduction velocity, which translates into an overall permanently diminished capacity for response to stimuli—also occur at low-level exposures. Even at the low levels found frequently in drinking water, lead can diminish the intelligence of any developing child. There appears to be no threshold for low-level lead poisoning.

Young children and fetuses are most susceptible to lead's effects. Excess lead in children can interfere with a wide variety of body processes including neurologic functions, mental development, formation of red blood cells, vitamin D metabolism, growth, and hearing. Excessive exposure in pregnant women also causes reduced gestation time and birth weight for fetuses.

Women who are pregnant and women who will have children must stay away from lead-tainted drinking water. In one 1974 study, published in the *American Journal of Obstetrics Gynecology,* the levels of lead in the blood of newborns upon birth were found to be already the same level as their mothers. The placental barrier is, in fact, no barrier. Lead has been known to have caused stillbirths and miscarriages in women working in the lead trades as early as the late nineteenth century.

Prenatal exposure to lead may result in damage to the brain. In one study, researchers identified seventy-seven retarded children and seventy-seven normal children who were matched for age, sex, and geography. Eleven of the retarded came from homes where their mothers drank water with a first-flush lead concentration that exceeded 800 parts per billion. No normal children came from such homes.

Lead's effect on the body is complex, and identifying blood lead levels at which there are no effects is difficult. Lead in drinking water is not an acute toxicity issue. It is the chronic, low-level exposure across the general population that makes it much more dangerous. A lot of little exposures end up being more than additive; they are multiplicative and compound.

Any well-done cost-benefit analysis would show that the benefits of getting lead out of our water more than offset the cost. There is no safe level of lead in the blood, and there is no tolerable level of lead in our tap water. The current government standard permits 50 parts per billion of lead in drinking water. However, in light of new data that suggest the effects of lead are adverse in the range of 4 to 15 ppb and above in blood, the EPA has considered tightening this standard to 7.5 parts per billion. EPA scientists believe that any lead is unacceptable, because there is no level that has been found that does not cause adverse effects. However, an MCL set at 5 parts per billion would cost $21 billion to implement while a standard of 7.5 parts per billion would cost only $5 billion. Estimates are that 15 to 20 percent of homes nationwide have drinking water lead levels above 20 ppb!

While every cut in lead is an improvement, a standard of 7.5 ppb will not be a great enough reduction to achieve a truly safe level of lead in our bodies. A concentration of 1 to 5 parts per billion lead in your tap water can contribute to significantly raising your blood lead level to the upper range of normalcy and bring your body levels to dangerous concentration. And, as I mentioned earlier, even low-level exposure to lead can diminish the intelligence of developing children.

We have seen in recent years that cutting lead in motor fuel has produced an across-the-board reduction of our nation's body-lead concentrations. This, we know, will make a serious contribution to overall improved health and mental capacity of Americans. The next significant reduction Americans must make is in drinking water. Write your legislators about this! We must have the proposed reduction to 7.5 ppb lead in water adopted, and then improved on! There is no excuse for dumping lead in our children's bodies. After all, our children are our future, and we must all act to make our government act on this subject. On a personal scale we must protect ourselves against lead contamination.

You can begin by finding out how much lead is in your water supply. Your supplier is required to tell you this. Older cities may still be using lead pipes in public water systems built before the 1930s. Any city with corrosive water—particularly in northeastern states such as Massachusetts and Pennsylvania where acid rain is a problem—could be delivering lead-tainted water. But government will test water only up to the point of delivery to your home. Once water flows through your home's plumbing, you are on your own. *And most lead exposures result from home plumbing.* So you have to do your own testing. You have to find out whether your plumbing is adding too much lead to your tap water. In the Personal Action Guide I recommend water-testing firms and explain how to contact them. Fortunately, having your water tested costs only about $35.00.

Ask your plumber to tell you what kind of solder was used in your system. The use of lead solder and copper plumbing should be a red warning flag. The combination of lead solder and copper pipes often produces a chemical reaction with an electrical activity level that causes copper to stay in place while the lead leaches out of the solder.

High-risk houses include old homes with plumbing installed before the 1930s, in the days when lead pipes and connectors were used. You should find out whether lead solder, lead service lines, lead plumbing, or any other lead materials were used in your distribution systems.

How to tell if your plumbing contains lead? Bang your plumbing with a pipe. If you hear a "thunk" rather than a "clang," it's probably lead, say experts from the Citizen's Clearinghouse for Hazardous Waste, in Arlington, Virginia. Color and texture are also signs. Lead is a soft dull gray metal that you can scratch with your fingernail, note the CCHW experts.

Some relatively new homes may also present problems, as new plumbing—including copper pipes with lead solder—can introduce lead to your water. New lead solders can release significant levels of lead into drinking water for up to five years, although they release less lead as they age and a hard mineral coating is formed on the inside of the pipe.

On the other hand, *some* older apartments and homes in areas where hard water is delivered may be safe. The dissolved minerals found in high concentrations in hard water form a physical barrier between water and plumbing materials. It takes about five years for enough dissolved materials to build up on pipes to form a protective shield. Until then your drinking water might have extremely high levels of lead.

If you find high levels of lead in your water, you can use reverse-osmosis and ion-exchange water filter systems to remove lead from your drinking water. I recommend installing an activated carbon/reverse osmosis water filter if you have children and if you find any lead at all in your water. If you have no children and are confident you will not have any, I recommend filtration for water-lead levels above two parts per billion.

Parents, be careful of water dispensers in public schools and day care centers. They can contribute unacceptably high amounts of lead. Water coolers may have higher lead levels because they may have lead-lined holding tanks and because they hold water a long time to cool it and because nobody flushes a water cooler. Your child could be drinking lead every day in school. See the Personal Action Guide for the telephone number and address of WaterTest Corp. of New Hampshire, which offers free lead tests for drinking water in schools and day care centers.

Use these safe-drinking-water tips to reduce your exposure to lead in drinking water.

• Do not use tap water first thing in the morning for drinking or making coffee. Water that sits in your pipes accumulates lead if there is any lead in your pipes. Often the first flush is the most poisoned. Use first-flush water for nonconsumptive purposes such as washing dishes or watering plants. Especially avoid giving first-draw water to children.

Most people don't know how significantly lead-contaminated first flush water is. An example: one New York City family concerned with the lead in their drinking water because of their newborn baby had their tap water tested for lead. The first flush test that they performed contained eight parts per billion lead. But when they tested tap water from late in the day, after running the water for a while, they found it contained no lead. Now this family knows firsthand how important it is to let water run a few minutes—especially after the supply water has been unused and left sitting several hours—before pouring a glass of water or preparing their baby's formula. Use first flush water for testing.

▪ After you do dishes at night, fill a bottle and put it on the counter. Leave it uncovered. That will be your purest water, and any VOCs in that water also will volatize and disperse in the ambient air, leaving the water even purer. Use this water for making coffee or juice in the morning instead of first-flush water.

▪ Never use hot water from the tap for baby formula because hot water has higher lead concentrations. When cooking for a baby, use cold water, after your system is flushed, heated on the stove.

▪ Structures built before 1930 may have service connectors made of lead. If you live in such a building or home, let the water run for two to five minutes or until the temperature of the water changes to flush service connectors.

Lead service connectors are common even now. In Washington, D.C., until 1987 and similarly in Chicago until 1988, most service connections were made from lead.

Radiation

Radiation is one of the most potent poisons in water. Its most serious effects include birth defects and cancer. Where possible, we should reduce exposure to radiation. And we *can* reduce our radiation exposure due to drinking water.

Naturally occurring forms of radiation, including uranium, radium, and radon, are found in drinking water supplies scattered across the country. Radium collects in the bones and damages the immune system. One expert has concluded that radium and its minor contaminants cause 17,000 to 51,000 cancer deaths a year in the United States. That is roughly 3 to 10 percent of all cancer deaths. As much as 20 percent of all childhood cancer may be the result of natural radiation, while medical X rays may account for another 6 or 7 percent of childhood cancer deaths. Naturally occurring radiation in drinking water in the form of radium, radon, or uranium is something to be concerned with. The federal standard for maximum radium levels in water is 5 picocuries per liter (abbreviated 5 pCi/L). I feel that a level of no more than 1 pCi/L is preferable. The 5 pCi/L level presents a risk experts have calculated as producing as many as forty excess cancers in one million persons from drinking normal amounts of radium-tainted water.

In New York State, radium in drinking water is one of the most important causes of birth defects. Florida has a major problem with radiation in its drinking water. The central part of the state is a major source of chemical (phosphate) fertilizer. In the process of extracting the phosphates, inevitable and natural by-products include radioactive compounds. These compounds are concentrated and then subsequently released into the groundwater. Not surprisingly, in Florida, elevated radium in drinking water has been shown to raise rates of leukemia and myeloid leukemia. In Iowa, an increased rate of cancers of the lung and bladder among males and cancer of the breast and lung among females was found in towns where radium levels in the water supply exceeded 5 pCi/L. As much as 10 percent of the population in Iowa could be affected. One can conclude that 1.6 to 3.1 percent of all cancer deaths in Iowa might be attributed to radium in the drinking water. In other words, 100 to 200 persons a year in Iowa might get cancer as a result of radium in drinking water. In South Dakota, radium in drinking water could be the cause of about one hundred childhood cancer cases a year. A study of North Carolina and Maine residents' drinking water with high radium concentrations found childhood leukemia rates that were nearly twice the normal rate. In view of accumulated evidence pointing to severe problems with this naturally occurring bone poison, it is important that we implement methods of self-protection.

You can tell sometimes by your natural surroundings if your water is at risk for radium contamination. Areas with granite rock outcroppings often have high radiation. Groundwater in these areas becomes more radiated than surface water, according to the New York State radium study. Women who drank from streams and lakes had fewer birth defects than women who got water from wells and springs.

Radon is another form of radioactivity found in drinking water, especially in areas in Maine, New Hampshire, Vermont, and Massachusetts. Radon is the breakdown product of radium. (Radium is itself the breakdown product of uranium.) Radon is found as a gas in homes, particularly in New Jersey, New York, and Pennsylvania. In its gaseous form, radon may cause 10,000 to 30,000 lung cancer deaths annually. In drinking water, radon may cause as many as 600 deaths nationally annually. Radon levels in your drinking water should not exceed 10 pCi/L. One method for removing radon gas from your water supply is to install an aeration unit that vents to the outside atmosphere before the water enters the home. I'll discuss atmospheric radon in Chapter 15: The Nontoxic Home.

Fortunately, you can remove uranium, radium, and radon from your drinking water by using filters. Reverse-osmosis systems will remove uranium and radium. Activated carbon filtration will remove radon. So by following the procedures for testing your water outlined later in this chapter and by installing the correct kind of water filter if there is radiation in your water, you can eliminate this particular toxic nightmare from your life.

Nitrate and Pesticide Contamination

Much of rural America's water is polluted with nitrates, which get into groundwater at dangerous levels from synthetic fertilizer. Nitrates can cause birth defects, and they are extremely toxic to babies. Nitrates can also cause adult cancer.

And, of course, pesticides used in agriculture poison our water. Large quantities of pesticides and nitrates are washed away by rain after they are applied to a crop or the soil. They end up in surface water supplies, or they seep down into groundwater. In the Little Switzerland region of northwest Iowa, wells could once be sunk to only 50 feet to tap a good water source. Today dairy farmers there have to go down 200 feet to find water free from nitrates, a result of the use of synthetic fertilizers. In rural California the pesticide DBCP has been found 400 feet down, in some of the deepest groundwater.

As many as 19 million Americans today are estimated to drink from private wells that may be contaminated by nitrates, pesticides, or both. Having water tested for nitrates is inexpensive—around thirty dollars—and can be done by laboratories listed in the Personal Action Guide. You can also do a home test for nitrates with a nitrate test strip; such strips allow you to constantly monitor your water supply as often as you would like. See the Personal Action Guide for more information. Ion-exchange and reverse-osmosis water filters will remove nitrates.

Pesticides taint water supplies across the nation, especially the farm states. Iowa is typical of agricultural states: in a 1988 study of Iowa wells, one or more pesticides were detected in 33 percent of the wells studied. The herbicide atrazine, which the EPA has recently learned may be a human carcinogen, was most commonly found, then alachlor, a probable human carcinogen, and 2,4-D, one of the chemicals for which there is a solid association between malignancy and pesticides in humans; particularly, according to a study conducted by researchers at the National Cancer Institute and published in the *Journal of the American Medical Association,*

2,4-D is among the herbicides associated with increased rates of non-Hodgkin's lymphoma among Kansas wheat farmers.

Alachlor is dangerous, too. It is one of the most potent pesticide carcinogens yet tested. It is also the most widely used herbicide in the United States. Every dose tested produced cancers in experimental animals. Most doses caused cancers in 100 percent of the animals. In one study, cancers were produced in three months or less in the animals. This pesticide is found in the drinking water supplies of every state in the union except Nevada and Alaska. It runs off into the surface waters and leaches into the groundwater. Standard water treatment does not remove it well. Yet the EPA has done precious little to cancel or ban this known and very dangerous chemical since it became aware of its carcinogenic potential in 1986.

Multiple pesticides in drinking water were frequently detected in the Iowa study. The atrazine lifetime health advisory level is 3 ppb. The median amount in the wells was .38 ppb, but some wells had atrazine at levels as high as 42 ppb. Nobody knows for sure how many years people drank these pesticides before they were detected. The problem in Iowa is not confined to rural areas. As many as seven pesticides pollute Iowa City's tap water at different times of the year.

Minnesota faces similar problems. One-third of five hundred wells tested in Minnesota contain pesticides. And in potato-growing regions of Wisconsin, the deadly pesticide aldicarb has been found in one-fourth of the wells tested. Unfortunately, we now know that the immune systems of women drinking aldicarb-tainted water may be significantly altered at supposedly safe levels. The improper handling of pesticides has resulted in eight sites in Wisconsin that have been identified as having polluted groundwater.

Along the eastern megalopolis, in heavily populated Suffolk and Nassau counties on Long Island, the upper glacial aquifer providing water to the region has been significantly contaminated with a number of volatile organic compounds as well as pesticides such as aldicarb. So bad is the pollution that drinking water must be trucked to parts of Long Island. Pesticides have been found in groundwater in Maine, Massachusetts, Rhode Island, Connecticut, New York, and Pennsylvania.

In California the pesticide 1,2-dibromo-3-chloropropane, known as DBCP, was used for years as a soil fumigant to control pests that afflicted fruit and vegetable crops. In the 1980s, DBCP was found to have become a widespread contaminant affecting the water supplies for one million Californians. Even the water supply to Disneyland, in Orange County, was contaminated by DBCP. In heavily agricultural Fresno County, 37 percent of wells tested had DBCP traces. In California alone DBCP has been discovered in 2,500 private and public drinking and irrigation wells. The manufacture of DBCP caused widespread sterility among males who produced the chemical, and its uses were severely restricted in 1979.

No one can predict for certain the long-term consequences of childhood exposures to DBCP. But researchers have discovered an excess amount of stomach cancer and leukemia among persons with traces of DBCP in their drinking water. The diseases were most prevalent where the water was most contaminated. One family called Dr. Richard Jackson, who conducted the study that demonstrated the human cancer toll of DBCP, and told him that their two children were suffering from leukemia. The family's well level of DBCP was sixty times greater than the safe level approved by government. The family's question, of course, was whether their children's illnesses could be related to the water contamination. I wish theirs were an isolated incident. Throughout America's farmlands, cancer caused by pesticides is a fact of life.

As for DBCP, the problem is not likely to disappear soon; the half-life of DBCP is 141 years.

In the small town of Fowler, California—with a population of only 3,000 —four children were afflicted with leukemia, a number far above normal. "We talked to some people about it, and pretty soon everyone in town wanted to know the answer: why did Fowler have so many children dying of leukemia?" Patricia Shepherd wrote in her journal. Patricia's daughter, Jennifer, was one of those afflicted. The Shepherds became convinced that pesticides such as DBCP had leached from the farm fields surrounding the town into the wells that provided the town's water supply.

The Shepherd family fought publicly to have the wells closed. But the town turned against them after state health officials flew in from Sacramento for a town meeting. One of these officials poured a glass of water from the Fowler water supply and, in front of the townspeople, drank the water. He licked his lips and told the people of the town they had nothing to worry about.

The townspeople of Fowler ridiculed the Shepherds after this humiliation. Dan Shepherd, a barber, lost much of his business. As he recalled in his journal, "I would stand in the door of my shop and watch all my old customers go in and out of the barbershop down the street. I had known some of them eighteen years. The pressure was on them to quit coming to my shop. I was very hurt. I felt we were fighting for their children and here they had gone and turned their backs on me. I knew we were being forced out of town." Eventually threats were made against Dan's life, for the people of Fowler wanted their town to enjoy economic growth, and if outsiders thought that the water was poisoned, nobody would come to live in the town.

In 1986, two years after their daughter was diagnosed with leukemia— and despite earlier assurances from state officials—the state of California announced that three of the town's five wells would be closed immediately. They had found traces of DBCP, another pesticide known as 1,2-dichloropropane, excessive levels of uranium, and even the industrial solvent perchloroethylene in the wells.

In the Midwest, most larger cities use shallow groundwater or surface water sources that routinely contain pesticide residues. What is the result of this low-level exposure? Is your child really suffering from a summer flu? Or could the real culprit be low-level chemical poisoning? We're beginning to learn that some chemicals are immune modulators. This means that they alter our immune systems, sometimes making us more susceptible to illness or acting as a warning that we already are ill. We're just learning to identify immune modulators, but the evidence we've uncovered already is quite disturbing. For example, we've learned that the pesticide aldicarb, which is legally used on potatoes, is an immune modulator. This pesticide contaminates wells throughout the country where it remains a relatively stable, persistent contaminant.

A critically noted study was conducted by government researchers in the Central Sands region of Wisconsin, where aldicarb has been widely used since 1980. More than 300 of 1,100 wells tested in the region have been found to have aldicarb residues ranging from 1 to 100 ppb. The study tested women exposed to aldicarb in their water (within government-set "safe" standards) and women who had not been exposed. In measures of T-cell subsets, the exposed and unexposed women differed significantly. T cells are white blood cells, the body's first line of defense against microbial invaders and other toxic substances.

In the case of the Wisconsin women, the aldicarb acted as a lymphocyte stimulant, resulting in an increase in the absolute number and percentage of T cells, which in some instances was outside the range of clinical normality, meaning that illness—even cancer or autoimmune diseases—could already be under way. Scientists simply are unsure of what these T-cell changes mean, but they are a warning. The researchers said this would be the first suggestion of T-cell changes in humans resulting from chronic exposure to an environmental contaminant. Because of the high water solubility of aldicarb and its presence in the drinking water of several states, the study's authors noted that the public health implications of continuing to expose large populations to it warrants careful review.

In a cautious and prudent response to this report, the Wisconsin Division of Health lowered its health advisory for aldicarb from 10 ppb to 1 ppb. Residents have been urged to stop drinking water with aldicarb at greater, than 1 ppb. I would urge residents—especially women who are pregnant —to avoid drinking untreated water with any amount of aldicarb, for even Wisconsin's prudent response may not be cautious enough to protect each individual's health.

Despite pronouncements from government and industry officials that our groundwater is safe, the Wisconsin study and many others demonstrate that groundwater contamination can pose the danger of chronic low-level nervous system poisoning and weakened immunity to cancer. The irony is clear: the new breed of organophosphate and carbamate pesticides is no safer for us or for the environment than were the old chlorinated hydrocarbon spray-gang dinosaurs (such as DDT and dieldrin) of our past. We've simply switched from one chemical fix to another. The fat-soluble chlorinated hydrocarbon pesticides of the 1960s are diminishing very slowly from our soil and water, but the newer water-soluble carbamate and organophosphate pesticides are appearing far too frequently in our drinking water. And the EPA is not doing well at assessing the risk of multiple exposures to the pesticides that are now typically found in our water. Theories about cumulative and synergistic toxin exposures are fairly new to the agency, and the EPA has not given top priority to investigating the pressing question of what happens to people who are exposed repeatedly not to just one carcinogen but to several.

In this ominous setting, the nation as of 1990 has developed no uniform policy or strategy for protecting our most precious resource. Various federal laws, such as the Safe Drinking Water Act, apply to groundwater pollution, and each state has regulatory agencies to monitor its water, but there is no integrated federal policy or effort to prevent such contamination. A recent survey of the National Conference of State Legislatures found that only twenty-four states have groundwater-protection statutes.

Water Testing

You may be among the fortunate millions whose tap delivers pure, safe, tasty water to your home. But the only way to be sure of this is to check for yourself.

You must take responsibility for the purity of your water. You can't trust government to ensure that your water supply is safe. The government has a way of valuing money above health concerns.

Here is what you can do: have your water tested; if the test shows pesticides, pollutants, radiation, or other dangers, you should invest in a good water filter system, or you can turn to bottled water.

Try to learn what you can about your water supply, so you will be aware of potential problems. What does your water look and taste like? Pollution sometimes provides perceptible clues. For example, water that is oily or that has a perfumed or chemical taste may well be polluted with industrial chemicals. Does your water have an oil or gas smell? Perhaps your water source is polluted with gasoline or is being polluted by a leaking underground fuel tank. Does your water smell like rotten eggs? The cause of such smells may be sewage intermingling with your water source and the presence of hydrogen sulfide, an extremely hazardous substance that, in low concentrations, can cause headaches, dizziness, and nausea and, at high concentrations, may inhibit cellular respiration, leading to coma and even death. A metallic taste may indicate high levels of iron or manganese. A salty, brackish taste could indicate that contaminants from road salting have intruded into your water supply. Very cloudy water could indicate too much organic matter or inadequate purification of water supplies by the public treatment plant before they reach the public. You should be concerned about the presence of carcinogenic THM compounds that form when chlorine interacts with organic matter. Blue-green stains on your sink and porcelain fixtures could result from corrosive water reacting with brass and copper fittings and pipes, bringing lead, brass, and copper into your tap water. If your fixtures or laundry turn black, that could mean you have too much manganese.

If you have a stainless-steel sink that has turned black or become pitted, there could be too much chloride in your water. Does your water smell like chlorine? The treatment plant could be adding excessive amounts of chlorine compounds to your water supply. Foamy water or water that smells like detergent could be the result of septic tank discharges polluting the water supply. Does your pot turn black when you brew tea? Does a thin film of grease form on your coffee? How does the water feel? After showering, do you break out in skin rashes? Can you taste anything faintly like gasoline or solvents? Does your clothing come out of the washer with tiny holes? If you answered yes to any of these questions, your drinking water and bathwater may well be polluted. Unfortunately, however, some of the most dangerous industrial pollutants and pesticides cannot be seen, smelled, nor tasted.

The addition of fluoride to water supplies has recently become a cause for concern. Many water systems add fluoride to protect customers' teeth. But the more that scientists learn about fluoride's biological properties, the more concern they express about the addition of fluoride to drinking water and about naturally occurring fluoride in some regional drinking water supplies. The National Toxicology Program announced in 1989 that experimental animals given fluoridated water experienced significantly higher rates of cancer of the mouth and bone growths that did not appear to be cancerous. Other animals in the study developed malignant bone tumors. The fluoride levels were high, and a broad community of scientific experts has not fully interpreted the study's results for its human implications. But the conclusion reached by one of the EPA's top scientific advisors is worth your consideration: because recent federal government tests have shown that fluoride appears to cause cancers at levels less than ten times the present maximum contaminant level, this would ordinarily require that all additions of fluoride to water supplies be suspended and treatment be instituted to remove naturally occurring fluoride. But the EPA has not yet reached a final determination and may not for years. Since these tests show fluoride may well be a carcinogen, you should undertake your own methods of self-protection and avoid drinking fluoridated water in addition to demanding that your locality remove it from its water supply if it is presently being added.

Your next step is to obtain a water report from your water supplier. I have already said that you should not trust what your public officials tell you about the chemicals in your water and their potential toxic effects. But you should nevertheless obtain a copy of your supplier's water-quality report for your records. Often the reports are quite accurate and quite revealing. They're interesting to examine and they might give you some valuable information about your water quality. In addition, you can compare this report with the report you obtain from a private laboratory. Do not be surprised if the information differs. Labs have different detection limits, and some private labs have much better detection capabilities than public laboratories. There are other ways to distort results. Your water supplier's report may say that your water contains only 1 ppb of some chemical. But that reassuring low number may be the result of statistical averaging. Public officials may average a pollutant's concentration over a period of time, or they may average one tainted well's toxic chemical concentrations with water from ten clean wells in another area. You may be drinking from the well with dirty water, but the report may imply that your water is relatively pure.

You can send the form letter that follows to your water supplier to make an official citizen's request for complete water quality reports. I have listed in the letter the tests you will want. You are entitled to this information by all applicable state and federal laws. All you have to do is reproduce the letter and send it to your water supplier.

If your water supplier's report shows nothing that concerns you—or even if it reveals impurities—you should still have your water tested by an outside laboratory. I've listed several reputable labs in the Personal Action Guide.

Compare the independent report with the official one. If *either* report shows any residues at all, even 1 ppb, of industrial pollutants, pesticides, or radiation, that should send up a red flag. Your water supplier may say the water is safe. But the ultimate responsibility for your safety rests in your hands, not the supplier's.

_____ 19__
(Date)

_____
(Your name)

_____
(Street address)

_____
(City, state)   (Zip code)

Dear Sir or Madam:

Please send me your most recent monitoring reports covering the last twelve months for water supplied to the above address.

These reports should specify weekly and/or monthly average measurements for:

Volatile organic chemicals and   Trihalomethanes and
    other industrial chemicals   chloroform
Bacteria   Metals
Total dissolved solids   Minerals (including fluoride)
Nitrates   Alkalinity
Pesticides
Radiation, radium, radon, and
    uranium

My request is supported by public right-to-know laws in this state. If you choose not to deliver this information, please notify me where I can get the information. I request a timely delivery of the above requested information.

                                    Sincerely,

NATIONAL
TESTING
LABORATORIES INC.
6151 Wilson Mills Road
Cleveland, OH 44143
(216) 449-2525

DRINKING WATER ANALYSIS RESULTS

NOTE: "*" indicates that maximum levels have been exceeded, or in the case of pH are either too high OR too low.
"nd" indicates that none of this contamination has been detected at or above our detection level.

Analysis performed	MCL (mg/l)	Detection Level	Level Detected
Microbiological:			
Total coliform (organism/100ml)	0	0.0	nd
Inorganic chemicals – metals:			
Arsenic	0.05	0.002	0.003
Barium	1.0	0.30	nd
Cadmium	0.01	0.002	nd
Chromium	0.05	0.004	nd
Copper	1.0	0.004	0.064
Iron	0.3	0.020	2.900*
Lead	0.05	0.002	nd
Manganese	0.05	0.004	0.044
Mercury	0.002	0.0002	nd
Nickel	0.15	0.02	nd
Selenium	0.01	0.002	nd
Silver	0.05	0.002	nd
Sodium	—	1.0	69.0
Zinc	5.0	0.004	0.230
Inorganic chemicals – other, and physical factors:			
Alkalinity (Total as $CaCO_3$)	—	2.0	90
Chloride	250	10.0	90
Fluoride	4.0	1.0	nd
Nitrate as N	10	0.5	nd
Nitrite	—	0.5	nd
Sulfate	250	10.0	100
Hardness (as $CaCO_3$)	—	20.0	200*
pH (Standard Units)	6.5–8.5	—	7.70
Total Dissolved Solids	500	20.0	500
Turbidity (Turbidity units)	1.0	0.1	35.0*
Organic chemicals – trihalomethanes:			
Bromoform	—	0.004	0.019
Bromodichloromethane	—	0.002	0.019
Chloroform	—	0.002	0.012
Dibromochloromethane	—	0.004	0.034
Total THMs (sum of four above)	0.1	0.002	0.084
Organic chemicals – volatiles			
Benzene	0.005	0.001	nd
Vinyl chloride	0.002	0.001	nd
Carbon tetrachloride	0.005	0.001	nd
1,2-Dichloroethane	0.005	0.001	nd
Trichloroethylene	0.005	0.001	nd
1,4-Dichlorobenzene	0.075	0.001	nd
1,1-Dichloroethylene	0.007	0.001	nd

Analysis performed	MCL (mg/l)	Detection Level	Level Detected
1,1,1-Trichloroethane	0.20	0.001	nd
Bromobenzene	—	0.002	nd
Bromomethane	—	0.002	nd
Chlorobenzene	—	0.001	nd
Chloroethane	—	0.002	nd
Chloroethylvinyl ether	—	0.002	nd
Chloromethane	—	0.002	nd
O-Chlorotoluene	—	0.001	nd
P-Chlorotoluene	—	0.001	nd
Dibromochloropropane (DBCP)	—	0.001	nd
Dibromomethane	—	0.002	nd
1,2-Dichlorobenzene	—	0.001	nd
1,3-Dichlorobenzene	—	0.001	nd
Dichlorodifluoromethane	—	0.002	nd
1,1-Dichlorethane	—	0.002	nd
Trans-1,2-Dichloroethylene	—	0.002	nd
Cis-1,2-Dichloroethylene	—	0.002	nd
Dichloromethane	—	0.002	nd
1,2-Dichloropropane	—	0.002	nd
Trans-1,3-Dichloropropane	—	0.002	nd
Cis-1,3-Dichloropropane	—	0.002	nd
2,2-Dichloropropane	—	0.002	nd
1,1-Dichloropropane	—	0.002	nd
1,3-Dichloropropane	—	0.002	nd
Ethylbenzene	—	0.001	nd
Ethylenedibromide (EDB)	—	0.001	nd
Styrene	—	0.001	nd
1,1,1,2-Tetrachloroethane	—	0.002	nd
1,1,2,2-Tetrachloroethane	—	0.002	nd
Tetrachloroethylene	—	0.002	nd
Trichlorobenzene(s)	—	0.002	nd
1,1,2-Trichloroethane	—	0.002	nd
Trichlorofluoromethane	—	0.002	nd
1,2,3-Trichloropropane	—	0.002	nd
Toluene	—	0.001	nd
Xylene	—	0.001	nd

**These test results are intended to be used for informational purposes only and may not be used for regulatory compliance.

WATER TEST RESULTS

These two pages depict a typical water-test analysis result sheet, which analyzes a consumer's drinking water for bacteria, metals, and inorganic and organic contaminants.

Results were presented in four columns. Column one tells the consumer what analysis was performed for a specific material. Column two shows the allowable levels of the material allowed by the Environmental Protection Agency or other federal agencies. Column three shows the detection level, which is the level at which the testing company's instruments and procedures are able to produce reliable results. Column four shows the level detected of the material, expressed in parts per million (ppm), which is also written in milligrams per liter (mg/L).

The term "nd" means that their analytical procedures did not find this material in your drinking water. An "*" or similar symbol indicates that the level detected exceeded the recommended allowable level set by the government.

This particular test cost $89, and it tells an interesting story about this home's drinking water. For example, the level of iron in this home's drinking water is almost ten times above the government's allowable standard. The level of turbidity was thirty-five times greater. Neither iron nor turbidity reflect direct health threats, though. On the bright side, the water had absolutely no detectable lead or industrial chemicals.

However, the level of chlorination by-products known as trihalomethanes (THMs) in the drinking water was a whopping 84 ppb, which is nearly equal to the allowable standard of 100 ppb. The chlorination of drinking water is associated with an elevated risk of cancer, and research repeatedly suggests that chlorination of drinking water is associated with breast cancer. A drinking water filtration system, including reverse osmosis and activated carbon filtration, would remove the THMs as well as decrease the turbidity and iron content of the water.

TABLE 2. ALLOWABLE CONTAMINANT LEVELS FOR TOXIC CHEMICALS IN DRINKING WATER

The Environmental Protection Agency has set allowable contaminant levels for toxic chemicals that are sometimes found in drinking water. They are listed below.

I feel that many of these levels represent compromises that endanger public health. However, if the government really protected our health by setting zero tolerance limits for these chemicals, many public water systems would be forced to close.

Some of these are official EPA Maximum Contaminant Levels, others are advisory levels set by the EPA for chemicals that have not gone through the process necessary for establishing MCLs.

Alachlor	.44 ppb
Arsenic	50 ppb
Aldicarb	10 ppb
Atrazine	3 ppb
Barium	1,500 ppb

Benzene	5 ppb
Bromacil	80 ppb
Cadmium	5 ppb
Carbon tetrachloride	.3 ppb
Copper	130 ppb
Cyanazine	9 ppb
Cyanide	154 ppb
2,4-D	100 ppb
Dacthal (DCPA)	3,500 ppb
DBCP	1 ppb
Dicamba	9 ppb
Dichlorobenzene	75 ppb
Dichloroethane	5 ppb
1,2-dichloroethane	5 ppb
1,1-dichloroethylene	7 ppb
1,3-dichloropropane	0.2 ppb
Dichloropropane	2 ppb
EDB (ethylene dibromide)	0.0005 ppb
Ethyl benzene	3,400 ppb
Fluoride	2,000–4,000 ppb
Lead	50 ppb
Lindane	4 ppb
Metolachlor	10 ppb
Metribuzin	175 ppb
Nitrate	10,000 ppb
Pentachlorophenol	21 ppb
PCE	3.5 ppb
Radium	5 pCi/L
Radon	10,000–20,000 pCi/L
Selenium	10 ppb
Simazine	35 ppb
Toluene	200 ppb
1,1,1-trichloroethane	200 ppb
Trichloroethylene	5 ppb
2,4,5-T (2,4,5-trichlorophenoxyacetic acid)	10 ppb
Trihalomethanes (THMs)	100 ppb
Vinyl chloride	2 ppb
Xylene	400 ppb

Compare the independent report with the official one. If *either* report shows any residues at all, even 1 ppb, of industrial pollutants, pesticides, or other toxins, that should send up a red flag. Your water supplier may say the water is safe. But the ultimate responsibility for your safety rests in your hands, not the supplier's.

You also should know that you can now purchase water test kits for lead and nitrates that give you your results at home. These are excellent for anybody but particularly home buyers, realtors, and persons drawing drinking water from private wells. See your Personal Action Guide.

You should definitely filter all the drinking and bathing water in your home or switch to bottled water if you know the water has high levels of THMs, radiation, industrial pollutants, nitrates, metals, certain minerals (such as fluoride or selenium), or pesticides. Filters and bottled water may be expensive, but the loss of your health or your child's and health care costs are even more expensive.

If you find out the water you drink is tainted with high levels of THMs or volatile industrial chemicals that can quickly become an airborne gaseous vapor, you need to take immediate steps to protect yourself. Increase ventilation by opening windows when you are washing, showering, or bathing. Take shorter showers and spend less time in steamy bathrooms. Ventilate the kitchen when you boil water. Children—particularly newborns and infants—should not be given long baths. Never allow children and infants to drink chemically tainted water regularly. Ventilate your laundry room. Open the kitchen windows when you use the dishwasher.

Welcome to American water.

Home Water Treatment

If you have industrial chemicals, pesticides, harmful bacteria, or other pollutants in your water supply, a water filter system will be a life-saving supplement to your home. But home filtering of your water should not take the place of your most important task—acting together with your neighbors to remove the source of the pollution.

There are many kinds of water filter systems. Some can be attached to the pipes under your sink, and others filter the entire water supply to your home. Still others are installed in pitchers for filtering drinking water only. Some filters use activated carbon; some use complex methods like reverse osmosis. The best combine various filtering methods. It's important to get the kind of system designed to filter out the particular pollutants your water contains.

Buying a water filter may seem like an intimidating task because there is so much you need to know. But a good filter is your best personal solution to water pollution. The technology is fantastic.

Some states have enacted legislation to restrict the sale of water filters, and with good reason. Some salespeople tell you all sorts of scary stories about water in general, but they do not know anything about your particular drinking water supply. Some salespeople offer to have your water tested and then return faked results. Others know nothing about water and just want to earn a few dollars on the side. Even a reputable company, Norelco, allowed a water filtration system to be sold for years that leached excessive amounts of methylene chloride into tap water.

One reason the choice of water filters is so vast is that there are many treatment methods. One method is not necessarily better than another, but filters do only what they are capable of doing and nothing more. An activated carbon filter may be great for pesticides, but it alone will not remove lead, which is best removed by reverse osmosis. Radiation is also removed by reverse osmosis, except in the case of radon, which is removed by activated carbon filters. Bacteria are killed by ultraviolet light. Sediment is strained out with a depth filter. Screen filters can remove bacteria such as *Giardia lamblia.* The best filtering systems combine several methods in a series of chambers and baffles through which the water runs.

Filters come in many shapes and sizes. Some countertop filters work just like a coffee filter. You pour the water into the filter, it trickles through, and presto! You get filtered water. Point-of-use filters are attached to the water faucet or installed under the sink. Don't bother with the tiny cheap ones that fit onto the faucet. They will eliminate rust and odors, but they are not very good at removing pesticides and other chemicals because they have a very small amount of activated carbon and drinking water remains in contact with it for only a short time. A filter works best when water remains in contact with the filter for a relatively long time. That requires a relatively large carbon block, which cannot fit on the end of a faucet.

Point-of-entry models will filter all the water in your home. If you have industrial pollutants in your water, you had better filter the water you use for showering and washing your face, because many industrial pollutants quickly become airborne gases that you could inhale or absorb through your skin. Such filter systems for the home run about $1,500 to $2,000.

The independent and respected National Sanitation Foundation of East Lansing, Michigan, certifies which home filter systems deliver on their claims, providing an NSF seal of approval only to systems that meet the foundation's high standards. I am very much in favor of this kind of legitimate third-party verification. Another good third-party institute that can give you information about filtration is the Water Quality Association of Lisle, Illinois. The WQA also guarantees performance standards for its members' products. See the Personal Action Guide for the NSF and WQA addresses. Their information will help you decide which water filter to purchase.

What kind of water filter should you buy? Many people like the combination of a carbon block filter with reverse osmosis. Other experts say to use distilled water. I will discuss each of the several kinds of filters, spending more time on the ones you are likely to invest in for your home.

Depth filters. Depth filters really do not do a good job of anything except removing a lot of dirt and other larger particles from your water without getting clogged. You can buy one for a few dollars. Depth filters are made from fabric such as cotton or wool, or from fiberglass or even porcelain. This material is formed into millions of tiny little channels through which the water must travel before reaching your faucet. The filter blocks out much of the debris and dirt, but it does not remove the smaller toxic-chemical particles from your water. Unless you have a lot of bugs, worms, leaves, and twigs in your water you probably do not need a depth filter.

The main thing to look for in a depth filter is its rating. One that is rated below 10 microns is too vulnerable to clogging to clean really dirty water with a lot of particulates; it will become clogged after only a short period of use. Buy a filter with a rating of 10 microns or above. That still is not going to remove much bacteria. To give you an idea of how small bacteria are, a human hair is about 100 microns thick; bacteria are as small as one micron, sometimes as large as 10 microns. So a depth filter is going to remove only fairly large particles. This is not what most people need.

Screen filters. Screen filters are very fine membranes that will effectively remove bacteria from water. Imagine an extremely fine screen door mesh; that is essentially how a screen filter works. Another kind of screen filter uses very finely meshed paper. The lower the rating, the better the screen will be at removing bacteria. Screen filters with a .2 micron rating are so good at removing bacteria that the medical profession uses them for sterilizing equipment that cannot be heated. If you have a problem with bacteria such as *Giardia lamblia,* a screen filter will remove them. Replacement membranes for screen filters can cost $100 or more, however, and must be replaced fairly frequently.

Activated carbon filters. Activated carbon filtration is one of the most commonly used and effective forms of treating home water to remove pesticides. It is one of the oldest methods—it's mentioned in the Bible—and one of the most effective for removing unpleasant odors and tastes and a wide range of synthetic chemicals including many pesticides. Activated carbon filtration is one of the systems you will probably want to seriously consider and combine with a supplemental method such as distillation or reverse osmosis (RO). Many complete systems combine charcoal filtration with RO or other supplemental filters.

Activated carbon works so well because it has the excellent quality of adsorption. Adsorption of contaminants in drinking water occurs when particles that are invisible to the naked eye are collected in the myriad channels in an activated carbon filter that is made from animal or vegetable materials and heat-treated to make it very porous. All its minuscule rivulets and channels, combined with its huge, super-compressed surface, make the activated carbon filter most adsorptive.

Pour-through activated carbon filters sit on your counter. You pour water through the filter and drink it after it is caught at the bottom. Many activated carbon filters fit underneath the sink into the cold water plumbing. (Always fit filters that have a carbon filter into the cold water line because hot water temperatures can damage the cartridge that contains the carbon; fortunately, shower water is not hot enough to damage cartridges, allowing the use of activated carbon filters in the shower for removal of volatile toxic chemicals.)

Activated carbon filtration systems are rated based on tests for the efficiency of their removal of iodine and phenols. Pay special attention to the iodine and phenol ratings. The higher the number in the iodine test the better the filter will be at removing toxic chemicals from your water supply. Look for systems with an iodine number of at least 1,000. The lower the phenol number the better. You want a filter with a phenol number of 15 or less. These two ratings for activated carbon filters are very important. If the salesperson does not know what you mean when you request the system's iodine and phenol numbers, you should deal with somebody else. You must not underestimate the significance of these numbers. Keep in mind that filter systems made by companies which are members of the NSF or WQA must undergo iodine and phenol removal testing verified by a third party.

In chemistry, like attracts like; that is why a carbon filter is so good at attracting organic chemicals, which are based on the carbon atom. But carbon also attracts bacterial life forms, which find the carbon a perfect breeding ground. After all, the carbon provides the host ground and then traps all these nutrients that bacteria need for nourishment. A perfect parasitic affair is going on in your own home filter. Bacteria proliferate in poorly working activated carbon filters. They also proliferate overnight while the water remains unused, which is why you should not use the first draw in the morning or after any period of nonuse. Instead, let water run for several minutes as you wash the dishes. Do not drink first flush water or use it in coffee or juice. Silver is embedded in some filters because it supposedly reduces the ability of bacteria to reproduce. But it is not a good idea to use a filter that contains silver. The metal can enter your water supply from your filter at dangerously high levels. In addition, silver probably does *not* reduce the concentration of bacteria in your water.

Most people use about four gallons of water a day for drinking and cooking. You should look for a filter that has a rated capacity of about 2,000 gallons— equivalent to 500 days of use—before requiring replacement.

Keep in mind that you want a structured carbon block or *granulated* activated carbon filtration system. An important consumer study noted that models using *powdered* activated carbon quickly lose efficiency and allow chloroform to enter the water supply. Indeed, these models have even been shown to concentrate the chloroform, so that levels are even higher in drinking water after it leaves the filter than they were when the water entered.

Some of the best activated carbon filter models, which have been consumer-tested by an independent thirty party, are models manufactured by Aqualux, Continental, Culligan, and Everpure.

Reverse-osmosis filters. Reverse osmosis is an effective method of removing a wide variety of contaminants. It's even used to make seawater drinkable! People drink salt water that has been reconditioned by reverse-osmosis systems in Rotunda and Venice, Florida.

Reverse-osmosis systems do a good job of removing bacteria, organic matter, inorganic substances, and particles.

RO membranes can filter many pesticides and they do an excellent job at lead removal. They have been shown to be effective filters of DDT, heptachlor, dieldrin, aldrin, malathion, and parathion. Other pesticides that can be removed include endrin and methoxychlor, and other contaminants, as well as nitrates, are removed very efficiently by the RO membrane, which also does a good job of removing PCBs from your water. A good RO membrane could remove as much as 99 percent of these contaminants.

Reverse-osmosis membranes are largely ineffective in removal of THMs, however, because chloroform and other THM molecules are small enough to pass through the membrane. So if your system is delivering high levels of THMs, you will want more than an RO filter. Fortunately most RO models combine reverse osmosis with activated carbon filtration.

Some combination RO-activated carbon filters have been extensively tested and proven to remove 95 to 97 percent of THMs from the first 1,000 gallons of water.

RO systems work slowly. Some units produce only 1.5 to 2 gallons of water a day. And these systems waste water. Many discard about 93 percent of incoming water.

How can you tell when you are looking at a good RO system? Look for the salt rejection percentage. The higher this percentage is, the better your system will work. You should search for a system with a rating of at least 90 percent.

In addition, look for dealers who know what they are talking about. How can you tell? RO membranes are very sensitive to water constituents including chlorine and pH. Good companies have salespeople who will use accurate home tests to check your water to make sure its level of chlorine and pH are known. Water that is chlorinated will have residuals of chlorine. A high chlorine level will mean that you must use a cellulose membrane, which is chlorine tolerant, rather than a polyamide membrane. If you were sold an RO system with a polymer membrane made from polyamide and your water had a fair amount of chlorine, your system would soon be ruined. Since most public drinking water is chlorinated, you probably will need a cellulose membrane. If the pH range of your water is between 4 and 8 you will have no problem with most RO membranes, and most drinking water falls within this pH range. But if your pH falls out of this range, you will need to add on a continuous feed system for acid or base to adjust the pH of your water.

Another helpful feature on the better RO units is an automatic membrane flush system that will occasionally clean the membrane. Also look for systems that shut down the storage tank if it is full. I would be wary of an RO system that does not require a depth prefilter upstream. All the best systems have depth prefilters that remove any sediment that could clog your RO membrane.

Costs for reverse-osmosis systems run from about $200 to as much as $700.

Activated alumina filters. Activated alumina filters have one duty: to remove fluoride from your water. Because fluoride may be a carcinogen, there may be no safe level for its presence in drinking water. At levels of 1 part per million, mottling of the teeth may occur; this is known as dental fluorosis. At levels of 4 parts per million, teeth can turn yellow or brown. Fluoride causes discoloration and pitting of teeth at the same time that it is known to help prevent cavities. It is also suspected to cause tumors. At high levels, fluoride is definitely toxic. In some areas, particularly the Midwest and Southwest, there are significant fluoride problems.

Activated alumina filters work just like activated carbon filters. But there is another trade-off that you need to consider here, for although an activated alumina filter does lower fluoride levels quite well—and arsenic levels, too—it adds a little bit of aluminum to your water. Since studies suggest that aluminum may contribute to the onset or exacerbation of Alzheimer's disease, adding any amount of aluminum to your diet is not recommended. So, unless you have exceptionally high fluoride levels, you may not want to trade less fluoride for more aluminum.

Water-softening. One of the most frequently asked questions by persons new to water-treatment technology is whether water softeners remove harmful toxic chemicals. Softening will not lower the level of THMs or other toxic organic chemicals in your water. Water softeners remove calcium and magnesium from hard water, hence the term "water softener."

Water softeners work on a very simple chemical principle. A column is filled with beads known as ion-exchange resins. The calcium and magnesium salts pass through the column with its sodium ions, and an exchange takes place in which the calcium and magnesium ions replace the sodium ions on the resin beads. The water itself still has the same amount of dissolved solids, but instead of calcium and magnesium, the water has sodium. This appears to be a very poor trade, for calcium and magnesium are two of our vital macronutrients, and studies show that water with calcium and magnesium can be very helpful in prevention of heart disease. The salt added when you soften water actually increases your risk of hypertension. One government study in Illinois found that water softeners increased the sodium levels in tap water by three to five times, raising the level above the government's recommended maximum. If your physician has put you on a low-sodium diet, you should know that softened water may very well greatly increase your sodium intake.

In addition, remember you cannot water plants and grass with softened water. Too much sodium could kill your grass. Too much sodium, for that matter, becomes very corrosive and could end up leaching more lead from pipes into your drinking water.

Distillation. Many people swear by distillation. Like reverse osmosis, distillation is very good at partially removing a wide range of undesirable substances from your water. But distillation alone cannot remove all of the contaminants, and despite enthusiastic advocates, distillation is not miraculous. It is simply a good process, which should be combined with an activated carbon filter.

Distillation works on a simple principle. Water has a lower boiling point than many contaminants. So water is boiled, turns to a gaseous steam, rises through a tube, and passes through a series of baffles. Then it is cooled and becomes water again, leaving many toxic organic chemicals behind. Unfortunately, many molecules such as THMs have a lower boiling point than water, so the THMs that evaporate along with the water could theoretically pass through the baffles and end up in the finished product. Chloroform, phenol, and trichloroethylene all have lower boiling points than water. That's one reason why our distillation systems need an activated carbon filter, too.

Distillation cannot kill all pathogens, either. Some pathogenic spores (hibernating bacteria) are fairly heat resistant.

In addition, water can become contaminated with bacteria when stored after distillation. For your own protection, do not store water longer than one week.

Distillers are also slow and take up quite a bit of room. An average distiller that sells for about $300 will provide only 3 to 6 gallons of water a day. A distiller that costs as much as $1,000 may produce 10 or 11 gallons a day.

Ultraviolet treatment. If dangerous bacteria are present in your water, ultraviolet treatment works extremely well. It will not eliminate all bacteria, but it will do an excellent job of killing off most of them, and it will prevent their reproduction. The system's ultraviolet rays change the molecular structure of the puny bacteria and wipe out their DNA. Hardier microorganisms such as parasites and viruses can survive ultraviolet radiation.

If you buy an ultraviolet system, it should have a prefilter. Too much particulate matter in water absorbs the ultraviolet radiation, decreasing its power to

TABLE 3. BEST FILTRATION METHODS FOR COMMON DRINKING WATER CONTAMINANTS

Contaminant	Best filtration methods
Bacteria	ultraviolet light, screen filter
Lead	distillation, reverse osmosis
Nitrates	reverse osmosis
Particulates	depth filter
Pesticides	activated carbon, reverse osmosis
Radium	reverse osmosis
Radon	activated carbon
Uranium	reverse osmosis
Volatile organic chemicals	activated carbon, reverse osmosis

kill bacteria. Your ultraviolet water treatment system should also have an ultraviolet absorption monitor to warn you when the water is absorbing too much ultraviolet radiation.

A good system will have built-in consumer-protection devices. Make sure you are not going to get a shock if you handle your system. Expect a cost of about $500.

BOTTLED WATER

Many people ask me about bottled water. Is it safer than tap water? Are all bottled waters the same? What is mineral water? What is hard water? Should people drink distilled water? Bottled water is expensive for families on a tight budget. Is it worth it? The answer is yes!

But I must add an important caveat. The recent discovery of traces of benzene in Perrier bottled water makes it clear that consumers must demand more government protection. Benzene occurs naturally. But it should have been filtered out, and the Perrier system of checks failed to discover that the filtration system was not doing its job. Standards ought to be promulgated at the federal and state levels that set up zero tolerance levels of harmful pollutants and bacteria that may be present in bottled water. Presently, bottled water is subject to the same standards as ordinary drinking water, which is not reassuring. Bottled water suppliers should be required by law to provide consumers with full disclosure on the labels of their products on the metal and mineral contents, including information on potentially harmful compounds such as aluminum, fluoride, nitrates, naturally occurring radiation, and sodium. And the federal and state governments ought to monitor the purity of bottled waters. The popularity of bottled water is largely dependent upon the public's perception that it not only tastes better but is safer than tap water that has undergone chlorination and may contain industrial and farm chemicals. Without this consumer confidence, the industry could lose a significant portion of its consumer base.

There are excellent bottled waters, however. I have reviewed nongovernment laboratory reports, which indicate that major brands of high-quality bottled water are free from industrial pollutants and pesticides. Unless you have had your water supply tested and are certain of its safety, or have installed a filter system that delivers you pure water, you may want to drink bottled water. Women who are or expect to be pregnant especially should drink bottled or filtered water. In California, the state Department of Health Services reports women who drink bottled or filtered water have an unusually low rate of miscarriages and birth defects compared with women who drink tap water.

Bottled waters vary in quality and mineral content. Brands that claim only to be "drinking water" may well have been drawn from a tap, but most are highly filtered. You should look for brands which state that the water is drawn from a spring or under pressure from an artesian well. An artesian well is a site where water gushes up from underground as a result of pressure exerted by layers of solid rock; often such water is especially rich in minerals. Overall, the bottled water industry is in the business of producing pure water, and companies try very hard, and successfully, to protect their water sources and locate new sources far from potential pollution. Today there are many popular bottled waters that are very pure, including Naya, Vittel, and Arrowhead.

What should you look for in a bottled water? I look for taste and mineral content (hardness), and I make sure there is not a high concentration of metals and certain minerals such as salt, lead, nitrates, and aluminum. The term "hardness" refers to the concentration of minerals—particularly calcium and magnesium—in the water. A good hard water is to be valued, for studies show that drinking hard water reduces your risk of heart disease. Examples of good hard waters? Mendocino is a super-rich calcium source. So are Vittel, Santé Mineral Water, Vichy Springs, and Rocky Minerals.

Water that has 500 parts per million total dissolved solids must legally be labeled as mineral water. Most mineral water has carbonation added during bottling; a few brands of bottled water are naturally carbonated. Carbonation in itself poses no threat to health. Mineral waters provide many important macro- and micronutrients such as calcium, magnesium, and iron, which we need for a healthy body.

When I travel I often drink bottled water because I don't always trust local water supplies. The San Joaquin Valley, for instance, is filled with pesticide-saturated farms and polluted wells. When I stop for a bite to eat, I order bottled water. Canada Dry Seltzer, which is widely available, is a decent bottled water that is highly filtered. Seltzer and club soda are usually carbonated tap water that is highly filtered.

Distilled bottled water is fine for drinking. It is very pure. But minerals will be lost in the distillation process; unless they are replenished after distillation, distilled water does not provide important nutrients such as calcium and magnesium that are present in mineral-rich waters. Some brands do have added minerals.

Choose bottled water that comes in glass, not plastic, bottles. Some relatively toxic chemicals may migrate in minute amounts from plastic containers into the water. Besides, plastic can impart an unpleasant odor to water. And plastic containers contribute significantly to this country's huge garbage pollution crisis. Glass is recyclable. If you buy water in plastic bottles, be sure to store it in a cool place out of the sun to protect it from off tastes.

Safe Shopping List: Bottled Water

I have analyzed the most popular American and international brands of bottled water to bring you this list, which you can use when you shop.

Some bottled waters have more minerals, making them more valuable to our bodies. Others have traces of naturally occurring toxins and metals that our bodies do not need. Check out your favorite brand. Most companies will supply laboratory reports upon request. You can also send samples of your favorite bottled water to the independent laboratories listed in the Personal Action Guide. Nitrate levels should never be more than 2 parts per million. Levels of other toxic metals and minerals should be very low or nondetectable.

In this case I have listed only those waters that fall in the Green Light category.

GREEN LIGHT

These American and international brands of bottled water lack significant concentrations of any harmful trace minerals. Many are rich sources of important minerals such as calcium.

Aiguad Andorra *(Andorra)*
à Santé Mineral Water *(Santa Rosa, California)*
Alhambra Crystal-Fresh Drinking Water *(San Francisco)*
Arrowhead Mountain Spring Water *(Los Angeles and Orange County)*
Artesia 100% Pure Sparkling Texas Mineral Water *(San Antonio)*
Big Spring Water *(Lewistown, Montana)*
Calistoga Mineral Water *(Calistoga, California)*
Chippewa Springs *(Chippewa Falls, Wisconsin)*
Contrexéville *(France)*
Crystal Bottled Waters Company *(Phoenix, Arizona)*
Crystal Geyser Sparkling Mineral Water *(Calistoga, California)*
Deer Park 100% Spring Water *(New York)*
Ephrata Diamond Spring Water *(Ephrata, Pennsylvania)*
Glenwood-Inglewood Spring Water *(Minneapolis, Minnesota)*
Good Hope Water Company *(Jacksonville, Florida)*
Hawaiian Sparkling Water *(Honolulu)*
Ice Mountain Maine Spring Water *(Mount Zircon, Maine)*
Kentwood Spring Water *(New Orleans)*
Madari Mineral Water *(Cyprus)*
Mendocino Mineral Water *(Mendocino, California)*

Mount Olympus Spring Water *(Salt Lake City, Utah)*

Moutoullas Mineral Table Water *(Cyprus)*

Napa Valley Springs Mineral Water *(Calistoga, California)*

Naya Spring Water *(Canada)*

Ozarka Spring Water *(San Antonio, Texas)*

Rock Crest Water Company *(Cheyenne, Wyoming)*

Rocky Minerals Brand Water *(Utah)*. This bottled water from Big Rock Candy Mountain is perhaps the richest bottled water source of calcium in America, with a whopping 1,500.9 parts per million. The water is well balanced, although its fluoride concentration is high.

San Pellegrino Pure Mineral Table Water *(Italy)*. An excellent source of calcium.

Sequoia Springs Natural Pure Mineral Water *(Escondido, California)*

Sparkletts Crystal Fresh Drinking Water *(Los Angeles)*

Tyler Mountain Water *(Charleston, West Virginia)*

Valser St. Petersquelle *(Switzerland)*

Vichy Célestins *(France)*

Vichy Springs Sparkling Mineral Water *(Ukiah, California)*

Vittel *(California)*. This brand carries the same name as the French bottled water Vittel, but it is drawn from an American spring, Bartlett Springs, in California; both waters are owned by the same company.

Volvic Natural Mineral Water *(France)*

Wissahickon Spring Water Company *(Manheim, Pennsylvania)*

Zephyrhills Bottled Water *(Central Florida)*

15. THE NONTOXIC HOME

L ike America's farmers, we have all had chemicals sold to us as the perfect solution to all our problems. The results include overreliance on prescription drugs and the use of unnecessary chemical formulations for housecleaning, deodorizing, lawn care, and insect control. There are safer, more ecologically sound ways to accomplish most of the things we've been trained to rely on chemicals for.

We all have chemical sensitivities. For millions of Americans with extreme sensitivities, even the smallest trace of a toxic chemical can create havoc in their bodies and send their immune systems into complete overreaction. Some people have multiple chemical sensitivities; they are like rain barrels that over the years have filled up with small amounts of toxic chemicals. One additional drop will cause the barrel to spill over, producing symptoms that can be quite severe.

Lynn Lawson, communications coordinator for the Human Ecology Action League (HEAL), notes:

Since World War II, over 70,000 new, synthetic chemicals (synthesized mainly from petroleum and coal tar) have been put into thousands of new products designed to create "better living through chemistry." Most of these chemicals have not been tested for long-term or even short-term toxic effects on human beings. Whether we like it or not, we are all guinea pigs for the Twentieth Century Chemical Revolution.

What are these products? They are all around us: detergents, scented or not; fabric softeners; deodorants, scented or not; deodorant soaps; perfumes and after-shave lotions (almost all are now derived from petrochemicals); synthetic and treated fabrics and fabric blends

243

(they contain formaldehyde and other chemicals); new carpeting, which contains poisonous chemicals and is usually mothproofed and sprayed with pesticides; anything newly dry-cleaned; and pesticides, herbicides, and fungicides. . . . Two things, especially, are not widely known: formaldehyde, known to be carcinogenic, is in 8 percent of the gross national product; and pesticides are sprayed almost everywhere. Because there are very few right-to-know laws, we do not realize that almost all stores, restaurants, churches, public gardens, and public buildings of all kinds are regularly sprayed with pesticides, again mostly untested for human health effects.

Do you see the omnipresence of our enemy? It is virtually everywhere! The life of one Los Angeles woman was severely disrupted simply because of fumes from a dry-cleaning plant. She was hospitalized for acute perchloroethylene toxicity. She returned home, sensitized, and found that whenever she opened her windows she suffered horrible, incapacitating headaches, disorientation, and irritability. That is how chemical sensitivity begins for many people. One day they're fine; then they get hit with a heavy-duty dose of a toxic chemical, and for the rest of their lives they're sensitized to that chemical and many others.

None of us is immune. Some of us cannot adapt, even imperfectly, to the chemical onslaught. For thousands of Americans, even the smallest trace of a toxic chemical can create physical havoc, bringing on an array of uncomfortable symptoms, even sending immune systems into complete overreaction and degeneration.

The EPA estimates that as many as 31,400 premature deaths occur *annually* as a result of indoor air pollution. Symptoms of poisoning from indoor air pollution are often only vaguely recognized. Some symptoms of low-level, indoor chemical poisoning in homes and offices include anxiety, inability to concentrate, fatigue, headaches, stomach problems, depression, muscle or joint aches and pains, and lack of thought clarity. If you have an ailment caused by indoor pollution, even your doctor probably won't diagnose it. According to a 1988 report released by the National Academy of Sciences, the medical profession is woefully uneducated when it comes to understanding the human health effects of environmental pollution. But the symptoms many people suffer are quite real.

People who are ill are unlikely to know that their headaches, sore throats, eye irritations, and respiratory problems could result from nitrogen dioxide released from poorly vented gas stoves and heaters. Sneezy, achy, feverish? Gases emanating from a new carpet could be the culprit. Particle board in many homes—especially mobile homes—can emit extraordinarily high concentrations of neurotoxic, cancer-causing formaldehyde. Across the country, whole families have been severely sickened with flulike symptoms, severe headaches, and illness as a result of formaldehyde fumes in mobile homes. EPA experts say formaldehyde used on fabrics and in home materials probably causes cancer in humans.

The list goes on: home and garden pesticides, we now know, can increase a child's risk of leukemia by nearly seven times, according to a recently published study. Fumes from the chemical paradichlorobenzene, which is used in mothballs and air fresheners and to mask odors in toilets, also probably contribute to human cancer. As David Rall, of the EPA's National Toxicology Program, has noted in an issue of *Science*: "Significant numbers of consumers are . . . exposed from the use of products containing *p*-dichlorobenzene." We have known for years that beauty care professionals were at a higher risk of cancer because so many aerosol products have contained the cancer-causing chemical methylene chloride, which they unsuspectingly inhaled, as a propellant. At work and even in our homes, methylene chloride has been used as a propellant in aerosol spray paint and in paint stripper. Secondhand cigarette smoke contains benzene, which puts children at a significantly increased risk of dying from cancer and leukemia when they are adults.

Our enemies are the tiny, cumulative poisons in everyday life, nemeses disguised in banality. For all of our sakes, the government must begin to regulate more tightly the safety of the seemingly innocent products we bring unsuspectingly into our homes, items whose chemical emanations and by-products invade our bodies. A 1989 EPA report estimates that eight of the most common indoor pollutants cost the nation more than $1 billion in medical costs from cancer and heart disease. In its report, the agency called for $100 million in research funds over a five-year period. In 1989, the Bush administration spent a mere $2.7 million on indoor air-pollution research. Yet, along with pesticide residues in our food, indoor air pollution is one of the nation's most personal and pressing health concerns, according to EPA experts.

Sure, we must win the war on outdoor air pollution. That is of paramount importance. But many of us spend 90 percent of our day indoors. Some, including the very young, elderly, and chronically ill, are indoors virtually 100 percent of the time.

Meanwhile, a recent EPA study found that toxic chemicals may be two hundred to five hundred times more concentrated in homes than outdoors.

Until the day government awakens to this problem, you must act on your own, gather knowledge, and protect yourself. You have the power to create an environmental sanctuary in your home. You can lead a nontoxic life-style.

You can start living a nontoxic life-style and feeling better today. I have carefully reviewed many common household products to show you how—in place of highly toxic chemicals invented in the laboratory—you can use safer, equally effective nontoxic alternatives.

THE KITCHEN

Kitchenware

A few examples of dangerously contaminated kitchenware and dinnerware will hammer home my point that household toxic exposures are a nemesis in disguise. You may drink tea from a glazed pot that you bought while traveling abroad. You may drink coffee from a handmade mug you picked up in Palermo. You may drink orange juice from a pitcher made in Sinaloa, Mexico, which you purchased at a local pottery shop. No doubt, you bought these glazed items of kitchenware because you liked their bright colors. However, makers of earthenware pottery and kitchenware often use cadmium and lead in their glazes; these metals brighten and highlight colors.

Even an innocent-looking glazed teapot or mug could be poisoning your body with toxic cadmium and lead. In a thirty-one month period between 1985 and 1988, some 271 lines of pottery and earthenware products were recalled by the federal government because way too much lead and cadmium were leaching from their glazes. Earthenware products from Italy, Spain, and Korea were named most frequently in recalls.

One family suffered acute lead poisoning after storing orange juice in a pitcher purchased in Mexico. A Washington State couple suffered debilitating illness and incurred extensive medical costs before they discovered they were being poisoned by lead leaching into their coffee from the ceramic glaze on their mugs.

As is often the case, doctors could not diagnose the cause of the Washington couple's sickness. Meanwhile, the husband, Don Wallace, lost 35 pounds. He could not sleep. He became irritable and impatient and suffered wrist pains. His wife, Frances, was misdiagnosed. One doctor told her she had the flu. A second told her she had porphyria, a rare, incurable metabolic disorder. She became dehydrated and anemic. Doctors feared she would die.

Finally, Don Wallace noticed that he and his wife drank coffee from the same set of imported mugs. Their son did not drink coffee or use those mugs; he was fine.

Testing revealed significantly elevated lead in his and his wife's blood, and the Wallaces discovered the cause of their illness: lead was leaching from their mugs into their coffee!

Another Washington couple, Patricia and James Apperson, were poisoned by a set of black- and gold-decorated tumblers and cocktail glasses she had bought from a Portland, Oregon, department store some forty years earlier. The Appersons had only recently begun to use their tumblers daily. Both of them developed anemia. Eventually their blood was analyzed for lead, and Mr. and Mrs. Apperson both had lead concentrations that were twice the danger level for industrially exposed workers. An industrial hygienist eventually traced their poisoning when gray smudges were noticed on the inside of their glasses.

The effects of consistent exposure to too much lead from kitchenware can be devastating. High levels of lead in the body can harm not only the nervous system, kidneys, and liver but also processes by which the blood is formed and the reproductive, cardiovascular, immunologic, and gastrointestinal systems. Human health problems are associated with *nearly* any amount of lead exposure. Children may be affected and exhibit symptoms that include apparent brain dysfunction, short attention span, restlessness, sudden bursts of impulsive behavior, and difficulty with coordination. There is evidence that low levels of lead cause permanent learning and behavioral disorders in children and can affect growth.

All of us should be on the alert whenever we purchase earthenware pottery for food service and storage. And remember: the price of kitchenware is not related to its safety.

Mexico's ceramic pottery ranks among the most dangerous. Many people use Mexican earthenware food-storage containers, juice pitchers, and coffee mugs. Some of these people are being poisoned with lead and do not even know it! Such beautifully decorated earthenware pottery is typically purchased at roadside stands and urban markets in Mexico, although it is also sold at fine Mexican art shops and stateside import and gift shops. These dishes are fine for decoration. Use them for flowers, not for food service and storage.

Some earthenware from Portugal and Spain also contains leachable lead and cadmium. Thousands of these items were sold in 1984 and earlier before the problem was identified. Spanish imports are known as *cazuelas* (cooking pans).

Unfortunately, there is no sure way to tell upon purchase how much, if any, lead and cadmium will leach from a piece of earthenware pottery. Glazed pottery is dangerous only when it has been improperly fired or when the glaze was improperly formulated. However, you can certainly tell whether your pottery has had glaze applied. Look for a thin glassy coating.

Here's what you should do to prevent dangerous lead and cadmium exposure from glazed kitchenware.

Buy glazed products from companies whose labels clearly state that lead-free glazes were used. If you are not sure whether a lead or cadmium glaze was used, do not use the earthenware pottery for food service or storage.

Do not store acidic foods in glazed kitchenware. Fruit and fruit juices are acidic. When stored in ceramic containers, they are particularly reactive and may absorb significant concentrations of lead and cadmium. Glass is a better choice for storing fruits and fruit juices. Other foods that should not be stored in glazed kitchenware and earthenware include soft drinks, wine, cider, vinegar, and foods containing vinegar, sauerkraut, tomatoes, and tomato mixtures. These are all highly acidic foods.

Drinking glasses with painted logos are often given away by service stations and markets; these items may contain lead-based glazes and paints. The logo may be on the outside of the glass, but that will not prevent lead exposure. Children may smear lead on their hands and then contaminate their food or lick their fingers. Lead is highly leachable, and such emblazoned glasses contribute to lead exposure. Throw out glasses with logos on them. They can expose children to excessive amounts of lead.

Old pottery-style dinnerware—including brightly colored earthenware and collectibles—produced before current safety codes were issued by the FDA in the early 1970s may not meet today's health standards. Certainly do not use antiques or collectibles to hold or serve food or beverages.

Liquor flasks disguised as colorfully glazed ceramic figurines may leach high concentrations of lead into whatever beverage is stored in them.

You can test your earthenware and kitchenware for leachable lead with a home test kit. If you have been using glazed earthenware pottery or kitchenware for food serving and storage, the test kit just might save your life. This kit was developed by Fran and Don Wallace, the lead poisoning victims from Washington. The kit is relatively precise, but your kitchenware must have high leachable cadmium and lead levels to be detected by this kit. A negative result does not imply total safety. Many earthenware items, however, do leach very high lead concentrations. For details, see the Personal Action Guide toward the end of this book.

These following countries export the most dangerous glazed earthenware, dinnerware, and kitchenware. Don't serve or store foods in earthenware pottery from these nations without first having it tested: Republic of China (Taiwan), People's Republic of China, Hong Kong, Italy, Macao, Mexico, Portugal, Soviet Union, Spain, India, North Korea, South Korea, Pakistan, and Thailand.

The following countries have a better record of safety. Their earthenware and kitchenware products leach less lead and cadmium overall, according to FDA inspection records: Brazil, France, Germany, Great Britain, the Maldives, Sri Lanka, and Chile. However, despite an overall good record, individual manufacturers from these nations may export products that do leach dangerously high lead and cadmium levels.

For your best protection, you should use a home lead test kit. You can use this to test glazed kitchenware that you will be eating or drinking from with any regularity. I strongly recommend doing this because of the failure of the FDA to act swiftly to force national and international manufacturers to reduce the amount of lead in their glazes and to use firing techniques sophisticated enough to prevent lead from leaching.

What's even stranger than toxic glazes? How about radioactive dinnerware? American manufacturers have, indeed, used uranium in dinnerware called Fiestaware in the recent past. Seems the uranium gave their dishes and plates an eerie, pleasing glow!

Fiestaware was sold under a variety of brand names, including Fiesta, Caliente, Early California, Edwin M. Knowles, Franciscan Pottery, Harlequin, Poppytrail, Stangl, and Vistosa before World War II and in the 1960s. It contained uranium compounds in its color glazes, which imparted a strange, bright orange-red, black, or yellow color to the ceramics. The dishes analyzed by the FDA had leachable uranium, however, and manufacture stopped. But plenty of these dishes made their way into the collections of American homeowners.

In the early 1980s, the New York State Department of Health tested dinnerware known to have uranium glazes. They reported that people who used the dinnerware would be exposed to a small amount of radioactivity. Indeed, in the early 1970s scientists calculated that continued use of uranium-glazed dinnerware could provide more than one-half of the annual maximum permissible dose of uranium for a single person. The display of these items does not pose a health problem, however—only their use in food service. People must be warned against serving and storing food in these products. Such exposure is easily avoidable.

Aluminum pans and aluminum foil can introduce aluminum into your body. If you use aluminum foil for storage, wrap your food in wax paper first; wax paper is the safest food-storage paper.

By avoiding aluminum exposure, you may well prevent intestinal disorders such as colitis, reduce hardening of the arteries, and obtain added protection from Alzheimer's disease and related disorders. Aluminum is great for lawn furniture, not your body. There is ample scientific proof that aluminum migrates from cookware into food. If you do not believe me, conduct your own experiment. Boil water for half an hour in an aluminum pan; then quickly pour this water into a clear glass container, and you will see flecks of aluminum in the water. Two doctors noted in the medical journal *Acta Medica Scandinavica* that colitis is associated with cooking in aluminum pots and pans. Doctors have also linked kidney and liver disease with aluminum ingestion. Aluminum can also deplete the body's nutrients and has been linked with hardening of the arteries. No wonder aluminum is considered a potentially toxic chemical.

Plastics

When shopping, remember that the largest use of plastics is in food packaging. One-quarter of all the plastics produced by the approximately 441 plastic resin plants in this country are used for packaging. The government noted in 1986 that five of the top six chemicals producing the most hazardous waste in this country are used in the manufacture of plastics. These five plastics are propylene, phenol, ethylene, polystyrene, and benzene. These chemicals are dangerous to the workers who manufacture them and who run a high risk of cancer—and all for packaging that is used once and then discarded. People living near plants that produce plastic products such as polyvinyl chloride also have an exceptionally high risk of liver cancer and brain cancer.

When shopping for eggs, buy only those eggs that come in cardboard cartons—preferably recycled cardboard. Don't buy eggs in plastic cartons.

Do not use Styrofoam cups, plates, or packing and packaging material, because they have a harmful effect on the ozone layer. The manufacture of Styrofoam releases chemical blowing agents called chlorofluorocarbons (CFCs)—which pump up the plastic with gas—into the atmosphere, helping to destroy the earth's protective ozone layer.

Even the use of Styrofoam products not manufactured with chlorofluorocarbons is ecologically unwise. These materials do not biodegrade at all or do so only very slowly, and they are crowding our nation's landfills. Beverage and food containers make up more than 12 percent of the solid waste produced in this country. Why not use glasses, plates, forks, and knives that can be reused?

Plastic is simply an ecologically poor choice when there is a recyclable substitute. We must ask whether it is wise to clutter up our landfills and our bodies—styrene appeared in 100 percent of human fat samples tested —with bits of burger boxes and disposable cups. Cups and containers are used for a few minutes and then thrown away. But they remain trash forever.

Limit your use of plastic bags; most do not biodegrade. Some, which are advertised as being ecologically friendly, biodegrade in sunlight, but very little sunlight reaches plastic packaging that is buried in a landfill. If your supermarket only has plastic bags, you can at least use them several times.

Take them with you when you shop and ask the bagger to put your groceries in your own bags. Many supermarkets recycle plastic bags and now have in-store recycling centers. Make sure your market is recycling. You can also buy natural fabric shopping bags and use them for years. Be brave. Dare to be different.

Recycle glass and paper. Use recycled paper. Its manufacture uses less energy and creates less pollution. This book is printed on recycled paper.

Cleaning Products

To remove tough hard lime deposits around faucets, use distilled white vinegar. (Use distilled white vinegar for all cleaning formulas that call for vinegar.) The deposits can be softened first for easy removal by covering them with vinegar-soaked paper towels. Leave the paper towels on for about an hour before cleaning.

Get out of the habit of storing cleaning chemicals such as carpet shampoos, furniture polishes, and drain cleaners in the kitchen. These chemicals contain volatile chemicals that can release low levels of toxic gases into the ambient air. Adults and children with respiratory problems such as asthma and bronchitis are especially sensitive to ammonia fumes. Keep these chemicals in the garage—under lock and key if you have children—or in a nonflammable area, away from people.

Use nontoxic substitutes for toxic household cleaners. Instead of caustic, irritating cleaners with ammonia and other disinfectants that can cause eye, lung, and skin irritation at even very low concentrations, combine 1 or 2 teaspoons of borax (available at supermarkets) and 1 quart hot water with a little lemon juice or distilled white vinegar. Mix it and put it in a spray bottle. This mixture will cut grease and can even help clean ovens. This mixture is pleasant to use, since there is no release of toxic vapors, as there is with chlorine- and ammonia-based cleaners. And this borax mixture works better than any of the high-priced supermarket brands! I use a borax–white vinegar mixture as an all-around kitchen cleaner; it leaves counters and stovetops sparkling. The residual smell of vinegar—light and sweet like fermented cider—does not last long.

Instead of corrosive, toxic oven cleaners containing potassium or sodium hydroxide and ammonia, sprinkle salt on spills in the oven when they are still warm and then scrub them off. If the spill has dried, lightly wet it before scrubbing. Another method is to dampen spills, sprinkle baking soda on them, and gently rub them with a fine steel wool pad. Also, occasionally dampen your sponge with vinegar and water before wiping out your oven. This will help prevent grease buildup.

Instead of drain cleaners, which contain dangerous lye, use a plunger. For prevention, every few weeks pour a half-cup of baking soda down the drain followed by a half-cup of white vinegar; cover the drain tightly for one to two minutes. Then pour a kettle of boiling water down the drain. This should help prevent clogging. Another nontoxic method of cleaning your drain is to mix one-half cup salt with one-half cup baking soda; pour this mixture down the drain, followed by about 6 cups boiling water. Let this mixture sit all night. In the morning, flush the drain with cold water.

Instead of chlorinated scouring powders, use one of the national brands whose labels state that they contain no chlorine. One such brand is Bon Ami cleaning powder. It is much less toxic than the chlorinated scouring powders whose chlorine fumes cause some people to suffer headaches and fatigue. Scouring powders may also contain talc, which can be contaminated with asbestos, a small amount of which becomes part of the ambient air. There is no safe level of asbestos exposure.

THE BATHROOM

Instead of mildew and mold cleaners, which might have traces of penta, kerosene, phenol, and formaldehyde that can be absorbed through the skin, use a mixture of 4 to 8 tablespoons of borax to 1 quart of equal parts water and vinegar in a spray bottle. Spray the mixture on the mildew and wipe the area clean. Borax is an excellent antibacterial agent, and unlike toxic supermarket cleaners, it leaves no disinfectant smell or fumes. Another solution is to bring a portable heater into your bathroom and turn up the heat. This will also kill mildew. But, parents and pet owners beware: keep children and pets away! And instead of germ killers, which have phenol, chlorine, and formaldehyde, use a mixture of water and borax. You get the same germ-free surfaces without toxic overload.

Instead of using toilet cleaners with corrosive toxic irritants such as hydrochloric or oxalic acid, paradichlorobenzene, and calcium hypochlorite, use a toilet brush with baking soda and a mild, nonchlorinated detergent such as Bon Ami.

Personal Care Products

It is important to keep in mind that many personal care products do contain toxic chemicals, and many of these products are tested—needlessly and with great cruelty—on animals. Other products rely extensively on animal ingredients.

Avoid cosmetics that contain mineral oil, polyvinylpyrrolidane (PVP), plastic resins, and formaldehyde. Use products made with natural ingredients or those that are hypoallergenic and unscented. Hair sprays may have plastics and formaldehyde.

Instead of deodorant soaps, which can have toxic chemicals such as formaldehyde, phenol, tricarban, and ammonia, use soaps without fragrance or dyes.

Antiperspirants and deodorants may contain toxins such as ammonia, formaldehyde, alcohol, and aluminum chlorhydrate. Baking soda dusted under the arms works fine. There are also many antiperspirants made without aluminum-based compounds and with natural, nonanimal ingredients.

Do not use talc—especially on babies. Talc may contain asbestos, which will become part of the air your baby breathes.

Mouthwashes and toothpastes often have phenol, formaldehyde, and cresol. Some toothpastes have artificial coloring and flavoring, including saccharin and sugar. Use natural toothpaste brands. Or brush your teeth with a little baking soda on your toothbrush.

Sculptured nail remover, which women use to remove artificial nails, contains 98 to 100 percent acetonitrile, which becomes cyanide when swallowed. Many poison-control experts say they would like to see such products banned because they are potentially hazardous to children. The FDA, however, is hamstrung by federal law and cannot take a product off the market unless injury results from its use according to instructions. Since swallowing sculptured nail remover is not part of the instructions, the FDA has no authority to act. For your toddler's sake, keep these products out of reach!

For a body emollient and skin cream, instead of using lanolin—an animal product, from sheep, that is contaminated with pesticides—use non-animal-based lotions such as aloe vera.

THE BEDROOM

Perchloroethylene fumes on dry-cleaned clothes can provoke a reaction in chemically sensitive people. Air your clothing outdoors for a few hours —after removing the plastic bag, of course—before putting it in the closet or wearing it.

Instead of toxic mothballs, which contain the cancer-causing chemical paradichlorobenzene, place cedar chips or sachets of dried lavender in drawers and closets.

THE LIVING ROOM

Stay away from carpet cleaners and shampoos that contain the solvent perchloroethylene. Some products may even contain naphthalene, a toxic inhalant. Our children should not have to crawl around on carpets and furniture, inhaling low-level fumes of cancer-causing perchloroethylene or toxins such as naphthalene. Instead, use nontoxic cleaning methods. To eliminate odors, sprinkle baking soda all over your carpet, covering the entire carpet. You will need several pounds of soda for a 9-by-12-foot rug. Wait at least fifteen minutes or even overnight. Then vacuum the rug. If odors persist, repeat this procedure. It will eliminate musty, moldy odors.

Carpet colors can be brightened with nontoxic methods. Mix one quart of white vinegar with three quarts of boiling water. Rub this mixture on the carpet with a moistened cloth. Moisten the nap only. Do not saturate the back! The rug will smell like vinegar at first, but it will dry odorless, and the colors will be very bright.

If you buy a new carpet or move into a home where there is new carpet, it is best to have the rugs professionally steam cleaned using hot water without detergents or other chemicals. This will help dissolve formaldehyde and other toxic chemicals that often accumulate in new fibers. The toxic inhalant known as 4-PCH (4-phenylcyclohexene) may be produced as a contaminant during the manufacture of glue and latex, which is used in some carpet backing. To avoid this potential problem, you might consider ordering carpet with a non-latex backing.

Over the last three years, the Consumer Product Safety Commission has received some 130 complaints about human illnesses linked with carpets. Symptoms include eye and throat irritation and sometimes nausea. People usually report illnesses and health problems immediately after new carpets are installed. You can limit your exposure to toxic chemicals in new carpets by requesting that the dealer air out the carpet before delivering it. Then you can allow the carpet to sit another day or two in your home, with all windows open, before having it installed. During installation, windows and doors should be open and as much ventilation maintained as possible.

This will not completely solve the problem by any means, because such toxic chemicals in carpets do not disappear in a few days. So if you are particularly chemically sensitive, seek floor covers such as hardwood or tiles instead of carpets; keep in mind, however, that even natural fiber carpets can have chemical dyes and backings, too.

Instead of furniture polish, which may contain toxic phenols and nitrobenzenes that can be inhaled and absorbed through the skin, polish your wood with plain mineral oil while wearing gloves. The main ingredient in furniture polish is oil; virutally any oil that the wood absorbs will work well. Mineral oil is the main ingredient in many commercial furniture polishes. When you use plain mineral oil, you do a great polishing job, and you avoid inhaling toxic solvents. You do not need mineral oil, however. You can even use mayonnaise. Yes, that's right: just rub some mayonnaise on a soft clean cloth and work it into your wood. The odor will linger for only a few minutes; you will be left with beautifully shined furniture! Another excellent furniture polish can be made with three parts olive or vegetable oil and one part white vinegar. Or dissolve one teaspoon of lemon oil in one pint of mineral oil to get a beautifully polished finish.

If your furniture is scratched, make a mixture of equal parts lemon juice and vegetable oil. Rub this combination into the scratches with a soft cloth until the scrapes disappear.

To eliminate water spots from furniture, rub them gently with a damp cloth smeared with toothpaste.

Wash wood, if necessary, with mild soap. Dampen a cloth with a solution of water and mild soap such as Ivory or Murphy Vegetable Oil Soap. Wring the cloth almost dry and wipe the furniture section by section. Be sure to dry each surface with a clean cloth as you go along, so that no section stays wet.

Refinish old furniture with Murphy Vegetable Oil Soap. Although you can use chemical finish removers, Murphy Vegetable Oil Soap, a simple nontoxic solvent, is a truly wonderful product. Use it first. It may be all the help your furniture needs.

To freshen the air in your living room, try leaving open a box of baking soda. Also try keeping fresh flowers and herbs in the room.

Remember to keep your gas heater clean. Inefficient gas heaters release unburned nitrogen dioxide into your home. Nitrogen dioxide can cause many symptoms, including throat irritation. Clean your furnace at least once a year—more often if you have pets or shag rugs.

Windows can be cleaned and brightened with a nontoxic mixture of equal parts water and white vinegar in a spray bottle. I never use cleaners with blue dyes or ammonia. Besides, this nontoxic cleaning mixture works much better!

Floors, such as no-wax linoleum, that are marred with a dull greasy film can be cleaned with one-half cup white vinegar mixed into one-half gallon of water. Your floor will look sparkling clean.

Wood floors can be shined with vegetable oil and vinegar. Mix equal parts oil and vinegar and apply a thin coat to your floor. Rub in well.

Brick and stone floors can be cleaned with vinegar. Mix one cup white vinegar in one gallon water. Scrub the floor with a brush and the vinegar solution. Rinse with clean water.

Ceramic tile can be cleaned with a quarter cup of white vinegar (more if very dirty) mixed in one gallon of water. This solution removes dirt without scrubbing and doesn't leave a film.

Wax can be removed from vinyl and asbestos tiles using club soda. Pour a small amount on a dry section. Scrub in well with a moist brush or cloth. Let it soak in a few minutes; wipe clean.

Wax can be removed from linoleum floors with isopropyl alcohol. Mix a solution of three parts water to one part rubbing alcohol. Scrub in well; rinse thoroughly. Be sure the area is well ventilated and wear gloves.

Black heel marks can be removed with a paste of baking soda and water. Don't use too much water or the baking soda will lose its abrasive quality.

Ventilate your home well when you install new products containing formaldehyde gas. Many products contain formaldehyde. They include particleboard, UF foam insulation, plastics, plywood, fiberglass, pressed wood furniture, insecticides, detergent, glue, antislip agents, nylon fiber, fiberboard, paint and wood finishes, electronic equipment, drapery and upholstery fabrics, carpets, and latex backing on carpets.

THE LAUNDRY ROOM

Laundry soap residue can be eliminated by pouring one cup of white vinegar into the washer during the final rinse cycle. Vinegar is too mild to harm fabrics but strong enough to dissolve alkalines in soaps and detergents. Vinegar also breaks down uric acid, so it is especially good for babies' clothes. To make wool and cotton blankets soft and fluffy, add two cups of white vinegar to your washer's rinse water when the tub is full. Do not use vinegar if you add chlorine bleach to your rinse water. The combination will produce harmful vapors.

Add one-quarter to one-half cup of baking soda to each wash load to make clothes feel soft and smell fresh. You can cut the amount of chlorine bleach you use in your wash by half when you add a half-cup of baking soda to top-loading machines or a quarter-cup to front loaders.

Instead of using corrosive, toxic bleach with sodium or potassium hydrazide, hydrogen peroxide, or sodium or calcium hypochlorite, try using a half-cup of white vinegar or a half-cup of baking soda.

THE HOBBY OR RECREATION ROOM

Hobby and art chemicals such as glue and oil-based paints and lacquers should be used in well-ventilated areas. Whenever possible, replace solvent-containing materials with water-based materials to eliminate solvent inhalation problems. This advice comes from New York's Center for Safety in the Arts. Set up your art or crafts studio carefully. If possible, do not have a studio in your home. If you must work at home, set up your studio in a separate room, not in a living area.

Store your art materials safely where children cannot reach them. Do not store materials in orange juice containers, soda bottles, or other beverage containers, because of the danger of accidental ingestion by you or others.

Wash chemical splashes off your skin with water. Do not wash your hands with solvents. Use soap and water. To remove oil paints, use baby oil and then soap and water.

Buy protective clothing and equipment. Wear special work clothes such as smocks or hair coverings. Use the right type of gloves, goggles, hearing protectors, and respirators. Make sure they are approved for the chemicals you are using and that they fit properly.

When you work with paints and paint strippers or other solvents, use a respirator, not a paper mask; make sure you work in a well-ventilated area.

And remove your work clothes before you enter your home's living space or other public places where you will be near other people. Some persons are very sensitive to toxic chemical vapors from work clothing. Work clothes should be washed separately from the family laundry, as a major exposure route for children is their parents' contaminated work clothes. If you work with solvents and you have young children, it is especially important that you do not expose them to saturated work clothing.

Don't dump workshop toxic chemicals in your trash. They can injure sanitation workers who handle them and lead to greater landfill contamination. Also don't pour toxic chemicals down the drain, and don't dump them onto the ground or pour them into the street. Take them to a waste disposal center where they can be properly disposed. And make sure you use them all up. If you cannot use up all the chemical, give it to a neighbor who needs that chemical.

For detailed information about hazards in the arts, write the Center for Safety in the Arts, 5 Beekman Street, Suite 1030, New York, NY 10038, or call (212) 227-6220. The center publishes many papers on health hazards in the arts as well as *Art Hazard News,* which appears ten times a year.

THE GARAGE

Don't let auto batteries sit around in your garage or yard. Be especially careful to avoid dumping or spilling antifreeze, transmission fluid, brake fluid, used oil, or battery acid on the floor or the ground. Take these fluids to a service station or reclamation center for recycling or save them until a household hazardous waste collection service comes to your neighborhood. Do not spill antifreeze, which is ethylene glycol, on the garage floor, and never pour it on the ground. Don't empty your oil into the topsoil. It may contaminate groundwater. And don't dump oil down a storm drain. The oil will eventually pollute our surface waters and may run into the sea or nearby rivers or streams. Instead, bring your oil to a service station that has an oil recycling program. If no service station in your area has one, present your elected local representative with a community petition requesting that one be set up in your neighborhood.

HOME AND GARDEN PESTS

In battling insects and pests in and around your home, you can reduce your exposure to dangerous insecticides by using natural, low-toxin pest-control methods. Supermarket pesticides such as Black Flag, D-Con, and Raid often contain cancer-causing and neurotoxic chemicals. Fly sprays, roach killers, pest strips, and pet products such as flea and tick sprays all contain dangerous pesticide compounds. Such highly volatile pesticides will contaminate surfaces and ambient air throughout your home. They also threaten children. The use of home and garden pesticides has been associated in one scientific study with significantly increased incidence of serious childhood illness such as leukemia. Home and garden pesticides really ought to be labeled clearly as presenting children with an increased risk of disease, if it is proven to be an established association. No such warnings can be found. What parent would buy a pesticide knowing that it would contribute to an increased risk of serious illness?

Instead of using pesticides try other methods that work as well without toxic side effects.

For eliminating flies try the old standby: a flyswatter. Close or screen windows and other openings where flies might enter your home. Keep your kitchen counters clean; do not leave out food, which attracts flies.

To eliminate cockroaches, keep your home and cupboards extra clean. Also use cement or screening to close off all gaps around pipes and electric lines where roaches enter the house. Use a nontoxic caulk to seal small cracks along baseboards, walls, and cupboards and around pipes, sinks, and bathroom fixtures. (See the Personal Action Guide for information about ordering nontoxic home products.)

Borax kills cockroaches. Try mixing 4 tablespoons borax with 1 tablespoon cocoa powder and 2 tablespoons flour. Set this sweet poison in easily accessible dishes in infested areas. Repeat three to five days later to kill newly hatched cockroaches. Parents and pet owners beware: borax can be toxic if eaten. Keep the mixture away from children and pets! You can also mix equal parts baking soda and powdered sugar and spread the mixture around the infested areas.

If this relatively nontoxic method doesn't eradicate the roaches, this stronger, nonvolatile toxin method should: try sprinkling blue-tinted technical boric acid in infested areas that are out of the way of children and pets. Boric acid is very toxic; a tablespoon ingested by a child could be deadly. So you do not want to sprinkle it in exposed areas. Nor should you use it around foods or in kitchen cabinets. But boric acid is essentially nonvolatile and emits virtually no fumes. By the way, be sure to buy *technical* boric acid, not the *medicinal* variety. *Medicinal* boric acid is white colored and could be confused for foodstuffs.

To eliminate ants, keep all food in sealed containers. Wash dishes immediately after each meal. Don't leave dirty dishes in the sink. Keep counters clean. Wipe up anything sticky that might attract ants. Be a sleuth. Follow the ants to where they have broken into your home. Seal that crack, hole, or crevice with nontoxic plaster and sealant, which you can buy through catalogs listed in the Personal Action Guide. Growing certain plants around your home may deter ants. Mint is reportedly a natural ant repellent, as are pennyroyal, southernwood, and tansy.

If ants persist, mix 1 cup flour with 2 cups borax. Spread the mix outdoors around the house foundation. The ants will eat this mixture, and the borax will kill them. Keep the borax out of reach of children and pets.

To eliminate rats and mice, set mouse or rat traps in strategic areas throughout your home. Change the location and replenish the bait every few days. Also make sure all food is stored and sealed.

To poison rats without the use of volatile toxic chemicals, mix one part plaster of paris with one part flour and a generous portion of sugar and cocoa. The rats will eat this sweet poison and die.

We have many nontoxic ways to deal with outdoor insect pests. Some

31 million American homes have gardens, and as many as 15 percent of America's home gardeners grow fruits and vegetables organically.

When a friend in Atlanta recently had a white fly infestation of his vegetable garden, I told him about a nontoxic control method and suggested that he use yellow sticky traps and a commercially available parasite, *Encarsia formosa*. To identify pests in your garden consult Rodale's *Garden Insect, Disease & Weed Identification Guide*. Check out Rodale's other publications for biological methods of pest control. See the Personal Action Guide for Rodale's address.

Lawns should not need pesticides. Healthy, rich soil is the key to luxuriant grass, not cancer-causing pesticides and synthetic fertilizers. When you mow your lawn, leave the clippings. They are a rich source of nitrogen and will build up the compost in your soil. Dandelions can be manually cut out at the root. They usually do not grow back if you dig several inches under the surface. Always water your lawn in the evening or early in the morning when there is less evaporation. Avoid overwatering, particularly in water-poor areas like southern California. Allow the lawn to dry out completely before watering it again. Lawns that are too moist are vulnerable to fungi. Allowing fungus-infested areas to dry out will help eliminate this pest. Plant a variety of grass that is suited to your area.

Be wary of lawn care companies. On February 17, 1988, New York Attorney General Robert Abrams filed suit on behalf of the people of the state of New York against Chemlawn Services Corporation because of alleged false and deceptive advertising that its lawn pesticides were safe and free from risk.

In his petition, Abrams cited examples of misleading safety assurances provided by Chemlawn. For example, the attorney general noted that Chemlawn asserts "a child would have to ingest the amount of pesticide found in almost 10 cupfuls of treated lawn clippings to equal the toxicity of one baby aspirin."

Further, the National Coalition Against the Misuse of Pesticides reports that "a Chemlawn application of the insecticide isofenphos in New York in 1985 was linked to the deaths of over 100 red-winged blackbirds. Analysis of the birds' gizzards showed 22.1 ppm of isofenphos, well over the lethal threshold dose."

Chemlawn is not the only major lawn care company that uses extremely toxic compounds. When you consider having an outside contractor care for your lawn, take a careful look at which pesticides are used. You might wish to further your knowledge of biological and organic lawn care methods that will not endanger you, your children, or local wildlife. Remember, we grew beautiful lawns in America long before an aging, tottering pesticide industry began peddling poisons to the home market.

Don't use or allow anyone else to use chlordane in your home to eradicate termites. As recently as 1988, three years after it was banned, Sears Roebuck continued to sell potent cancer-causing chlordane compounds to kill termites around the home. The further manufacture of chlordane was banned because of its high toxicity, environmental persistence, and tendency to build up in maternal breast milk. Its cancer-causing potential is rated three times greater than that of pure DDT.

So what are the solutions? In the Los Angeles area, the Tallon pest-control company uses nitrogen gas at $-350°F$. to literally freeze termites. This revolutionary treatment is effective and nontoxic. You can use other less toxic chemicals such as copper chromate, crylite, or a nonvolatile termiticide. Boric acid is one of the least toxic poisons. Commercial grade boric acid (also known as technical boric acid) is blue in color and should be sprinkled in exposed termite areas. Keep children and pets away from these areas.

Prevention is protection. Make sure you keep the wood dry in your home. Use the best wood if you are building a home or adding to an older home. Insect- and mold-resistant woods include cedar, redwood, cyprus, and jarrah.

Pests that damage your wood do well in damp soil. Make sure you maintain excellent soil drainage around your home.

Flea collars and flea and tick powders for pets contain pesticides that can have profound effects on chemically sensitive animals and persons. And we are not talking about strictly physiological effects. Some involve personality changes. Dog and cat collars may contain as much as 5 percent carbaryl. *The New Yorker* reported recently that carbaryl was linked with violence that affected both a man and his cat. When the man dusted his cat with flea powder, the breeze would blow the dust into his face. The dust would rise in a white cloud each time the cat brushed against him or the breeze blew, and the owner would inhale a whiff of carbaryl, but the owner was barely conscious of this and thought nothing of it. After one week, the cat, with a history of docility, began killing birds and mice. It would bring in mice and claw them for hours. The man wondered what had happened to make the cat so violent.

A companion of the cat's owner noted that the changes were not only in the cat. The cat's owner had begun giving menacing replies to innocent questions, his face flushed. When his friend pointed this out, the man became so angry that he kicked his pet, and his companion fled, fearing for his own life.

In a sudden burst of insight, the cat owner saw that both he and his cat had become violent and menacing. He made the connection between the flea powder and their violent behavior. The symptoms—tearing eyes, fatigue, and aching joints—were all signs of anticholinesterase intoxication associated with low-level carbaryl poisoning. The violent changes that overtook man and beast subsided after he stopped using the flea powder.

I have examined labels of products that contain carbaryl. On these labels are some of the very same messages that may confront you in supermarkets and garden shops. They are deceptive. Carbaryl is not a safe pesticide for use on a flea collar, in flea or tick powder, in a home or garden spray, or on your produce. Carbaryl is a poison. The main ingredient of carbaryl is methyl isocyanate, the poison that formed the toxic cloud that killed and maimed thousands of men, women, and children in Bhopal, India. Ironically, a simple six dollar nontoxic flea comb can do a wonderful job of rooting out these pests.

I have brought your attention to just a few of the nontoxic alternatives that are available today. Your nontoxic life-style will make your home a true haven from outside pollution and will allow you to contribute to cleaning up our planet as well.

The Personal Action Guide lists some of the major suppliers of these and other low-toxicity and nontoxic products.

LEAD IN THE HOME

Lead in old paint poses terrible health problems. Old plaster is dangerous, too; it was colored white with lead carbonate. So old, flaking plaster can be just as toxic from lead as the paint that covered it.

During home renovation be especially careful of lead poisoning. Home renovations have recently come under serious reevaluation because of the real potential for poisoning children with lead-contaminated dust. Scraping of paint during home renovations is common, yet few people are aware of the danger of lead poisoning from handling old paint chips.

Lead poisoning can cause a variety of symptoms in children: hyperactivity, impatience, impulsive behavior, and lowered creative and cognitive thinking. Lead that has accumulated in the body can be removed through a process called chelation, in which toxic materials are bound to an agent and excreted from the body. This process can help reverse some symptoms and reduce chances later on that the lead will promote cancer when the child becomes an adult. But chelation is only an emergency measure. Prevention is your best method of protection.

Experts believe that most neighborhoods with homes sixty to one hundred years old will present lead toxicity problems. In Charleston, South Carolina, one disturbing study reported that among low-income children tested for lead in their blood, about 40 percent had levels that significantly exceeded toxic levels. Since the recent publication of articles about lead poisoning in Charleston, testing has begun on children from wealthier families, and lead poisoning is occurring among these children, too. Wealth will not protect your children. In older home renovations, children are not always kept away from lead-contaminated materials, and the lead dust is not cleaned up properly. Elevated blood levels of lead have been found in children in about 75 percent of these cases.

This terrible legacy has a long history that is now catching up with us. Parents with children who have learning problems are only now recalling that they renovated their homes when their children were toddlers. The symptoms then were vague, and only now are parents beginning to realize that their children were poisoned. Children who are born developmentally normal can become mentally impaired if they become lead poisoned. And the damage done by lead poisoning is not totally reversible, even after blood lead levels are reduced.

The federal government estimates that some 12 million children live in housing where they will be exposed to lead, often at incredibly high toxic concentrations. Government experts believe that as many as 4 million children in America already have toxic levels of lead in their bloodstream. Lead poisoning is probably the most common preventable disease among infants and toddlers. Removing paint from your home is serious business. When you sand or scrape old layers of paint or burn them off with a heat gun, invisible dust and vapors of toxic lead paint are created, and your entire home can be coated with lead dust. Although adults are susceptible to lead poisoning, too, recent studies indicate that children absorb five times more lead than adults. In addition, children tend to put things in their mouths, and these things could be covered with lead dust. Further, young children often are anemic and their reduced iron supply makes them even more vulnerable to lead poisoning.

The problem is insidious. In Baltimore alone an estimated 2,000 children *per year* suffer permanent brain damage and neurological damage as a result of lead paint poisoning. As the lead content in paint chips increases, they taste sweeter, making it more likely that children will eat them.

Prevention is the best protection. Follow these tips to protect yourself and your family:

• Don't use innocence as an excuse. Even home remodeling jobs can end in tragedy, and sanding lead paint can lead to poisoning. Repainting an older home without testing for lead is asking for tragedy.

• Determine if your home has lead paint. The federal government banned most uses of lead paint in 1977. How do you know if your home has lead-based paint? You have several ways to tell. First, if your home was built prior to the 1970s, there's a good chance that lead paints were used. Second, obtain a surface wipe lead dust test. That will tell you about the lead contamination in and around your home. Third, have an X-ray fluorescence (XRF) examination. Homes have many painted surfaces, so it is impractical to take samples to a laboratory for analysis. Trained technicians use XRF machines in the home to test surfaces for lead.

▪ Be especially careful of problem areas, such as windows in older homes. Home builders once preferred lead paint because of its resistance to temperature and humidity changes. Raising and lowering the sash grinds the paint, turning it into fine lead dust that can be blown throughout the home.

▪ Do not be fooled by new-looking older walls. Lead paint wall surfaces tend to oxidize and chalk off. While the surface may appear relatively clean and new, the chalked-off paint becomes lead dust that cannot be seen.

▪ Lead abatement is not a do-it-yourself job. It is dangerous, and the government has developed strict guidelines that include the use of a respirator with a High Efficiency Particle Air (HEPA) filter and disposable coveralls, shoe coverings, hair coverings, and gloves. Constant blood testing is strongly recommended for workers involved in lead abatement. All furniture must be removed, and all nonremovable furniture, including sinks and radiators, as well as vents and other openings, must be sealed off. All floors must be covered with plastic. Whenever anyone is scraping lead paint in your home, stay out. Be sure to remove all furniture, toys, and other household items from the home before a renovation begins. Drywall, paneling, and sometimes fiberglass are often recommended for sealing surface areas. Cleanup is complex, its proper execution critical. The entire area must be HEPA vacuumed several times. Any attempt to vacuum with a home or shop machine will only spread lead dust throughout the home. Phosphate detergents must be used along with further HEPA vacuuming. Needless to say, only trained professionals should carry out lead abatement and cleanup. Make sure that your professional knows that the U.S. Department of Housing and Urban Development (HUD) has contracted with the National Institute of Building Sciences to develop strict guidelines for identification, abatement, cleanup, and disposal of lead hazards.

▪ Do not reoccupy the home until a thorough cleanup has been done by experts in removing lead contamination hazards.

▪ Have surface lead levels in different areas of your home checked periodically for at least a month before you return.

These steps are costly, but they will give you peace of mind.
Another alternative is to cover walls that have lead-based paint on them

with paneling or Sheetrock. Also, lead-based paint covered with modern paint is usually well sealed. But if the lead-based paint is flaking or peeling, you must remove children and family members from the room until the premises have undergone professional lead removal. When children are present, make sure they wash their hands frequently and do not put any potentially contaminated objects in their mouths. Teach your child not to eat objects that might be dusted with lead.

One warning flag of lead poisoning in children and adults is anemia. Very few doctors know how to test for lead or will even suspect lead poisoning as the cause of your child's illness or behaviorial or learning problems. Thus, anemia may act as a warning to you of toxic lead exposures. Any blood level of lead above 5 parts per billion may require medical treatment. The federal government recommends treatment at 25 parts per billion, but I believe this standard is too high to protect children.

You should consider having your children tested for lead if you live in a community near a major highway with heavy traffic or near hazardous-waste sites or industries. Testing need not always require taking blood samples from the baby or child; hair can be tested for lead, too, and can provide an excellent indication of exposure.

RADON

Every home should be tested for radon, a naturally occurring radioactive gas. The EPA estimates that some 10 percent of all homes in the nation may have elevated concentrations of radon. In Georgia, 1,438 homes were tested by commercial laboratories and the state Department of Natural Resources. About 15 percent had radon levels above 4 pCi/L, usually between 4 pCi/L and 20 pCi/L. Eighty-seven percent of the homes with elevated levels were located in thirteen north Georgia counties where granite and granite-gneiss rock formations probably contain uranium. How dangerous is radon? The EPA estimates that 5,000 to 20,000 lung cancer deaths annually result from radon exposure; in 1988, there were about 139,000 lung cancer deaths in the United States, according to the American Cancer Society. In some cases, the amount of radon gas to which a family has been exposed has equaled smoking more than 135 packs of cigarettes a day! Radon enters homes, as the natural decay product of uranium and radium, through floors, drains, sumps, and cracks in concrete walls. The radon gas breaks down into stable isotopes called radon daughters that we inhale and that then decay in the lungs, initiating cancer.

You can test for radon with an inexpensive radon detector. There are two basic kinds. Charcoal canisters are exposed to the home environment for two to seven days. Alpha track detectors are exposed for one month or longer. The alpha track detectors are often recommended as being superior to the charcoal canisters. See the Personal Action Guide for order information. You can also request from the EPA its two radon information pamphlets, *A Citizen's Guide to Radon* and *Radon Reduction Methods: A Homeowner's Guide*.

Any level of radon in the home above 4 picocuries demands your attention; any level above 20 picocuries demands immediate attention. Fortunately, we can mitigate the concentration of radon in homes. The Consumer Products Safety Commission recommends source control measures that include sealing cracks and other openings in your basement, ventilating crawl spaces, installing basement ventilation, and using air-to-air heat exchanges. Radon reduction may require covering exposed earth with cement and sealing porous walls and cracks in concrete.

HOME IMPROVEMENT

There are other things you need to know about nontoxic home improvements. Today we can use a wide variety of low-toxicity products, from flame-retardant treatments for wood-shingled rooftops to low-odor, non-reactive paints and wood stains. Incredibly, you often cannot smell paint in a home that has been freshly coated with a nonreactive, low-toxicity paint. You will be surprised at how few fumes there are in such homes. Low-toxicity paints do not contain bactericides or fungicides such as phenol and formaldehyde.

If your home has surfaces that are producing fumes, you can use a water seal that will create a very tight film. This product dries to a dull gloss finish and reduces the emission of fumes from walls, ceilings, and floors. You can even find low-toxicity products formulated to replace adhesive glues, lacquers, rust remover, and strippers that contain hazardous solvents. See the Personal Action Guide.

There are several options for improving home air quality. One simple, effective method is increased ventilation. Provided outside air is superior to indoor air and that you do not live near a busy highway, opening windows and doors, if weather permits, is an excellent way to increase air ventilation. Opening windows and doors is especially important if you are engaged in intense, indoor air polluting activities like painting, paint stripping, welding, soldering, sanding, or other hobby and crafts work.

You can also use plants. The National Aeronautics and Space Administration performed studies with typical houseplants to test their ability to remove air toxins in a controlled environment. While the studies are by no means conclusive, they do offer suggestive evidence that certain plants may play a contributing role in improvement of our homes' air quality. According to the NASA study, plants that have proven effective under experimental conditions for removing formaldehyde gases include spider plants, gold pothos vine *(Scindapsus aureus)*, and varieties of philodendron. For removal of benzene, chrysanthemums and gerbera daisies have proven effective under experimental conditions. Other good detox plants include Chinese evergreen, English ivy, peace lily, bamboo palm, and mother-in-law's tongue. Seek plants that reproduce new leaves very quickly; they provide the greatest source of oxygen.

Home air filters are available. If you buy a high-efficiency particle air (HEPA) filter, be sure that you distinguish between an actual HEPA filter and HEPA-type filters. The difference is slight, and HEPA-type filters are also adept at air filtration. True HEPA filters will remove particulates with 99.7 percent efficiency at the 0.3 micron size. HEPA-type filters will remove about 95 percent of the particulates at the 0.3 micron size. HEPA and HEPA-type filters are adept at removing the particulates in air pollution. For removal of chemicals, gases, and odors, the system should also come with a carbon filter. The best systems contain carbon filters made from granular coconut shell.

Filtration is an excellent way of purifying our air from smoke and toxins. Good air filters cost $200 to $400 or more with prices up to $1,000. They come in several kinds of systems and can be either tabletop or console models.

For a large room—say, 9 by 12 or larger—you should buy an air filter that has a clean air delivery rating of at least 250. This rating is arrived at by using a formula based on how long it would take the system to clean 90 percent of the smoke from a 9-by-12-foot room.

All air filters make noise at high levels. Be sure to take note of this and avoid models that make noises you don't like.

An excellent model is the AllerMed Air Star-5C, which is listed at $349 but can be obtained for about $100 less at some outlets. This air filter comes with a granular coconut carbon filter and will purify a 15-by-18-foot room. It has a HEPA-type filter.

For freeway commuters, there are excellent auto air filters such as the AllerMed Autoaire-II and the Aireox Model 22. If you do a lot of commuting on jammed metro freeways, an auto air filter can really help clean up the air you breathe.

16. PREGNANCY AND TOXIC CHEMICALS

A woman's diet is more important during pregnancy and the months just before becoming pregnant than at any other time in her life. Extraordinary demands for calcium, protein, and other nutrients are placed on a woman's body as a child grows within her. And toxins in a woman's diet can do irreparable harm at this time. The developing fetus is exquisitely sensitive to even minute amounts of toxic chemicals. The poisons in our food, water, and air are responsible for thousands of miscarriages and stillbirths, and they contribute hugely to birth defects. Some of their worst effects are subtle but insidious: these chemicals often affect the brain, resulting not in gross malformation but in lost mental abilities.

In 1988, some 1.8 million American babies were born. Four to five percent of them were born with mild to severe birth defects.

We would like to think that in these technologically advanced times we've made progress in preventing birth defects. Let me put that myth to rest: we have not.

In fact, the occurrence of many birth defects has increased dramatically in recent years. Between 1970 and 1985, eighteen of the twenty-seven most common birth defects increased in incidence. Some common birth defects went up in incidence as much as 1,700 percent. Seven decreased in incidence. The rates of two of the twenty-seven defects remained relatively stable during the period 1970 to 1985.

There are many reasons for this dramatic increased incidence, not the least of which is better diagnosis and reporting of birth defects. The ingestion of alcohol, cigarette smoking, and drug use by women during pregnancy are also factors that must be included in the skyrocketing incidence rates for birth defects. But increased toxin levels in the environment must also be counted. There is little doubt that these changes are linked, in part, to our environment's saturation with toxic chemicals. The changes have appeared too fast to be considered a result of natural evolution. The evidence is unavoidable that the unborn child is affected when parents are not careful about the quality of the food they eat and the water they drink. One California state study found that women who drank tap water had significantly higher incidences of birth defects and miscarriages than did women who drank bottled or filtered water. And this study just hints at the tip of the iceberg.

How many parents know about this study or other studies that point to the same conclusion? Government experts do far too little to educate people about toxic chemical hazards during pregnancy. I am very concerned about this. Erik Jansson, coordinator of the National Network to Prevent Birth Defects, in Washington, D.C., one of the nation's leading experts on the causes and prevention of birth defects, says that *a 50 percent reduction in birth defect rates could be achieved through a combination of improved diet and toxic exposure reduction.*

The evidence is remarkably clear when we talk about the effects of prenatal toxic exposures. Heart defects have skyrocketed in incidence since 1970, and any pediatrician versed in the literature can tell you that their increased incidence is in part the result of toxic chemicals in food, water, and our environment. We simply cannot deceive ourselves and attribute this increase solely to better reporting. Nor can we rationalize the startling 1,700 percent increase in lung agenesis, which occurs when a baby is born without fully developed lungs. There has been a 700 percent increase in endocardial cushion defects, which occur when a baby's heart lacks a septum, the partition between its chambers. There has been a 540 percent increase in patent ductus arteriosus, which occurs when the artery-like blood vessel, the ductus arteriosus, fails to close after birth, resulting in loss of oxygen to body and brain; and a 450 percent increase in pulmonary artery anomaly, which occurs when pulmonary blood circulation circumvents the lungs and the blood is circulated to the rest of the body without enough oxygen.

Ventricular septal defects, another defect in which the baby is born without a septum between the ventricles, went up 150 percent. Tetralogy of Fallot went up 117 percent. Tetralogy of Fallot includes four distinct defects that, when they occur in tandem, are, remarkably, not fatal. The occurrence of any one of these defects alone, however, could be deadly. At least two of the parts of tetralogy of Fallot are on the increase. Coarctation of the aorta occurs when a baby is born with a pinched aorta and the heart becomes enlarged. This defect, which can be deadly if it is severe, increased 100 percent. Transposition of the great arteries, which occurs when the aorta crosses the vena cava and the heart pumps backward, went up 67 percent. Many of these heart defects can be linked with toxic chemical exposures.

We need only look in our own backyard—in Tucson, Arizona; San Jose, California; and Woburn, Massachusetts—for evidence of the link between toxic chemicals and birth defects. These towns' tragedies are not isolated. They've merely become symbols of a widespread insidious toxic threat to our children. A recent study by the University of Arizona Health Sciences Center in Tucson found that there were 2.5 times more heart defects among babies born to parents who drank water contaminated with the solvent TCE at home or at work. The solvent had leached, throughout the last fifteen or twenty years, into public drinking wells from pits and ponds at the Hughes Aircraft Company. The study counted about 1,200 children with heart defects in a portion of Tucson where the residents unknowingly drank TCE-tainted water. An earlier study in San Jose, California, examined the effects of another solvent, TCA, and found that birth defects among exposed parents increased by a factor of three. Again, heart defects were a primary result.

In Woburn, Massachusetts, increases in the number of birth defects were associated with drinking water from wells polluted with industrial solvents including TCE. High incidences of leukemia, perinatal death, lung and respiratory disorders, and kidney and other urinary disorders were clearly associated with polluted wells. The pollution stemmed from a toxic chemical waste dump that leaked the solvents into the underground freshwater supply.

These are our sirens. They are wailing, telling us that we will lose our war against birth defects unless we accept zero tolerance for industrial pollution and pesticides in our drinking water, our food, and the air we breathe.

Prescription Drugs

Most physicians are very attuned to the risks of birth defects from taking pharmaceuticals, and medications carry a category label so their effects can be easily checked. A number of medications are known to be safe, such as penicillin, and physicians use these whenever possible. Sometimes medical conditions demand that the doctor use medicines that he or she would prefer not to use in order to save the mother's life or the fetus's. For example, fetal hypoxia resulting from maternal seizure may be a greater threat to the baby than the possible birth defects from a seizure medication.

But there are still problems. Often, physicians do not know that their patient is pregnant. She may be in the first weeks of pregnancy and not even know it herself, and physicians do not always ask women of child-bearing age whether they believe they might be pregnant. Nor do they always test for pregnancy before writing out a prescription. Women of childbearing age should ask questions about possible effects on a fetus of any medication prescribed to them. The first two months of pregnancy represent a period when vital organs are rapidly developing and the unborn child is most vulnerable to toxic chemical exposures.

Therapeutic drugs prescribed by doctors have been linked with birth defects. A study published in *Obstetrics and Gynecology* in 1981 by Michael Bracken and Theodore Holford found that 44.5 percent of all pregnant women in five Connecticut hospitals received prescription drugs such as antiemetics, hormones, antibiotics, antihistamines, tranquilizers, narcotic analgesics, antidepressants, and diuretics, and that these prescription drugs contributed about 13 percent to the total birth defect rate. One such drug, the anticonvulsant medication valproic acid, has been linked with neural tube birth defects in a small percentage of pregnancies. Other drugs, like Dilantin (also known as phenytoin), when administered during pregnancy, may cause mild or even moderate mental deficiency in children in addition to birth defects. Valium, too, has been shown to cause visible brain damage as well as birth defects.

The overmedication of pregnant women is a problem that is potentially as serious as our overmedication of the elderly. No pregnant woman should be on any therapeutic drug that could cause birth defects or that has not been thoroughly tested, unless there is an absolute medical necessity.

I am talking even about aspirin. A common drug like aspirin, we now know, could cause bleeding in the brain of the baby during pregnancy and its regular ingestion by the mother could result in significant learning impairment with as much as a 7 percent reduction in intelligence. Common mood-altering drugs, such as lithium and Xanax, can cause birth defects. Recently, we learned that the acne medicine Accutane causes gross birth defects.

Doctors used to tell pregnant women to use Benedictin, which contained the antihistamine doxylamine, for morning sickness. Unfortunately, many women who are pregnant do not know that a large number of popular cold remedies, including Nyquil and Vicks Formula 44, contain, or have contained, doxylamine. The sleeping pill Unisom also contains this antihistamine. The jury is still out on this antihistamine's potential to cause birth defects. But as a precaution, pregnant women may want to avoid drugs that contain this antihistamine.

Unfortunately, appropriate warnings for pregnant women are not always given for prescription and over-the-counter drugs. Colace, Comfolax, Correctol, Dialose, Kasof, and Regutol are stool softeners that relieve constipation. But they all contain docusate (dioctyl sodium sulfosuccinate). Although constipation is a common condition of pregnancy, there is evidence that docusate may cause birth defects, and pregnant women would be well advised to avoid the use of any products that contain docusate. To relieve constipation, they would do much better to make sure their diet is high in fruits, vegetables, and fiber-rich grains.

Women with allergies and asthma also need to be careful of the drugs they use. Nasal sprays like Beclovent and Vanceril contain beclomethasone, which has caused birth defects in experimental animals. Some bronchodilators such as Slo-Phyllin and Theo-Dur contain theophylline, whose residues have been found in nursing mothers' breast milk. Further, there is evidence that theophylline causes an increased risk of birth defects among experimental animals, according to one study. Feldene, manufactured by Pfizer Laboratories, is used to relieve inflammation due to arthritis, as well as pain. Feldene contains piroxicam, which may cause birth defects, according to experimental animal studies; piroxicam also may inhibit milk production in nursing mothers.

Before using any prescription or over-the-counter drug, pregnant women should consult the *Physicians' Desk Reference* or *The New People's Pharmacy* for information on the drug's potential to cause birth defects or cancer.

I would like to see the government force manufacturers to post warnings on cosmetics, diuretics, and antihistamines that can form high levels of nitrosamines. Any sensible person will agree that a woman who uses antihistamines or diuretics during pregnancy should not have to run the risk of cancer in her child. And all easily nitrosable drugs that contain chemicals that can be converted to carcinogens and teratogens once in the mother's body should be supplemented with vitamin C, for this would significantly reduce the risk.

If you must take drugs, prefer well-established drugs that have been in use for ten to twenty years. Today's newer drugs may not have been fully tested for their potential to cause human birth defects. Follow-up studies have been done on older drugs and any problems will probably have been detected. Obviously, newer drugs have not been around long enough for the follow-up studies to be conducted.

It goes without saying that so-called recreational drugs such as cocaine and marijuana are serious threats to the unborn and must be avoided by women who are pregnant.

Smoking

No matter how careful you are about your food and water, if you smoke you could possibly harm your unborn child. One of the biggest single causes of mild birth defects is cigarette smoking. *Just don't smoke during pregnancy.* Smoking is a toxic exposure that will decrease birth weight and possibly harm the overall health and vitality of the newborn, resulting in other symptoms of prenatal toxic exposure, including increased risk of childhood respiratory illness. Even secondhand smoke is a potent source of cancer-causing nitrosamines. Avoid cigarette smoke!

Alcohol

Alcohol can also cause birth defects and other symptoms of toxic exposure such as lower than normal birth weight and shorter than normal pregnancy. Doctors with whom I have spoken tell me that a beer or glass of wine once in a while during pregnancy may not be dangerous. But regularly drinking alcohol is dangerous. I consider alcohol a toxic chemical just like PCBs or any other birth defect–causing industrial solvent. Indeed, researchers note that fetal alcohol syndrome is one of the leading causes of mental retardation in the United States.

Many women remain unaware of their pregnancy until several weeks have passed. They may refrain from drinking alcohol once they know they are pregnant, but by then it may be too late. During the first month of pregnancy, many critical embryonic developments have already occurred. If you think you might become pregnant, you should refrain from drinking alcohol.

Coffee

Drinking one or two cups of coffee a day is probably not dangerous. But drinking four, five, or more cups a day could have a serious impact on an unborn child. High doses of caffeine have been shown to cause serious birth defects.

Furthermore, coffee may make it more difficult for couples to conceive. Natural stimulants such as caffeine are associated with reduced chance of pregnancy.

PCBs and Pesticides

Smoking, drinking, and using drugs are conscious choices people make. But what about involuntary exposures?

Chemicals such as heptachlor and PCBs, found in some foods, decrease the unborn child's capacity for intelligence and increase chances of birth defects and diseases.

Michigan studies indicate that PCB exposure during pregnancy causes a delay of brain development of the infant, resulting in slower neuromuscular development and decreased head circumference, birth weight, and gestation period. Severe adverse effects were seen among infants whose mothers ate only two or three Great Lakes fish a month over several years, long before they ever considered the effects that such toxins could have on their pregnancies.

In Oahu, Hawaii, milk cows were fed pineapple leaves contaminated with heptachlor. (This contamination affected only the outer portions and leaves of the pineapples fed to cows; few incidences of heptachlor contamination of the portions of pineapples humans eat have surfaced.) The heptachlor had been used to grow pineapples in 1982, despite its ban elsewhere in America. The milk many Hawaiian mothers drank subsequently was contaminated with heptachlor. A researcher who studied 120 of the births that occurred in 1982 among exposed women found that their babies demonstrated several symptoms of toxic chemical exposure: lower birth weight, higher rates of jaundice, smaller head circumference, and increased birth defect rates. Sixteen of the babies became seriously ill. One Kapiolani Children's Medical Center pediatrician said it was her feeling that there were too many serious illnesses, that 10 percent of babies studied becoming seriously ill was too high a figure to be called anything but abnormally elevated.

The severity of the health effects increased as exposure to the heptachlor-tainted milk increased; women with the highest body concentrations of heptachlor had the most infants with birth defects and with the most severe symptoms of fetal toxic exposure.

Even moderate levels of heptachlor contamination were associated with lower infant intelligence test scores, decreased birth weight, smaller head circumference, and increased cases of jaundice. Some experts fear these studies, done at four and eight months, indicate potential for significant learning disabilities later in the life of each child.

What makes this disaster in Oahu even more disconcerting is that as early as 1979 the EPA had released a study of clusters of unexplained low birth weights. Low birth weights are important warning flags because they provide early notice of subsequent increased risk of disease such as cerebral palsy, learning difficulties, and difficulty in processing information later in life. One such cluster of low birth weights was identified in Oahu as early as 1979. It is quite possible that toxic chemicals such as heptachlor may have gotten into the milk supply and gone undetected for several years prior to the discovery of the contamination in 1982.

There is strong evidence that a father's exposure to some toxic chemicals can also produce cancer in his children. Researchers working in Florida found that the male sperm count was reduced by 30 percent as a result of some twenty chlorinated chemicals found in sperm and semen. One of the chemicals found was our old friend, penta, which turned up in its highest concentration, insidiously, not in semen, but in sperm. If penta is proven conclusively to be a human mutagen or teratogen it may start interfering with cell processes at the moment the sperm fertilizes an ovum. And the seed of childhood cancer may be planted at the moment of conception. Both parents must be very careful to reduce their toxic exposures even before pregnancy begins.

Women whose tap water is contaminated with the pesticide aldicarb at any level should be concerned. Aldicarb concentrates in the brains of laboratory animals' babies at levels that are higher than those found in the mothers. Some experts believe aldicarb exposure may result in decreased ability to engage in informational processing necessary for optimal learning.

Aldicarb remains relatively stable in water, and women in states such as California, Wisconsin, Rhode Island, and New York, where wells have aldicarb residues, should find an alternative water source, especially if they are pregnant or going to be pregnant.

One study of women who worked in the vineyards of Andhra Pradesh, India, found significant genetic damage and miscarriages after the women were exposed to nine pesticides: DDT, lindane, quinalphos, diethan, metasytox, parathion, copper sulfate, diclorvos, and dieldrin. The exposed women had a 44 percent spontaneous abortion rate compared to 7.5 percent among unexposed families. The most damaging chromosomal changes were found among women who were most exposed to the pesticides; their chromosomes were transformed into abnormal shapes. Pregnant women should never work around pesticides, nor should they use home and garden pesticides.

Because some seafood can deliver exceptionally high levels of toxins, expectant or nursing mothers should be especially selective about the seafood they eat. Women who are pregnant or who hope to become pregnant are at high risk if they eat even moderate amounts of PCB-contaminated fish. See the seafood chapter for information on which fish may have PCBs.

These women also need to be especially careful of the extraordinarily potent toxin dioxin. They should avoid eating any fish from the Great Lakes because many are contaminated with dioxin. The safest fish for such women are deep-water saltwater species that are not mercury accumulators.

Methyl mercury is a fetal toxin found in fish and shellfish as a result of pollution and natural exposure. Birth defects can occur in children of women who have had no symptoms of mercury intoxication. Fetuses are estimated to be ten times more sensitive to mercury contamination than adults are. Thus, women of childbearing age should avoid these mercury accumulators: freshwater bass, carp, catfish, perch, pike, rock cod, red snapper, sablefish, shark, smelt, striped bass, swordfish, tuna (canned and fresh), turbot, and walleye. Fresh tuna is also rich in omega-3 fatty acids. (Women who want fresh tuna for its omega-3 fatty acids should limit consumption to once a week.)

Other potent pesticide accumulators that pregnant women should avoid are bluefish, buffalo fish, chub, drum, eels, herring, lake trout, mullet, and whitefish.

Metals

Exposure to excessive amounts of nine common industrial and naturally occurring metals—aluminum, arsenic, cadmium, chromium, cobalt, lead, lithium, manganese, and mercury—can affect a child's reading, spelling, and coordination. In fact, researchers can predict which children will be learning disabled based on their past exposure to toxic metals.

During pregnancy, even a seemingly small amount of lead in tap water can promote birth defects. Researchers believe that lead exposure during pregnancy may play a primary or supporting role in as many as 45 percent of the birth defects today, including subtle effects. In an early 1970s study, half the hyperactive children in one Brooklyn neighborhood were found to have elevated blood lead levels. But with a lead chelation program using the drug EDTA, which binds metals and helps the body excrete them, these dangerously high lead levels were reduced.

Exposure to cadmium may produce birth defects. Cadmium compounds are used to make plastics, stabilizers, and pigments. Birth weight can be reduced by cadmium exposures, as demonstrated in a study of infants born to industrial workers who were exposed to cadmium-laced smoke. Europeans in particular have become concerned about their children's exposure to industrial metals and naturally occurring metals. In the 1980s, a concerted effort to reduce all cadmium discharged into the environment was launched throughout Europe, partly as a result of exceedingly elevated cadmium levels in beef, fish, cereals, potatoes, mushrooms, and mussels in German products. In America, our public officials have not shown nearly the same concern over cadmium contamination and its toxic effects on the developing fetus.

Nitrates and Nitrites

We are exposed to nitrates in our drinking water as a result of the overuse of synthetic fertilizers on our farmlands. Nationwide, the water in about 3 percent of rural wells exceeds government standards for nitrates. I believe these are low estimates. In north central states, about 6 percent of rural wells exceed the government standard. Water companies must notify customers if nitrate levels exceed government standards, and private well owners should have their wells regularly checked. Any level above one or two parts per million indicates contamination, a situation that is healthy for neither adults nor babies.

In newborns, nitrates deplete the blood of oxygen. This condition is known as blue baby syndrome, or methemoglobinemia. Babies' intestinal tracts are not sufficiently acidic to prevent the growth of bacteria that convert nitrates to toxic compounds known as nitrites, and a heavy intake of nitrates can quickly lead to toxic levels of nitrites in the blood, which impede the red blood cells from carrying oxygen to the rest of the body. At toxic levels the baby turns blue. The baby will die if not immediately treated for nitrate poisoning. Parents in rural areas should note that exposure causes a visible color change in a child, and one can see that something is terribly wrong. The baby needs immediate hospital attention.

The present government standard is ten parts per million nitrates in water. But any level above one or two parts per million represents nitrate pollution in your water. That is because one or two parts per million usually is the highest natural level of nitrates in water, with the exception of highly mineralized waters.

Women who are pregnant or who will have children should know that nitrates are associated with birth defects. Australian studies indicate that the U.S. standard of ten parts per million has resulted in sharp increases in birth defects among exposed babies. Nitrates have had perhaps their greatest impact in pregnancies on neural tube birth defects, which can occur when the spinal column does not fuse and form a protective tube around the spinal cord or when the meninges, the soft tissue sheath surrounding the spinal cord, fails to fully develop. The Australian studies on birth defects indicate that the drinking water standard for nitrates needs to be reduced to less than five parts per million, since birth defect rates more than doubled at the five to fifteen parts per million range.

Have your water tested for nitrates if you live near farmlands. If the level exceeds five parts per million, find an alternate safe water source or have your water filtered. See the chapter on water for information on filters. Pregnant women drawing drinking water from private wells in agricultural areas should regularly monitor their water supply if there is any evidence of a nitrate problem. See the Personal Action Guide for information on nitrate home test kits.

Pregnant women should know that diet is a strong ally in the fight against nitrates. A diet rich in vitamin C and vitamin E will significantly inhibit the transformation of nitrates into birth defect–causing chemicals. Vitamin C is an important aspect of the low-toxin diet. It will also help block nutrient depletion that might arise as a result of nitrate-induced vitamin deficiency.

Mothers should avoid sidestream cigarette smoke, another potent source of nitrosamine-containing substances.

Nitrates in water are not our only problem. Similar chemicals called nitrites are added to our food. Eating nitrite-rich foods even once a week significantly raises the risk of birth defects. Eating nitrite-rich foods two or more times a week could more than double the risk of giving birth to a baby with a birth defect. There is clearly a need to begin the systematic reduction of nitrite preservatives in our food supply. Eating preserved meats such as ham and bacon and salted or smoked fish has been shown in several independent studies to be the cause of brain cancer in children who were exposed during gestation. A study in England reported that women who eat cured meats with nitrites during pregnancy are more likely to give birth to babies with neural tube birth defects. An American study found higher rates of brain cancer in children whose mothers were exposed to nitrogen compounds during pregnancy.

Limit your consumption of nitrite-rich foods such as bacon, ham, sausage, hot dogs, salami, and cold cuts to less than once a month during pregnancy. If you do eat cured meats and salted fish, eat plenty of oranges and strawberries and swallow a vitamin C tablet; these vitamin C–rich foods will inhibit the formation of birth defect–causing chemicals.

Vitamin C is an important weapon in the battle against nitrites. In 1978, the government's agriculture department, under pressure from consumers and scientists, reduced the amount of nitrites that could be added to bacon roughly in half, down to 120 parts per million. In addition, the changes in the law mandated that vitamin C be added to processed meats, in part because it is known to inhibit the conversion of nitrites to birth defect–causing compounds. I believe that nitrite levels in meat should be brought down to no more than 40 parts per million. Such proposals in the past were killed in Congress as a result of heavy industry lobbying.

We have an urgent need in America to reduce our exposure to nitrates, nitrites, and nitroso-compounds. I believe we must reduce our exposure by 50 percent. Individuals on the low-toxin high-energy diet can accomplish this without trouble, for the diet is designed specifically to root out these very dangerous toxic chemical exposures.

Radiation

There is no safe level of radiation during pregnancy. Radiation is a major contributor to birth defects and childhood cancer.

American researchers report that fallout from the April 1986 Chernobyl disaster caused a significant increase in U.S. infant mortality. Radiation from the Soviet Union reached the United States about May 7, 1986, less than two weeks after the Chernobyl nuclear power station accident. Two of America's most prestigious radiation researchers, Dr. Jay Gould, of the Council for Economic Priorities, and Dr. Ernest Sternglass found that a large number of American babies appear to have been killed by the fallout of radioactive iodine 131. This report is dramatic. But you cannot doubt the scientific credibility of its authors. Gould is currently the principal investigator of a Radiation and Public Health Research Project and served on the EPA Science Advisory Board from 1977 to 1980. Sternglass is Emeritus Professor of Radiological Physics in the Department of Radiology, University of Pittsburgh School of Medicine, where he was director of the Radiological Physics and Engineering Laboratory. Gould and Sternglass reported in 1989 in *Chemtech* that 20,000 to 40,000 deaths were accelerated as a result of worldwide nuclear fallout in the four summer months following the meltdown. For the United States as a whole, there was an 8.2 percent increase in infant mortality during the month of June 1986, over the previous year, one of the highest increases noted since 1934. States with the highest amount of iodine 131 in the milk supplies— including Washington, New Jersey, and Pennsylvania—were hit hardest. In states like New York, where residents were warned by environmental groups not to drink the milk and where milk consumption declined, infant mortality actually declined, making the increases in states like Washington, New Jersey, and Pennsylvania even more significant. In Washington, infant mortality went up 254 percent in June 1986 compared to June of the previous year. Monthly live births fell dramatically in June in Massachusetts. In California we kept telling ourselves that surely our milk would remain untouched. But, in fact, our milk supply received substantial boosts in its iodine 131 content; not surprisingly, 80 percent of the miscarriages, fetal deaths, and stillbirths in the United States between May and August 1986 occurred in California, according to Gould and Sternglass in a paper presented at the first Global Radiation Victims Conference in New York in September 1987. These occurrences struck California's wildlife, too. In the Point Reyes Bird Observatory during the summer months, the number of newly hatched birds dropped more than 60 percent, according to observations by David De Sante, who documented the massive and unprecedented reproductive failure of land birds between May 15 and August 15, 1986.

In northern Alberta, Canada, birth defects nearly doubled between 1959 and 1961. The culprit proved to be atmospheric fallout from Soviet nuclear explosions. Other studies, particularly a study in Kerala, in southern coastal India, indicate that as background radiation increases, the rate of birth defects, including mental retardation, also increases. A March of Dimes–financed study of pregnancies among Navajo women indicates that exposure to radioactive uranium mine wastes and radioactive releases from milling significantly increased retardation rates among Navajo newborns.

The use of X rays during pregnancy can result in damage to the fetus in about one percent of all cases. The fetus should absolutely not be exposed to X rays. The chilling related effects include premature death of the child, changes in a mother's fertility, and learning disability in the child if radiation exposure occurs between the eighth and fifteenth week of the pregnancy. There is no safe level of radiation for pregnant women. I am telling you to be careful here, for many doctors still allow X rays during pregnancy. But even a small exposure may cause later learning disability and hyperactivity. The fetus is as much as sixteen times more sensitive to radiation than adults are, and development of the brain is most susceptible to chronic low-level radiation. You should even avoid dental X rays during this crucial period.

Unfortunately, physicians often do not know that a woman is pregnant when they order X rays. If there is even a tiny chance that you might be pregnant, you should avoid X rays unless absolutely necessary.

It seems now that earlier studies of the effects of X rays seriously underestimated the dangers of these low-level exposures. Radiation exposure seems to be very intense at low levels. One study in Baltimore discovered children exposed to medical diagnostic X rays when they were in the womb died at a 40 to 50 percent faster than normal rate before the age of ten.

Every X ray facility in the country has lead pregnancy shields to protect the fetus, and they are often used on all women of childbearing age, whether known to be pregnant or not. There is no question that X rays cause birth defects, particularly in the first trimester, as all medical personnel should know. Sometimes, of course, X rays are imperative for a pregnant woman. For example, after a severe automobile crash, when a cervical spine fracture is suspected and the patient has been immobilized in full spinal restraints, removing the restraints without first verifying by X ray that there is no fracture has led to unnecessary paralysis in highly publicized cases. But a pregnancy test should be routinely ordered by all physicians prior to abdominal X rays on women of childbearing age, unless emergency circumstances prohibit this precaution.

Steps for a Safe Pregnancy

We want to provide the greatest opportunities for our children so that they can grow up smart, creative, and healthy and fulfill all their human potential. These guidelines will help you defend yourself and your children against the ravages of toxic chemicals.

Eat pure foods. Women who will have children should follow the dietary guidelines presented in this book in order to cut down their intake of toxic chemicals. Always choose the purest foods available. Organic should be your first choice; low-toxic green light foods will be your alternative.

Drink filtered or bottled water. A study by the California state Department of Health Services reported that women who drank bottled or filtered water had significantly lower rates of spontaneous abortions and birth defects than ones who drank tap water.

Use vitamin supplements. Judicious use of nutritional supplements are recommended during pregnancy. Numerous toxic chemicals, such as lead, nitrates, nitrites, and some pesticides and therapeutic drugs, tend to deplete vitamins from the body. Vitamin deficiencies, in turn, have been linked with neural tube defects in several studies. Studies show that women who used multiple vitamins have lower rates of spontaneous abortions and babies with birth defects. The federal Centers for Disease Control report that the incidence of neural tube defects was lower among mothers who took multivitamins during and at least three months before pregnancy. Even mothers who waited to use multivitamins until during their pregnancy had slightly lower risk for neural tube defects.

Be careful to consult your physician about any possible fetal toxicity with vitamins, notably vitamin A. Don't just start loading up with vitamins and minerals. Consult a registered dietician or a physician trained in nutrition.

When buying a supplement, remember that the form in which vitamins and minerals are delivered is very important. Calcium carbonate, for example, is difficult for many women to absorb because of their low stomach acid production. Both calcium and magnesium supplements are best when they come in capsules or tablets mixed with citrates. The citrates will help prevent the formation of kidney stones. Your best choice is to take about 1,000 milligrams of calcium citrate daily.

It is also important to take 300 to 400 milligrams of magnesium citrate daily. Magnesium also helps prevent kidney stones. Other macronutrients you will want to supplement are zinc and copper. You will need an iodine supplement if you eat fewer than three servings of seafood each week during pregnancy. Be sure to supplement selenium and chromium, two essential micronutrients, during pregnancy. Because there is a fine line between helpful and toxic amounts of chromium and selenium, consult a registered dietician or physician for advice on the best amounts. You should take 25 milligrams daily of vitamin B_6. Women often are deficient in this vitamin, which is essential for proper functioning of the immune system. Also supplement folic acid and take about 200 international units of vitamin E daily.

Do not take choline or lecithin; these nutrients produce chemicals that can potentially affect the behavior of the baby.

Don't burn incense. Burning incense in the house exposes the fetus to high levels of nitroso-compounds and benzopyrene and is associated with childhood leukemia, according to recent research published in the *Journal of the National Cancer Institute.*

Don't use pesticides unless they are biologically benign products. (See the gardening section in the chapter on the nontoxic home for safe pest remedies.) Pesticide use has been shown to increase chances of children being born with birth defects or later contracting leukemia. The odds were nearly seven times greater that children would contract leukemia in families that used garden pesticides once a month, according to a 1987 study. The message is, don't use pesticides in the home. Certainly, pregnant women should not spray pesticides around the home or the garden.

Do not diet. Dieting promotes the release of toxic chemicals, stored in your fatty tissues, into the bloodstream. Weight gain is going to occur during pregnancy. Women at normal weights will gain 25 to 35 pounds. Many doctors advise pregnant women to eat six small meals daily instead of three larger meals.

Eat a variety of high-fiber, low-fat foods.

Emphasize calcium-rich foods. Salmon, figs, beans, organic spinach, almonds, and walnuts have generous amounts of calcium. You should eat organic cheddar cheese daily; it's a wonderful calcium source. Or eat canned salmon with the bones. The bones, which are very soft, having been cooked before being canned, are the richest source of calcium. Eat four calcium-rich meals daily. Include nonfat yogurt, nonfat milk, and organic cheese. Drink several glasses of nonfat milk daily. You might even want to drink one of the calcium-rich waters listed in the water chapter.

Omega-3 fatty acids are of vital importance during pregnancy. Omega-3 fatty acids help nourish your immune system, which is undergoing a literal depression. During pregnancy the immune system must become slightly subdued, so it does not attack the embryo. Unfortunately, some doctors recommend eating fish such as mackerel, herring, and bluefish. This is bad advice! The best fish for omega-3 fatty acids include Oregon, Washington, and Alaska salmon and limited amounts of fresh, not canned, tuna. Only fresh tuna contains significant amounts of omega-3 fatty acids. But limit tuna to twice a week, because it is a moderate mercury accumulator.

Get plenty of iron and zinc. Organic lean red meat has these minerals, which provide essential help for metabolizing omega-3 fatty acids. Vegetarians should substitute almonds, pecans, sesame seeds, soybeans, lentils, chickpeas, and lima beans, which are rich sources of iron and zinc. Most beans are a good bet. Eat several cups of beans each week during pregnancy. To avoid gas, change the water several times while you are cooking the beans, or soak the beans overnight and then discard the water. Troublesome complex sugars disappear with the discarded water.

Vegetarians should be careful to get enough protein during pregnancy. When nutritionists plan substitutions for meats and poultry, they use one egg or one-half cup seeds and nuts in place of three ounces of meat. Eggs are an excellent trade-off, during pregnancy, for meat. Eggs tend to be significantly less contaminated with heavy-duty pesticides than beef. Buy eggs that are guaranteed to be from fertile chickens raised without hormones or antibiotics and not artificially colored.

Eat three or four servings of fruits and vegetables daily. Be sure to substitute organically grown produce for the most chemically saturated fruits and vegetables. Your baby will need the ultimate protection now from toxic invaders, and foods rich in vitamin A and vitamin C will enhance your immunity and stimulate those sentinels we call lymphocytes to gobble up invaders and get them out of the bloodstream.

Eat four servings of whole grains daily. Always buy whole grains. Fiber will help you reduce your exposure to unwelcome toxic chemicals by absorbing and binding them and then removing them. Whole grain cereals and breads are great sources of fiber.

Abstain from alcohol and limit caffeine to no more than two cups of coffee daily. Black tea, cocoa, chocolate milk, and cola also contain caffeine.

Stay away from artificial sweeteners. NutraSweet and Equal contain aspartame. This sweetener appears to have damaged the brains of laboratory animals and presently its effect on the human fetus remains unclear. In addition, soft drinks often have phosphoric acid, which interferes with your body's use of calcium and magnesium.

Breast-Feeding

Industrial chemicals and pesticides can concentrate in breast milk. In most women, the breast-milk contaminants are at a low enough level that the benefits of breast-feeding, physiologically and psychologically, out-weigh the risks. The American Academy of Pediatrics asserts that breast-feeding provides important immunological and nutritional benefits that are not available in formula.

But women who do not reduce their exposure to toxic chemicals could expose their babies to industrial pollutants and pesticides by breast-feeding. Remember, dangerous pollutants, such as DDT and PCBs, con-centrate in fatty tissues, and breast milk is fatty.

The proper time for concern is before pregnancy. Women can find out about the levels of pollutants in their blood before they become pregnant. If the levels are high, women can detox and purge these contaminants. See the Detoxification chapter for information on background levels of different chemicals in your blood. Once lactation begins, any woman who suspects she may have been contaminated should have her breast milk analyzed for organic pollutants.

Breast milk contamination is quite serious in this country. Women in Arkansas and Hawaii have had their breast milk contaminated with hepta-chlor as a result of food contamination and have been warned against breast-feeding their children as a result. Many women living in the Mid-west and along the Great Lakes have breast milk contaminated with dan-gerously elevated levels of dioxin. In a survey of Illinois mothers, high levels of toxaphene were found in their breast milk. A survey of Michigan mothers found that fifty percent had PCBs in their breast milk at levels that equaled or exceeded FDA safety standards.

I believe we should begin a full-scale national program to reduce breast milk contamination. We need to learn more about how we can prevent pollutants from concentrating in breast milk. I am certain that the findings would lead to increased purity of our nation's food supply and would con-tribute to the health of our children.

Mothers—and fathers, too—might want to consider a largely vegetarian diet. One study shows that women who are vegetarians have one-one-hundredth the DDT pollution of average American mothers. Compared with the average American mother, vegetarian mothers had one-fourteenth the BHC pollution, one-forty-eighth the chlordane, one-fiftieth the heptachlor, and two-thirds the PCB pollution. Since we know that breast-feeding is extremely important, women of childbearing age can help themselves and their children by watching their diet long before they be-come pregnant and by avoiding the industrially contaminated and pesticide-laden foods that pose the greatest threat to infants.

17. BABY FOODS

Baby food is in pretty much the same situation as adult food: some products have very few pesticide residues; others are quite heavily saturated. But babies are much more vulnerable to toxins than adults are. It is imperative that we take steps to limit babies' intake of pesticides and other residues.

Some scientists say we do not know why childhood cancer rates skyrocketed nearly 1 percent a year between 1950 and 1985, an increase of 32 percent over thirty-five years. But, no doubt, part of this increase must be attributed to our increased reliance on synthetic chemicals and to babies' exposure to toxic chemicals in food and water.

Government records indicate that from 1978 to 1982 more infants than ever were exposed to many of the most carcinogenic and neurotoxic pesticides, including captan, carbaryl, chlorobenzilate, chlorpyrifos, diazinon, dicofol, dimethoate, endosulfan, penta, and tecnazene. Many of our children's favorite fruit juices are saturated with pesticides, including carbaryl, chlorobenzilate, dicofol, dimethoate, endosulfan, ethion, malathion, parathion, and phosalone. Is this what we want our babies to be ingesting three to six times a day?

Infant susceptibility to toxic chemicals in food is much greater than that of adults. A baby's liver still lacks certain enzymes and cannot break down pesticides effectively. Babies' and toddlers' immune systems are not as strong as those of adults; they may not be able to vanquish toxic invaders. In addition, "Cells undergoing rapid growth [may be] more susceptible to carcinogens than cells that are more static," Dr. Richard Jackson, chairman of the American Academy of Pediatrics environmental hazards committee, told *Newsweek.*

Toxins ingested by a baby can affect it for its whole life. A baby's neurological system undergoes important growth during the first few years, but many of the pesticides in baby food are neurotoxins, which can disrupt nerve transmissions from the brain, upsetting this development. What may be happening is that chronic toxic exposures during late pregnancy and soon after birth can interfere with the normal proliferation of the brain's microneurons, which contribute to the fine circuitry of a given brain region. This can lead to subtle, permanent nerve deficits in a child, which can lead to learning disabilities and hyperactivity. Also, 55 percent of the lifetime cancer risk we face from carcinogenic pesticides in foods can occur by age six, according to a Natural Resources Defense Council (NRDC) estimate.

The EPA tolerance-setting procedures have always been for adults. "There is little question that children face a higher risk from pesticides and that, until the past few years, EPA has not factored this into its calculations," says *Science* magazine. In addition, tolerances for most of the 600 to 700 chemicals used in pesticides were set years ago with much less testing than is now required.

Some of the so-called inert ingredients found in pesticides in baby foods as well as all other foods may be more toxic than their actual active ingredients. For example, one of the inert ingredients of the herbicide glyphosate is anywhere from 100 to 500 times more toxic to fish than the active ingredients. Other pesticides contain carbon tetrachloride as an inert ingredient; yet carbon tetrachloride is so toxic to humans that it is no longer allowed to be used as an active ingredient. The situation for adults is absurd and risky. But for babies and children, whose natural defense systems are so poorly developed, the situation is downright dangerous.

The NRDC estimates that 5,500 to 6,200 of our present preschool children may develop cancer some time in their lives as a result of exposure by the age of six to just eight of the pesticides that can contaminate produce, and this probably underestimates the overall cancer risk severely. In its study, NRDC examined only twenty-three out of the approximately three hundred pesticides that can contaminate our foods. Furthermore, the study neglects to examine the pesticide burden posed by the most dangerous food groups such as meat and dairy foods.

Although there is much we do not know, we do know what our common sense tells us: these chemicals are toxic. They definitely are not nutrients; in fact, they are antinutrients. They have no positive role in baby food. Companies can get them out completely if we make our dollars vote in the supermarket by purchasing the least toxic baby foods and organic baby foods. We are the ones who must lead this revolution. Nobody can do it for us. We want our babies' bodies to be pure. So we must learn about the dangerous pesticides in baby food and then take protective action.

And do not be fooled by claims from the nation's leading producers of baby food. Gerber, Heinz, and Beech-Nut all allow pesticides to be used on the produce with which their foods are made. They all make claims that sound good. In 1986, H. J. Heinz & Co., of Pittsburgh, announced that it would stop buying for use in its baby foods and juices crops treated with the chemicals alachlor, aldicarb, captafol, captan, carbofuran, carbon tetrachloride, cyanazine, daminozide, dinocap, linuron, and TPTH. That is a good start, but it leaves open hundreds of other pesticides that may be used. Gerber says that its suppliers' produce has very low pesticide residues. Beech-Nut says produce cannot have pesticides that are more than one-quarter of the legal limit for each particular chemical. But these limits are not strict enough for our babies' health and future growth. Send these companies a clear message that we want *no* pesticides in baby food.

Many of the foods toddlers and older children love are the most pesticide-laden around. Some of the highest levels in our diet of benzene hexachloride (BHC)—a carcinogen nineteen times more potent than DDT—are found in butter, processed cheese, beef frankfurters, and milk chocolate.

Peanut butter is one of the most thoroughly pesticide-saturated foods in the American diet. Grape jelly has residues. Virtually all doughnuts, coffee cakes, Danish pastries, and pumpkin pies contain high levels of malathion. Chocolate cake and chocolate chip cookies contain diazinon. In the Total Diet Study, raisins were found to contain more than one hundred residues. Fast-food hamburgers, french fries, milk shakes, pizza, grapes, chocolate chip cookies, potato chips, ice cream, bologna, sandwich cookies, and macaroni and cheese all contain hordes of pesticides, and many of these foods also have additives and preservatives. They can affect children's behavior as well as their health. They really do not belong in our children's diets if we are concerned about their exposure to toxic chemicals and behavior-altering additives.

Baby Food Survival Guide

GREEN LIGHT

You will note that the low-toxin foods in the adult diet and the low-toxin foods for babies are pretty much the same. Feed these foods to your baby as often as you like. They are outperformed only by organic baby foods. Best of all, buy organic produce and make your own baby foods.

Bananas and pineapple. Bananas and pineapple had one pesticide residue, malathion.

Carrots. Carrots had only four pesticide residues including DDT and parathion.

Chicken and noodles. Chicken and noodles had only five pesticide residues including chlorpyrifos, diazinon, malathion, and parathion.

Corn. Creamed corn had only one pesticide residue, chlorpyrifos.

Fruit dessert with tapioca. Fruit dessert with tapioca had only seven pesticide residues including chlorpyrifos, DDT, dicofol, and parathion.

Milk-based infant formula with iron. Milk-based infant formula with iron had only one pesticide residue, penta.

Milk-based infant formula without iron. Only two pesticide residues, chlorpropham and penta, were found in milk-based infant formula without iron.

Mixed vegetables and garden vegetables. These baby foods had only seven pesticide residues including chlorpropham, dicloran, malathion, and parathion.

Peas. Only two residues were found in peas: DCPA and tributyl phosphate.

Pudding and custard. Pudding and custard (any flavor) had only four pesticide residues including diazinon, dicofol, lindane, and phosalone.

Tomatoes with beef and macaroni. This baby food had only nine industrial chemical and pesticide residues including chlorpyrifos, DDT, diazinon, dicloran, EDB, malathion, and tributyl phosphate.

Turkey and rice. Turkey and rice had only four pesticide residues including chlorpropham, chlorpyrifos, and DDT.

Vegetables with bacon and ham. Vegetables with bacon and ham had eleven pesticide residues including chlorpropham, chlorpyrifos, diazinon, lindane, malathion, and tecnazene. Be sure to check the label for nitrites; limit your baby's consumption of this food if nitrites are, in fact, used. Also, be aware that some pork products may contain sulfa drugs.

Vegetables with turkey and chicken. Vegetables with turkey and chicken had four industrial chemical and pesticide residues: chlorpropham, chlorpyrifos, tecnazene, and tributyl phosphate.

YELLOW LIGHT

Feed your child foods from this group less often.

Apple betty. This apple combination contained eighteen pesticide residues. The wide variety detected included BHC, chlorpyrifos, DDT, dicloran, dicofol, ethion, parathion, and phosalone. At least half the pesticides detected can cause cancer. They are virtually all neurotoxic chemicals.

Apple juice. Plain apple juice, apple-cherry juice, and apple-grape juice contain twenty pesticide residues. Carbaryl and dimethoate—both acute neurotoxins—were detected in at least half the samples. Acephate and omethoate also were detected.

Beef. Beef had twenty-six pesticide residues. Every sample contained low levels of DDT. Other pesticides detected included dieldrin, HCB, lindane, and octachlor. Beef may also have hormone residues that are not good for your baby.

Chicken and turkey. Chicken and turkey baby food contained thirty pesticide residues. Virtually every sample contained DDT. Half the samples contained dieldrin. Traces of heptachlor, HCB, and octachlor were also detected.

Green beans. Twenty-eight pesticide residues were found in green beans. More than half the samples contained the acute neurotoxin methamidophos. Other pesticides detected included acephate, BBC, DDT, dicloran, dieldrin, endosulfan, parathion, and pentachloroaniline.

Beef and vegetables. This baby food had twenty-three pesticide residues. DDT was detected in half the samples and dieldrin in a quarter of the samples. Other pesticides detected included chlorpropham, chlorpyrifos, diazinon, ethion, heptachlor, malathion, and penta.

Ham and vegetables. Seventeen pesticide residues were found in this food. DDT was found in nearly three-fourths of the samples. Other pesticides detected included dieldrin and penta.

Infant mixed cereal. This cereal combination had nineteen pesticide residues including malathion in fourteen of the sixteen samples and penta in three of the sixteen. The other pesticides detected included chlorpyrifos and diazinon. As for other baby cereals, follow the advice in the section about grains for finding the least toxic varieties.

Oatmeal with applesauce. This baby food had twenty-one pesticide residues. More than three-quarters of the samples contained malathion; other pesticides detected included chlorpyrifos, endosulfan, parathion, and phosalone.

Orange juice. Both orange juice and orange-pineapple juice contained twenty-four pesticide residues. The carcinogen chlorobenzilate was detected in more than three-fourths of the samples. Other pesticides detected included carbaryl, endosulfan, ethion, methiocarb, and omethoate.

Prunes or plums with tapioca. These mixtures contained twenty-seven pesticide residues. At least half the samples contained the carcinogen dicofol. Other pesticides detected included DDT, endosulfan, parathion, and phosalone. Both DDT and parathion are carcinogens; endosulfan can cause kidney damage.

Spinach. Creamed spinach contained twenty-seven pesticide residues. More than three-quarters of the samples contained DDT. Other pesticides detected included chlorpyrifos, EPN, EDB, methamidophos, penta, and permethrin.

Sweet potatoes with yellow squash. This vegetable mixture contained nineteen pesticide residues. More than 80 percent of the samples contained dicloran. A quarter contained dieldrin. One contained pentachloroaniline.

Vegetables with beef. Vegetables with beef had sixteen pesticide residues. DDT was detected in half the samples. Other pesticides detected included BHC, chlordane, chlorpropham, chlorpyrifos, and malathion.

RED LIGHT

Strictly limit your child's consumption of these foods.

Applesauce. Both plain applesauce and applesauce mixed with other fruit contained thirty-eight pesticide residues. The wide variety included acephate, chlorpyrifos, DDT, dicofol, dimethoate, endosulfan, omethoate, parathion, phosalone, and phosmet.

Peaches. Peaches contained thirty-three pesticide residues. There was a wide variety including chlorpyrifos, DDT, dicloran, dicofol, endosulfan, parathion, and phosalone. Nearly half of them cause cancer.

Pears. Plain pears and pears with pineapple contained fifty-two pesticide residues. More than half the samples contained endosulfan and phosalone. Other pesticides detected included chlorpyrifos, DCPA, DDT, dicofol, ethion, and parathion.

Pork. Pork contained fifty-two residues. More than half the samples contained DDT and penta. Other chemicals detected included dieldrin, heptachlor, HCB, nonachlor, octachlor, and pentachlorobenzene. Most of these chemicals can cause cancer.

Shopping Tips

What to do? Buy low-toxin or organic foods and make your own baby food. Or buy organic baby food. Companies that make such products are growing fast. Why not? They use pesticide-free organic crops, which are the safest that you can give your children. It comes down to common sense. Knowing what we know, who wouldn't want to buy organic baby food?

Earth's Best, of Middlebury, Vermont, requires all growers to be certified organic by independent third-party groups, and growers must go through a three-year transition from chemical farming to organic farming. Their baby foods are available at 5,000 health and natural food stores nationwide as well as by mail and through home delivery.

Simply Pure, of Bangor, Maine, uses strictly organically grown produce from farms where no pesticides have been used for at least three years. Most Simply Pure produce comes from farms that have been organic for much longer than that. Produce is frequently tested at the University of Maine laboratories for pesticide residues and toxins. Their foods are also certified kosher. You may order by mail from Simply Pure. See the Personal Action Guide for details.

A pesticide residue may occasionally find its way into even organic baby food. But overall the exposure is so low that this is really not a concern when compared with nonorganic baby foods that are high in pesticides.

You can use trips to the supermarket to teach your children good nutrition. There are wonderful games you can play with children in the supermarket. Get them involved in handling fruits and vegetables. Tell your children you want something yellow, something red, something orange, and something green. If you are at a store with a good selection of produce, tell the children to find something purple—you may end up with purple cabbage or purple potatoes. Never refuse a vegetable, even if it is unfamiliar. If your child brings you a purple potato, well, there are plenty of good dishes to be made with purple potatoes. A crookneck yellow squash cooks just as easily as zucchini.

Another fun idea is baking whole grain pizzas. You can pretend that the pizza is Mr. Pizza Man or Ms. Pizza Woman and decorate the face with a variety of organically grown vegetables. Alfalfa sprouts can be the hair, mushrooms eyes, tomatoes the cheeks. Use red sweet pepper for lips and zucchini slices for a beard. And use a good organic cheese or organic soy substitute cheese.

For children's parties, serve granola bars, plum drops, and pineapple and coconut clusters. Serve organic potato chips. These should not be diet staples, of course. But they are much purer than pesticide-laden milk chocolates and ice cream. Try nonfat yogurt with organic sweet conserves and fresh organic fruits. Kids love these desserts. Serve muesli crackers and organic whole grain cookies. Instead of soda pop, serve organic strawberry cider or fruit spritzers.

A final important consideration for new parents is diapers. Nearly 85 percent of all diapers used are disposables, which means that each year more than eighteen billion disposable diapers are tossed into landfills where they will last without breaking down for centuries. It is estimated that as much as 3 percent of solid waste in landfills consists of soiled disposable diapers; about five million tons of disposable diapers are buried in landfills in the United States every year. These diapers can take as long as five hundred years to decompose once they are buried. Furthermore, traces of the highly toxic industrial contaminant dioxin can be found in disposable diapers, adding to the child's early toxic chemical body burden. For all these reasons, disposable diapers are not a way of promoting good ecology. We *must* change our ways, especially when our actions can be modified so easily!

One ecologically correct course of action, which also saves money, is to use cloth diapers and a diaper service. You get your diapers washed by professionals and delivered, at a fraction of the cost of disposables, and you play your role in promoting good ecology for our nation. Furthermore, studies show that babies who wear cotton diapers get rashes five times less often than those who wear disposables. See the Personal Action Guide for details on home delivery diaper services. At least ten major urban diaper delivery services also sell Earth's Best organic baby foods. What a deal!

And if you must use disposable diapers, at least look for brands that easily biodegrade. Such environmentally sound products are becoming increasingly available at supermarkets nationwide.

Safe Shopping List: Baby Foods

Green Light	Number of Residues
Bananas and pineapples	1
Corn (creamed)	1
Milk-based infant formula with iron	1
Milk-based infant formula without iron	2
Peas	2
Carrots	4
Pudding and custard (any flavor)	4
Turkey and rice	4
Vegetables with turkey and chicken	4
Chicken and noodles	5
Fruit dessert with tapioca	7
Mixed vegetables and garden vegetables	7
Tomatoes with beef and macaroni	9
Vegetables with bacon and ham	11

Yellow Light	Number of Residues
Vegetables with beef	16
Ham and vegetables	17
Dutch apple and apple betty	18
Infant mixed cereal	19
Sweet potatoes with yellow squash	19
Apple, apple-cherry, and apple-grape juice	20

Oatmeal with applesauce	21
Beef and vegetables	23
Orange juice and orange-pineapple juice	24
Beef	26
Prunes or plums with tapioca	27
Spinach (creamed)	27
Green beans	28
Chicken and turkey	30

Red Light	Number of Residues
Peaches	33
Plain applesauce and applesauce with other fruit	38
Plain pears and pears and pineapple	52
Pork	52

18. DETOXIFICATION

Back in the fall of 1985, when I first learned of the toxins in seafood caught in Santa Monica Bay, I had my blood serum analyzed during the course of the study I was conducting on fish eaters poisoned by DDT-contaminated local sport fish. That study, published in 1989 in *Environmental Toxicology and Chemistry,* concluded that Los Angeles fish eaters had levels of DDT that were as much as ten times higher than the levels of people who did not eat local fish. The PCB levels of some fish eaters were similarly elevated.

My blood analysis contained levels of DDT and PCBs that were quite elevated for someone my age; I was then thirty. I wasn't surprised. Since I'd started eating fish from the polluted waters of Santa Monica Bay as a teenager, I knew I was likely to be poisoned.

If I'd been better informed, I would not have fished in the bay and eaten my catch. Even today, when I visit Marina del Rey near Los Angeles and see children with buckets full of contaminated fish, I am amazed to see no warning signs. We get poisoned in a lot of ways.

I cannot adequately describe to you the sense of betrayal I felt about public officials who had let me go on fishing and eating contaminated fish, with DDT and PCBs building up in my tissues, endangering my mind and body. They knew. They stayed silent. I was their victim.

I came to realize that if I continued to eat the local fish and other poisoned foods, my blood pollution concentrations could only get worse. I had to know the toxic levels of all the foods I ate so that I could avoid the most highly contaminated foods and always make nontoxic choices. This period—while I was learning more about the scientific, medical, and ecological aspects of food—marked the beginning of a new consciousness for me. I rarely ate meat after that, and when I did I made absolutely sure that it was a very low-toxic cut or an organic meat and that the animal had been raised humanely. I ate far more fruits, vegetables, and grains than I had before. The only flesh foods I ate were low-toxin ones, such as safe seafood. As I cut fatty foods and animal foods down to a small part of my diet and ate more satiating, wholesome plant foods, I felt as though I were being reborn. I felt better than I remembered feeling since the carefree days of childhood, and I had a new vision of personal health and planetary ecological commitment.

Yet I remained troubled by the pesticides that I knew were stored in my fat and were circulating in my bloodstream at levels that were too high. Despite the assertions of most medical professionals that there was no way to reduce these levels, I decided to find a way to reduce my body burden of pesticides and other toxins. Those chemicals lodged in my fatty tissues could be the cause of a cancer later in my life or they could be affecting my moods or alertness or mental stamina. I wanted to find out how much better I could feel, and I wanted to be sure that those chemicals I'd ingested over the years weren't lurking inside my body, capable of future harm.

I found a way. It works. I'll show you how you can do the same for yourself.

For years doctors have believed that persistent pesticides such as BHC, chlordane, DDT, dieldrin, and heptachlor could not be eliminated from the human body, that once those poisons got into our bodies we were stuck with them. One prominent researcher called exposure to DDE—a metabolite of DDT—a lifetime fatty tissue burden, asserting that "elimination of DDE would require the better part of a man's natural life span." I suspect that one reason for this school of thought is that for forty years after World War II, human exposure to contaminants was so constant and profound that there was little opportunity to detoxify. Few of us knew enough about the value of pure food and water. Until recently, virtually everybody—except for a few knowledgeable and far-seeing individuals—munched on pesticides. There was no escape. The contamination problem today is still dire, but in the 1970s levels of some of the most dangerous bioaccumulating chemicals were even higher.

And now we know it *is* possible to eliminate or markedly reduce our body's burden of toxins.

For the past five years I have been documenting what I believe to be some of the world's most revolutionary research on detoxifying toxic chemicals that have accumulated in the human body. The program is being carried out at a clinic called HealthMed, in the Los Angeles area. In the scientific community, this nonprofit organization's results have been widely disseminated and reported on by organizations as prestigious as the Swedish Royal Academy of Science, the World Health Organization's International Agency for Research on Cancer, the American Society of Civil Engineers, and many other scientific and medical groups. Thousands of individuals have gone through the HealthMed program with successful reductions in toxic levels and great improvements in overall health and spirit. So important is the detox work at HealthMed that I want to tell you more about it.

The successes of this program tell the story:

▪ In 1973, a fire retardant consisting predominantly of polybrominated biphenyls (PBBs) was substituted for a cattle feed supplement in the state of Michigan. Milk and meat were consequently contaminated. In 1978, some 97 percent of individuals tested in Michigan had detectable PBBs in their fatty tissues. A small group of Michigan residents had undergone constant monitoring of their fatty tissue levels by environmental contamination experts at the Mount Sinai School of Medicine in New York and the concentration of toxic chemicals in their fatty tissues had not been reduced in any way in the six years since their initial exposure. When these exposed persons underwent a supervised detoxification program at HealthMed, they experienced a 21.3 percent reduction on average of sixteen of the most common toxic chemicals found in fat, including PBBs, which had been stored in their fatty tissue. But these results were just the immediate post-therapy measurements. Four months after treatment, toxic chemical reductions continued and had been reduced an average of 42 percent. Researchers concluded that the treatment used on the Michigan residents enhanced their bodies' ability to continue to eliminate toxic chemicals—after six years in which there had been no significant changes in their PBB body burdens.

▪ A thirty-three-year-old Vietnam veteran with a history of dioxin exposure and symptoms suggestive of Agent Orange toxicity—eye problems and shortened attention span—was treated. Although a fat biopsy failed to reveal dioxin residues (the limit of detection was 5 parts per trillion), it did show a whopping 7,900 parts per billion DDE and 670 parts per billion PCBs. In a nine-month period, that included both the treatment and the post-treatment phase, 97 percent of the DDT was removed from his body along with 27 percent of the PCBs. His symptoms disappeared.

▪ A young woman employed at a factory in the Yugoslavian town of Semic was heavily exposed to PCBs used in the manufacture of electrical capacitors. She tested approximately twenty thousand small capacitors a day for leakage, working by hand with little or no protection. She began to develop serious health problems including severe abdominal complaints, liver problems, acne, joint pains, and an unusual spontaneous bluish breast discharge. Detoxification reduced the levels of PCBs in her fat tissues by 63 percent. The breast discharge ceased entirely, and her symptoms improved markedly.

• Some one hundred fire fighters and police officers responded to a fire involving a transformer explosion at Louisiana State University in 1987. Some suffered acute exposure to PCBs and dioxins. Several fire fighters became ill. Seventeen underwent detoxification at HealthMed. Prior to treatment, five exhibited clinical symptoms of nerve damage including numbness in the extremities, burning sensations, and tingling, which are all symptoms of a condition known as peripheral neuropathy, which is often regarded as irreversible. According to a report in *Clinical Ecology*, all five showed significant improvement in their peripheral neuropathy and reductions in their body burdens of these chemicals.

• A fifty-four-year-old former library clerk in a public school, whose predecessor had died of cancer of the liver, became ill and began to feel very tired. Her feet hurt so much that she could not walk. After she had seen nine doctors, a neurologist told her she had chemical poisoning. She discovered that the library where she worked had been sprayed once a month with pesticides including Dursban (chlorpyrifos) and Ficam. The employees were not notified of the spraying. She had the books in the library tested and learned that they contained DDT. She arrived at the HealthMed clinic for treatment so sickened by her chemical exposure that she had a hard time leaving her hotel room. After going through detoxification, however, she felt a weight taken off her shoulders. Fat biopsies showed that she had undergone an 80 to 90 percent reduction in toxic chemicals. She also regained hearing in her right ear, which she had lost when one doctor prescribed Indocin and sixteen aspirin tablets a day to relieve the pain in her feet.

Most of these patients' toxic levels, although elevated, were not extraordinary. The bodies of millions of Americans are similarly polluted. A toxic chemical at a concentration that has no effect on one person may have a significant impact on a person who is more highly sensitized. Toxic exposure is present throughout the population. An estimated 23 million American workers are exposed to thirteen commonly used solvents. Some 3.5 million workers are exposed to trichloroethylene in short high-level bursts. Some 3.4 million workers are exposed to carbon tetrachloride either directly or indirectly. And we have all been exposed to low-level contamination in our food, water, and air.

The long-term toxic effects of residues of drugs such as marijuana, cocaine, and LSD can also be modified by detoxification. Many of these drugs are stored in the fatty tissues just like industrial chemicals and pesticides. Persons with historical residues will be amazed at the clarity of mind they experience as they purge their bodies of contaminants and street drugs.

It would be helpful if there were establishments like HealthMed in every major city across America, where people could come to cleanse their bodies internally and purify themselves of the lingering effects of toxic chemicals and drugs. And it would be wonderful if everybody who needed to be purified could afford the approximately $3,000 the HealthMed program costs. That's not cheap, but considering the results and the fact that one is being medically supervised for several hours a day for twenty to forty-five days, it's a considerable bargain.

Unfortunately, there are only two HealthMed clinics at present, in Los Angeles and Sacramento; their addresses are listed in the Personal Action Guide. If you suspect that you are really chemically ill, if you feel sick and disabled, I recommend that you contact HealthMed and inquire whether the program could help you.

The HealthMed detoxification program is designed to flush toxic chemicals out of the human body, first by releasing them into the circulatory system from the fatty tissues in which they are stored, then by making sure they are excreted from the body through several pathways.

The basics of the program were discovered in the 1950s, when researcher L. Ron Hubbard, working with veterans of atomic bomb testing, found that a low dose of niacin (vitamin B_3) would cause a red, prickly flushing of the skin in patients.

There is some controversy over precisely how niacin causes flushing and other symptoms. The answer may be that niacin causes the body to release histamine. Niacin also could cause the dilation and increased permeability of blood vessels. The dilation of blood vessels alone could cause the flush; the release of toxic chemicals stored in fatty acids could contribute to other symptoms.

The one thing researchers do know is that niacin is a significant ally in flushing toxic chemicals from the human body. If a patient continued to take the same dose of niacin for several days, the flushing would cease. A higher dose would then cause the flushing to resume. Eventually, as the dose of niacin was gradually increased, the patient would reach a level at which the flushing effect no longer occurred.

Hubbard also found that niacin could precipitate other effects besides the flush, such as flu symptoms, hives, and aching bones, but that if the dose was continued and gradually increased, these reactions would eventually cease.

The detoxification program builds on the discovery of the effects of niacin. The release of toxic chemicals from fat deposits is the underpinning of HealthMed's deep-reaching, thoroughly purifying detoxification regimen.

In the program used at HealthMed, powdered niacin is given to patients in ever-increasing doses. Fortunately, the vast majority of people can take niacin without adverse effects. In fact, physicians for years have routinely prescribed niacin as a vital part of a cholesterol reduction program at much higher doses than those used in the detoxification program. One beneficial side effect of this program is that cholesterol levels are usually reduced by it. In addition, niacin is an excellent supplement to fight the onset of Alzheimer's disease, particularly failing memory and confusion, according to convincing evidence presented by Michael Weiner, Ph.D., in *Reducing the Risk of Alzheimer's*. The program starts with 100 milligrams daily of niacin. Patients stay at 100 milligrams until they have a very slight reaction, if any. The physician does not advance the niacin dose to 200 milligrams until the individual's body can handle 100 milligrams. Over a period of two to six weeks, the niacin dosage, in constellation with balanced doses of other vitamins and minerals, is gradually increased to a level of perhaps 5,000 milligrams.

Between 100 milligrams and 1,000 milligrams, most patients climb up the ladder in 100 milligram steps. At 1,000 milligrams, most progress in 500 milligram steps.

Some experts condone long-term elevated niacin supplementation, but my advice is to consult a knowledgeable physician and work slowly on detox. Remember, detox is not a race where the fastest finisher wins.

The niacin mobilizes fatty acids, moving them from the fat into the bloodstream. To enhance this mobilization, patients run, jog, or do other physician-directed aerobic exercise for about thirty minutes a day. This gets the blood circulating through all layers of body tissues, so chemicals can be helped along into the circulatory system.

After exercise mobilizes the chemicals into the bloodstream, they need to be excreted from the body. This is encouraged in several ways. Patients at HealthMed eat a diet that includes pure, high-fiber foods. They drink lots of fluids. And after exercise, they spend time in a low-heat sauna. Some toxic chemicals appear to be excreted through the sweat as efficiently as through the urine, according to many scientific reports. Sauna time is a vital component of the HealthMed detox program.

The last major component of the HealthMed detox program is the use of polyunsaturated oils. Polyunsaturated oils help circumvent the circular route of the enterohepatic pathway. The body is unwilling to give up its fatty acids if it senses it needs them. Eating polyunsaturated fats allows the body to replace fatty acid compounds that were previously stored in fat. So doses of pure, unpolluted polyunsaturated fats can enhance elimination of contaminated stored fats. In addition, polyunsaturated fatty acids enhance elimination of toxic chemicals by stimulating the production of bile. Into bile go toxic compounds as they pass through the liver. The bile goes from the liver to the gallbladder to the gastrointestinal tract, where a diet high in fiber plant foods will bind the bile and its toxic chemicals, helping to eliminate them completely. By supplementing the diet with polyunsaturated oils, people actually initiate a fat exchange, replacing dirty fat with cleaner, purer fats.

At HealthMed this detox program is carried out under intense medical supervision and is continually modified to suit each patient's progress. The patients' diets are carefully monitored, including nutritional supplements not described here. Their rate of success is extraordinary. But beware of programs set up in imitation of HealthMed. I have looked into some and been appalled by their fly-by-night nature.

A HOME DETOX PROGRAM

By using simple detoxification principles that anybody can employ, I was able to reduce my DDT blood level from 15 parts per billion to about 4 parts per billion—a reduction of 70 percent. My PCB blood concentration went from 7 parts per billion to about 4.5 parts per billion, a reduction of 36 percent.

After detoxing on my own, I underwent a supervised detoxification program at HealthMed. Since completion of this intense supervised program, I have continued to slough off accumulated toxic chemicals; further lab analyses indicate that my PCB levels have gone down even lower, to about .4 parts per billion, a 90 percent reduction. My DDT levels are down to less than 4 parts per billion. I feel better, too. With my changes in diet and life-style and this detox program, I have cleaned up my body. You can do the same.

One last note: detoxification also helps in weight loss. Many persons report shedding many of their excess pounds after undergoing detoxification. The reason for this is not established. But weight loss does appear to be an unplanned benefit of detoxification.

There are many people who sense the need to detox. They know they have been exposed to a variety of pollutants and are perhaps suffering from common complaints like headaches, fatigue, irritability, and mental fogginess. Active detoxification can help these people feel better. So, after consulting with experts affiliated with HealthMed and other scientists and physicians, I have developed a home detox program, which I'll outline in the pages ahead. It does not require the intense supervision that a niacin-based program requires. So it is perfect for just about anybody who wants to detox on their own.

The components of the program are really quite simple: a low-toxin diet, exercise, time spent in a sauna, and basic nutritional support. Many health-conscious, active individuals will discover that they are already doing many of the right things to detoxify. The details presented in these pages will crystallize a hands-on approach so that anybody can take advantage of the purifying effects of exercise and sweating.

Will this program help you? Should you embark on a detoxifying life-style? I can answer the first question. There is ample evidence that the steps I will detail below can enhance your body's ability to detoxify toxic chemicals. As for the second question, you must answer that for yourself. I believe we can all gain greater health and mental clarity by going through a detox program.

Persons suffering serious effects from chemical exposures should work with trained specialists. People who have been heavily or acutely exposed should do the same. I cannot stress this strongly enough. And everyone undertaking this program should first discuss it with a physician and get periodic medical checkups during its course.

And finally, any detoxification regimen involving exercise and sauna is inadvisable for persons with coronary artery disease or any other major physical disabilities unless it is done under the direct supervision of a physician familiar with exercise physiology who is willing to work out a specific exercise, sauna, and vitamin program for the patient.

Now that you know the basic principles and have thought seriously about these warnings, let's begin.

Blood Tests

Tell your physician that you want to undertake detoxification. As I've said, many physicians know little about toxicology. You may have to look around awhile to find one who will work with you. Show your doctor this book. Find one who will work with you.

Ask your doctor to help you get some basic tests done. Blood serum and urine should be checked for normal functions. For serum, these tests would include hematocrit, hemoglobin, red cell count, MCV, MCH, MCHC, white cell count, neutrophil segs, lymphocytes, monocytes, eosinophils, basophils, and platelet count. Urine should be checked for color, appearance, specific gravity, reaction pH, glucose, protein, ketone, occult blood, bilirubin, UA routine micro, RBC/HPF, WBC/HPF, and mucous threads. All these are standard tests covered under most insurance plans. Your doctor will know what they are for.

You may want to have your blood serum tested for industrial pollution and pesticide concentrations before you start, so that you can measure your progress later on. This is not absolutely necessary, but a pre-program blood analysis will provide you with a good benchmark for your detox success. Then at the end of the program—in about a year's time—you can have your blood serum tested for the same industrial pollutant and pesticide concentrations. Make sure all tests are done by the same lab to avoid any interlab variability. Such tests, conducted before and after the program, will cost $130 to $400, depending on how many chemicals you have measured. Ask your doctor if such tests can be covered by your health insurance.

Physicians who are not familiar with chemical toxicology may be reluctant to check blood for industrial chemicals and pesticides. But it is really quite simple. All they need to do is draw a blood serum sample. Testing labs provide containers and instructions. Two labs that do these tests are listed in the Personal Action Guide. Once results are provided, the labs will give advice on their interpretation.

The detection limits at which the chemistry laboratory operates are crucial. They must be capable of measuring chemical pollutants at a level of a fraction of a part per billion. Many laboratories' instruments are not sensitive enough to detect chemical pollutants in the bloodstream. The testing firms listed in the Personal Action Guide have this capability.

Have your blood serum analyzed for the chemicals listed on the following table. I've provided typical ambient background levels for these chemicals. Levels above these typical background levels could mean that somewhere along the line you suffered an extraordinary exposure. If this is the case, you should go over your test results in consultation with a physician who is well trained in interpreting such data.

TABLE 4. TYPICAL BACKGROUND LEVELS OF PESTICIDES AND INDUSTRIAL CHEMICALS IN THE BLOOD

Chlorinated Hydrocarbon Pesticides and Industrial Pollutants	Typical Background Level in the Blood
Benzene hexachloride	.3 ppb
Chlordane	.8 ppb
DDT (total)	1 to 5 ppb
Dieldrin	less than .3 ppb
Heptachlor	.3 ppb
Hexachlorobenzene	less than .3 ppb
Lindane	less than .3 ppb
Pentachlorophenol (penta)	12 ppb
PCBs	1 to 2 ppb

Halogenated Volatile Hydrocarbons

Chloroform	less than 1 ppb
Dichlorobenzenes	less than 1 ppb
Dichloromethane	less than 1 ppb
Perchloroethylene	1.1 ppb
1,1,1 trichloroethane	1.6 ppb
Trichloroethylene	less than .5 ppb

Aromatic Solvents in Blood

Benzene	less than 1 ppb
Ethylbenzene	less than .5 ppb
Styrene	less than 1 ppb
Toluene	.6 ppb
Xylenes	1.5 ppb

Ketone Solvents in Blood

Methyl ethyl ketone (MEK)	less than 20 ppb
Methyl isobutyl ketone (MIBK)	less than 20 ppb
Methyl n-butyl ketone (MBK)	less than 20 ppb

Compare your laboratory results with the "normal" levels in the second column. Obviously, in an ideal world, there are no "normal" levels of industrial pollutants and pesticides in the bloodstream; the lower the concentrations the better. But in this poisoned world, one has to be realistic enough to accept that some contamination of one's body is inevitable. Fortunately, you can reduce the concentrations of many of these chemicals by switching to low-toxin foods and water and by embarking on a detox regimen.

Once you've consulted your doctor, had your tests done, and gone over the results with your doctor, you're ready to get down to business.

Vitamins, Exercise, and Sauna

To start, you must make a firm commitment to clean living, keeping your food and water sources pure, cleaning up your home environment, and reducing your exposure to air pollution. Follow the low-toxin high-energy diet. Don't undermine your gains by reintroducing industrial chemicals and pesticides into your body.

Begin detoxification slowly, one day a week or on two consecutive days, for the first few weeks. You will need three to four hours each day.

Eat well on a detox day. Be sure to eat plenty of fruit and green vegetables.

Start detox with exercise. If you have not been exercising, you could start with an easy twenty-minute run. When you exercise you should try to raise your pulse rate to 114 to 156 beats a minute.

The intensity with which you exercise will depend on your physical condition. You may use exercises such as jazzercise, striding, or even fast walking. The point is not to strain but simply to set your blood in motion, circulating it to the deep layers of your body. Anyone who has not been exercising regularly should start with brisk walking. Starting right in running can put too much stress on people who aren't ready for it.

Now, with exercise, you have mobilized body fats in which toxic chemicals are stored. Mobilization alone, however, is not the answer. You also want enhanced elimination.

Elimination of toxic chemicals occurs through a variety of channels: urine, feces, and sweat. Researchers have found that substances such as industrial solvents, pesticides, methadone, amphetamines, morphine, and antiepileptics can be excreted through sweat. We excrete heavy metals in our sweat, according to studies, and cadmium is more concentrated in sweat than in urine. So shortly after you exercise you should try to visit a sauna or a steam bath. Most YMCAs and health clubs have saunas or steam baths.

The health benefits of sauna have been known for centuries. In Spain, cinnabar miners have for hundreds of years used sweating as a means of eliminating mercury from their bodies. Certain Native Americans have used sweat lodges for purification purposes. Many other cultures have used sweating for health betterment. The period spent in the sauna is the perfect, safe enhancement of our body's ability to excrete toxic chemicals.

Saunas at health clubs can work well for detoxifying. Many saunas can be regulated for heat by the user. If your club's sauna is too hot, its steam bath's temperature may be significantly lower. The key factor is a temperature between 140 and 160 degrees so you can stay in for a reasonable amount of time and really feel the sweat run down your body. I have actually found toxic chemicals such as DDT in samples of my sweat that I took while detoxing.

To start, you should have two sauna sessions of fifteen to twenty minutes at most. Stay for only as long as you can comfortably tolerate. Because of the length of time you will spend in the sauna or steam bath, the temperatures should be slightly lower than normal. Most health club saunas operate at a temperature of approximately 180°F. or higher. The ideal temperature for a detox sauna is lower, 140°F. to 160°F.

You should carefully inspect the sauna at any health club you are contemplating joining. An ideal sauna will have a clock so you can keep track of time. It should be free from perfumes, air fresheners, and other chemicals.

It should be comfortable and have several levels where you may sit to adjust your heat exposure. You will find significant differences in temperature by sitting high or low. Heat rises. Thus, when you sit on a lower level or on the floor, the temperature will be cooler.

Do not sleep in the sauna, and do not prolong your stay. You can build up gradually to sessions of thirty minutes. Remember, each body is different. This is not a race.

If possible, to increase air circulation, leave the sauna door slightly ajar with a towel. You will need pure water, so bring a thermos or a bottle of water with you or make sure that your facility has good pure water. With prolonged sweating, you will need to consume additional amounts of water. You can tell if you've lost too much water by weighing yourself before the sauna and after. You should not lose weight during a session. Your weight should remain stable or perhaps increase slightly as a result of your consumption of liquids.

Be careful not to overstress your body in the sauna. When your body is overstressed you will not sweat very well, anyway. If you feel clammy, end your sauna. Look for these symptoms: cold skin, dizziness, no sweating, or nausea. If the symptoms persist even after you've taken salt and other tablets, get out. Take a cool or lukewarm shower. Relax for ten or fifteen minutes. When you feel ready, reenter the sauna. After your first day's sauna, relax; let your body cool down naturally. Then shower.

Eat a good, healthy, toxin-free meal and then get a good night's sleep.

Finally, vitamin supplementation is one of the most important aspects of the detox diet. In this toxic world, vitamin supplements are absolutely essential.

Vitamins and minerals play an essential role in helping your body break down and eliminate toxic chemicals. Supplements enhance the body's natural immunity to invasive toxic pollution.

Supplement your diet with vitamin A in its natural beta carotene form, vitamin C as calcium ascorbate or ascorbyl palmitate (avoid ascorbic acid alone), vitamin E as d-alpha tocopherol, and selenium as yeast-free amino acid mineral chelate (such as selenomethionine).

Be sure to buy the safest, highest-quality supplements. Buy capsules; heat, pressure, and numerous additives are used in the manufacture of tablets. Look for naturally made vitamins and minerals whose labels specifically state that they were not made with petroleum chemicals that have hydrocarbon contaminants. Buy hypoallergenic products that are free from common allergens such as corn, wheat, milk, soy, yeast, fish oils, and other animal products. Make sure the label clearly states that no additives of any kind were used. Do not be fooled by claims that no *synthetic* additives are used. You want a product without *any* additives. Avoid children's supplements with additives such as artificial coloring and sweeteners.

Fish oils may have traces of pesticides. Calcium and magnesium from oyster shells, bone meal, or dolomite might have traces of pollution.

Follow this program of vitamins, exercise, and sauna one day a week or twice a week on consecutive days. Always detox on consecutive days so you will excrete the toxins you've mobilized. Some weeks you may want to detox on three or four consecutive days.

Move slowly. It is essential that you do not rush detoxifying. Realize that with every detox day, the body is becoming purer.

Eventually most individuals can stay in the sauna, when kept at appropriate temperature, for thirty minutes at a time without any problems. You will tolerate the sauna very well as long as you begin slowly and increase your time gradually. Of course, you will never stay in the sauna longer than thirty minutes at a time, tops. Many people may stay in only twenty minutes at a time.

Remember, detoxing toxic chemicals does not happen overnight but over a period of months and even years, so take your time with this program. On the other hand, you will experience periods when your body demands consecutive days of detox. It is very important not to end your detox until you feel good about your physical and psychological state.

About once a month now I take a sauna for two or three days in a row after running or engaging in other aerobic exercise. I stay in the sauna for two or three 20 to 30 minute sessions. That seems to be all that I need now, probably because my body is becoming less contaminated as I learn more about a nontoxic life-style.

Remember, when you begin sweating profusely in the sauna, that is a good sign; it tells you that you are detoxifying your body. You will be amazed at how quickly you feel better. Your mind will be much clearer as soon as you begin excreting the neurotoxins your body has accumulated.

Now that you know how to eat properly and how to detox your body whenever you feel the need, you will feel healthier. In our lives we need a sense of constant renewal. Toxic chemicals build up in our bodies, and following this detox program can become a major source of purification.

You really can virtually eliminate your exposure to toxic chemicals through your food and drinking water, the water with which you wash and bathe, and to an extent even the air you breathe. I have presented you with effective, easily accomplished solutions. When you have adopted these solutions together with the home detoxification guidelines, you will gradually be able to lower the toxic burden in your body. All of these active methods of detoxification will gradually evolve into an exciting, liberating new life-style. And as the chemical fog lifts you will see even more clearly why we all need to become ecologically committed to the health of our planet and our bodies.

19. SAFE EATING IN THE REAL WORLD

Two cars, two jobs, two schedules. Check the calendar for a date with your mate. Dinner? I'll pick up something on the way home. Welcome to twentieth-century eating habits.

This is the way many of us live. I've had to learn safe eating habits that fit this life-style. If it's midnight, and I've just gotten home from teaching a night class, there's no food in the house, and I'm hungry, that pizza parlor down the road starts to look mighty inviting. Maybe if I took the cheese off . . .

I've had to find ways to eat safely in all kinds of circumstances. When I go shopping, I buy lots of tasty, safe foods so that pizza doesn't seem so tempting. I've learned what foods I can buy in a supermarket and which ones to buy only in an organic food store. I now know what foods are safe to eat in most restaurants and coffee shops. I've learned to eat safely everywhere and all the time, not just at home. In this chapter I'll try to show you how I've made the low-toxin high-energy diet a reality for me. Maybe you can apply these ideas in your life, too.

I know how hard it would be to make changes in your diet if the new foods didn't taste good. After all, the fine taste of foods is one of the great pleasures of living. Nobody knows this better than I do. I love to eat!

I once was the worst eater in the world. I would stuff my body with fast-food hamburgers, milk shakes, french fries, pepperoni pizza, butter, cheese, fried chicken, and spareribs. I ate ice cream almost every night. I was doing everything wrong. No wonder my DDT and PCB levels were so elevated. The poisons in the toxic fish I ate were in good company. But once I began stocking my home with good, pure foods, I lost my desire to pig out at fast-food joints and to eat pesticide-saturated cheese omeletes at greasy spoon restaurants. I got smart about food. Today I feel better than ever, and I enjoy eating more than ever.

Once you fall in love with great-tasting whole grain pastas, organic pasta sauces, whole grain breads, and low-toxin fruits and vegetables, you are not going to want to eat a poisoned frozen pizza or other fatty foods laced with industrial chemicals, pesticides, nitrites, and additives. Why? Because you will feel great and you will not want to lose that feeling by consuming poisoned, pesticide-saturated, antibiotic-laced foods.

It is most important always to have safe foods that you love on your kitchen shelves and in the refrigerator, foods to which you can always turn when you need a little comfort, old reliable friends that know exactly how to make you feel better.

For breakfast, instead of sulfa- and pesticide-saturated sausage, ham, or bacon, I eat cornflakes with organic raisins, millet flakes, crisped rice, oatmeal, cream of rice, or one of the many other widely available whole grain cereals, topped with skim milk or soy milk. Even if these cereals are not organic, they will still help you significantly reduce your exposure to sulfa drugs, industrial pollutants, and pesticides. The sheer industrial pollution and pesticide saturation of a bacon- or sausage-and-egg breakfast is incredible. With each bite, you are being poisoned with three or four hard-core carcinogenic pesticides, the kind that build up in your body and bioaccumulate over your life. Just like a few grains of arsenic in your coffee.

For lunch, instead of nitrite- and pesticide-laced cold cut sandwiches, I eat complex carbohydrates such as whole grain rice and pasta, vegetables, whole grain breads, and fruits or whole grain cookies. These foods, particularly if they are grown organically, offer the safest route you can take for protection from exposure to industrial pollution and pesticides. You will significantly reduce your exposure to dangerous cancer-causing and neurotoxic chemicals.

Staples I like to keep on hand include whole grain breads, organic peanut butter, organic jams, whole grain graham crackers, and cookies and muffins whose ingredients include organic or low-toxin fruits and no additives. And there's always whole grain pasta in the cupboard. I cook the pasta and eat it with tomato sauce and just a little oil, or with steamed vegetables. A pollution-free meal in fifteen minutes.

Often when I work at home I make rice with beans and all sorts of organic fresh vegetables, from broccoli and chard to spinach and zucchini. I like to add an organic soy sauce for seasoning. To make sure I eat enough fruit, I make a fruit salad of diced organic apples with bananas, grapefruit, oranges, watermelon, and whatever else is safe and in season.

I always keep plenty of fresh fruit and vegetables on hand for snacking. I used to feel guilty when I first started eating healthfully, because I'd often end up throwing out fresh produce that went bad before I could eat it. But

I realized that I shouldn't feel guilty. The benefits of having fresh, safe, delicious foods on hand are so great that it pays to have plenty of them around. It's better to have to throw a little out at the end of the week than not to have enough on hand when I feel like snacking, and perhaps turn to something not as healthful. And now I'm so addicted to fresh fruits and vegetables that there's hardly any waste.

I buy food in season. In the spring, from April through June, organic kiwi fruit is in season, so I eat lots of it. I also buy organic Valencia oranges in season from December to May for fifty cents a pound. Unlike chemically grown oranges with food dye and fungicides in the peels, organic oranges are wonderfully pure. Organic grapes come in June and keep coming through the winter in big, bountiful bunches, selling for about a dollar a pound. As for vegetables, from late fall through early winter I may munch on lettuce, steamed broccoli, carrots, cauliflower, or even garbanzo beans. I like to arrange vegetables in a colorful palette. Since each color vegetable has different anti-cancer properties, I don't bother to memorize how much vitamin A is in a carrot or how much vitamin C is in broccoli. I just make a colorful selection. This is a key to nutritional eating. My meals always include mixed vegetables as a side dish. Remember always to choose the deepest-colored vegetables, for they are the richest in the antioxidant, pollution-fighting vitamins you need to fight off the damage done by free radicals and other poisons introduced into your body by toxic chemical pollution.

I always try to buy U.S.-grown produce. I never buy chemically grown Mexican foods. Who would eat Mexican produce knowing about the frequency of residues of dieldrin, heptachlor, endrin, and DDT? That is just asking to be dosed. One of these days, we will stop shipping our poisons to Third World nations and smarten up enough to realize that they come right back to us on brightly colored Mexican produce trucks. Someday the Mexican farmers will be forced to quit their excessive pesticide applications when we tighten up the loopholes that allow these banned and unregistered pesticides back into this country on popular produce items such as squash, cucumbers, pumpkins, and cantaloupe.

For dinner once in a while I like to eat very rich foods, so I stock my refrigerator with wholesome brands of these otherwise pesticide-saturated foods: organic whole grain pizzas with soy cheese; organic whole grain macaroni and soy cheese; potpies made with virtually all organic ingredients; and tofu frankfurters. Instead of eating ground beef, I keep tofu burgers in the fridge. I can pop them in the toaster and eat them with whole grain hamburger buns and organic tomatoes and relish. I use organic relish, mustard, salsa, salad dressing, and sauces. My herbs and spices are often organic and are never irradiated.

I travel pretty often and I enjoy eating in restaurants. So I have learned how to eat safely in the restaurant jungle. It is rarely perfect. But I can do a pretty good job of low-toxin dining no matter where I am. When I eat out, I look for the purest foods available, those that are most likely to be free from industrial pollution and pesticides.

When I eat breakfast out, I order cornflakes or rice crisps with nonfat milk and fruit, or I choose pancakes or waffles with fruit. I definitely avoid omelets, sausage, and bacon.

For lunch and dinner, I look to seafood as my saving grace. For example, whether I am dining in Cape Cod or Washington State, I can always order sea bass, grouper, orange roughy, red snapper, or Pacific salmon. I know these foods will be relatively free from pesticides. I tell the waiter I do not want butter or butter-based sauces on my seafood or vegetables. I frequently order rice, which is relatively free from pesticides, and high-fiber vegetables. Their fiber helps prevent absorption of industrial pollution and pesticides. Other dishes I feel very comfortable ordering include skinless breast of chicken, duck, chicken salad, and pasta with tomato sauce. For dessert, I order sherbet or sorbet, which are relatively low in industrial pollution and pesticides. Instead of drinking the restaurant's tap water, I order a pure bottled water such as Evian or Calistoga. My next choice is bottled seltzer because it is highly filtered and likely to be contaminant free.

Sometimes I travel to cities known for great regional foods. I do not deprive myself of Cajun cooking when I am in New Orleans, and in Kansas City I can't pass up barbecued ribs, but I try to eat safely. I know that crawfish étouffée, a Cajun favorite, is a fine low-toxin dish, for instance, but I also know that an unsafe meal like Kansas City ribs once or twice a year won't hurt me. I enjoy the meal, then go right back to my usual low-toxin high-energy eating habits.

In foreign countries, I look for good bottled water and worldwide safe foods such as rice and low-toxin vegetables. When I fly, I order vegetarian meals ahead of time. Airlines will serve vegetarian dishes if you make arrangements early. They're much tastier and healthier than the usual airplane fare. I also bring sandwiches and pure, wholesome snack foods on the flight.

I try to surround myself always with tasty, wholesome, low-toxin foods. Sometimes eating this way costs a little more, but I don't believe it's wise to skimp when it comes to health. A few dollars extra for organic groceries every week is a smart investment when you consider the improved health and peace of mind it gives you.

20. POSTSCRIPT: PESTICIDES IN OUR FOOD

I want to tell you briefly how it is that our food came to be laced with poisons.

In the late 1800s, American farmers began using chemicals to control pests. They used botanical pesticides such as nicotine, which was made from tobacco leaves; pyrethrum, made with chemicals found in the painted daisy flower; and sabadilla, made from a chemical in the seeds of a Caribbean lily. They also used inorganic pesticides such as arsenic; copper sulfate; Paris green, an arsenic-based pesticide; and Bordeaux, a copper sulfate–lime mixture.

Insecticide sales in the United States totaled $20 million by 1910. That figure climbed after World War I, stimulated by the manufacture of complex synthetic poisons that were used as tear gas during the war and as insecticides afterward.

The breakthrough in pesticide use came with the arrival of DDT in America after it was developed by Paul Mueller, a Swiss chemist. The first samples came in 1943 and were immediately put to use by the army to control lice and mosquito larvae. In 1945 the use of DDT dust halted an outbreak of mosquito-carried typhus in Naples, Italy. Meanwhile, back home, field tests indicated that DDT killed a number of crop pests. New York and Wisconsin potato yields immediately increased by more than 50 percent, and farmers dreamed of fields without pests. The green revolution was proclaimed. Research papers extolled the new era of agriculture, detailing all the possibilities of synthetic chemicals spawned by DDT, such as BHC, chlordane, and dieldrin. Scientific journals devoted more and more pages to the synthetic chemicals and fewer to the subtle science of biological pest control, which is so much kinder to the earth. By 1948, BHC was being applied to Nebraska cornfields, and farmers across the nation were switching to chemical farming techniques. They learned to consult pest control analysts, many of whom worked on commission for the chemical companies who manufactured pesticides, when insects became a problem. Of course the "analysts" recommended more and newer pesticides.

This. period of unbridled optimism was short-lived. Over time insects would develop a resistance to a chemical. In Naples, Italy, for example, a few years after successful spraying, DDT-resistant mosquitos returned in larger swarms than before. Increased applications would help for a while, then not at all, so manufacturers kept inventing new pesticides that would do the trick. In late 1954, scientists learned that the boll weevil was resistant to DDT. Thirty years later scientists had counted some 447 pesticide-resistant crop pests. And explosions of new crop pests emerged because pesticides killed all kinds of insects, including those that were the natural enemies of the crop pests. In Central America, among United Fruit Company's banana plantations, selective breeding was occurring. New populations of significant banana pests, such as moths and butterflies, began to emerge; additional spraying could not destroy them. The pests' populations swelled as their natural enemies were wiped out by the pesticides. In 1959, United Fruit Company entomologists confirmed that the crop pests were resistant to dieldrin. So dieldrin was replaced by carbaryl. By 1962, the pests had become resistant to carbaryl. Plantations sometimes applied carbaryl twelve times a season, but still the pests were destroying the banana crops.

Newer pesticides that were even more toxic were needed. The spiral accelerated, and the use of pesticides began to multiply astronomically. We used pesticides in our schools and in public buildings, on our lawns, and on our bouquets. Very acutely toxic, cancer-causing pesticides were sold in spray cans right beside food in supermarkets. Some 320 million pounds of active ingredients were applied to croplands in 1965. By 1982, that number had peaked at 880 million pounds, more than four pounds of active ingredients for every man, woman, and child in America.

The extra applications did not seem to help. Whereas preharvest crop loss before DDT, in 1940, was 7 percent, by 1975, losses had nearly doubled to 13 percent.

The pest control boom was a boomerang.

And it wasn't just the continued resistance of pests to the pesticides that was backfiring. The pesticides were killing animals and farmers and field workers as well.

Although the pesticides initially seemed completely safe, disturbing signs of their toxicity soon became evident. At Clear Lake, California, a form of DDT known as DDD was sprayed in 1949. Western grebes in the area, which fed on fish, began dying in large numbers five years later. The poison magnified in concentration as it accumulated from water to plankton to fishes and birds.

Soon bird species began disappearing from the East Coast and the Midwest. The bird kills continue today. In 1986, in southwest Spain, between the city of Seville and the Bay of Cádiz, more than thirty thousand migratory birds, including spoonbills, royals, geese, herons, plovers, curlews, and flamingos, were poisoned by pesticides. The number killed equaled roughly one-seventh of the total migratory population of these birds. The pesticides malathion and methyl parathion, used in the growing of rice in nearby paddies, is blamed.

In New York, the application of the pesticide diazinon on a Long Island golf course resulted in the death of some seven hundred Atlantic brant geese after they fed on the pesticide-saturated grass. In 1984, best estimates were that for the entire state of New York, the Atlantic brant population is only 2,500.

In total, sixty bird kills—all linked with diazinon—involving more than twenty species—have been documented throughout the nation in recent years.

In the Midwest, granular carbofuran applied to corn and sorghum crops resulted in so many bird kills, sometimes numbering in the thousands, that in 1989 the government was finally forced to recommend a ban on the pesticide, which had had sales of 6 to 9 million pounds annually.

Of course it is not just birds that pesticides kill. They kill other animals, too. By the late 1980s, the survival of more than half of the 450 endangered American animal species was further threatened by use of pesticides. And they kill humans as well. DDT and its close cousins, such as BHC, chlordane, and dieldrin are superpoisons that, once sprayed, or dumped in a landfill, lake, or ocean, cannot be easily destroyed. Their ability to poison living things persists for decades.

Tests indicate that DDT and the many other chemicals it has spawned cause cancer in animals such as fish, dogs, rats, monkeys, and mice. Surely a significant proportion of cancer today is the result of exposure to toxic industrial chemicals and pesticides such as DDT.

But scientists on the cutting edge of chemical toxicology no longer believe that cancer is the primary danger of low-level chemical exposure. It is a serious danger, yes, but more dangerous still is the fact that toxic chemicals such as DDT act as neurotoxins, impairing the affected person's mental ability. In the normally functioning body, impulses pass from nerve to nerve with the aid of a chemical called acetylcholine, which quickly disappears after completing its nerve transmission function. Indeed, if it didn't disappear, we would be overcome by waves of nerve impulses; our movements would become convulsive, and we would suffer muscular spasms and tremors. The result would be death.

Fortunately, our bodies also contain an enzyme called cholinesterase, which destroys acetylcholine. Many pesticides kill insects by destroying cholinesterase. The insects' neurons fire uncontrollably and they die in convulsions. These pesticides have the same effect on *our* bodies. Chronic low-level exposures slowly destroy our ability to manufacture cholinesterase, allowing acetylcholine to build up.

Even at the very low levels that are now present in the bodies of millions of Americans, chemicals such as DDT have a profound effect on mental clarity and on the ability to think, comprehend, and react to outside stimuli. They also deaden peripheral nervous systems, which can lead to diminished sensations in the extremities. Research shows that when people detoxify their bodies, ridding themselves of these industrial pollutants and pesticides, their IQ usually rises.

Many farm workers have been killed by pesticides because of their acute neurotoxicity. One man who worked for the state of California reached into a tank of the pesticide penta and died within a day. Children across the country have died after eating pesticides. In South America, an infant went into convulsions while nursing because of the acutely toxic levels of pesticides in the mother's breast milk. By the 1970s, one person was killed by pesticides in the Third World every hour and 45 minutes. Around the world, half a million to one million people suffer sublethal sickness from pesticides each year.

These chemicals have many other dangerous effects. DDT causes decreased lactation; a North Carolina study found that mothers with the highest levels of DDT in their bodies are able to breast-feed for a much shorter period than mothers with very low DDT body burdens. DDT's relatives are teratogens that can cause birth defects in a developing fetus. Their effects include slowed motor reflexes and reactions, decreased muscular coordination, smaller head circumference, and decreased mental function—for example, a loss of ten to fifteen points off the child's IQ. It is important to note that toxic chemicals that decrease fetal gestation time will, in turn, increase the child's chances later on of mortality and childhood diseases.

And these chemicals *do* cause cancer. By 1985, four separate studies had reported that DDT was present in higher than usual concentrations in humans dying from cancer. Other studies found higher levels of these chemicals in the breast tissues of women with breast cancer. Additional adverse health effects associated with elevated pesticide concentrations include hypertension and heart disease. These studies provide a clear signal that these are broadly toxic lethal compounds.

DDT and its related chemicals are persistent and are attracted to fatty tissues, so they build up in the bodies of living organisms. Fish and carnivorous birds, for example, end up accumulating large amounts of DDT. The accumulation begins with plankton, which filter water contaminated with DDT. Fish that eat plankton consume the DDT accumulated by thousands or millions of plankton. And fish that eat other fish accumulate DDT from all the fish that have eaten all the plankton. Carnivorous birds like the bald eagle, which eat fish-eating fish (which eat the fish that eat the plankton that first filtered the water contaminated with the pesticide), accumulate even larger doses of DDT. Human beings, many of whom eat fish-eating fish and other animals, have among the highest concentrations of DDT and other pesticides to be found in any living creatures.

By the 1960s, the natural world was exhibiting signs of pesticide-induced population stress. With calcium synthesis disrupted by DDT, causing production of fragile, soft eggshells, the ospreys of Gardiners Island, off the eastern end of Long Island, New York, suffered such severe reproductive failures that their once-vibrant population decreased from hundreds of pairs in the 1940s to fewer than ten. On California's south coast, coastal bald eagles virtually disappeared along with other fish-eating birds such as the brown pelican.

In 1972, the newly formed U.S. Environmental Protection Agency banned DDT. Unfortunately, the chemicals manufactured after DDT were even more deadly. Benzene hexachloride (BHC) is nineteen times more powerful as a carcinogen than DDT. Chlordane is four times more powerful than DDT. Dieldrin is forty-seven to eighty-five times more powerful as a carcinogen than DDT. Heptachlor is fifteen to thirty times more powerful as a carcinogen than DDT.

The industrial chemical polychlorated biphenyl (PCB) is twenty-three times more powerful as a carcinogen than DDT. Thus, in the following two decades, many of these other cancer-causing chemicals, including BHC, chlordane, dieldrin, heptachlor, and PCBs, were banned. These chemicals are all closely related; all are highly complex compounds that can be synthesized only in a chemistry laboratory, and all are made with durable chains of carbon, hydrogen, and chlorine atoms; they're all persistent, fat-soluble chemicals that build up in the environment and move up the food web in ever-increasing concentrations. I call this family of chemicals— including DDT, BHC, chlordane, dieldrin, endrin, HCB, and heptachlor— the old-time spray gang because they were often applied by aerial spraying. The very strong toxicity and persistence in the environment of these chemicals is the reason they are still of concern today, nearly twenty years after DDT was banned for virtually all common uses in this nation. Indeed, as former EPA administrator Russell Train noted, "Dieldrin-caused tumors in both mice and rats appear at a variety of sites within the body, including the liver, lungs, lymphoid tissue, thyroid, uterus, and mammary glands. These tumors have resulted at highly statistically significant levels from dietary dosages as low as 0.1 parts per million in the diet, which is the lowest dosage ever tested in any animal species. In short, even the lowest levels of dieldrin produced significant cancerous effects. Furthermore, the evidence indicates that exposure to dieldrin for periods as brief as several weeks is sufficient to cause highly significant carcinogenic effects in test animals."

PCBs are among the most troubling chemical formulations found in seafood today. They were one of the first and most widely used "miracle" chemicals. But PCB exposure has exacted a tremendous toll on people's health. Factory workers as early as the 1930s reported severe chloracne cases from PCB exposure. One San Diego hotel worker who periodically cleaned PCB-contaminated transformers throughout the 1970s accumulated such a large dose that his teeth fell out, he lost coordination, and he suffered joint numbness and slurred speech. Michigan researchers have found a cancer rate as much as eleven times higher than normal among a small group of farm families who ate meat and dairy products accidentally tainted with PCBs. As I fear we shall see, this finding has direct implications for consumers of seafood from the Great Lakes and Long Island Sound, which are thoroughly contaminated with PCBs.

In the mid-1970s further manufacture of PCBs was prohibited by federal law, although the government allowed industry to use up supplies on hand. However, the damage was done; the legacy of PCBs will continue into the twenty-first century. PCBs remain widely present today in industry. They are used as high-temperature lubricants and heat shields in transformers and capacitors because of their stability. It is estimated that approximately half of all the PCBs ever manufactured remain in use today. So we must be very careful even today about PCB contamination of our seafood.

PCBs are also potent neurotoxins. Among the first signs of low-level PCB exposure is subtle neurotoxicity, which affects mental clarity and can include loss of mental acuity, nervousness, inability to concentrate, and degeneration of peripheral nerve conduction. Joint numbness, aches, and sudden intense sweats have also been linked with PCB exposure. In addition, accumulation of body burdens of PCBs at levels commonly found in the general population may have adverse effects on blood pressure and possibly cholesterol levels. Such findings are of particular concern to seafood lovers, since seafood is the only regular major source of PCBs today in the American diet.

When Rachel Carson was working on her book, the broad-based human studies that would have provided her with the final link in the chain of pesticide poisoning had barely begun. Still, *Silent Spring* put down strong, cogent theories on how harm results from the use of pesticides despite the lack of population studies that would have proved each point. In the years since its publication dozens of studies have confirmed the human toxicity of pesticides:

- In Nebraska, mortality from leukemia was higher among farmers than among any other work group.

- Wisconsin farmers who work with large amounts of herbicides and insecticides have an increased risk of non-Hodgkin's lymphoma.

- Iowa farmers are at higher risk for non-Hodgkin's lymphoma in counties where herbicide use is prolific.

- Washington farmers and industrial populations exposed to herbicides have excess numbers of soft-tissue sarcomas.

- Minnesota farmers and Washington ranchers have elevated mortality rates from cancer of the brain and central nervous system.

- Washington, Oregon, Wisconsin, Iowa, and Texas farmers have elevated incidences of multiple myeloma.

- Multiple myeloma in the north central United States occurs most frequently among farmers.

- Maryland children with brain cancer are more likely to have lived on farms than are children without such cancers.

- Cotton-growing regions from Minnesota to Texas have leukemia rates that are steadily increasing where pesticide use is a common practice.

- Pregnant women who live in agricultural regions of California have a greater than average chance of giving birth to babies with severe birth defects.

- A second California study puts the rate of farm workers' children born with severe birth defects, including deformed limbs, at 5.2 per 1,000 births, a rate thirteen times above that of the general population.

In southwest Kansas, a region known as the nation's Wheat Belt, farmers combat broadleaf weeds that threaten grain crops by spraying herbicides. These herbicides are rarely detected in the food supply because they break down quickly in the environment. But unfortunately for the farmers, they do not break down quickly enough, and repeated exposures have apparently had a cumulative effect on the farmers. Medical scientists and epidemiological detectives have difficulty finding traces of these toxic criminals, many years after the fact, in the farmers' tissues. But the cancers and other diseases are there, years after the pesticides that caused them are gone. The farmers who apply the poisons know all too well the diseases that are caused by chemical exposure.

In 1987, some 350 new cases of non-Hodgkin's lymphoma and 175 deaths from it were reported in Kansas, the American Cancer Society estimated. In America more than 126,000 newly diagnosed, similar soft tissue cancers are recorded annually. Many of these cancers are the result of exposure to environmental toxins including the farmers' exposure to phenoxy-herbicides. Today Kansas's stretch of high-yield wheat fields has come to be known as the nation's Cancer Belt. There the cancer rate for non-Hodgkin's lymphoma, which in the 1950s mirrored the national trends, has increased steadily—as has the farmers' reliance on herbicides–and now ranks among the most concentrated in the nation. About 90 percent of the nation has lower rates of non-Hodgkin's lymphoma.

What accounts for this shocking cancer devastation of Kansas farmers? Researchers found recently that Kansas farmers who work regularly with chemicals were six to eight times more likely to get non-Hodgkin's lymphoma. The link is strongly suggestive of cause and effect. The risk rose with exposure. Men exposed to herbicides more than twenty days a year had a sixfold increased risk of contracting non-Hodgkin's lymphoma compared to non-farmers. Frequent users who mixed or applied the herbicides themselves had an eight times greater risk. Similar findings are not confined to Kansas wheat farmers. All through the grain belt, increased risk for cancers among farmers is now linked with herbicide exposure. Death from chemical exposure is as real for those who raise Washington wheat as it is for Iowa corn farmers.

This is only a tiny example of the human toll of pesticide use. I can only hint at the anger, anguish, anxiety, frustration, and helplessness that victims and their families feel when a loved one is struck down by the pesticide plague and they learn that the government that they thought would protect them actually condones the use of the poisons that have destroyed their health. In the course of researching the decline of our environment, I have heard many people describe how they were poisoned because they grew or picked the food we set on our tables or because they just happened to be in the wrong place at the wrong time.

Willoughby Houk, age sixty, of Firebaugh, California, farmed a variety of crops, from cotton, alfalfa, walnuts, cantaloupes, and corn to feed grains. The manufacturers let him use the pesticides without telling him to wear a mask and protective equipment. In 1986 he was diagnosed with lymphoma. In an eight-mile area around his farm, six people have died from lymphoma. In Firebaugh, west of Fresno, with a population of 3,500, fifty-four people have died from cancer in the past two years. Many of the cancer victims were farm owners and workers. Everybody in the valley knows that people are dying early from pesticide-linked cancer. The cancer clusters are scattered up and down the vast San Joaquin Valley, from Bakersfield to Firebaugh, but not all of the cases have been reported because no state agency has ever kept a cancer log. When researchers looked, however, they found a link between higher incidences of cancer and pesticide exposure. The link was confirmed for cancer and the pesticide DBCP. And more than one million Californians have drunk water tainted with DBCP.

In 1985, six-year-old Jared Johnson was diagnosed with diabetes, a disease researchers assert can be brought on by toxic pesticide exposure. His mother, Joyce, blames the pesticide paraquat. One year before Jared was diagnosed, another boy who attended the same school was diagnosed with diabetes at the same time of year, November. Their school is surrounded by cotton fields, and at that time of year it would be smothered for weeks in paraquat vapors. Jared's mother said crop planes flew within a quarter-mile of the school while children were in class. They all breathed paraquat. Some people might have a genetic tendency to become diabetic. All it takes to trigger this tendency is a shock to the body that makes the immune system go crazy and kill off beta cells in the pancreas, which create insulin. Jared's mother feels strongly that exposure to paraquat provided that shock. The boy's doctors also suspect paraquat.

Ed Davis, a respected adviser on agricultural pest control in Kern County, California, says that years have been shaved off his life because of his pesticide exposures. As a pest control adviser, Davis spends much of his time in farm fields. Often he must enter fields that were sprayed just a few days earlier. He has been sickened due to pesticide exposure five times in ten years.

When Connie Rosales of McFarland, California, became pregnant in 1981, she learned that farm chemicals had polluted their town wells. She was concerned for the child she was carrying, but at the time she knew little about the damage that nitrates and pesticides could do, and she did not think that the contamination posed a serious threat for older children. So after her daughter's birth, Ms. Rosales continued to give her baby bottled water; because she suffered from toxemia, her doctor also recommended that Connie herself drink distilled bottled water. That left her oldest child, Randy, to drink contaminated water from the tap.

Randy was diagnosed with lymphoma. He is one of sixteen children within a several-block area of McFarland who contracted cancer or leukemia. Eight have died. The families' homes are built on a pesticide dump, and their drinking water contains the pesticide DBCP, which is linked with increased human cancer incidence. California officials have declared the area a cancer cluster—one of many clusters, official and unofficial, dotting the San Joaquin Valley—but they have not made a public statement about the cause of the illnesses of the children. Most of the children who were sickened, however, drank tap water that was polluted with nitrates and the pesticide DBCP. The names of the deceased children of McFarland, like epitaphs on a tombstone, are our reminders that we all share responsibility for their deaths because of our food and water decisions.

Ramona Franco, who lives in Delano, a town near McFarland, worked as a grape picker in a vineyard that had been sprayed with the fungicide captan during the first three months of her pregnancy. Her son Felipe was born without arms or legs. Doctors blame this birth defect on her captan exposure.

Captan is one of the most widely used fungicides in California vineyards. Once it has broken down in the environment, it bears molecular resemblance to the sedative thalidomide, which was used by pregnant women in the United States and Europe in the 1960s and which caused thousands of infants to be born without arms or legs. Captan residues taint fruit crops, including berries, grapes, and stone fruit such as peaches and cherries throughout the world. Because captan is not acutely toxic, it is considered safe. Nevertheless, it is a proven carcinogen and teratogen. Yet it is even used as a home pesticide. It can be found regularly in fruits at levels of one to two parts per million, a pretty large dose for a toxic chemical.

These accounts of people who are dying or ill because of pesticide exposure are deeply disturbing in themselves, but they also give us warning of what pesticides will do to the general population over time. Every time we eat unwisely chosen plant and animal foods, all of us are consuming the same chemicals that killed or sickened these people. A report by an expert committee of the National Academy of Sciences said that pesticide residues contaminating the foods that people enjoy every day—tomatoes, potatoes, oranges, lettuce, apples, peaches, beans, carrots, and grapes—could be responsible for thousands of cancer deaths.

The most disturbing trend is the wide variety and increasing number of pesticides that are being detected at low levels in our foods. These chemical cocktails could truly be time bombs ticking away in the bodies of tens of thousands of people.

We know from the historic record that many pesticides once hailed as safe were later proven dangerous and banned, and government officials admit that many chemicals in use today are dangerous and probably will be banned in the future. Government takes twenty years to ban a chemical. But the danger to your health is immediate. You should not wait until a ban is in place. The government has allowed our bodies to absorb unsafe amounts of chemicals for years. The EPA has set many tolerance levels without firmly establishing the actual long-term health risks of the pesticides, and tolerance levels have seldom been updated or revised even after the government has received new facts about potential risks from a certain pesticide.

Many experts do not believe the guidelines set by the government offer the consumer enough protection. Most people do not realize that the government regulates pesticides on the basis of "risk versus benefits"—

that is, risks to *your* health versus benefits to the food industry's profits— rather than primarily to protect human health. For example, according to a report published in the *Arizona Republic*, the government spent one decade studying the harmful effects of lead arsenate, but while they were doing the study, they permitted Florida growers to use this pesticide on grapefruits so that the fruit growers could market their crop two months earlier, adding an additional $10 million to their profits. Lead is known to cause disorders of the human brain and nervous system. Arsenic, a known human carcinogen, can severely damage the nervous system and internal organs. Both substances can harm a human fetus. This is how the government protects our health.

What researchers do know from their limited studies is that consumers are accumulating poisons in their bodies. A doctoral student at the University of California at Davis was surprised to find that her study of pesticide residues in human urine indicated a high incidence of pesticides in people who claimed they never were exposed. The urine of one-third of the subjects had five pesticides commonly used on crops. It was quite disturbing that the pesticides left such obvious and chronic patterns of exposure.

A larger federal study of 28,000 people in sixty-four communities across America reported significant pesticide concentrations circulating in the bodies of people among the general population with regular detections of residues of carbaryl, chlorpyrifos, dimethoate, dicamba, malathion, and many other chemicals. All of these chemicals are either carcinogens or neurotoxins.

And what about our children? A 1989 study by the Natural Resources Defense Council (NRDC) asserts that children face a greater risk than adults from pesticides, and that much of our risk as adults stems from childhood exposures. The NRDC scientists estimate that 5,000 to 6,200 preschool children alive today could get cancer as a result of exposure to just eight carcinogenic pesticides at levels that have actually been measured in raw produce. The report said that the average preschooler receives more than five times greater exposure to the fungicide mancozeb, nine times greater exposure to the neurotoxic organophosphate azinphosmethyl, and twelve times greater exposure to UDMH, the carcinogenic metabolite of Alar, than adults do. Of course, the study was attacked vigorously by the pesticide industry. But what do you expect? It was so on target that it worked: it got the chemical Alar off the market (it should have been taken off years earlier). The sorry fact is that the leaders of the apple industry knew long ago that Alar was a dangerous chemical. They should have moved on their own much earlier to voluntarily end the use of Alar before the NRDC report was published.

In fact, the overall cancer rate for children as a result of pesticides is probably much higher than what NRDC predicted it to be when you factor in other childhood pesticide exposures, from pesticides in our kids' other favorite foods such as hot dogs, raisins, milk chocolate, and ice cream.

If you think the U.S. government is going to protect you from unhealthful levels of pesticides on crops, think again. It's up to us now to turn that tide by supporting organic farming and biological pest controls.

Even after the government gets around to banning dangerous pesticides, they still find many ways into our diets. Their manufacturers are often allowed to produce them for sale abroad or to sell their huge existing stockpiles abroad. Although dangerous pesticides such as aldrin, chlordane, DDT, dieldrin, endrin, and heptachlor were banned for use in the United States during the 1970s and 1980s, manufacturers shipped supplies to Mexico and other Third World nations, where farmers sprayed them on their crops and then returned them to this country on produce, completing the circle of poison.

And as for inspections to detect excess residues, forget it. Less than 1 percent of produce coming in to U.S. markets is checked. And even when shipments with illegal residues are detected, stopping infiltration into the vast American market is tough. A report by the General Accounting Office found that in 1986 only 73 of 164 shipments found to have illegal pesticide residues were recovered and prevented from being sold. The rest, with illegal, potentially dangerous residues, were consumed by the public. For most FDA laboratories, the average pesticide analysis takes nearly one month. By that time the suspect fruits and vegetables have been sold.

When it comes to produce coming into the United States from abroad, you have to take responsibility yourself. You can't count on the government to test it for you. Nearly half the winter produce sold in this country comes from Mexico, and many chemicals not allowed to be used here are in use there. In 1986, I went through the FDA crop records for Mexico for several years preceding and found an unnerving number of reports of detections of dieldrin, eldrin, heptachlor, and other toxic chemicals that had been banned in the United States.

The only protection we have is FDA inspection points along the U.S.-Mexico border. In a study I did for a report in the *Arizona Republic* I learned that on at least 140 days during 1987 *no inspections of produce* were made at the most important border crossings for Mexican produce coming into this country. I spent two days in April 1988 watching hundreds upon hundreds of trucks loaded with peppers, squash, tomatoes, watermelons, and many other fruits and vegetables come uninspected into this country. Yet one government study shows 18 percent of imported produce is in violation of regulations!

Only four FDA inspectors are present at New York's Kennedy Airport to inspect more than 1,500 shipments of produce that arrive daily. For the entire country, FDA has only 750 inspectors.

And the tests that are made are often inadequate. Although more than five hundred pesticides can legally be used on foods, government analytical procedures detect, at most, only half. The test methods used by the Seattle, Dallas, Minneapolis, San Francisco, and Los Angeles government laboratories cannot detect some of the potentially most harmful pesticides registered for use on apples, grapes, corn, lettuce, and cabbage. A group of chemicals called EBDCs is used throughout the world to prevent fungus in fresh produce. Breakdown products of the EBDCs are probable human carcinogens, and yet, between 1978 and March 1986, the FDA did not test any imported foods for their presence. Further, detection limits are often so high that pesticides on your food go undetected.

The bottom line is that chemically grown produce is saturated with pesticides that cause cancer in farm workers and rural residents, who also become sick from acute and chronic exposures in their air and drinking water. The effects in the general population have not been measured, but the overall environmental toxic properties of pesticide residues in fruits and vegetables probably contribute to the development of thousands, tens of thousands, or even more human cancers each year.

Farmers have become increasingly aware of the dangers of pesticides, and as it has become clear that they will never win the war of eradication, they have led the search for safer ways to raise crops.

And as they look in that direction, farmers are learning that pesticide withdrawal does not decrease their yields. Often it increases them. The government of Peru has pioneered in this direction. After the use of pesticides began in Peru in 1949, new crop pests emerged, forcing farmers to spray even more chemicals. Yet yields dropped dramatically. In 1956, the Ministry of Agriculture banned the use of synthetic pesticides. The populations of beneficial insects rose, populations of the new pests declined, and successful agriculture returned. Cotton yields, after the pesticide withdrawal, increased tremendously to an all-time high.

In 1973, insect specialists with experience in biological control persuaded the United Fruit Company to stop spraying pesticides in the Golfito region of Costa Rica. By the mid-1970s, the new crop pests had disappeared, populations of beneficial insects had increased tremendously, and other pest populations decreased accordingly. One pest, the banana rust thrip, still caused problems, but those problems were solved by slipping plastic bags over the fruit as it grew on the trees. My study of residues on bananas indicates that today you can go to any market and buy bananas with the reassuring knowledge that they contain few, if any, pesticide residues, regardless of where they were grown. The same story is told in

Texas. Between 1964 and 1976, Texas cotton farmers were able to control pests with only one-tenth of the pesticides they formerly used. The farmers of Texas are learning that pesticides sometimes are used to mask poor farming techniques. And in 1989, Washington apple growers are learning that with proper pruning they do not need to use Alar any longer to produce a quality crop. Chemical farming is on its outward passage, and biological methods, more closely attuned with the environment, are the new heroes. Farmers are now paying attention to pest populations, learning to recognize the point at which they can reach damaging levels, and deciding only then, as a last resort, to bring down populations by spraying.

The American pesticide experiment is winding down.

We have learned that the sooner we get off the pesticide treadmill, the better off our ecology and our bodies will be. The crops will, as usual, do well.

The overall economic benefits of pesticide use today are suspect. Since the introduction of pesticides we have had far more water pollution and cancer. Pre-harvest crop loss is on the increase. Responsible stewards of the land are asking how much is really needed and how much is too much. We now know that chemical farmers have been on overkill, applying toxic chemicals by the calendar, not always to meet real need. Today they are learning safer effective means of pest control.

Organic farming methods are on the rise. There is more organic produce available now than at any other time in the past several decades; still, it is only a minuscule fraction of total American crop production. We have a long way to go. But at least people are more aware of the problems of chemical farming now. We've begun the process of correction.

For now, chemically grown food is cheaper than organic food. But the difference only adds up to a few dollars a week. And isn't it worth it to be confident you're eating food that is free of poisons that could give you or your loved ones cancer or other diseases?

And actually the lower price of chemical crops is only an illusion! When you go into your local supermarket and buy chemical crops, you buy into the poisoning of the earth. You support an outmoded form of chemical agriculture that is poisoning our land and our seas and our drinking water. You support a system that exploits workers in the fields, who become poisoned and complain of feeling tired all the time when they spray pesticides, because the neurotoxic pesticides are destroying their nervous systems. You buy into tainted water that has caused children in towns across the land to develop leukemia, other cancers, and many other illnesses. You buy into the total financial devastation of family after family that buckles under the weight of medical costs because of severe pesticide-linked illnesses including birth defects, cancer, and other diseases such as diabetes. You buy into toxic waste dumps with leaking barrels of pesticide-tainted wastes polluting groundwater throughout the Midwest. You buy into the loss of America's freshwater fishery due to pesticide contamination, and you buy into the disappearance of our wildlife.

If these ecological costs were factored in, people would see that chemical crops cost many times more than organically grown fruits and vegetables.

There is a solution. Use the safe shopping lists in this book to find the safe foods, the ones with the fewest chemical residues. You'll find plenty of good-tasting safe fruits, vegetables, and meats and lots of dairy, poultry, and seafood. Photocopy the safe shopping lists and use them in markets that sell chemically grown foods. Check off your nontoxic selections.

As people become more aware of the damage pesticides do, more and more retailers are making organic produce available. Organic farming is now a billion dollar industry, and major supermarket chains such as D'Agostino's in New York, Kroger in the East, HEB in Texas, Farm Fresh in the South, Stop & Shop in New England, Ralph's, Raley's, Fred Meyer, and Von's in the far West, and many others have begun to stock organic produce. I've listed suppliers of organic foods in the Personal Action Guide, but this is a fast growing area—by the time you read this book, the number of suppliers could have doubled.

Want to join the revolution? Go to your supermarket and say something subversive like, "Do you have organically grown apples?" Every time you buy organically grown produce and every time you ask for it, you send a strong, clear message to supermarkets and farmers that biological growing methods are good *and* profitable.

In the supermarket today you will find a variety of certified organic produce that is labeled in different ways. Some fruits and vegetables are said to have been grown by *sustainable agriculture*, others by *transitional agriculture*, and yet others by *integrated pest management*. Some kinds of agriculture are said to be *biodynamic*. What do all these terms mean?

Let me put this simply: you want *organic* or *biodynamic* produce. Both methods of farming are done without toxic herbicides, pesticides, or fungicides and without synthetic fertilizers. All the rest—sustainable agriculture, transitional agriculture, and integrated pest management—are second choices.

The "sustainable agriculture" label is supposed to indicate low pesticide use, but in fact, sustainable produce items could be pesticide saturated. If farmers need pesticides they use them.

Integrated pest management (IPM) is another name for sustainable agriculture. IPM combines pesticides use with biologic methods. The produce could be remarkably clean or it could have fresh residues. Do not buy IPM produce believing it is pesticide-free.

Transitional foods are those grown without pesticides but on land where pesticides have been used in the recent past. These fruits and vegetables may have some pesticide residues in them. Still, transitional produce makes a pretty good choice. After several years, crops from these farms will be able to be labeled organic.

The terms *organic, premium organic,* and *biodynamic* are used for foods that have been grown without chemical fertilizers, pesticides, herbicides, or fungicides. This is what you want. Don't panic. Buy organic!

Organically grown crops really are much purer than chemically raised crops. I did my own testing to prove the point. And I studied extensive lab analyses of crops from Washington State's certified organic crop program and from the records of other laboratories. Washington officials report that no detectable pesticide residues have been found in any organically grown crops analyzed since 1988. Other labs report similar results. The bottom line: organically grown food is the real McCoy and a taste treat that's good for your body, good for your children's bodies, and good for the ecology of the planet.

Appendixes

Spend your money wisely. If you and others like you buy low-toxin foods or organic foods instead of foods grown with chemical fertilizers, pesticides, and herbicides, farmers and food producers will see that there's a growing market for safe foods. So what if the cost, at present, is higher? It's worth it to pay more for safe foods to compensate retailers and farmers for not poisoning us or our land. It's worth it because you know your cucumbers won't kill you.

Identify the enemy. Shun the non-food products made by manufacturers of chemical pesticides. Learn to use fewer plastics and chemical products. Our grandparents kept clean homes without them and so can we.

And finally, learn to influence the lawmakers. It was public pressure that brought down Alar and, earlier, the spray gang dinosaurs. Public expressions of outrage can do it again. Write to your local, state, and federal representatives. Suggest government incentives for organic farmers and higher taxes for manufacturers and users of chemical fertilizers and pesticides. We end up paying to clean up after them through our taxes—disposing of toxic wastes, trying to purify our water supplies, paying the huge medical bills for cancer treatments. Let's tax the polluters up front. More ideas will come to you as you write. You have the power of your dollars and power of your vote. Learn to speak loudly with the way you exercise both!

SAFE FOODS
SHOPPING LIST

To help you remember the safe-food basics, I have combined all the green light shopping lists into one ultimate shopping list you can copy and take with you to the supermarket. Now whenever you shop you can buy the safest, purest low-toxin foods available. Overall, these foods have the least industrial chemical and pesticide saturation of any nonorganic foods produced in America today. They will help keep you healthy and free from excessive toxic exposures.

GREEN LIGHT FOODS

Fruits

Applesauce	Guavas	Peaches
Avocados	Grapefruit	(canned)
Bananas	Lemons	Pears (canned)
Bitter melons	Limes	Pineapples
Coconuts	Oranges	Plantains
Dates	Papayas	Tangerines
Figs	Passion fruit	Watermelons
Fruit cocktail		

Vegetables

Alfalfa sprouts	Corn	Pinto beans
Asparagus	Daikon	Radicchio
Adzuki beans	Fava beans	Rapini
Bamboo shoots	Fennel root	Red beans
(canned)	Garlic	Red chard
Bean sprouts	Jicama	Rhubarb
Beets	Kidney beans	Shallots
Black-eyed peas	Leeks	Snap green beans
(cowpeas)	Lima beans (mature)	Snow peas
Brussels sprouts	Mixed vegetables	Tomatoes
Cabbage	(canned)	(canned)
Carrots	Mushrooms	Watercress
Cassava	Navy beans	Yams
Cauliflower	Onions	
Chives	Peas	
Cilantro		

Nuts and Seeds

Almonds	Pecans	Sunflower seeds
Chinese pine nuts	Pistachios	Walnuts
Flax	Pumpkin seeds	Water chestnuts
Hazelnuts	Sesame seeds	Watermelon seeds

Juices

Apricot nectar	Lemonade	Prune juice
Cranberry juice	Lime juice	Mixed vegetable
Grape juice	Pineapple juice	juice

Miscellaneous Produce

Aloe vera	Cole	Rombuton
Arrowroot	Durian	Seaweed seasoning
Burdock root	Langon	Shredded bamboo
Cactus	Lotus root	Taro
Cardoni	Pai kon	

Grains

Biscuits	Granola	Popcorn
Corn bread	Grits	Rice
Cornflakes	Oat rings	Saltines
Crisped rice cereal	Oatmeal	Shredded wheat
Egg noodles	Pancakes	cereal
Farina	Pasta	Tortillas

Meat and Poultry

Chicken (roasted)
Game (alligator, buffalo, duck, frogs' legs, goose, rabbit, escargot, turtle, domestic venison)
Lamb chops
Pork roast
Turkey
Turkey breast luncheon meat (without nitrites)

Seafood

Abalone
Arctic char
Crawfish
Dover sole
Dungeness crab
English sole
Fish sticks
Flounder
Grouper
Haddock
Halibut
Imitation crab (surimi)
Mahimahi
Marlin
Menpachi
Monkfish
Octopus
Orange roughy
Pacific salmon
Red snapper
Scallops
Sea bass
Sea urchin roe
Shrimp
Sole
Spiny lobster
Squid
Talapia
Tuna
Wahoo
Whiting
Yellowtail

Dairy Products and Dairy Substitutions

Buttermilk
Cream substitute
Fruit sorbet
Low-fat chocolate milk
Low-fat cottage cheese
Low-fat milk
Low-fat and nonfat yogurt
Low-fat and nonfat frozen yogurt
Nonfat yogurt cheese
Sapsago cheese
Sherbet
Skim milk
Soy cheese
Soy milk
Water ices

Convenience Foods

Canned beef broth
Canned chicken noodle soup
Canned cream of tomato soup
Canned pork and beans
Canned spaghetti in tomato sauce
Canned vegetable beef soup (and other uncreamed soups)

Desserts and Sweet Snacks

Apple pie
Gelatin dessert
Instant pudding
Yellow cake

Condiments and Snacks

Brown gravy
Pancake syrup
Honey
Italian salad dressing
Mayonnaise
Sugar

Vegetable Oils

Avocado oil
Olive oil (virgin or extra-virgin)
Organic oils
Sesame oil

PERSONAL ACTION GUIDE

VEGETABLES AND FRUITS

MAIL-ORDER ORGANIC PRODUCE SOURCES

No matter where you live today it is easy to get organically grown fresh fruits, vegetables, nuts, and seeds. Many nationwide distributors have mail-order service and home delivery.

I've checked virtually all the sources listed with tough interviews, and I've tried to find out about their growing practices and their certification procedures. In some cases, I have even had their products analyzed for pesticide residues. I am pleased to say that organic is the real thing. This list constitutes an endorsement.

Ahler's Organic Date and Grapefruit
  Garden
P.O. Box 726
Mecca, CA 92254
(619) 396-2337

  Organic dates by mail.

Lee Anderson's Covalda Date
  Company
51-392 Highway 86
P.O. Box 908-N
Coachella, CA 92236
(619) 398-3441

  Organically grown dried apples, apricots, black mission figs, peaches, pears, and Thompson seedless raisins by mail.

Arjoy Acres
HCR Box 1410
Payson, AZ 85541
(602) 474-1224

  Mail-order organically grown Swedish brown beans, kidney beans, pinto beans, garlic, peas, shallots, and garlic braids.

Beekeeper
Karel Rehka Products
880 Northwood Drive, N.E.
Salem, OR 97301
(503) 364-9701

  Honey, pollen, beeswax, and royal jelly, as well as organic garlic, prunes, and filberts.

Blooming Prairie Warehouse, Inc.
2340 Heinz Road
Iowa City, IA 52240
(319) 337-6448

  Organic produce by mail in nine-state Midwestern region.

Blue Heron Farm
P.O. Box 68
Rumsey, CA 95679
(916) 796-3799

  Organic nuts by mail.

Community Mill and Bean, Inc.
R.D. 1, Route 89
Savannah, NY 13146
(315) 365-2664
Fax: (315) 365-2690

  Organic beans by mail.

Dach Ranch
P.O. Box 44
Philo, CA 95466
(707) 895-3173

Organically grown apples, pears, and vinegars by mail throughout the nation.

Deer Valley Farm
R.D. 1
Guilford, NY 13780
(607) 764-8556

Organic fruits and vegetables such as squash, cabbage, celery, oranges, and grapefruit sold by mail throughout the nation. Also offers home delivery in New York City, Long Island, Westchester, western Connecticut, northern New Jersey, Albany, Utica, Ithaca, Binghamton, Buffalo, and Rochester.

Dharma Farms
Star Route, Box 140
Osage, AR 72638
(501) 553-2550

Apples and pears mailed throughout the country.

Diamond K Enterprises
R.R. 1, Box 30
Saint Charles, MN 55972
(507) 932-4308

Organically grown dates and raisins by mail.

Ecology Sound Farm
42126 Road 168
Orosi, CA 93647
(209) 528-3816

Organically grown navel and Valencia oranges, plums, Asian pears, Fuyu persimmons, and kiwi fruit available by mail nationwide.

Garden Spot Distributors
438 White Oak Road, Box 729A
New Holland, PA 17557
(717) 354-4936

Organically grown nuts, dried fruits, seeds, and beans. In shops, look for their retail brand name, Shiloh Farms.

Golden Acres Orchard
Route 2, Box 2450
Front Royal, VA 22630

Organically grown apples, apple juice, and apple cider vinegar.

Golden Angels Apiary
P.O. Box 2
Singers Glen, VA 22850
(703) 833-5104

Pesticide-free honey by mail.

Great Date in the Morning
P.O. Box 31
Coachella, CA 92236
(619) 398-6171

Mail-order dates.

Greek Gourmet Ltd.
195 Whiting Street
Hingham, MA 02043

Organic olives by mail.

Green Knoll Farm
P.O. Box 434
Gridley, CA 95948
(916) 846-3431

Organically grown kiwi fruit by mail.

Hill and Dale Farm
R-2, Box 1260
Putney, VT 05346
(802) 387-5817

Northern Vermont mountain apples (Spy, McIntosh, Red Delicious) available by mail.

Stanley and Marina Jacobson
1505 Doherty
Mission, TX 78572
(512) 585-1712

Organically grown grapefruit, picked fresh after you order, shipped throughout the nation.

Jaffe Brothers
P.O. Box 636
Valley Center, CA 92082
(619) 749-1133

Organically grown dried fruits, nuts, and seeds by mail.

Kennedys' Natural Foods
1051 West Broad Street
Falls Church, VA 22046
(703) 533-8484

Dried fruits, nuts, and hardy produce by mail. The Kennedys have an excellent mail-order catalog with many diverse and useful organic products.

Joseph T. Miller
R.R. 3, Box 202
Dixon, MO 65459

Organically grown sweet potatoes and artichokes by mail.

Millstream Market
1310 A. G. Tallmadge Avenue
Akron, OH 44310
(216) 630-2700

Organically grown produce, dried fruits, and nuts.

Mountain Ark Trading Company
120 South East Avenue
Fayetteville, AR 72701
(800) 643-8909

Organically grown honey by mail.

Nature Grown
Winnsboro, TX 75494
(214) 342-3657

Organically grown fruits and vegetables shipped anywhere in the United States.

Nature's Corner
Route 2, Box 302
Iowa Falls, IA 50126

Organically grown crops by mail.

New Hope Homestead
Route 5
Murphy, NC 28906

Honey gathered from the fields and forests of the Chattahoochee National Forest.

Organic Foods Express
11003 Emack Road
Beltsville, MD 20705
(301) 937-8608

A full line of fresh organically grown produce, including herbs, shipped throughout the United States.

Ozark Organic Growers Association
Ozark Mountain Wildflower Honey
HCR 72, Box 34
Parthenon, AR 72666
(501) 446-5783

Honey without pesticide or antibiotic residues. (Yes, some farmers feed antibiotics to bees, too!) No heat is used in the extraction or processing of this honey, which is minimally filtered through cheesecloth. Heavy filtration is a primary reason why all brands of chemically grown honey look and taste alike.

Red Fox Farm
R.D. 1, Box 7
Sharon Springs, NY 13459

Maple syrup and maple candy without chemicals, additives, or formaldehyde.

Rising Sun Organic Food
P.O. Box 627 PA 150/I-80
Milesburg, PA 16853
(814) 355-9850

Organically grown fruits and vege-
tables by mail.

Star Organic Produce, Inc.
P.O. Box 561502
Miami, FL 33256-1502
(305) 262-1242

Tropical fruits organically grown in
Florida.

Leo Tew Organics
7120 Benhart Drive
Raleigh, NC 27612
(919) 782-9338

Organic sweet potatoes.

Walnut Acres
Penns Creek, PA 17862
(717) 837-0601

A wide variety of fresh produce
available by mail. Walnut Acres is the
exclusive mail-order distributor of
Earth's Best organic baby food.

Water Wheel Sugar House
Route 2
Jefferson, NH 03583
(603) 586-4479

Maple syrup by mail throughout the
nation.

The Wright Farm
Enosburg Falls, VT 05450
(802) 933-4775

For more than thirty years, the
Wrights have been selling pure Ver-
mont syrup by mail throughout the na-
tion. Their syrup has no additives or
chemicals.

ORGANIC CERTIFICATION GROUPS

One of these groups will be able to tell you about organic produce growers
and retailers in your area.

California Certified Organic Farmers
    (CCOF)
P.O. Box 8136
Santa Cruz, CA 95061
(408) 423-2263

Farm Verified Organic Program
    (FVO)
Mercantile Development, Inc.
274 Riverside Avenue
P.O. Box 2747
Westport, CT 06880
(203) 226-7803

Maine Organic Farmers' &
    Gardeners' Association (MOFGA)
Nancy Ross
P.O. Box 2176
Augusta, ME 04338
(207) 622-3118

Natural Organic Farmers'
    Association (NOFA)–Connecticut
153 Bowers Hill
Oxford, CT 06483
(203) 888-9280

NOFA–Massachusetts
153 N. Main St.
Natick, MA 01760
(508) 655-2204

NOFA–New Hampshire
Route 1, Box 516
Andover, NH 03216
(603) 648-2521

NOFA–New York
5403 Barber Road
Avon, NY 14414
(716) 226-6412

NOFA–Vermont
15 Barre Street
Montpelier, VT 05602
(802) 223-7222 or (802) 229-0800

Ohio Ecological Food and Farm
   Association
7300 Bagley Road
Mount Perry, OH 43769

Organic Crop Improvement
   Association (OCIA)
125 West Seventh Street
Wind Gap, PA 18091
(215) 863-6700
   or:
P.O. Box 729A
White Oak Road
New Holland, PA 17557

Organic Foods Production
   Association of North America
   (OFPANA)
P.O. Box 31
Belchertown, MA 01007
(413) 323-6821

Organic Growers and Buyers
   Association
P.O. Box 9747
Minneapolis, MN 55440
(612) 674-8527

Organic Growers of Michigan
Lewis King
3031 White Creek Road
Kingston, MI 48741
(517) 683-2573
   or:

Lee Purdy
3928 S. Sheraton Road
Lennon, MI 48449
(313) 621-4977
   or:
Joe Scrimager
Bio Systems
Marlette, MI
(517) 635-2864

Ozark Organic Growers Association
P.O. Box 1528
Fayetteville, AR 72702
(501) 521-COOP

Texas Department of Agriculture
Organic Certification Program
P.O. Box 12847
Austin, TX 78711
(512) 463-9883

Tilth Producers' Cooperative–
   Oregon
Yvonne Frost
P.O. Box 218
Tualatin, OR 97062
(503) 692-4877

Tilth Producers' Cooperative–
   Washington
1219 East Sauk Road
Concrete, WA 98237
(206) 853-8449

Virginia Association of Biological
   Farmers
Box 252
Flint Hill, VA 22747

GRAINS

Reasonably priced organically grown grains and grain-based products are widely available through the mail and at natural food stores. Look for the seal certifying the product as truly organic. This list constitutes an endorsement of these products.

MAIL-ORDER GRAIN SOURCES

Baldwin Hill Bakery
Baldwin Hill Road
Philipston, MA 01331
(508) 249-4691

Berkshire Mountain Bakery
P.O. Box 785
Housatonic, MA 01236

Bread Alone
Route 28
Boiceville, NY 12412
(914) 657-3328

Totally organic breads including farm bread (a coarse-grain wheat and rye), six-grain bread, miche (yeast-free sourdough), whole wheat walnut, and many others.

Community Mill and Bean
R.D. 1, Route 89
Savannah, NY 13146
(315) 365-2664
Fax: (315) 365-2690

Organic whole grain flours, mixes for pancakes, gingerbread, and corn bread, organic grains, and organic dried beans.

Diamond K Enterprises
R.R. 1, Box 30
Saint Charles, MN 55972
(507) 932-4308 or 932-5433

Organic whole grains in bulk, from alfalfa and barley to oats and soybeans as well as flours and mixes.

Garden Spot Distributors
Kathy Clough
438 White Oak Road
New Holland, PA 17557

A wide variety of organic grains: barley, buckwheat, millet, rye, rice, sprouted grain breads, and pesticide-free granolas.

Mill City Bakery
1566 Randolph Avenue
St. Paul, MN 55105
(612) 698-4705

Some of the best tasting, purest sourdough breads in the nation.

Nokomis Farms
3293 Main Street
East Troy, WI 53120
(414) 642-9665

Sourdough bread made with certified organically grown grains. Nokomis also sells organically grown flour.

Northern Lake Wild Rice Company
P.O. Box 28
Cass Lake, MN 56633

Organically grown wild rice.

Pacific Bakery
429 South Hill Street
P.O. Box 950
Oceanside, CA 92054
(619) 757-6020

Multigrain and oat bread.

Rising Sun Organic Food
P.O. Box 627 PA 150/I-80
Milesburg, PA 16853
(814) 355-9850

Organically grown grains. Rising Sun also sells organic breads made by the Baldwin Hill Bakery and the Women's Community Bakery; Sprout's Delight, which uses no yeast; and organic flours, cereals, and granola.

Sunrise Sourdough Bakery
Bill Hotchkiss
P.O. Box 727
Philomath, OR 97370
(503) 929-3237

Sourdough bread by mail throughout the western states.

MEATS AND POULTRY

Producers of top-quality meats and poultry can be found in virtually every region of the country. Because these firms use neither subtherapeutic doses of antibiotics or hormones, the farm animals are more likely to be raised humanely; sometimes, overcrowding and inhumane conditions force ranchers to use antibiotics and hormones. If you cannot find organic meat and poultry locally, you can order it through the mail. The USDA runs a meat and poultry hot line; if you have questions about food safety, you can call (800) 535-4555. In the Washington, D.C., metropolitan area the number is (202) 447-3333.

Antibiotic- and hormone-free meats are available at many retail outlets. These are among the major brands which you should seek:

Coleman Natural Beef of Colorado is available at supermarkets throughout the nation, including Grand Union stores in the New York City area as well as Purity Supreme in New England, A&P in New York and New Jersey, Bread & Circus in the Boston area, Big Y Foods in Massachusetts, and Farmer Jack's stores in the Detroit area. Coleman Natural Beef supplies just about the purest beef in the nation. Samples of Coleman Natural Beef have been lab tested for pesticides without any positive detections at extremely low detection levels. Free from antibiotics and hormones. Hot dog lovers will be heartened by the arrival of Coleman Natural Beef hot dogs.

Foster Farms poultry is available throughout the western United States. Foster Farms has a rigorous pesticide residue elimination program, screening all shipments of grain for pesticides and rejecting shipments with detectable levels of pesticides. Subtherapeutic doses of antibiotics are not used in the feed.

Holly Farms poultry is available throughout the eastern United States and Midwest. Holly Farms has a pesticide residue elimination program, screening all shipments of grain for pesticides and rejecting shipments with detectable levels of pesticides. Subtherapeutic doses of antibiotics are not used in the feed.

Kohler Farms of Wisconsin supplies hormone-free beef to supermarkets in Wisconsin and the Chicago area including Treasure Island. Look for the PURElean BEEF trademark.

Larsen Beef, produced without antibiotics or hormones, can be found in Kroger stores in Atlanta, Georgia, as well as King Kullen on Long Island, Kash 'N Karry in the Tampa and Orlando, Florida, areas and Dominicks in the Chicago area.

Laura's Lean Beef, produced without hormones, is available at Kroger stores in Kentucky and Southern Indiana.

Maverick Ranch Lite Beef is produced without hormones or antibiotics and is lab tested for pesticide residues; any beef cuts that show positive pesticide detections are not sold under the Maverick trademark. Maverick Ranch Lite Beef is available at King Sooper markets in Denver, Schnucks in Saint Louis, Kings Supermarkets in New Jersey, and Clemens in Philadelphia.

Organic Cattle Co. beef is certified organic and available at markets in the New York City area.

Quality Steaks produces hormone-free beef that is available at Star Markets in Massachusetts, First National Supermarkets in New England, and ABCO in the Phoenix, Arizona, area.

MAIL-ORDER ORGANIC AND HORMONE-FREE MEAT AND POULTRY SOURCES

Brae Beef
45 John Street
Greenwich, CT 06831
(203) 869-0106

Hormone-free beef and poultry by mail worldwide.

Mike Brodman
6409 East Scipio Top Road 8
Republic, OH 44867
(419) 585-5852

Organic beef.

Dakota Lean Meats
136 West Trip
Winner, SD 57580
(800) 727-5326

Hormone-free beef.

David Feldman
402 North Pine Meadow Drive
De Bary, FL 32713-2307
(407) 668-6361

Organic beef and pork by mail.

Garden Spot Distributors
438 White Oak Road
Box 729A
New Holland, PA 17557

A wide variety of organic meat and poultry products including whole chickens and turkeys, chicken and beef hot dogs, ground beef, and bologna. No nitrites, coloring, fillings, or binders in any products. All organic grains fed to their animals.

Green Earth Natural Foods
2545 Prairie Avenue
Evanston, IL 60201
(800) 322-3662

Organic beef, chicken, and pork.

Jordan River Farm
Cory Koral and Miriam Harris
Huntly, VA 22640
(703) 636-9388

Certified organic beef and veal.

Lean & Free
R.R. 3, Box 53
Ackley, IA 50601
(800) 383-BEEF

Hormone-free beef.

Organic Beef, Inc.
P.O. Box 642
Mena, AK 71953
(501) 387-7111

Beef raised without antibiotics or hormones.

Organic Cattle Company
Helen Tahmin
P.O. Box 355
White Plains, NY 10605
(914) 684-6529

Beef without hormones or antibiotics. Cattle are fed organic grains.

Piedmont Foods
Roy Baldwin
7419 Highway 64 East
Knightdale, NC 27545
(919) 266-7773

Organic beef and pork delivered to your home. Service available throughout the country.

Rising Sun Organic Food
P.O. Box 627 PA 150/I-80
Milesburg, PA 16853
(814) 355-9850

Certified organic chicken, turkey, beef, lamb, and pork.

Roseland Farms
27427 M-60 West
Cassopolis, MI 49031
(616) 445-8987

Organic beef.

Stapleman Meats
Brent Stapleman
Route 2, Box 6A
Belden, NE 68717
(402) 985-2470

Organic beef and pork. No antibiotics or hormones are used in their organic beef.

Summerfield Farm
HCR 4 Box 195A
Brightwood, VA 22715
(703) 948-3100

Veal products available from humanely raised calves. Lamb and game birds are also available.

Wolfe's Neck Farm
R.R. 1
Freeport, ME 04032
(207) 865-4469

Certified organic beef air-shipped throughout New England.

ACTIVIST GROUPS

The Humane Farming Association
1550 California Street, Suite 6
San Francisco, CA 94109
(415) 485-1495

The Humane Farming Association has been in the forefront of the movement to treat farm animals humanely.

Food Animals Concerns Trust
P.O. Box 14599
Chicago, IL 60614-9966
(312) 525-4952

FACT is actively involved in taking farm animals out of crates and cages and putting them in more humane settings. Contact for sources of humanely raised veal.

A SAFER GRILL

Hermelin, Inc.
130 McCormick Avenue, Suite 109
Costa Mesa, CA 92626

Manufacturers of the Vertikal Grill, which allows grilling without cancer-causing PAHs. Costs about $59.

SEAFOOD

Pure seafood is something you need to buy directly from a local seafood shop rather than through the mail. You can help save our rivers, lakes, streams, coastal waters, and oceans by joining a clean water group in your area.

DAIRY PRODUCTS

MAIL-ORDER ORGANIC
CHEESE SOURCES

Brier Run Farm
Route 1, Box 73
Birch River, WV 26610
(304) 649-2975

Brier Run Farm goat cheese (chèvre) is certified organic and sold by mail nationwide; it can be found at Bread & Circus supermarkets in Boston, Zabar's, Balducci's, Dean and Deluca, and other shops in New York City, and Sutton Place Gourmet and other shops in Washington, D.C.

Other stores in Pennsylvania, Virginia, Ohio, North Carolina, and Connecticut carry Brier Run products, too. Call the number above for stores in your area that carry their cheese.

Millhopper Marketing, Inc.
1110 N.W. 8th Avenue, Suite C
Gainesville, FL 32601

Manufactures a yogurt cheese funnel which you can use to make nonfat cheese at home. $9.95.

EGGS

Look for Nest Eggs brand eggs at stores nationwide. Nest Eggs come from humanely raised chickens. For more information about where to find Nest Eggs brand eggs in your area, contact:

Food Animal Concerns Trust
  (FACT)
P.O. Box 14599
Chicago, IL 60614-9966
(312) 525-4952

PREPARED FOODS

CONVENIENCE FOODS

Many companies sell prepared foods made without harmful additives and artificial chemicals. This list constitutes an endorsement for these products. They are among the best available today.

Amy's Kitchen vegetable potpies are completely free from additives and contain only organically grown grains and vegetables. They do contain butter. Amy's macaroni and cheese is made with organic soy ingredients.

Arrowhead Mills Spanish-style quick brown rice uses ingredients grown without herbicides, pesticides, or synthetic fertilizers.

Colonel Sanchez chicken tamales are made with certified organically grown blue corn and Foster Farms poultry. Foster Farms has a pesticide residue elimination program. No food additives are used.

De Bole's whole wheat macaroni and cheese dinner is made with organically grown durum whole wheat flour and cheddar cheese.

Graindance Pizza uses real cheese, which probably contains pesticides, but the crust is 100 percent organic whole wheat flour, and no nitrites or additives are used.

Health Valley chicken broth is made with chicken broth, chicken fat, honey, onion powder, turmeric, and other natural spices. Health Valley vegetarian amaranth is made with organically grown amaranth, oats, pearl barley, brown rice, and rye. It cooks in three minutes. Health Valley oat bran pastas use organically grown grains.

Heart & Soul spinach quiche and broccoli quiche are made with organically grown tofu and mozzarella- and Monterey Jack–style cheese alternatives made from tofu, soy oil, and casein. The crust is made from 100 percent whole wheat flour, soy oil, and sea salt. Heart & Soul also makes an excellent tofu lasagne with organically grown soybeans, nondairy cheese substitute, and eggless whole wheat noodles.

Jaclyn's line of all natural soups include barley and mushroom, split pea, and vegetable. Although organically grown vegetables are not used, these soups do have an impeccable ingredients list. Jaclyn's also markets organic frozen breaded mushrooms and breaded cauliflower.

Lima brand ratatouille potage is made with organically grown tomatoes, zucchini, onion, egg, peppers, garlic, olive, thyme, bay leaves, and sea salt. Lima Sietan is made with organic whole wheat, organic soy beans, tamari soy sauce, kombu seaweed, and herbs. Lima brand *sietan* is known as the "vegetable meat" and can be used in most recipes instead of meat.

Legume produces an excellent line of low-calorie nonmeat and nondairy frozen dinners from cannelloni to enchiladas. Although not made with organically grown ingredients, these are among the best weight watcher–style frozen dinners available today.

Medallions salmon patties are made with Washington salmon, which is among the purest of seafoods. The rest of the ingredients, although not organic, have low pesticide saturation.

Old Chicago Pizza-Lite brand pizzas with mozzarella soy cheese use organically grown whole wheat.

Pizsoy makes great pizzas with organic whole wheat flour crust and tofu mozzarella made with organic soybeans.

Soy Deli Tofu Burgers are made with organic tofu and nonorganic carrots and onions. They are an excellent substitute for pesticide-saturated beef hamburgers.

Soy Powder savory baked tofu is made with organically grown soybeans, water, soy sauce, spices, and nigari.

The Specialty Grain Company's organically grown popcorn is an excellent snack food.

Wildwood tofu products are made with organically grown grains.

CONDIMENTS

Arrowhead Mills peanut butter is made without herbicides and pesticides, and the peanuts are allowed to dry naturally on the vine, virtually eliminating aflatoxin contamination.

Cascadian Farm fruit conserves, sweet pickle relish, pickles, and potato chips are made with organically grown ingredients.

Jaclyn's whole wheat bread crumbs are made with organically grown stone-ground whole wheat flour, unrefined safflower oil, barley malt, herbs, and spices.

Marantha almond butter is made with roasted organic almonds.

Nasoya Vegi-Dip is made with tofu, pressed sunflower oil, brown rice syrup (for sweetener), apple cider vinegar, lemon juice, onions, sea salt, and vegetable gum. Nasoya Creamy Italian tofu dressing is a no-cholesterol dressing made with well water and tofu from organically grown soybeans. Nasoya Garden Herb vegi-dressing is made with organically grown tofu. Nasoya Nayonnaise is a good mayonnaise substitute with half the calories of regular mayonnaise.

Senor Felipe's salsa, enchilada sauce, and barbecue sauce are all made with organically grown produce.

The ingredients of Soya Kaas cream cheese–style spreads include tofu made with organically grown soybeans, soy oil, vegetable gums, calcium sulfate, and calcium sodium caseinate.

Tree of Life salsa is made with organically grown tomatoes, carrots, and garlic.

Westbrae soy sauce is made with organically grown soybeans, whole wheat, and sea salt.

DESSERTS AND SWEET SNACKS

Beware of products with highly saturated palm, palm kernel, or coconut oils. These oils may actually raise cholesterol levels.

El Molino orange ginger spice cookies are baked with organically grown whole wheat flour.

Glenny's Fruit Drops are made with rice syrup, oil of orange, rose hips, hibiscus, orange peel, lemon peel, cream of tartar, natural vegetable color, and natural flavors.

Health Valley desserts and snacks are made with organic grains and other ingredients. Their amaranth graham crackers are made with organically grown whole grain amaranth and pure fruit concentrates. Health Valley apple bakes have organically grown grains including whole wheat, amaranth, and rolled oats.

Pride o' the Farm muesli crackers are baked with organically grown whole wheat flour and use fruit juice concentrate as sweetener.

Rebel Bakers, of San Diego, makes carrot cupcakes with organically grown grains, fruits, and nuts.

Westbrae makes organic cookies. Their gingersnaps are made with organic whole wheat and whole rye flours with non-alum baking powder. The sweetener is rice malt syrup with sustaining complex sugars.

BEVERAGES

MAIL-ORDER ORGANIC WINE SOURCES

Chartrand Imports
Paul Chartrand
P.O. Box 1319
Rockland, ME 04841
(207) 594-7300

Mail-order distributor for French and California organic wines.

Fitzpatrick Winery and Lodge
Brian Fitzpatrick
7740 Fairplay Road
Somerset, CA 95684
(209) 245-3248

A variety of organic wines such as Sauvignon Blanc, Chardonnay, blushes, white zinfandel, white cabernet, chenin blanc, and on the red side, zinfandel, Kings Red, Cabernet Franc and Cabernet Sauvignon, and Merlo and Petit Sirah. They sell by mail order throughout the nation. They try to limit their use of sulfites.

Four Chimneys Farm Winery
R.D. 1, Hall Road
Himrod-on-Seneca, NY 14842
(607) 243-7502

Excellent vintages with absolutely no added sulfites, available by mail throughout the country.

Frey Vineyards
14000 Tomki Road
Redwood Valley, CA 95470
(707) 485-5177

Organic wines available nationwide. Call for information on local availability.

The Organic Wine Company
54 Genoa Place
San Francisco, CA 94133
(415) 433-0167

Sells certified organic French wines in the western U.S. Contact for information on location of retail outlets in your area.

ADDITIVES

Feingold Association
P.O. Box 6550
Alexandria, VA 22306
(703) 768-3287

An international organization providing information on food additives and related health problems. Contact for the location of the nearest Feingold support group in your area. Publishes an excellent newsletter, Pure Facts, ten times annually.

National Organization Mobilized to Stop MSG (NOMSG)
P.O. Box 367
Santa Fe, NM 87504
(800) 288-0718

A nonprofit consumer group formed to educate consumers about MSG dangers.

IRRADIATION

These are groups fighting to stop irradiation of food. Support them. Get involved.

Arizona

International Alliance of Atomic
Veterans
P.O. Box 32
Topoc, AZ 86436
(602) 768-7515

California

Berkeley, California, Coalition to
Stop Food Irradiation (CSFI)
2129 Oregon Street
Berkeley, CA 94705
(415) 848-4424

Citizens Against a Radioactive Dublin
(CARD)
6979 Portage
Dublin, CA 94568
(415) 828-5263

Dublin Against a Radioactive
Environment (DARE)
6997 Dublin Boulevard
Dublin, CA 94568
(415) 828-8199

Food Irradiation Response
Box 5183
Santa Cruz, CA 95063
(408) 426-2734

Graphic Communications
International Union Local 583
2301 Ocean Avenue
San Francisco, CA 94127
(415) 239-7700

Los Angeles, California, CSFI
P.O. Box 3294
South Pasadena, CA 91030
(818) 353-2543

Mid-Peninsula, California, CSFI
Box 2384
Stanford, CA 94309
(415) 323-5321

Napa, California, CSFI
2411 Soda Canyon Road
Napa, CA 94558
(707) 252-8757

National Coalition to Stop Food
Irradiation
P.O. Box 59-0488
San Francisco, CA 94159
(415) 626-2743

National Nutritional Foods
Association
125 East Baker Avenue, #230
Costa Mesa, CA 92626
(714) 966-6632

Sacramento, California, CSFI
2517 O Street, #2
Sacramento, CA 95816
(916) 421-6369

San Mateo County, California, CSFI
Box 1211
Burlingame, CA 94011
(415) 344-9778

Sausage Makers Union, Local 203
United Food & Commercial Workers
4120 Mission Street
San Francisco, CA 94112
(415) 584-6550

Sonoma County, California, CSFI
P.O. Box 524
Petaluma, CA 94953
(707) 578-6018

Southwestern Regional Council of
United Food & Commercial
Workers
3550 Watt Avenue, #190
Sacramento, CA 95821
(916) 488-2300

Colorado

Colorado Alliance to Protect Our
  Food
8332 Peakview, #H-6
Fort Collins, CO 80525
(303) 663-0811

District of Columbia

Environmental Policy Institute
218 D Street
Washington, DC 20003
(202) 544-2600

Florida

Broward County, Florida, Coalition
  to Stop Food Irradiation (FCSFI)
3100 Riverside Drive, #211
Coral Springs, FL 33065

Citizens Against a Radioactive
  Environment (CARE)
P.O. Box 14644
Gainesville, FL 32604
(904) 374-6675

Consumers Alliance to Protect Our
  Edibles (CAPE)
P.O. Box 5835
Titusville, FL 32783

Dade County, Florida, FCSFI
4329 North Bay Road
Miami Beach, FL 33140
(305) 672-8044

Florida Consumers Opposed to Food
  Irradiation
Box 13042
Saint Petersburg, FL 33733
(813) 327-7690

Hillsborough County, Florida, FCSFI
30 Landing Way
Oldmar, FL 34677
(813) 787-2011

Palm Beach County, Florida, FCSFI
P.O. Box 05 70 86
West Palm Beach, FL 33405
(407) 964-8937

Pinellas County, Florida, FCSFI
P.O. Box 1722
Dunedin, FL 34697
(813) 449-0766

Southwest Florida FCSFI
4411 Bee Ridge Road, #310
Sarasota, FL 34233
(813) 371-7960

Indiana

Hoosiers Concerned About Food
  Irradiation
4175 Meander Bend, 3-B
Indianapolis, IN 46268
(317) 875-0927

Kansas

Lawrence, Kansas, CSFI
Community Mercantile
700 Main Street
Lawrence, KS 66044
(913) 749-1592

Maine

Citizens Against Nuclear Trash
  (CANT)
P.O. Box 701
South Casco, ME 04077
(207) 655-4661

Maryland

Health and Energy Institute
P.O. Box 5357
Tacoma Park, MD 20912
(301) 585-5541

Massachusetts

Boston Area CSFI
P.O. Box 2192
Cambridge, MA 02238
(617) 787-1524

Minnesota

Brainerd, Minnesota, CSFI
Sunberry Food Buying Club
8800 County Road 77 West
Brainerd, MN 56501
(218) 929-6811

Twin Cities CSFI
6724 Colfax Avenue North
Brooklyn Center, MN 55430
(612) 561-0814

New York

Food & Water, Inc.
225 Lafayette, #612
New York, NY 10102
(212) 941-9340

Hudson Valley CSFI
2 Maiden Avenue
Saugerties, NY 12477

New York Public Interest Research
    Group
9 Murray Street
New York, NY 10007
(212) 349-6460

Oklahoma

Grassroots Environmental Action
    Team (GREAT)
Box 2
Snow, OK 74567
(405) 298-2803

Pennsylvania

Coalition for Alternatives to Nutrition
    and Healthcare (CANAH)
P.O. Box B-12
Richlandtown, PA 18955

Texas

American Fruitarian Society and
    Organic Food Network
P.O. Box 17128
Austin, TX 78760
(512) 385-2841

San Antonio, Texas, CSFI
238 Senisa Drive
San Antonio, TX 78228
(512) 732-4181

Vermont

Vermont Alliance to Protect Our
    Food
P.O. Box 237
Vergennes, VT 05491
(802) 877-3289

Vermont Public Interest Research
    Group
43 State Street
Montpelier, VT 05602
(802) 223-5221

Virginia

National Health Federation
5001 Seminary Road, #1330
Alexandria, VA 22231
(703) 379-0589

Poultry producers are contemplating using irradiation on their products. Tell them you will not purchase poultry products from a company that supports or uses food irradiation. Most of these companies have toll-free numbers:

Tyson Foods: (800) 643-3140
Con Agra: (501) 863-1600
Holly Farms: (800) 334-7251
Perdue, Inc.: (800) 638-1150
Gold Kist: (404) 393-5000

WATER

WATER TESTING

These firms can test your water for lead, bacteria, metal, minerals, nitrates, industrial solvents, and pesticides. Costs range from around $30 to over $200 for all contaminants.

David Diagnostics, Inc.
46-01 Broadway
Astoria, NY 11103
(718) 278-7676

Nitrate test strips for screening well water for nitrate contamination.

International Diagnostic Laboratories
16100 Chesterfield Village Parkway
Chesterfield, MO 63017

Nitrate test strips.

National Testing Laboratories
6151 Wilson Mills Road
Cleveland, OH 44143
(800) 458-3330
(216) 449-2525

Complete line of water testing kits, reasonably priced.

Suburban Water Testing
  Laboratories
4600 Kutztown Road
Temple, PA 19560
(800) 433-6595
(215) 929-3666

Offers a complete line of water-testing services. Kits shipped to customers with sampling instructions.

Watertest Corporation of America
33 South Commercial Street
Manchester, NH 03101
(800) 426-8378

Complete line of water analysis services priced from $29 to $298. Watertest will analyze the water from a school or day care center for lead at no charge.

CERTIFIERS OF WATER FILTERS

National Sanitation Foundation
3475 Plymouth Road
P.O. Box 1468
Ann Arbor, MI 48106
(313) 769-8010

Water Quality Association
4151 Naperville Road
Lisle, IL 60532

WQA will send you general information about water quality problems and point-of-use technologies that can be used in the home or office.

PORTABLE WATER FILTERS

General Ecology
151 Sheree Boulevard
Lionville, PA 19353
(800) 441-8166

Manufacturer of a small portable water filter, called the First Need Portable Drinking Water Purifier.

LEAD

A booklet, *Lead in Drinking Water,* is available from the Environmental Protection Agency, Washington, D.C. 20460

Frandon Enterprises
P.O. Box 300321
Seattle, WA 98103
(800) 359-9000

The Frandon Lead Alert Kit for Drinking Water enables consumers to test for lead at home, work, or school, for levels down to 10 to 20 parts per billion.

THE NONTOXIC HOME

LEAD

Frandon Enterprises
P.O. Box 300321
Seattle WA 98103
(800) 359-9000

The Frandon Lead Alert Kit offers consumers a method of self-protection against lead contamination by allowing them to conduct home tests for excessive lead leaching in food service and storage containers like earthenware, ceramics, enameled metal, and lead-soldered-seam cans. The kit can also be used to test for lead paint and lead-soldered seams in plumbing. Cost is $29.95 plus $2.50 for shipping, handling and insurance.

The U.S. Pottery Association has a surveillance program of members to make sure they use safe glazes. Look for products with the USPA approval seal.

Potters and hobbyists can obtain a book on using safe glazes by writing to the Lead Industries Association, Inc., 292 Madison Avenue, New York, NY 10017.

LOW-TOXIN HOME RENOVATION PRODUCTS

AFM Enterprises, Inc.
1140 Stacy Court
Riverside, CA 92507
(714) 781-6860

PEST CONTROL

Bio-Integral Resource Center
P.O. Box 7414
Berkeley, CA 94707
(415) 524-2567

A nonprofit corporation undertaking research and education in integrated pest management and organic pest control. Publishes the IPM Practitioner 10 times a year and the Common Sense Pest Control Quarterly and many other booklets on nontoxic methods of pest control.

Natural Gardening Resource Center
P.O. Box 149
Sunman, IN 47041
(812) 623-3800

Natural Gardening Resource Center is a source for a variety of biological controls for gardening and reduced

toxicity gardening products as well as a free catalog that contains information on plant disease and treatment.

Rodale Press
33 E. Minor Street
Emmaus, PA 18098
(215) 967-5171

An excellent resource center for organic gardening.

Unique Insect Control
5540 Sperry Drive
Citrus Heights, CA 95621
(916) 961-7945

A national distributor of beneficial insects for biological control of pests. Products include ladybugs, praying mantis eggs, lacewing, fly parasites, and red earthworms. Also provides information and instructions.

RADON TEST KITS

Many companies sell radon testing kits. For sources, consult the *Healthy House Catalog* (see under Safe Home Products, below).

SAFE HOME PRODUCTS

Environmental Hazards Management
  Institute
Box 932
Durham, NH 03824
(603) 868-1496

A state-chartered institute that provides educational materials about home and water hazards associated with industrial pollution and natural causes.

Household Hazardous Waste Project
  (HHWP)
901 South National Avenue
Box 108
Springfield, MO 65804
(417) 836-5777

A nonprofit group dedicated to educating communities in Missouri about

the safety, storage, and disposal of household hazardous products and waste. They publish an excellent guide to hazardous products around the home.

Housing Resource Center
4115 Bridge Avenue
Cleveland, OH 44113
(800) 222-9348

Housing Resource Center publishes the Healthy House Catalog, *which provides excellent directions for creating a nontoxic home environment. Its directory of products and services is a resource that anybody interested in an environmentally pure home atmosphere will want. Cost, $19.95 plus $3 shipping.*

Human Ecology Action League
(HEAL)
P.O. Box 49126
Atlanta, GA 30359

HEAL provides a support network for environmentally sensitive persons as well as information on physicians who work with environmentally ill persons. HEAL also publishes an excellent quarterly magazine.

Nigra Enterprises
5699 Kanan Road
Agoura, CA 91301
(818) 889-6877

SAFE HOME TEST KIT

DIET FOR A POISONED PLANET SAFE HOME AND SAFE FOOD TEST KITS

325 North Oakhurst Drive
Suite 404
Beverly Hills, CA 90210
(213) 550-7600

To help people detect and eliminate environmental pollutants, pesticides, and animal drugs in their homes or in their food and water, I am presenting inexpensive home test kits. In many cases you will be able to get immediate results. These sampler test kits will help you test for toxic gases and other toxins in your home or kitchenware, such as asbestos, carbon monoxide, formaldehyde, lead, molds, nitrogen dioxide, radon, and even secondhand cigarette smoke. Homebuyers should purchase the homebuyer's safe home test kit before they buy their homes. Other test kits will help you to test for sulfa drugs, pesticides and lead in your food and water. Each kit is a sampler, allowing you to test for a variety of toxins.

Please call or write for product information.

Sells air filters, paints, sealants, caulks, grout, joint compounds, adhesives, furniture, shoe polish, soap, and a wide variety of other low-toxic and nontoxic products.

Seventh Generation
10 Farrell Street
South Burlington, VT 05403
(802) 862-2999

Sells recycled paper products, nontoxic cleaning products, biodegradable diapers and trash bags, low-flow shower heads, solar products, and home test kits for formaldehyde, gas, radon, and contaminants in water.

BABY FOODS AND SUPPLIES

Earth's Best
P.O. Box 887
Middlebury, VT 05753
(800) 442-4221

Simply Pure
RFD 3, Box 99
Bangor, ME 04401
(800) IAM-PURE

Tell the big baby food companies you don't want pesticide-contaminated baby foods.

Beech-Nut: (800) 523-6633
Gerber: (800) 4-GERBER
Heinz: (800) USABABY

DIAPERS

National Association of Diaper
  Services
2017 Walnut Street
Philadelphia, PA 19103
(215) 569-3650

DETOXIFICATION INFORMATION AND SUPPLEMENTS

HealthMed
R. Michael Wisner, Administrative
  Director
314 North Harper
Los Angeles, CA 90048
(213) 653-0837
  or:
HealthMed
1 Scripps Drive
Medical Building Suite 201
Sacramento, CA 95825
(916) 924-8060

For further information on a structured, clinical detox program, contact HealthMed.

AccuChem Laboratories
990 North Bowser Road, Suite 800
Richardson, TX 75081
(800) 558-0069
In Texas (214) 234-5412

Performs a complete array of pesticide and industrial chemical analyses for blood, urine, and body tissues.

Pacific Toxicology
1545 Pontious Avenue
Los Angeles, CA 90025
(213) 479-4911

Performs a complete array of pesticide and industrial chemical analyses for blood, urine, and body tissues.

The Winning Combination
11920 West Olympic Boulevard
Los Angeles, CA 90064
(800) 332-7799

The Winning Combination sells vitamin supplements by mail and publishes an excellent free booklet called Understanding Vitamin-Mineral Supplements.

POSTSCRIPT: PESTICIDES IN OUR FOOD

PESTICIDE REFORM ORGANIZATIONS

These organizations are working to bring you a safe and nontoxic planet.

Americans for Safe Food/Center for Science in the Public Interest
1875 Connecticut Avenue, NW
Washington, DC 20009-5728
(202) 332-9110

California Agrarian Action Project
P.O. Box 464
Davis, CA 95617
(916) 756-8518

Publishes a directory of organic food wholesalers, farm suppliers, and other sources.

Mothers and Others for Pesticide Limits
P.O. Box 96641
Washington, DC 20090

At work to strengthen pesticide laws.

National Coalition Against Misuse of Pesticides (NCAMP)
701 E. Street, SE Suite 200
Washington, DC 20003
(202) 543-5450

Dedicated to standing up for victims of pesticide poisoning, disseminating information, and acting as the national umbrella group for the many local grass roots groups working to change pesticide laws in their states and counties. Publishes an excellent newsletter.

Natural Resources Defense Council (NRDC)
90 New Montgomery Street
San Francisco, CA 94105
(415) 777-0220

Working on all issues from producing reports on pesticides to effects of acid rain on the New York City water supply.

Northwest Coalition for Alternatives to Pesticides (NCAP)
P.O. Box 1393
Eugene, OR 97440
(503) 344-5044

Five-state coalition of the Northwest that has fought the U.S. Forest Service on herbicide spraying. Publishes the Journal of Pesticide Reform, *a quarterly.*

Organic Food Network
American Fruitarian Society
6600 Burleston Road
P.O. Box 17128
Austin, TX 78760-7128
(512) 385-2481

Publishes a directory of organic food growers and shippers.

Organic Network–Eden Acres, Inc.
12100 Lima Center Road
Clinton, MI 49236

Publishes a directory of organic food suppliers, primarily growers, listed by state and zip code and indexed by commodity.

Pesticide Action Network–North America Regional Center (PAN)
P.O. Box 610
San Francisco, CA 94101
(415) 541-9140

Worldwide umbrella organization of people and groups from across the world who are opposed to the proliferation of pesticide use.

CANADIAN NATIONAL DIRECTORY OF ORGANIC FOOD SOURCES

Organic farming and ranching is booming in Canada. Shopping for organic foods by mail can be done in Canada but not nearly to the extent that it is in the U.S. On the other hand many farms and ranches sell directly to consumers, and there are many retail stores, too.

For a shortcut on finding organic foods in Canada, I highly recommend a publication called *The Directory*. It is a fantastic source book for locating suppliers of organic foods from produce to meat and poultry to convenience foods. *The Directory* lists farms and stores providing all necessary information. Since the 1989 directory is sold out, order early for the 1991 version. Cost is $10 (Canada), $15 (U.S.). Write to:

Canadian Organic Growers (COG)
Box 6408, Stn. "J"
Ottawa, Ontario, Canada K2A 3Y6
(416) 485-3534/(613) 395-5392/
(519) 747-5660

GLOSSARY OF PESTICIDES AND
TOXIC CHEMICALS

Acephate. An insecticide introduced in 1972 and used on thirty-four different food crops, primarily citrus. A relatively weak cancer-causing chemical.

Acifluorfen. An herbicide introduced in 1980 and used to control weeds and grasses around peanuts, soybeans, and rice. May be contaminated with dioxin, a suspected teratogen, embryotoxin, carcinogen, and co-carcinogen. Excessive exposure may cause liver and kidney damage and delayed fetal development. A possible human carcinogen.

Alachlor. An herbicide introduced in 1969, used on twenty-five different food crops, primarily corn and soybeans. A probable human carcinogen. May cause ocular lesions, prenatal and postnatal damage.

Alar. A growth regulator used on apples and peanuts from 1967 until withdrawn from use by Uniroyal in 1989 after a report issued by the Natural Resources Defense Council, which concluded some 5,500 to 6,000 children would contract cancer as a result of childhood exposure to this chemical in apples and apple products including apple juice. A probable human carcinogen.

Aldicarb. Also known as Temik, this dangerous pesticide was introduced in 1970 and has been used on a variety of crops, particularly potatoes. Even a drop absorbed by the skin can send a man into convulsions; it first came to the nation's attention when levels of this dangerous chemical, measured in parts per billion in California watermelon, sickened more than 1,000 persons during the July 4, 1985, weekend. Although most victims suffered acute flulike symptoms that included nausea, vomiting, and diarrhea, some victims suffered seizures and irregular heartbeat. At least two women reported stillbirths after their exposure. There is no way to tell whether the victims will suffer long-term degenerative central nervous system damage. Aldicarb contaminates about 5 percent of the chemically grown potatoes in supermarkets. Levels at which it is found in some foods and certainly in well water could very well cause babies and infants to become sick with flulike symptoms such as vomiting, nausea, blurred vision, stomach pain, sweating, and muscular weakness in the arms and legs. In Wisconsin, where aldicarb has been used on potatoes, Dr. Michael Fiore studied women who were exposed to aldicarb and discovered that the chemical is a potent immune modulator that, at levels in the parts per billion range, can change the ratio of T8 and T4 white blood cells into a clinically abnormal range. Although the precise clinical significance is unclear, the abnormal ratio may indicate that the women's immune systems were being stressed, possibly undergoing significant permanent damage. Before the 1985 aldicarb-tainted watermelon contamination incident, the Pesticide Incident Monitoring System reports on aldicarb from 1966 through 1982 contained 165 incidents associated with human injury. Aldicarb is highly toxic to mammals, birds, estuarine and marine organisms, and freshwater organisms. Aldicarb has also been found to pose a threat to an endangered species, Attwater's greater prairie chicken, which resides in or near aldicarb-treated fields in the Texas counties of Aransas, Austin, Brazoria, Colorado, Galveston, Goliad, Harris, Refugio, and Victoria. A California state scientific panel has called for a complete ban on aldicarb because of its dire threat to water quality and exposed humans. However, the state's Department of Food and Agriculture has, thus far, refused to ban the pesticide. Aldicarb sulfone and aldicarb sulfoxide are two breakdown products of the parent compound aldicarb.

Aldrin. An early insecticide that has been banned, aldrin is rarely seen in today's food supply. It is a strong liver toxin and probable human carcinogen.

Atrazine. An herbicide introduced in 1963 for weed control on corn, sorghum, sugarcane, pineapple, citrus, banana, and coffee crops worldwide. Excessive exposure at levels found in drinking water may cause chromosomal damage as well as damage to the lungs, liver, and kidneys. It may affect the adrenal glands and the nervous system and may delay fetal development. A relatively strong mutagen and possible human carcinogen.

Azinphos-methyl. An insecticide introduced in 1956 and used on seventy-eight different crops, primarily peaches and some other fruits. This acute neurotoxin, which can also cause severe eye and skin irritation, is a mutagen that causes cancerous liver tumors in animals.

Baygon. An insecticide used against cockroaches, flies, and mosquitoes. It may cause inhibition of the cholinesterase enzymes, which could result in nausea, blurred vision, stomach pain, sweating, muscle weakness in arms and legs, and vomiting.

Benomyl. A fungicide introduced in 1972, applied to forty-three different food crops, primarily as a post-harvest fungicide on citrus fruits such as grapefruit, mandarins, oranges, tangelos, and tangerines as well as rice, soybeans, and stone fruits. It is a possible human carcinogen and an animal teratogen that has been implicated in decreased sperm counts in animal studies.

Benzene. A common drinking water contaminant. A known human carcinogen, it is produced during the refining of petroleum, used in gasoline to increase octane and as a chemical intermediate during synthesis of compounds such as styrene, synthetic rubber, phenol, nitrobenzene, and cyclohexane, and produced naturally at low levels during some biological processes. Acute exposure produces central nervous system effects such as dizziness, giddiness, exhilaration, nausea, vomiting, headache, drowsiness, staggering, loss of balance, narcosis, and coma. It also causes acute leukemia, immune system depression, susceptibility to tuberculosis and pneumonia, and chromosomal aberrations.

Benzene hexachloride. A pesticide introduced in 1945 and now banned; production ceased in 1976. BHC is considered a probable human carcinogen.

BHC. See benzene hexachloride.

Bromacil. An herbicide used for general weed and brush control in non-crop areas and on citrus fruits and pineapples. A possible human carcinogen. Sheep exposed to high doses develop weakness in the legs and lack of coordination, which may last several weeks. Long-term high exposure may result in decreased weight gain, reduced food intake, and mild histological changes in the thyroid and liver. It also appears to be weakly mutagenic.

Butylate. An herbicide first introduced in 1967, used to control grassy weeds in corn. Long-term exposure in laboratory animals has resulted in testicular lesions and significant effects on blood clotting at all doses. Other studies have noted kidney and liver lesions and profound developmental effects in fetuses. It may be weakly mutagenic and is a possible human carcinogen.

Butylated hydroxyanisole (BHA) and butylated hydroxytoluene (BHT). Introduced in 1947 and used to prevent fats, oils, and fat-containing foods from becoming rancid, BHA or BHT may also be added to food packaging materials. Researchers report that BHA in the diet of pregnant mice results in brain enzyme changes in the newborn offspring including a 50 percent decreased activity in brain cholinesterase, which is responsible for the transmission of nerve impulses. In addition, the behavior of animals receiving either BHA or BHT in the diet differed from that of control animals with respect to sleep, aggression, and freezing behavior. Animals receiving BHA or BHT also exhibited a marked decrease in the explorator reflex as well as a reduction in weight. A subsequent study reported altered behavioral patterns among laboratory animals. The authors of the study speculated that BHA and BHT could affect the normal sequence of neurological development in young animals. Many consumers eat nearly 20 milligrams or more of BHA or BHT daily. Babies are estimated to ingest as much as 8 milligrams.

Captan. A widely used fungicide introduced in 1951, captan is used on apples, strawberries, blueberries, raspberries, and stone fruits. It is a probable human carcinogen and teratogen. One of its breakdown compounds appears to be very similar to the sedative thalidomide, which was used by pregnant women in the 1960s, causing thousands of children to be born with deformed limbs or without limbs. On June 21, 1985, the EPA proposed to cancel all uses of captan on food crops. At present, however, it remains in widespread use. Many home and garden pesticide formulations available at supermarkets and garden supply shops contain captan.

Carbaryl. A broad-spectrum insecticide introduced in 1958, carbaryl is used on more than 1,000 different crops including citrus, fruit, nuts, fodder, trees, bushes, and shrubs. It may be a carcinogen and definitely is a mutagen that causes kidney damage in animals. In humans, carbaryl may cause behavioral effects including antisocial and violent behavior, central nervous system lesions, heart defects, immune system suppression, renal tubular damage, and weight loss. Isocyanate, an ingredient in carbaryl, was the toxic agent present in the death cloud that killed and maimed thousands of persons in Bhopal, India, during the mid-1980s.

Carbofuran. A widely used broad-spectrum pesticide introduced in 1969 to control insects, mites, and nematodes in corn, carbofuran interferes with acetylcholinesterase production in the body. Symptoms include mild and reversible symptoms such as malaise, light-headedness, nausea, blurring of vision, hypersalivation, and vomiting. Symptoms that may occur with more severe poisoning include chest tightness, muscular twitching, convulsions, and coma. There is strong evidence that carbofuran may be mutagenic. It is a ravager of wildlife, particularly birds, which eat the pellets as they grub for food in farm fields. The EPA has reported that a single granule may be fatal to a small bird. More than forty separate bird kills attributed to carbofuran have occurred throughout the country. These kills involved as many as 1,000 birds of various types per incident. Secondary poisoning incidents have killed bald eagles, red-tailed hawks, red-shouldered hawks, northern harriers, loggerhead shrikes, and other birds of prey. These species are attracted to dead or dying smaller birds and small mammals affected by granular carbofuran. The Fish and Wildlife Service of the U.S. Department of the Interior indicated in its biological opinion of carbofuran that the Aplomado falcon, Attwater's greater prairie chicken, and the Aleutian Canada goose were endangered bird species jeopardized by the use of carbofuran. Because of the bird kills, carbofuran has been put under special review by the EPA, which is proposing to ban the use of the granular formulations of the pesticide on all sites.

Carbon tetrachloride. The major use of carbon tetrachloride, a probable human carcinogen, has been in the production of chlorofluorocarbons, which are used as refrigerants, foam-blowing agents, and solvents. It is also used in fumigants and pesticides, as a solvent in metal cleaning, and in the manufacture of paints and plastics. It was extensively used in the past in grain fumigation and was responsible for numerous deaths from acute and chronic long-term exposure before it was banned in the mid-1980s. The human liver, kidney, and lungs are most vulnerable to damage from carbon tetrachloride, which causes cancer—mainly liver cancer—in animals such as mice, rats, and hamsters. Among workers exposed to carbon tetrachloride, increased lymphosarcoma and lymphatic leukemia have been noted.

Carbophenothion. This is an organophosphate pesticide whose toxic effects include inhibition of cholinesterase, which results in immediate uncontrollable physiological responses as well as long-term central nervous system damage. It may cause prenatal damage as well as severe physiological damage including coma, confusion, convulsions, dizziness and vertigo, hallucinations, headaches, liver damage, psychosis, salivation, shock, sweating, vomiting, and extreme weakness. Carbophenothion may be synergistic with other organophosphate pesticides. It is highly toxic to freshwater, marine, and estuarine organisms and to upland game birds.

Chloramben. A widely used herbicide introduced in 1960 and used to control weeds in soybeans, chloramben is mutagenic in animals.

Chlordane. A member of the organochlorine family of pesticides, chlordane is closely related to DDT, but it is an even more potent and direct carcinogen. It has been frequently used in termite control. One of the most common forms of pesticide poisoning today has resulted after homes were fumigated with chlordane. Effects include mutagenicity, prenatal and postnatal damage, and reproductive system effects. Most uses of chlordane have been strictly limited. It may be used sporadically throughout the United States for termite control and is widely used in other nations.

Chlorobenzene. Acute exposure to this chemical, which is used in the manufacture of numerous pesticides, may cause drowsiness, incoherence, and liver damage. Points of attack include the respiratory system and the central nervous system.

Chlorobenzilate. This insecticide, introduced in 1956 and used on citrus fruits, is a possible human carcinogen. The EPA canceled all uses of chlorobenzilate in 1979 *except* for use on citrus. It may be a reproductive toxin and has been shown to have especially damaging effects on animal testes.

Chlorothalonil. This funguicide, introduced in 1961 and used on forty-seven different food crops—primarily fruits, peanuts, and vegetables—is a probable human carcinogen. It may cause kidney damage and impairment of the thyroid and liver.

Chlorpropham. An herbicide and plant growth regulator used especially on potatoes to control post-harvest sprouting, this is a carcinogen and teratogen.

Chlorpyrifos. This insecticide was introduced in 1965 and is used to control rootworms and cutworms in corn and in other grain crops as well as pests that attack a wide range of vegetable and fruit crops. It is also used on lawns, ornamental plants, and in and around homes and is directly applied to stagnant water. Chlorpyrifos is extremely toxic to fish, birds, and other wildlife. Symptoms of poisoning include headache, dizziness, extreme weakness, ataxia, tiny pupils, twitching, tremor, nausea, slow heartbeat, pulmonary edema, and sweating. Continual worker exposure may result in flulike symptoms including weakness, anorexia, and malaise.

Cyanazine. A widely used pre- and post-emergence herbicide introduced in 1971 for control of annual grasses and broadleaf weeds in corn. Toxic effects in laboratory animals include poor appearance, skin sores, increased mortality in the female animals, increased relative brain weight in both sexes, increased liver weight among females as well as anemia among females. Studies indicate that cyanazine is tumorigenic and causes teratogenic effects and developmental toxicity.

Dacthal. An herbicide used to control grasses in turf, ornamentals, and certain crops. Excessive exposure may cause liver damage. Dacthal may be contaminated with dioxin.

DCPA. See dacthal.

DDT. An insecticide introduced in 1942 and banned in 1972, DDT is a probable human carcinogen and neurotoxin. Metabolites include DDD and DDE.

DEF. An organophosphate pesticide. Acute exposure can cause a variety of effects: ataxia, central nervous system impairment, coma, confusion, convulsions, diarrhea, hallucinations, hepatic damage, and hyperthermia as well as salivation, shock, sweating, vomiting, and weakness.

Demeton-s. An insecticide introduced in 1955 for use on vegetables and orchard crops, it is an acute nervous system toxin that may cause birth defects and mutagenic effects. However, studies are considered inadequate by the EPA for determining its carcinogenicity, teratogenicity, and reproductive toxicity.

Diallate. An herbicide introduced in 1963 that is used on corn, soybeans, and sugar beets. Chronic effects of diallate include carcinogenesis, neurotoxicity, and reproductive system damage. Acute exposure may result in coughing, respiratory mucous membrane irritation, sneezing, skin irritation, and eye irritation.

Diazinon. An acutely toxic insecticide used on crops, pastures, ranges, grasslands, ornamentals, and golf courses, diazinon is responsible for hundreds of bird kills.

1,2-dibromo-3-chloropropane. A soil fumigant used throughout the 1970s to control nematodes on vegetables, fruits, and nuts. In 1979, the EPA suspended all registrations for DBCP except for use on pineapples in Hawaii. Researchers in California discovered that stomach cancer was far more prevalent in areas where residents drank DBCP-contaminated water. One-third of the males involved in manufacturing this pesticide suffered sterility. It may also be a mutagen and is a probable human carcinogen.

Di-butyl phthalate. A colorless, oily liquid used in plastics and as an insect repellant. Points of attack include the respiratory and gastrointestinal systems. Its presence in food may be due to packaging or to its use as an insecticide.

Dicamba. A widely used post-emergence herbicide introduced in 1967 and used to control weeds in corn and small grains and to control brush and vines in non-crop areas. Workers exposed to dicamba have developed muscle cramps, dyspnea, nausea, vomiting, skin rashes, loss of voice, or swelling of cervical glands.

1,2-dichloroethane. This chemical is used in the production of vinyl chloride; as a starting material for the production of other solvents; as an additive (lead scavenger) in gasolines; for metal degreasing and textile cleaning; in paints, coatings, and adhesives; as a grain fumigant, varnish, and finish remover; in soaps and scouring compounds; and as a wetting and penetrating agent. It is strongly mutagenic and is a probable human carcinogen.

1,1-dichloroethylene. The major use of this chemical is in the production of polymers. Effects on exposed workers, in combination with other vinyl compounds, include liver function abnormalities, headaches, vision problems, weakness, fatigue, and neurological sensory disturbances. It is a mutagen and a possible human carcinogen.

2,4-dichloro-6-nitrobenzenamine. A pesticide metabolite, possibly very similar to dicloran.

2,4-dichlorophenoxyacetic acid (2,4-D). An herbicide introduced in 1948 and widely used to eliminate weeds in wheat, corn, sorghum, and barley and on lawns, rangeland, and pasture. Occupational exposure to 2,4-D may result in reduced nerve conduction velocity. Population studies in Scandinavian countries indicate that exposure to 2,4-D and other phenoxy herbicides results in excess risk of developing soft-tissue sarcomas and malignant lymphomas. May be a weak teratogen and, in the first months of pregnancy, toxic to the developing embryo. This chemical may also lead to functional disturbances in the brain and to growth depression, and it is strongly suspected of being a mutagen.

1,2-dichloropropane. Used as a solvent for oils and fats, in dry-cleaning and degreasing operations, and as a component of soil fumigants. It is a mutagen and a probable human carcinogen.

Dicloran. A fungicide first registered for use in 1961 on peaches, plums, cherries, grapes, other fruits, and vegetables. Very little is known about its acute or long-term effects. Dicloran has been shown to have significant liver effects in animals.

Dicofol. An insecticide and acaricide introduced in 1955 and used particularly on citrus crops and cotton. It contains DDT as a contaminant and is a probable human carcinogen.

Dieldrin. An insecticide introduced in the late 1940s and banned in 1974, dieldrin is one of the most violent, persistent insecticides whose residues appear in significant concentration in the food supply. It is a strong neurotoxin and probable human carcinogen that attacks the liver and causes a rare form of hepatitis.

Dimethoate. A systemic insecticide and acaricide introduced in 1963 to control a wide variety of insects and mites in farm buildings, corn, soybeans, fruits such as grapes, and vegetables such as tomatoes. Limited evidence indicates that dimethoate, a neurotoxin, may also be a carcinogen and may cause birth defects, reproductive toxicity, and mutagenic effects.

Dioxin. Formed as a by-product in the manufacture of a number of chlorinated phenolic compounds, dioxin can also be present in fly ash and flue gases of incinerators. A probable human carcinogen, it is among the most potent carcinogenic substances ever studied by the EPA; it is 480,000 times more potent than DDT. It may be mutagenic; it displays an unusually high degree of reproductive toxicity; it is teratogenic and fetotoxic; and it reduces fertility.

Diphenyl 2-ethylhexyl phosphate. An industrial chemical that enters the food supply as a result of migration from processed-food packaging.

Disulfoton. An insecticide and acaricide introduced in 1958 for use on insects and mites on grains, strawberries, pineapples, and vegetables. In one incident, three carpenters were sprayed accidentally with disulfoton while the compound was being applied by airplane to a wheat field adjacent to their work site. The older two carpenters had heart attacks. Disulfoton is a mutagen and is extremely toxic.

Endosulfan. An organochlorine pesticide. Limited evidence suggests that the long-term chronic effects of endosulfan exposure may include liver and kidney damage and testicular atrophy. Breakdown products include endosulfan II and endosulfan sulfate.

Endrin. This chemical was widely used in the United States until its use was canceled in 1979. Exposure to even minute amounts of endrin may cause sudden convulsions, headaches, dizziness, sleepiness, and weakness. A number of deaths have been caused by swallowing endrin. Several cases of endrin poisoning from contaminated flour have been reported. In Wales, bread made from endrin-contaminated flour resulted in fifty-nine poisoning cases in 1956. Incidents have occurred in Doha, Qatar, and in Hofuf, Saudi Arabia. Eight persons were severely poisoned after ingesting endrin-contaminated tortillas in southern California in 1988.

EPN. An organophosphate pesticide that is extremely toxic to bees in areas of blooming crops and weeds. Acute exposure to EPN may cause headaches, tight chest, wheezing, salivation, nausea, abdominal cramps, diarrhea, convulsions, and low blood pressure. Points of attack include the central nervous system and the respiratory system. Many uses of EPN were canceled in 1983 because of its extreme toxicity. Other uses—on cotton, soybeans, corn, pecans, and other food crops—were strictly limited.

EPTC (S-ethyl dipropylthiocarbamate). A widely used selective herbicide introduced in 1969 to control annual and perennial grasses in corn and potatoes. Acute exposure may cause coughing, skin irritation, respiratory mucous membrane irritation, and sneezing.

Ethion. An insecticide that is known to be teratogenic.

Ethylene dibromide (EDB). Developed in the 1920s for use as an additive in leaded gasoline and as a fumigant and insecticide, EDB replaced DBCP, which was banned in the late 1970s. EDB, however, is even more carcinogenic than DBCP. It causes very high rates of cancer among virtually all laboratory species. It also causes birth defects and can cause sterility. It was banned in the mid-1980s.

Fenitrothion. An organophosphate pesticide, acute exposure may cause a variety of symptoms including ataxia, cholinesterase inhibition, central nervous system impairment, coma, confusion, convulsions, diarrhea, dizziness and vertigo, hallucinations, headaches, liver damage, nausea, pallor, psychosis, salivation, shock, sweating, vomiting, and weakness.

Fonofos. A widely used pre-emergence insecticide introduced in 1967 to control corn rootworm, wireworm, and cutworm. Very few data are available on the effects of human exposure. Laboratory studies indicate that high levels induce moderate inhibition of serum and red blood cell cholinesterase activity.

HCB. See hexachlorobenzene.

Heptachlor. A member of the organochlorine family of insecticides, heptachlor has been used on corn, alfalfa, hay, and vegetables and as a termiticide in homes. During the mid-1970s, the use of heptachlor on food crops was phased out because of the persistence of the chemical. Currently, heptachlor is used only as a termiticide and on a very limited number of crops. Evidence of transplacental transfer of heptachlor or heptachlor epoxide in humans comes from a study in which the pesticide was detected in the adipose tissue, brain, adrenal glands, lungs, heart, liver, kidney, and spleen of ten stillborn babies and two babies who died soon after birth and in twenty-seven of thirty samples of cord blood from healthy babies. Clinical case studies of humans with acute exposure to chlordane containing heptachlor document a pattern of central nervous system effects similar to those found in animals: irritability, salivation, labored respiration, muscle tremors, and convulsions. Several blood diseases, including anemia and leukemia, are associated with heptachlor exposure. Other researchers reported an insignificant increased incidence of lung cancer and a significant increase of cerebrovascular disease in 1,403 white male workers employed for seventy-three months in the production of chlordane and heptachlor. Heptachlor is a potent carcinogen and mutagen. It has been implicated frequently throughout the 1980s in mass population contamination and poisoning over widespread American regions. In both Arkansas and Hawaii, mothers who were exposed to heptachlor through dairy and meat products have been advised against breast-feeding their babies. In the environment, heptachlor undergoes a substantitive change and becomes a chemical known as heptachlor epoxide, which is twice as toxic as its parent compound, simple heptachlor. Heptachlor was banned in America in the mid-1980s, but farmers have enormous supplies on hand. Enough heptachlor is stored around the country—60,000 to 80,000 gallons—to last for eighty years at current rates of use.

Hexachlorobenzene (HCB). An ingredient of imported fungicides, hexachlorobenzene is not manufactured as a commercial product in the United States. The exposure of humans to seed wheat contaminated with HCB in Turkey from 1955 through 1959 caused an epidemic of HCB-induced porphyria turcica, which is manifested as disturbed porphyrin metabolism, cutaneous lesions, and hyperpigmentation. In children under one year of age, pink sores were observed and there was 95 percent mortality. Follow-up studies conducted with patients twenty to twenty-five years after the onset of porphyria showed that a few patients—about 10 percent—still had active porphyria; 78 percent exhibited hyperpigmentation; and 83 percent had scarring and other dermatologic, neurologic, and skeletal features of HCB toxicity. Enlarged thyroids were diagnosed in 60 percent of the female patients. Mice exposed to HCB during pregnancy exhibited numerous teratogenic responses including cleft palate and decreased fetal weight. HCB is a probable human carcinogen.

3-hydroxycarbofuran. A metabolite of carbofuran.

Iprodione. A broad-spectrum fungicide used on grapes, stone fruits, and berries.

Isopropyl phenyl phospates, mixed. Industrial chemicals that enter the food supply through environmental contamination or as a result of packaging.

Isopropyl-3-chloro-4-methoxy-phenylcarbamate. A metabolite of chlorpropham or a similar chemical.

Lindane. Used as an insecticidal treatment for hardwood logs and lumber, seed grains, and livestock and in dog shampoos and dips for treatment of fleas, ticks, lice, sarcoptic mange, and scabies. Flea collars may contain lindane, and it is sometimes used in moth sprays, shelf paper, and household sprays. As a scabicide (against lice), it may be present in lotions, creams, or shampoos. Lindane is a possible human carcinogen whose long-term human health implications include aplastic anemia and liver and kidney damage. Many uses have been severely restricted.

Linuron. A widely used herbicide introduced in 1966 to control weeds in corn and soybeans, linuron is a possible human carcinogen.

Malathion. An organophosphate pesticide. According to research results published in *Environmental Research,* malathion and its oxygen analog, malaoxon, are quite carcinogenic and have been linked with increased incidences of leukemia in animals. Other researchers contend malathion does not cause cancer. Very low doses of malathion—not much lower than what humans ingest—have produced direct mutagenic effects. Disturbingly, subsequent exposures to malathion, using much smaller doses, produced more chromatid breaks, an indication that the effects are cumulative. This chemical is a potent sensitizer of the skin and causes allergic dermatitis in human beings after a single exposure. Some people who are exposed will be sensitized to malathion and will develop skin eruptions on subsequent exposure, even to very weak dilutions. In addition, contact with malathion is likely to elicit allergic reactions ranging from a mild rash to severe asthmalike symptoms. Neurological abnormalities occurred in rats exposed to low levels even though the chemical was undetectable in blood samples.

MCPA, or (4-chloro-2-methylphenoxy)-acetic acid. An herbicide introduced in 1952 to control annual and perennial broadleaf weeds in small grains and on grasslands and non-crop areas. Chronic exposure at high doses may damage kidney and liver function. MCPA has caused delayed skeletal development in newborns, according to laboratory animal studies. It stimulates liver peroxisomal proliferation, which has been implicated in carcinogenicity.

Methamidophos. One of the most acutely toxic pesticides used in agriculture. Found on tomatoes and bell peppers.

Methidathion. This pesticide—frequently found in citrus fruits and products such as oranges, orange juice, and lemonade—is a possible human carcinogen. Despite its widespread use, there is not sufficient information about the cancer-causing potential of methidathion and its ability to cause birth defects and reproductive toxicity.

Methiocarb. Acute exposure to the pesticide methiocarb, a pesticide, may cause excess amounts of acetylcholine to accumulate at cholinergic neuroeffector junctions, which can damage central nervous system functioning. It may also alter the body's enzyme systems. Acute exposure effects include abdominal pain, coma, skin irritation, diarrhea, disorientation, dizziness, muscle twitching, nausea, psychosis, tremors, and vomiting. Effects of long-term exposure may include muscle weakness, central nervous system degeneration, and impaired nerve conduction.

Methomyl. An insecticide introduced in 1963 to control a broad spectrum of insects in agricultural and ornamental crops. Excessive exposure may cause kidney, spleen, liver, and bone marrow damage. It may be a mutagen. Acetamide, a metabolite, is a possible human carcinogen.

Methoxychlor. An insecticide registered for use on eighty-seven crops and used in dairy barns. Some experts believe it is a carcinogen; government officials contend it is not. According to Rachel Carson, "Methoxychlor may not be as free from dangerous qualities as it is generally said to be, for recent work on experimental animals shows a direct action on the uterus and a blocking effect on some of the powerful pituitary hormones—reminding us again that these are chemicals with enormous biologic effect. . . . If the liver has been damaged by another agent, methoxychlor is stored in the body at *100 times* its normal rate, and will then imitate the effects of DDT with long-lasting effects on the nervous system. Yet the liver damage that brings this about might be so slight as to pass unnoticed."

Methyl ethyl ketone (MEK). A colorless liquid solvent used extensively in the synthetic rubber industry; in processes involving gums, resins, cellulose acetate, and cellulose nitrate; in production of paraffin wax and high-grade lubricating oil; and in household products such as lacquer and varnish, paint remover, and glue. Studies indicate that MEK is embryotoxic, fetotoxic, and teratogenic. Although there is no evidence to date that MEK is carcinogenic or mutagenic, evidence suggests it may be injurious to the fetus at high maternal doses. Low-level chronic exposure has been shown to cause decreased memory and impairment of the central nervous system.

Methyl parathion. An organophosphate insecticide introduced in 1954 to control various insects such as the boll weevil on grains, peanuts, berries, and many other fruits and vegetables. A strong human mutagen upon acute exposure, it causes degenerative effects on nerve tissue, birth defects, reproductive effects in animals, and cataracts. There is some evidence of carcinogenicity in animals.

Metolachlor. An herbicide introduced in 1976 for use on corn and soybeans. Signs of human intoxication include abdominal cramps, anemia, ataxia, dark urine, methemoglobinemia, cyanosis, hypothermia, collapse, convulsions, diarrhea, gastrointestinal irritation, jaundice, weakness, nausea, shock, sweating, vomiting, depression, dizziness, dyspnea, liver damage, heart failure, skin irritation, corneal opacity, and adverse reproductive effects. A possible human carcinogen.

Metribuzin. A broad-spectrum herbicide introduced in 1973 to control grassy and broadleaf weeds in soybeans. Does not appear to be either a carcinogen or a mutagen.

Mevinphos. An acutely toxic pesticide used on many crops including strawberries, collards, and lettuce. Mevinphos is a deadly toxic pesticide that attacks the respiratory system, lungs, central nervous system, and cardiovascular system.

Nitrate and nitrite. Naturally occurring inorganic ions that make up part of the nitrogen cycle. Levels of nitrate in water can be significantly raised as a result of contamination by nitrogen-containing fertilizers or by human and animal wastes. Because nitrate is taken up by plants during their growth and converted back to organic form, nitrates occur naturally in a number of foods, particularly vegetables. The major use of nitrates is in inorganic fertilizers. The major sources of nitrates and nitrites in the average diet are vegetables, cured meats, breads, and drinking water. Both nitrate and nitrite are used in curing meats. In adults, nitrite in the stomach can react with secondary amines and other amine substrates such as carbamate pesticides to form N-nitroso compounds that are carcinogenic. Vitamin C and vitamin E inhibit the formation of N-nitroso compounds.

Nonachlor. A metabolite of chlordane.

Octachlor. Also known as chlordane. A probable human carcinogen. May cause birth defects and reproductive toxicity. Although uses were canceled for agriculture in 1978 and for termite control in 1987, existing supplies may remain in use.

Omethoate. A breakdown product of the pesticide dimethoate and a pesticide in its own right, omethoate is much more acutely toxic than dimethoate. Its use is not allowed on crops grown in the United States. However, residues are frequently found on grapes imported from Mexico. Based on toxicological data gathered for dimethoate, omethoate will have nervous system effects such as inhibition of cholinesterase. It may be a mutagen, and it may cause reproductive effects in animals. There is also some evidence of carcinogenicity in animals.

Oxamyl. An insecticide and nematocide used on a variety of fruit and vegetable crops including potatoes, peanuts, soybeans, and cotton, oxamyl inhibits cholinesterase in laboratory animals and has caused an increase in cholesterol levels. In a study of its neurotoxicity on hens, the fowls showed sudden depression, lethargy, ruffled feathers, slight respiratory difficulty, ataxia, and incoordination immediately after exposure. Depression and nervous signs lasted twelve hours. In a reproductive study of rats fed oxamyl, the litter size, viability, and lactation of exposed animals were lower at high doses.

Parathion. An organophosphate pesticide, parathion is acutely toxic. One chemist swallowed a mixture of about .00424 ounces of parathion, believing he would learn about its toxic properties through subjective research. He was immediately paralyzed. He had prepared antidotes but could not act quickly enough to swallow them. He died. In Finland, parathion is a favorite means of committing suicide. Hundreds of deaths have been reported in India, Syria, and Japan as a result of parathion poisoning. Even entering fields sprayed with parathion a month after application can cause serious injury to farm workers, as was proven in California when orchard workers collapsed and went into shock. Fatalities were avoided only through proper and immediate medical attention. Parathion is also deadly to wildlife. Indiana farmers once instructed a pilot to apply parathion to river bottomland where thousands of blackbirds congregated. Approximately 65,000 blackbirds and starlings were killed by their exposure to parathion.

PCNB. See pentachloronitrobenzene.

Penta. See pentachlorophenol.

Pentachlorobenzene. Used in the manufacture of the fungicide pentachloronitrobenzene. Ingestion of pentachlorobenzene by pregnant rats produced developmental effects and decreased body weight in fetuses. One study indicates it may be carcinogenic.

Pentachlorobenzonitrile. An industrial chemical or metabolite of PCNB.

Pentachloronitrobenzene. Also known as quintozene and PCNB, this is a soil fungicide introduced in 1955 for use on specialty crops, including cotton, peanuts, and vegetables, and on lawns. It is contaminated with the carcinogen hexachlorobenzene.

Pentachlorophenol. Also known as penta, this chemical is used as a wood preservative to protect against fungus decay and termite attacks. It was once used as an insecticide and herbicide, but registrations have been canceled for all non-wood uses, and other uses have been restricted. Penta is so powerful that a California tank truck driver applying penta to a cotton crop was killed when the spigot he was using to draw the chemical drum fell out of the drum and he reached into the liquid with his bare hand. He washed immediately, but by the next day he was dead. Metabolites include pentachlorophenol methyl ether and pentachlorophenol methyl sulfide.

Perchloroethylene (PCE). Major uses are in the textile and dry-cleaning industries and in metal degreasing. Liver and kidney damage and central nervous system depression have been observed in humans who were occupationally exposed to PCE. Chronic exposure may cause impairment of brain function and decreased memory. Signs of exposure include malaise, dizziness, headaches, increased perspiration, fatigue, incoordination, and impaired mental acuity. It is a probable human carcinogen.

Permethrin. An insecticide introduced in 1978 for use on vegetables, permethrin is a possible human carcinogen.

Perthane. A pesticide rarely used today, in part because pests have become resistant to it.

Phorate. An insecticide introduced in 1959 to control a wide range of insects in corn, soybeans, and other crops. Metabolites include phorate sulfone and phorate sulfoxide.

Phosalone. An organophosphate pesticide that causes central nervous system damage.

Phosmet. A pesticide that is a possible human carcinogen and mutagen.

Phosphamidon. An organophosphate insecticide used against sucking insects and aphids on a variety of crops. It attacks the central nervous system, causing acetylcholine to build up at nerve junctions, leading to muscular and nervous convulsions. Phosphamidon appears to be a mutagen.

Picloram. A broad-spectrum herbicide introduced in 1963 to control broadleaf and woody plants in rangelands, pastures, and rights-of-way. Among its acute effects are skin irritation, eye irritation, nausea, nervous system disorders, and respiratory tract irritation. It is suspected of being a carcinogen, and it causes hepatic, prenatal, and reproductive system damage.

Pirimiphos-methyl. An organophosphate pesticide that attacks the central nervous system, causing acetylcholine buildup at nerve junctions. Symptoms of acute exposure include alkyl phosphates in urine, anoxia, aphasia, ataxia, confusion, convulsions, cyanosis, dermatitis, diarrhea, dizziness and vertigo, hallucinations, headache, hypertension, hypotension, hyperthermia, incontinence, tenesmus, nausea, pallor, paresis, psychosis, renal damage, vomiting, and weakness. This chemical also appears to be a mutagen.

Propachlor. A widely used herbicide introduced in 1965 to control grasses and broadleaf weeds in corn. Acute exposure may cause abdominal pains, anemia, chills, collapse, convulsions, diarrhea, eye irritation, jaundice, muscular weakness, nausea, shock, sweating, and darkened urine and may cause the blood to turn brown. Chronic exposure can cause anemia, dermatitis, dizziness, dyspnea, hepatic damage, and nephritis. Two chemicals analogous to this compound—alachlor and acetochlor—were found to be oncogenic in two animal species. Propachlor may also be a mutagen.

Ronnel. A member of the organophosphate pesticide family, ronnel has been banned for use in the United States. It may cause cancer, prenatal damage, and reproductive system effects.

Simazine. An herbicide introduced in 1957 to control grasses and broadleaf weeds in corn. Its toxic effects include ataxia, carcinogenesis, convulsions, cyanosis, dyspnea, miosis, paralysis, tearing, tremors, and weakness. Simazine may disturb the metabolism of thiamine and riboflavin. It has caused mutations in human tissue, and it induces thyroid and mammary tumors in females.

Styrene. Used in styrene plastics. Points of attack include the central nervous system, respiratory system, lungs, eyes, and skin. There is suggestive evidence that the human fetus is more sensitive than the adult body is to the toxic effects of styrene. Styrene has been linked with spontaneous abortions among Finnish chemical workers. Finnish women who worked in the reinforced-plastics industry and who were regularly exposed to styrene, polyester resin, and acetone during pregnancy were more likely to give birth to children with central nervous system defects. In fact, there appeared to be more than a 300-fold increased rate of central nervous system defects in the reinforced-plastics industry during the study period. Styrene oxide, a major metabolite of styrene, has been demonstrated consistently to be mutagenic in laboratory studies. It is a possible human carcinogen.

Sulfur. An element of the earth's crust, sulfur has been used as a miticide and fungicide for centuries. Sulfur is probably not carcinogenic or mutagenic and is of low toxicity to bees, aquatic organisms, birds and fish. Chronic human exposure to sulfur in mines and refineries has resulted in serious respiratory disturbances including chronic bronchitis and sinus problems. Agricultural incidents usually result in skin and eye irritations. In 1980–81, the California Department of Food and Agriculture reported 302 poisoning incidents linked with sulfur. Sulfur is one of the least toxic pesticides for both agricultural workers and wildlife and beneficial insects.

Tecnazene. A fungicide used mainly on potatoes, tecnazene is chemically similar to pentachloronitrobenzene. It is also used as a plant growth regulator.

Terbufos. A widely used pesticide introduced in 1974 to control rootworms, insects, and nematodes in corn. There is no evidence that terbufos is a carcinogen and very little evidence that it is a potent mutagen. Exposed farm workers have shown no indication of harmful physiological effects.

2,3,5,6-tetrachloroaniline. A metabolite of tecnazene.

2,3,5,6-tetrachloroanisidine. A metabolite of tecnazene.

Tetrachlorobenzenes. Industrial chemicals that enter the food supply from environmental contamination.

Tetrachloro (methylthio) benzene. A metabolite of tecnazene.

Tetrahydrofuran. A solvent used to dissolve synthetic resins such as polyvinyl chloride and vinylidene chloride copolymers. Among the symptoms of exposure are nausea, dizziness, headaches, dry skin, dermatitis, and central nervous system disorders. In experimental animals, liver and kidney damage have been reported.

Toluene. Used as a raw material in the production of benzene and organic solvents, toluene is itself a solvent. It is used mainly in paints, coatings, gums, oils, and resins and as a gasoline additive to elevate octane ratings. Points of attack are the central nervous system, liver, kidneys, and skin. Symptoms of low-level exposure include headaches, dizziness, fatigue, muscular weakness, drowsiness, incoordination with a staggering gait, collapse, and coma. Toluene does not appear to be mutagenic, and there is inadequate animal data to determine its carcinogenic potential.

Toxaphene. An insecticide introduced in 1948, toxaphene was widely used on soybeans, cotton, corn, wheat, and other crops until 1982 when most common uses were canceled as a result of its potential to cause tumors and its decimation of wildlife. It is a probable human carcinogen.

Tri (beta-chloroethyl) phosphate. An environmental contaminant.

Tri (2-butoxyethyl) phosphate. An environmental contaminant.

Tri (2-ethylhexyl) phosphate. An environmental contaminant.

Tributyl phosphate. An antifoaming agent, plasticizer, and solvent for cellulose esters; its presence in the food supply is usually the result of the containers in which food is packed. Points of attack include the respiratory system, skin, and eyes.

1,1,1-trichloroethane. A colorless, nonflammable liquid used in the cleaning and vapor-degreasing of fabricated metal parts, in the synthesis of other chemicals, as a spot remover and film cleaner, and as an additive in metal-cutting oils. Acute exposure symptoms include dizziness, incoordination, and drowsiness. Chronic low-level exposure to 1,1,1-trichloroethane has been found to cause decreased memory and impairment of the central nervous system. It appears to be mutagenic and carcinogenic.

Trichloroethylene (TCE). Used as a solvent in vapor degreasing, once for extraction of caffeine from coffee, as a dry-cleaning agent, and in the production of pesticides, resins, paints, and varnishes. Once used as an anesthetic, TCE is highly toxic to the nervous system. Points of attack include the respiratory system, central nervous system, heart, liver, kidneys, and skin. TCE appears to be a mutagen and is a probable human carcinogen.

Trihalomethanes (THMs). This family of chemicals is formed when chemicals used for the chlorination of drinking water interact with organic material such as leaves, insects, and humus in the water. Among the chemicals that belong to this family are bromodichloromethane, bromoform, bromomethane, chlorodibromomethane, chloroform, and chloromethane. The THM family of chemicals has been strongly linked with increased incidences of cancer at many sites in the human body.

Triphenyl phosphate. Used to impregnate roofing paper and as a plasticizer for cellulose esters in lacquers and varnishes. May cause minor changes in blood enzymes, muscular weakness, and paralysis. Presence in the food supply is usually the result of migration from plastic in which foods are packed.

Trichlorobenzene. An herbicide intermediate and a potential insecticide against termites, this chemical causes drowsiness, incoordination, and unconsciousness. Animal exposures have produced liver damage, and chronic exposure may result in liver, kidney, and lung damage.

1,2,3-trichlorobenzene. A moderately toxic termiticide that irritates the eyes and the respiratory tract.

2,4,5-trichlorophenoxypropionic acid (2,4,5-T). An herbicide used to control weeds and plants on industrial sites and rangeland. Along with 2,4-dichlorophenoxyacetic acid, it was half of the formulation known as Agent Orange, which was used as a defoliant in Vietnam. It is a proven teratogen. Case-controlled epidemiological studies of people in the Scandinavian countries who were exposed to the phenoxy herbicides (as well as other chemicals and contaminants) indicate excess risk of developing soft-tissue sarcomas and malignant lymphomas. Data on mutagenicity and reproductive effects are unavailable. All registration for herbicides containing 2,4,5-T were canceled in 1985.

Trifluralin. A widely used herbicide introduced in 1963 to control annual grasses and broadleaf weeds in soybeans as well as on golf courses and rights of way. Excessive exposure may cause kidney and liver damage and effects on blood. Trifluralin is considered by the EPA to be a possible human carcinogen.

Vinclozolin. A fungicide with moderate toxicity used on grapes, strawberries, soft fruits, vegetables, ornamental flowers, and turf grasses.

Vinyl chloride. Used as raw material in the plastics, rubber, paper, glass, and automotive industries, in the manufacture of electrical wire insulation and cables, piping, industrial and household equipment, medical supplies, food packaging materials, and building and construction products. Increased incidence of liver cancer and tumors of the brain, lung, and lymph tissues have been associated with occupational exposure to vinyl chloride. Chronic inhalation of this chemical induced liver cancer and other cancers in both rats and mice. It is a known human carcinogen and is strongly mutagenic. There is an association between human exposure to vinyl chloride and an increase in birth defects and fetal losses.

Volatile organic chemicals. Also known as VOCs, volatile organic chemicals comprise a family of industrial compounds such as perchloroethylene and trichloroethylene, which are often found in drinking water. When exposed to the environment VOCs often become gaseous and move from the water to the air. However, when found in groundwater, they become much more stable and remain in the water supplies. VOCs may cause acute illness and even death upon high exposure. The levels at which they are commonly found in drinking water bring up the problem of chronic long-term health effects such as cancer, central nervous system damage, and immune system impairment, which may occur after twenty to thirty years of chronic low-level exposure.

Xylenes. These chemicals are used as solvents for paints, inks, and adhesives and as components of detergents and other industrial and household products. Points of attack include the central nervous system, eyes, gastrointestinal tract, blood, liver, kidneys, and skin. Although they are clearly neurotoxins, xylenes have not been classified yet for carcinogenicity. They do not appear to be mutagenic.

PRINCIPAL SOURCES

I used hundreds upon hundreds of sources, ranging from interviews and newspaper articles to highly scientific studies. Many have been mentioned in the text. I also used many of my own studies. The following list contains some of the principal sources used in this book.

INTRODUCTION

Pages 1–3:
Citron, Alan. "Warning Issued on Fish Caught off Southland." *Los Angeles Times,* April 22, 1985.

1. AN END TO FOOD ANXIETY

Pages 4–6:
Weissman, Joseph. *Choose to Live.* New York: Grove Press, 1988.
Pages 6–8:
Annual Cancer Statistics Review Including Cancer Trends: 1950–1985. Bethesda, Md.: National Cancer Institute, Division of Cancer Prevention and Control, U.S. Department of Health and Human Services, Public Health Service, National Institutes of Health, 1987.
Cantor, Kenneth; Hoover, Robert; Hartge, Patricia; Mason, Thomas; Silverman, Debra; Altman, Ronald; Austin, Donald; Child, Margaret; Key, Charles; Marrett, Loraine; Myers, Max; Narayana, Ambati; Levin, Lynn; Sullivan, J. W.; Swanson, G. Marie; Thomas, David; and West, Dee. "Bladder Cancer, Drinking Water Source, and Tap Water Consumption: A Case-Control Study." *Journal of the National Cancer Institute* 79, no. 6 (December 1987), pp. 1269–79.
The Surgeon General's Report on Nutrition and Health. Washington, D.C.: U.S. Department of Health and Human Services, Public Health Service, 1988.

Wasserman, M. "Organochlorine Compounds in Neoplastic and Adjacent Apparently Normal Breast Tissue." *Bulletin of Environmental Contamination and Toxicology* 15 (1976), pp. 478–84.
Page 8:
Weiner, Michael. *Reducing the Risk of Alzheimer's.* New York: Stein and Day, 1987.
Pages 9–10:
Ashford, Nicholas. "New Scientific Evidence and Public Health Imperatives." *The New England Journal of Medicine* 316, no. 17 (April 23, 1987), pp. 1084–85.
McAuliffe, Kathleen; Gilbert, David; Kistner, William; Weir, David. "Legally Clean, but Questions Remain." *U.S. News & World Report,* November 16, 1987.
Masterson, Mike. "The Poison Within: A Special Report." Phoenix: *The Arizona Republic,* January 29 to February 3, 1989.
Nigim, Chun-Han, and Devathasan, Gobinathan. "Epidemiologic Study on the Association Between Body Burden Mercury Level and Idiopathic Parkinson's Disease." *Neuroepidemiology* 8 (1989), pp. 128–41.
Root, David; Katzin, David; and Schnare, David. "Diagnosis and Treatment of Patients Presenting Subclinical Signs and Symptoms of Exposure to Chemicals Which Bioaccumulate in Human Tissue." *Proceedings of the National Conference on Hazardous Wastes and Environmental Emergencies,* May 14–16, 1985.
Page 10:
Role of the Primary Care Physician in Occupational and Environmental Medicine. Washington, D.C.: National Academy Press, 1988.
Page 11:
Houk, Vernon. "What's the Health Concern?" *Pesticides and Groundwater: A Health Concern for the Midwest.* Proceedings of the Freshwater Foundation conference, October 16–17, 1986, Navarre, Minn.
Pages 11–12:
Gunderson, Ellis. *FDA Total Diet Study, April 1982–April 1986: Dietary Intakes of Pesticides, Selected Elements, and Other Chemicals.* Arlington, Va.: Association of Official Analytical Chemists.

2. PLANT FOODS

Pages 13–24:
Liebman, Bonnie. "Are Vegetarians Healthier Than the Rest of Us?" *Nutrition Action Health Letter,* June 1983.
Liebman, Bonnie. "Carrots Against Cancer?" *Nutrition Action Health Letter,* December 1988.
Nutritive Value of Foods. Washington, D.C.: U.S. Department of Agriculture, 1981.
Robbins, John. *Diet for a New America.* Walpole, N.H.: Stillpoint Publishing, 1987.
The Surgeon General's Report on Nutrition and Health. Washington, D.C.: U.S. Department of Health and Human Services, Public Health Service, 1988.

Weiner, Michael. *Reducing the Risk of Alzheimer's.* New York: Stein and Day, 1987.

3. VEGETABLES AND FRUITS

Pages 25–44:
Food and Drug Administration Pesticide Monitoring Crop Reports for Fruits and Vegetables, 1985–88, Washington, D.C.
Gunderson, Ellis. *FDA Total Diet Study, April 1982–April 1986: Dietary Intakes of Pesticides, Selected Elements, and Other Chemicals.* Arlington, Va.: Association of Official Analytical Chemists.
Pages 44–47:
Bashin, Bryan Jay. "The Freshness Illusion: A Few Good Words for Frozen Food and Some Serious New Questions About the Content of Supermarket Produce." *Harrowsmith,* January–February 1987.
"Safety and Labelling of Waxed Fruits and Vegetables." Compliance Policy Guides. Washington, D.C.: Associate Commissioner for Regulatory Affairs, U.S. Food and Drug Administration, November 1, 1980.
The Wax Cover-Up: What Consumers Aren't Told About Pesticides on Fresh Produce. Washington, D.C.: Center for Science in the Public Interest, 1989.
Pages 47–48:
Cunningham, William. Author's interview with Cunningham of the Food and Drug Administration, Center for Food Safety and Applied Nutrition, Division of Contaminants Chemistry, Washington, D.C., April 1989.
Cunningham, William; Stroube, William; and Baratta, Edmond. "Radionuclides in Domestic and Imported Foods in the United States, 1983–1986." *Journal of the Association of Official Analytical Chemists* 72, no. 1 (1989), pp. 15–18.
Pages 48–49:
Mott, Lawrie, and Snyder, Karen. *Pesticide Alert.* San Francisco: Sierra Club Books, 1988.
Pages 49–54:
Food and Drug Administration Pesticide Monitoring Crop Reports for Fruits and Vegetables, 1985–88, Washington, D.C.
Gunderson, Ellis. *FDA Total Diet Study, April 1982–April 1986: Dietary Intakes of Pesticides, Selected Elements, and Other Chemicals.* Arlington, Va.: Association of Official Analytical Chemists.

4. GRAINS

Pages 55–61:
The Surgeon General's Report on Nutrition and Health. Washington, D.C.: U.S. Department of Health and Human Services, Public Health Service, 1988.
Pages 61–68:

Gunderson, Ellis. *FDA Total Diet Study, April 1982–April 1986: Dietary Intakes of Pesticides, Selected Elements, and Other Chemicals.* Arlington, Va.: Association of Official Analytical Chemists.
Pages 68–70:
Weiner, Michael. *Reducing the Risk of Alzheimer's.* New York: Stein and Day, 1987.
Winter, Ruth. *A Consumer's Dictionary of Food Additives.* New York: Crown Publishers, Inc., 1984.
Pages 70–71:
Gunderson, Ellis. *FDA Total Diet Study, April 1982–April 1986: Dietary Intakes of Pesticides, Selected Elements, and Other Chemicals.* Arlington, Va.: Association of Official Analytical Chemists.

5. ANIMAL FOODS

Pages 72–75:
"Loss of Tainted Chickens Won't Hurt Prices: Analyst." *Supermarket News,* March 20, 1989.
Masterson, Mike. "The Poison Within: A Special Report." Phoenix: *The Arizona Republic,* January 29 to February 3, 1989.
Steinman, David. "Human Blood Serum Levels of Chlorinated Hydrocarbon Compounds." Unpublished data, 1988–90.

6. MEAT AND POULTRY

Pages 76–77:
Schell, Orville. *Modern Meat: Antibiotics, Hormones, and the Pharmaceutical Farm.* New York: Random House, 1984.
Pages 77–78:
Harr, James (U.S. Department of Agriculture). Interview with author on sulfamethazine residues in meat, Nov. 7, 1988.
Marbery, Steve. "Sulfa Offers No Easy Choices." *Hog Farm Management,* May 1988.
Meeker, David (Director of Research and Education, National Pork Producers Council). Interview with author, December 1988.
Pages 78–81:
Burns, Jim. "What's the Beef? Trade Uproar Focuses Attention on American Meat." *Los Angeles Herald-Examiner,* January 19, 1989.
Davis, Darnise. "Abnormal Sexual Development." Transcript from the news broadcast on Cable News Network, February 7, 1985.
Meat and Poultry Inspection: The Scientific Basis of the Nation's Program. Washington, D.C.: National Academy Press, 1985.
Schell, Orville. *Modern Meat: Antibiotics, Hormones, and the Pharmaceutical Farm.* New York: Random House, 1984.
Pages 81–83:
Malko, Constance. "Raley's Range-Fed Veal Gets Positive Response." *Supermarket News,* July 31, 1989.
Malko, Constance. "Veal Quality Assurance Begun to Allay Drug Residue Concern." *Supermarket News,* September 25, 1989.

Miller, Brad (director of the Humane Farming Association, San Francisco). Interview with author, June 1989.

Puzo, Daniel. "Animal-Rights Group Claims Poor Treatment of Calves, Calls for Boycott." *Los Angeles Times,* June 22, 1989.

Residue Monitoring Program Yearly Data Summary (Domestic/Imports for the Years 1983–1988). Washington, D.C.: Food Safety and Inspection Service, U.S. Department of Agriculture.

Wilson, Noel. "Bill Aimed at Veal Calf Raising Revived." *Los Angeles Times,* March 9, 1989.

Page 83:

Lohr, Steve. "Swedish Farm Animals Get a Bill of Rights." *New York Times,* October 20, 1988.

Pages 84–85:

Anthan, George. "Contamination Rate Reaches 80 Percent at Some U.S. Poultry Plants." *The Des Moines Register,* April 12, 1987.

Anthan, George. "Salmonella Poisoning: More Than an Upset Stomach." *The Des Moines Register,* April 13, 1987.

Anthan, George. "Poultry Firms Allowed to Vacuum Away Pus, U.S. Inspectors Say." *The Des Moines Register,* June 16, 1987.

Cohen, Mitchell, and Tauxe, Robert. "Drug Resistant *Salmonella* in the United States: An Epidemiologic Perspective." *Science* 234 (November 21, 1986), pp. 964–969.

"Keeping Our Food Safe from Animal Drugs." *FDA Consumer,* July–August 1986.

Zuckerman, Sam. "The Overuse of Antibiotics in Animal Feed." *Nutrition Action,* January–February 1985.

Pages 86–93:

Gunderson, Ellis. *FDA Total Diet Study, April 1982–April 1986: Dietary Intakes of Pesticides, Selected Elements, and Other Chemicals.* Arlington, Va.: Association of Official Analytical Chemists.

Residue Monitoring Program Yearly Data Summary (Domestic/Imports for the Years 1983–1988). Washington, D.C.: Food Safety and Inspection Service, U.S. Department of Agriculture.

Pages 93–97:

"Imported Meat and Poultry Samples Analyzed for Radiocesium by the Food Safety and Inspection Service Following the Chernobyl Accident, May 1986 Through December 1988." Washington, D.C.: U.S. Department of Agriculture.

Pages 97–99:

Lefferts, Lisa. "Great Grilling." *Nutrition Action Health Letter,* July–August 1989.

Parmley, Mary Ann. *The Safe Food Book: Your Kitchen Guide.* Washington, D.C.: U.S. Office of Consumer Affairs, 1985.

Pages 100–101:

Gunderson, Ellis. *FDA Total Diet Study, April 1982–April 1986: Dietary Intakes of Pesticides, Selected Elements, and Other Chemicals.* Arlington, Va.: Association of Official Analytical Chemists.

Residue Monitoring Program Yearly Data Summary (Domestic/Imports for the

Years 1983–1988). Washington, D.C.: Food Safety and Inspection Service, U.S. Department of Agriculture.

7. SEAFOOD

Pages 102–103:

Gossett, Richard; Wikholm, Gary; Ljubenkov, John; Steinman, David. "Human Serum DDT Levels Related to Consumption of Fish from the Coastal Waters of Los Angeles." *Environmental Toxicology and Chemistry* 8 (1989), pp. 951–55.

Pages 103–11:

Industrial Chemical/Pesticide Monitoring Reports for Seafood 1982–88. Washington, D.C.: U.S. Food and Drug Administration.

Pages 112–13:

Hokama, Yoshitsugi. *Detection of Ciguatoxin and Related Polyethers in Fish Tissues Associated with Ciguatera Poisoning by the Stick Enzyme Immunoassay.* A paper presented before the National Academy of Sciences Committee on Evaluation of Safety of Fishery Products, Woods Hole, Ma., July 26, 1989.

Pages 113–17:

"Seafood Safety: Present and Future." Presentation made by U.S. Food and Drug Administration at the Institute of Food Technologists meeting in Chicago, June 1989.

Wastes in Marine Environments. Washington, D.C.: U.S. Office of Technology Assessment, April 1987.

Pages 117–19:

Ruttenberg, Michael. "Safe Sushi." Letter to the editor in *The New England Journal of Medicine,* September 28, 1989, p. 900.

Kure, Katsuhiro, and Yokoi, Masahiko. Letter to the editor in *The New England Journal of Medicine,* September 28, 1989, p. 900.

Page 120:

Industrial Chemical/Pesticide Monitoring Reports for Seafood 1982–88. Washington, D.C.: U.S. Food and Drug Administration.

8. DAIRY FOODS

Pages 121–22:

Nutritive Value of Foods. Washington, D.C.: U.S. Department of Agriculture, 1981.

Weiner, Michael. *Reducing the Risk of Alzheimer's.* New York: Stein and Day, 1987.

Pages 122–23:

Blume, Elaine. "Stalking the Deadly Listeria." *Nutrition Action Health Letter,* July–August 1987.

"Brie and Mexican Cheese Recalled." *FDA Consumer,* May 1986.

Pages 123–37:

Cimons, Marlene. "Dioxin Detected in Milk, FDA Says." *Los Angeles Times,* September 2, 1989.

"Drug Residues Found in Milk." *New York Times,* April 14, 1988.

Gunderson, Ellis. *FDA Total Diet Study, April 1982–April 1986: Dietary Intakes of Pesticides, Selected Elements, and Other Chemicals.* Arlington, Va.: Association of Official Analytical Chemists.

Parrad, Marc. "Listeriosis Scare Sends Shiver Through French Town That Is Famous for Its Cheese." *Los Angeles Times,* April 16, 1989.

"Sulfamethazine Survey of Residues in Milk from Major U.S. Cities." Washington, D.C.: Food and Drug Administration, 1988.

"Firm Recalls Mexican Cheese." *Los Angeles Times,* January 31, 1988.

Young, Frank. "Keeping Drug Residues Out of Milk: A Lesson in Industry Education." *FDA Consumer,* March 1989.

9. EGGS

Pages 138–39:

Nutritive Value of Foods. Washington, D.C.: U.S. Department of Agriculture, 1981.

Pages 139–42:

Burros, Marian. "Eating Well: Salmonella Study Suggests That Eggs Should Be Treated with Great Caution." *New York Times,* April 13, 1988.

Hanson, Amy, and Bennett, William. "Trojan Eggs." *New York Times Magazine,* July 30, 1989.

Leary, Warren. "Research Links Eggs to Recent Outbreak of Food Poisoning." *New York Times,* April 7, 1988.

Leary, Warren. "U.S. Begins Testing to Fight Rise in Egg Contamination." *New York Times,* September 16, 1988.

"Raw Eggs May Be Bad Eggs." *University of California, Berkeley, Wellness Letter,* June 1988.

"British Health Aide Quits After Furor over Eggs." *Los Angeles Times,* December 17, 1988.

Pages 142–43:

Malko, Constance. "Sales of Free-Range Eggs Reported to Be Increasing." *Supermarket News,* September 25, 1989.

"Scrambled Priorities." *Watchdog* (published by the Humane Farming Association), Spring 1989.

Yaeger, Don. "Low-Cholesterol Eggs Get Push in Saint Louis." *Supermarket News,* February 6, 1989.

10. PREPARED FOODS

Pages 144–48:

Goodman-Malamuth, Leslie. "Junk Foods Go Hollywood." *Nutrition Action Health Letter,* September–October 1985.

Pages 148–51:

Gunderson, Ellis. *FDA Total Diet Study, April 1982–April 1986: Dietary In-*

takes of Pesticides, Selected Elements, and Other Chemicals. Arlington, Va.: Association of Official Analytical Chemists.

Lefferts, Lisa, and Schmidt, Stephen. "Microwaves: The Heat Is On." *Nutrition Action Health Letter*, January–February 1990.

Pages 151–57:

Gunderson, Ellis. *FDA Total Diet Study, April 1982–April 1986: Dietary Intakes of Pesticides, Selected Elements, and Other Chemicals*. Arlington, Va.: Association of Official Analytical Chemists.

Pages 157–61:

Erasmus, Udo. *Fats That Heal, Fats That Kill*. Petaluma, Calif.: Spectrum Naturals, 1987.

Galland, Leo. *Superimmunity for Kids*. New York: E. P. Dutton, 1988.

Pages 161–65:

Duggan, Reo; Corneliussen, Paul; Duggan, Mary; McMahon, Bernadette; and Martin, Robert. *Pesticide Residue Levels in Foods in the United States from July 1, 1969 to June 30, 1976*. Washington, D.C.: U.S. Food and Drug Administration, 1983.

Gunderson, Ellis. *FDA Total Diet Study, April 1982–April 1986: Dietary Intakes of Pesticides, Selected Elements, and Other Chemicals*. Arlington, Va.: Association of Official Analytical Chemists.

11. BEVERAGES

Pages 166–72:

Ethyl Carbamate (EC) Levels in Alcoholic Beverages Analyzed by FDA (1986–1988). Washington, D.C.: Center for Food Safety and Applied Nutrition, U.S. Food and Drug Administration, 1989.

Mitchell, Charles, and Jacobson, Michael. *Tainted Booze: The Consumer's Guide to Urethane in Alcoholic Beverages*. Washington, D.C.: Center for Science in the Public Interest, 1989.

Pages 172–77:

Food and Drug Administration Pesticide Monitoring Crop Reports for Fruits and Vegetables, 1985–88, Washington, D.C.

Gunderson, Ellis. *FDA Total Diet Study, April 1982–April 1986: Dietary Intakes of Pesticides, Selected Elements, and Other Chemicals*. Arlington, Va.: Association of Official Analytical Chemists.

12. ADDITIVES

Pages 177–195:

Eddins, Sheryl. "School Vetoes Junk Food." *Pritikin Research Foundation Newsletter*, Summer 1982.

Egger, J.; Graham, P. J.; Soothill, J. F.; Carter, C. M.; and Gumley, D. "Controlled Trial of Oligoantigenic Treatment in the Hyperkinetic Syndrome." *Lancet*, March 9, 1985.

Food and Drug Administration Food Additive Process Followed for Aspartame. Washington, D.C.: U.S. General Accounting Office, 1987.

Janssen, Wallace. "The Squad That Ate Poison." *FDA Consumer*, December–January 1982.

Quarterly Report on Adverse Reactions Associated with Aspartame Ingestion. Washington, D.C.: Center for Food Safety and Nutrition, U.S. Food and Drug Administration, April 1, 1988.

Reexamination of the GRAS Status of Sulfiting Agents. Springfield, Va.: National Technical Information Service, U.S. Department of Commerce, January 1985.

Schoenthaler, Stephen; Doraz, Walter; and Wakefield, James, Jr. "The Impact of a Low Food Additive and Sucrose Diet on Academic Performance in 803 New York City Public Schools." *International Journal of Biosocial Medical Research*, 8, no. 2 (1986), pp. 185–195; and "Testing of Various Hypotheses as Explanations for the Gains in National Standardized Academic Test Scores in the 1978–1983 New York City Nutrition Policy Modification Project." *International Journal of Biosocial Medical Research*, 8, no. 2 (1986), pp. 196–203.

Winter, Ruth. *A Consumer's Dictionary of Food Additives.* New York: Crown Publishers, Inc., 1984.

13. IRRADIATION

Pages 196–97:

MacFadyen, Tevere. "Immortal Shrimp and Other Fruits of the Gamma Ray—Irradiated Food: The Latest Panacea from the Same Folks Who Brought Us Atoms for Peace." *Harrowsmith*, January–February 1986.

Pages 197–98:

"Australian Scientists Find Cancer Link to Food Irradiation." *Consumer Interpol Memo* (a publication of the International Organization of Consumer Unions), April 6, 1989.

Bhaskaram, C., and Sodasivan, G. "Effects of Feeding Irradiated Wheat to Malnourished Children." *American Journal of Clinical Nutrition* 28 (February 1975), pp. 130–35.

"The Irradiation Industry Hall of Shame, Part 1." *Food Irradiation Alert!* 3, no. 2 (March 1989).

"The Irradiation Industry Hall of Shame, Part 2." *Food Irradiation Alert!* 3, no. 3 (June 1989).

Jacobs, Sanford. "U.S. Jury Convicts Former President of Radiation Firm." *Wall Street Journal*, July 14, 1988.

Johnsrud, Judith. "Food Irradiation: Its Environmental Threat, Its Toxic Connection." *The Workbook*, 13, no. 2 (April–June 1988).

Pages 199–201:

Somer, Noel (lecturer and post-harvest pathologist, University of California, Davis). Personal letter to Paul T. Libassi, editor, *The Sciences*, New York Academy of Sciences, March 5, 1985.

14. DRINKING WATER

Pages 202–206:

Dean, Norman. *Danger on Tap: The Government's Failure to Enforce the Federal Safe Drinking Water Act.* Washington, D.C.: National Wildlife Federation, October 1988.

Gabler, Raymond, and editors of Consumer Reports Books. *Is Your Water Safe to Drink?* Mount Vernon, N.Y.: Consumers Union, 1987.

Masterson, Mike. "Chemical Pollution Taints Country's Ground Water." *The Arizona Republic,* January 31, 1989.

Masterson, Mike. "U.S. Says Ground Water Is 'Good,' But Its Claims Prove Deceptive." *The Arizona Republic,* January 31, 1989.

Pages 206–209:

Cantor, Kenneth; Hoover, Robert; Hartge, Patricia; Mason, Thomas; Silverman, Debra; Altman, Ronald; Austin, Donald; Child, Margaret; Key, Charles; Marrett, Loraine; Myers, Max; Narayana, Ambati; Levin, Lynn; Sullivan, J. W.; Swanson, G. Marie; Thomas, David; and West, Dee. "Bladder Cancer, Drinking Water Source, and Tap Water Consumption: A Case-Control Study." *Journal of the National Cancer Institute* 79, no. 6 (December 1987), pp. 1269–79.

Gabler, Raymond, and editors of Consumer Reports Books. *Is Your Water Safe to Drink?* Mount Vernon, N.Y.: Consumers Union, 1987.

"National Interim Primary Drinking Regulations; Control of Trihalomethanes in Drinking Water; Final Rule." Washington, D.C.: *Federal Register,* November 29, 1979.

Pages 210–14:

Feldman, Robert; Chirico-Post, Jeanette; and Proctor, Susan. "Blink Reflex Latency After Exposure to Trichloroethylene in Well Water." *Archives of Environmental Health* 43, no. 2, (March–April 1988), pp. 143–48.

Masterson, Mike. "Chemical Pollution Taints Country's Ground Water." *The Arizona Republic,* January 31, 1989.

Masterson, Mike. "U.S. Says Ground Water Is 'Good,' But Its Claims Prove Deceptive." *The Arizona Republic,* January 31, 1989.

Pages 215–18:

Bellinger, David; Leviton, Alan; Waternaux, Christine; Needleman, Herbert; and Rabinowitz, Michael. "Longitudinal Analyses of Prenatal and Postnatal Lead Exposure and Early Cognitive Development." *The New England Journal of Medicine* 316, no. 17 (April 23, 1987), pp. 1037–43.

Jansson, Erik. "Comments on Preliminary Summary of Draft Proposal to Revise Standard for Lead in Drinking Water." Letter from Erik Jansson, director of the National Network to Prevent Birth Defects, Washington, D.C., to Greg Helms of the Task Force on Lead in Drinking Water, Office of Drinking Water, U.S. Environmental Protection Agency, January 15, 1988.

Rosov, Eugene (president of WaterTest Corporation of Manchester, N.H.). Testimony before the Congressional Subcommittee on Health and the Environment, July 13, 1988.

Pages 218–19:

Gabler, Raymond, and editors of Consumer Reports Books. *Is Your Water Safe to Drink?* Mount Vernon, N.Y.: Consumers Union, 1987.

Jansson, Erik. *New Studies Indicate That Radium in the Drinking Water Produces as Many Cancers and Birth Defects as Airborne Radon and That EPA Has Understated Radium as a Health Hazard.* Washington, D.C.: National Network to Prevent Birth Defects, August 3, 1987.

Page 220:

Mueller, William. "Dark Waters: Scientists Discover Agricultural Chemicals Running Deep in the Nation's Aquifers, and One Farm State Takes Action." *Harrowsmith,* November–December 1987, pp. 69–79.

Nielsen, Elizabeth, and Lee, Linda. *The Magnitude and Costs of Groundwater Contamination from Agricultural Chemicals.* Washington, D.C.: U.S. Department of Agriculture, 1987.

Page 221:

Pesticides and Groundwater: Surveys of Selected Minnesota Wells. Minneapolis: Minnesota Department of Health and Minnesota Department of Agriculture, February 1988.

Fiore, Michael. "Chronic Exposure to Aldicarb Contaminated Groundwater and Human Immune Function." *Pesticides and Groundwater: A Health Concern for the Midwest.* Proceedings of the Freshwater Foundation conference, October 16–17, 1986, Navarre, Minn.

Jackson, Richard. "DBCP and Drinking Water in California." *Pesticides and Groundwater: A Health Concern for the Midwest.* Proceedings of the Freshwater Foundation conference, October 16–17, 1986, Navarre, Minn.

Pages 222–23:

Shepherd, Dan (Fowler, California, resident whose daughter contracted leukemia allegedly from contaminated drinking water). Interview with the author. August 10, 1988.

Pages 223–24:

Fiore, Michael. "Chronic Exposure to Aldicarb Contaminated Groundwater and Human Immune Function." *Pesticides and Groundwater: A Health Concern for the Midwest.* Proceedings of the Freshwater Foundation conference, October 16–17, 1986, Navarre, Minn.

Pages 224–39:

A Consumer's Guide to Protecting Your Drinking Water. Boston: National Toxics Campaign, 1989.

Gabler, Raymond, and editors of Consumer Reports Books. *Is Your Water Safe to Drink?* Mount Vernon, N.Y.: Consumers Union, 1987.

King, Jonathon. *Troubled Water: The Poisoning of America's Drinking Water —How Government and Industry Allowed It to Happen, and What You Can Do to Ensure a Safe Supply in the Home.* Emmaus, Pa.: Rodale Press, 1985.

Lester, Stephen, and Lipsett, Brian. *Drinking Water Filters: What You Need to Know.* Arlington, Va.: Citizens Clearinghouse for Hazardous Wastes, January 1988.

Szejnwald Brown, Halina; Bishop, Donna; Rowan, Carol. "The Role of Skin Absorption as a Route of Exposure for Volatile Organic Compounds (VOCs) in Drinking Water." *American Journal of Public Health* 74, (May 1984), pp. 479–84.

Your Drinking Water—How Bad Is It? Cleveland, Ohio: National Testing Laboratories, 1985.

"Water Sense Wheel" (presents explanations of symptoms of water quality problems). Durham, N.H.: Environmental Hazards Management Institute, 1988.

Pages 240–42:

Ballentine, Carol, and Herndon, Michael. "The Water That Goes into Bottles." *FDA Consumer,* May 1983.

Paddock, Richard, and Stein, Mark. " 'Unusually Low' Miscarriage Rate Linked to Drinking Bottled Water." *Los Angeles Times,* May 24, 1988.

Von Wiesenberger, Arthur. *H₂O: The Guide to Quality Bottled Water.* Santa Barbara, Calif.: Woodbridge Press, 1988.

15. THE NONTOXIC HOME

Pages 243–44:

Lawson, Lynn (communications coordinator for the Human Ecology Action League). Letter to author, Aug. 1, 1988.

Page 245:

"EPA Sees Cancer Link to Formaldehyde." *Chicago Tribune,* April 17, 1987.

The Inside Story: A Guide to Indoor Air Quality. Washington, D.C.: U.S. Environmental Protection Agency, Office of Air and Radiation, September 1988.

Pages 246–67:

Dolan, Maura. "Renovations Stir Up New Poison Fear." *Los Angeles Times,* July 9, 1989.

Guide to Hazardous Products Around the Home. Springfield, Mo.: Household Hazardous Waste Project, 1989.

Hazardous Waste in Our Homes—And in Our Water. Navarre, Minn.: Freshwater Foundation, 1985.

Hazards in the Arts. New York: Center for Occupational Hazards.

Lead and Cadmium in Dinnerware Reported by Fiscal Year and Country. Washington, D.C.: U.S. Food and Drug Administration, 1989.

Lecos, Chris. "Pretty Poisons: Lead and Ceramic Ware." Washington, D.C.: *FDA Consumer,* July–August 1987.

Roueché, Berton. Letter to editor of *The New Yorker,* February 29, 1988.

Silver, Lori. "EPA Cites Indoor Pollution Hazards." *Los Angeles Times,* Nov. 11, 1988.

16. PREGNANCY AND TOXIC CHEMICALS

Page 268:

Jansson, Erik. "Components of a National Program to Reduce Birth Defect, Learning Disability, Very Low Birth Weight, and Child Abuse Rates by 50 Percent and Childhood Cancer by 30 Percent." Washington, D.C.: National Network to Prevent Birth Defects, October 21, 1987.

Jansson, Erik. "Recent Findings about the Preventative Effects of Vitamins and Minerals upon Human Health." Washington, D.C.: Physicians Committee for Responsible Medicine, January 20, 1989.

Pages 268–70:

"Rates Skyrocket in 15 Years." Washington, D.C.: *Birth Defect Prevention*

News. Washington, D.C.: National Network to Prevent Birth Defects, Fall 1988.
Page 270:
Kay, Jane. "Solvent Linked to Defects." *San Francisco Examiner,* September 6, 1987.
Pages 270–72:
Graedon, Joe. *The New People's Pharmacy.* New York: Bantam Books, 1985.
Jansson, Erik. *Medical, Environmental, and Economic Information on: Nitrates, Nitrites, and Nitroso-Compounds. Why American Exposure to Nitrates, Nitrites, and Nitroso-Compounds Needs to Be Reduced by More Than 50 Percent.* Washington, D.C.: National Network to Prevent Birth Defects, August 1, 1987.
Meggs, William, M.D. Letter to the author from Meggs, of East Carolina University School of Medicine, North Carolina, on situations in which therapeutic drugs could be needed during pregnancy, March 5, 1990.
Wikholm, Gary, M.D. Author's interview with Dr. Wikholm, a family practice physician in Ventura, Calif., on guidelines for women on use of therapeutic drugs during pregnancy, February 4, 1990.
Page 273:
Willhite, Calvin; Hendricks, Andrew; Burk, Dorothy; Book, Steven. "Warnings and the Hazards of Drinking Alcoholic Beverages During Pregnancy." Letters. *Teratology* 37, August 3, 1987.
Pages 274–76:
Elkington, John. *The Poisoned Womb.* New York: Viking Penguin, 1985.
Fein, G. G.; Jacobson, J. L.; Jacobson, S. W.; Schwartz, P. M.; and Dowler, J. K. "Prenatal Exposure to Polychlorinated Biphenyls: Effects on Birth Size and Gestational Age." *Journal of Pediatrics* (1984), pp. 315–20.
Jansson, Erik. "Petition for a Breast Milk Purity Strategy." Petition from Jansson, director of the National Network to Prevent Birth Defects, Washington, D.C., to Lee Thomas, Administrator, U.S. Environmental Protection Agency, March 1, 1985.
Pages 276–77:
Jansson, Erik. "Comments on Preliminary Summary of Draft Proposal to Revise Standard for Lead in Drinking Water." Letter from Jansson, director of the National Network to Prevent Birth Defects, Washington, D.C., to Greg Helms, Task Force on Lead in Drinking Water, Office of Drinking Water, U.S. Environmental Protection Agency, January 15, 1988.
Jansson, Erik. "Petition on the Need to Address Other Toxic Metals Besides Lead." Petition from Jansson, director of the National Network to Prevent Birth Defects, Washington, D.C., to Lee Thomas, Administrator, U.S. Environmental Protection Agency, January 9, 1986.
Pages 277–79:
Jansson, Erik. *Medical, Environmental, and Economic Information on: Nitrates, Nitrites, and Nitroso-Compounds. Why American Exposure to Nitrates, Nitrites, and Nitroso-Compounds Needs to Be Reduced by More Than 50 Percent.* Washington, D.C.: National Network to Prevent Birth Defects, August 1, 1987.
Pages 279–81:
Galland, Leo. *Superimmunity for Kids.* New York: Dutton, 1988.

Gould, Jay, and Sternglass, Ernest. "Low-level Radiation and Mortality." *Chemtech*, January 1989.

Jansson, Erik. "Supporting Medical Information on Low Dosage Radiation: Why American Exposure to Radiation Needs to Be Reduced by 50 Percent, and Petition Item Summary." Submitted by Jansson, director of the National Network to Prevent Birth Defects, Washington, D.C., to Administrator, U.S. Environmental Protection Agency, and Secretaries of the Department of Health and Human Services, Department of Energy, Department of Defense, Department of Housing and Urban Development, Chairman of the Nuclear Regulatory Commission, and Chairman of the Tennessee Valley Authority, December 1, 1986.

"New Studies Indicate That Radium in the Drinking Water Produces as Many Cancers and Birth Defects as Airborne Radon and That EPA Has Underestimated Radium as a Health Hazard." Washington, D.C.: National Network to Prevent Birth Defects, August 3, 1987.

Pages 281–83:

Galland, Leo. *Superimmunity for Kids.* New York: Dutton, 1988.

Jansson, Erik. "Cancer in Children: Principal Causes and Prevention." Washington, D.C.: National Network to Prevent Birth Defects, September 29, 1987.

Jansson, Erik. *Recent Findings About the Preventative Effects of Vitamins and Minerals Upon Human Health.* Washington, D.C.: Physicians Committee for Responsible Medicine, January 20, 1989.

Pages 283–84:

Jansson, Erik. "Petition for a Breast Milk Purity Strategy." Petition from Jansson, director of the National Network to Prevent Birth Defects, Washington, D.C., to Lee Thomas, Administrator, U.S. Environmental Protection Agency, March 1, 1985.

17. BABY FOODS

Pages 285–90 and 292–93:

Gunderson, Ellis. *FDA Total Diet Study, April 1982–April 1986: Dietary Intakes of Pesticides, Selected Elements, and Other Chemicals.* Arlington, Va.: Association of Official Analytical Chemists.

18. DETOXIFICATION

Page 294:

Citron, Alan. "Warning Issued on Fish Caught off Southland." *Los Angeles Times,* April 12, 1985.

Steinman, David. "Poisoned Fish? Poisoned Fishermen?" *L.A. Weekly,* November 1, 1985. Volume 7, number 49.

Pages 294–95:

Steinman, David. "We Are All Sick." *The Reader,* September 1, 1989.

Pages 296–97:

Kilburn, Kaye; Warshaw, Ralph; and Shields, Megan. "Neurobehavorial Dysfunction in Firemen Exposed to Polychlorinated Biphenyls (PCBs): Possible

Improvement After Detoxification." *Archives of Environmental Health,* November–December 1989, pp. 345–50.

Roehm, D. "Effects of a Program of Sauna Baths and Megavitamins on Adipose DDE and PCBs and on Cleaning Symptoms of Agent Orange (Dioxin) Toxicity." *Clinical Research* 31, 1983.

Tretjak, Z.; Beckmann, S.; Tretjak, A.; and Gunnerson, C. "Occupational, Environmental, and Public Health in Semic: A Case Study of Polychlorinated Biphenyl (PCB) Pollution." *Proceedings of the Annual Meeting of the American Society of Chemical Engineers,* New Orleans, October 1989.

Pages 297–300:

The program used by HealthMed was originally developed by L. Ron Hubbard, based on research he conducted in the 1950s on the effects of niacin on radiation victims. Hubbard later went on to develop the entire program of niacin supplements, exercise, sauna, and polyunsaturated oil that is now used by medical professionals throughout the country for detoxification of pesticides, industrial chemicals, and recreational drugs. Hubbard's work in this area has been verified by numerous independent researchers whose studies have been published in peer-reviewed scientific medical journals.

Connor, William; Witiak, Donald; Stone, Daniel; and Armstrong, Mark. "Cholesterol Balance and Fecal Neutral Steroid and Bile Acid Excretion in Normal Men Fed Dietary Fats of Different Fatty Acid Composition." *Journal of Clinical Investigations* 48 (1969), pp. 1363–75.

Nye, E. R., and Buchanan, H. "Short-term Effect of Nicotinic Acid on Plasma Level and Turnover of Free Fatty Acids in Sheep and Man." *Journal of Lipid Research* 10 (1969), pp. 193–96.

Shepherd, J.; Stewart, J.; Clark, J.; and Carr, K. "Sequential Changes in Plasma Lipoproteins and Body Fat Composition During Polyunsaturated Fat Feeding in Man." *British Journal of Nutrition* 44 (1980), pp. 265–71.

Pages 300–301:

Wisner, Michael, Administrative Director of HealthMed, Los Angeles. Correspondence with author, August 25, 1989.

Pages 301–303:

"Population Serum Averages: Toxic Compounds." Richardson, Tex.: Accu-Chem Laboratories, September 26, 1989.

Steinman, David. "Human Blood Serum Levels of Chlorinated Hydrocarbon Compounds." Unpublished data, 1988–90.

Pages 303–306:

Beckmann, Shelley. Correspondence from Beckmann, science director of Foundation for Advancements in Science and Education, with author November 17, 1989.

Bulow, J. "Adipose Tissue Blood Flow During Exercise." *Danish Medical Bulletin* 30 (1983), pp. 85–100.

Carlson, L. A. "Nicotinic Acid; Its Metabolism and Its Effects on Plasma Free Fatty Acids." Gay, K. F., and Carlson, L. A., editors. *Metabolic Effects of Nicotinic Acid and Its Derivatives,* 1971.

Cohn, James, and Emmett, Edward. "The Excretion of Trace Metals in Human Sweat." *Annals of Clinical and Laboratory Science* 8 (1978), pp. 270–75.

Root, David, and Lionelli, G. T. "Excretion of a Lipophilic Toxicant Through the Sebaceous Glands: A Case Report." *Journal of Cutaneous and Ocular Toxicology* 6, no. 1 (1987), pp. 13–17.

Wisner, Michael, Administrative Director of HealthMed, Los Angeles. Interview with author. November 13, 1989.

19. SAFE EATING IN THE REAL WORLD

Pages 307–10:

Lusk, Albert. Author's interview with Lusk, owner of Albert's Organics in Los Angeles, a nationwide wholesale distributor of certified organic produce, 1989.

20. POSTSCRIPT: PESTICIDES IN OUR FOOD

Pages 311–12:

Hansen, Michael. *Escape from the Pesticide Treadmill: Alternatives to Pesticides in Developing Countries.* Mount Vernon, N.Y.: Institute for Consumer Policy Research, Consumers Union, 1987.

Pages 313–14:

Carson, Rachel. *Silent Spring.* Boston: Houghton Mifflin Company, 1962.

Graham, Frank, Jr. *Since Silent Spring.* Boston: Houghton Mifflin Company, 1970.

Mott, Lawrie, and Snyder, Karen. *Pesticide Alert.* San Francisco: Sierra Club Books, 1988.

Page 314:

Weir, David, and Schapiro, Mark. *Circle of Poison.* San Francisco: Institute for Food and Development Policy, 1981.

Pages 314–18:

Blair, Aaron. "Cancer and Pesticides Among Farmers." *Pesticides and Groundwater: A Health Concern for the Midwest.* Proceedings of the Freshwater Foundation conference, October 16–17, 1986, Navarre, Minn.

Blair, Aaron; Fraumeni, Joseph; and Mason, Thomas. "Geographic Patterns of Leukemia in the United States." *Journal of Chronic Disease* 33 (1980), pp. 251–60.

Blair, Aaron, and Thomas, Terry. "Leukemia Among Nebraska Farmers: A Death Certificate Study." *American Journal of Epidemiology* 110, no. 3 (1979), pp. 264–73.

Dalton, Bill. "Risks for Farmers Rise with Pesticide Use." *Kansas City Star,* October 20, 1987.

Hoar Zahm, S.; Blair, Aaron. "Geographic Variation in Lymphoma Incidence." Letter to the editor. *British Journal of Cancer* 57 (1988), p. 443.

Saftlas, Audrey; Blair, Aaron; Cantor, Kenneth; Hanrahan, Larry; and Anderson, Henry. "Cancer and Other Causes of Death Among Wisconsin Farmers." *American Journal of Industrial Medicine* 11 (1987), pp. 119–29.

Pages 318–22:

Auerbach, Jan (U.S. Environmental Protection Agency Office of Pesticides). Interview with author about pesticides undergoing agency special reviews, July 18, 1988.

Guidance for the Reregistration of Pesticide Products Containing Captan as the Active Ingredient. Washington, D.C.: U.S. Environmental Protection Agency, March 6, 1986.

Houk, Willoughby (Fresno County farmer from San Joaquin Valley, California, diagnosed with lymphoma). Interview with author, April 1989.

Johnson, Diane (mother of Jared Johnson, who contracted diabetes allegedly as a result of his exposure to the pesticide paraquat). Personal interview. April 1989.

Kutz, Frederick; Carra, Joseph; Cook, Brion; Stroup, Cindy; Settergreen, Susan; Potter, Frank; and Murphy, Robert. *Toxic Substance Residues and Metabolites in Human Blood and Urine from a General Population Survey.* Presented at the annual meeting of the American Public Health Association, Dallas, Tex., November 16, 1983.

Masterson, Mike. "Debate in U.S. Focuses on Effect of Pesticides." *The Arizona Republic,* February 1, 1988.

Masterson, Mike. "Kids' Deaths in Clusters Haunt Parents Across U.S." *The Arizona Republic,* January 29, 1988.

Masterson, Mike. "Our Tainted Food Chain: Serving Disease and Death." *The Arizona Republic,* January 29, 1988.

Rosales, Connie (mother of Randy Rosales, a McFarland, Calif., cancer victim who survived.) Interview with author. June 7, 1988.

Sewell, Bradford, and Whyatt, Robin. *Intolerable Risk: Pesticides in Our Children's Food.* San Francisco: Natural Resources Defense Council, February 1989.

Taylor, Ronald. "Crop Dusting—Ill Winds of Arizona?" *Los Angeles Times,* July 30, 1979.

Taylor, Ronald. "DBCP Still Used Despite Dangers." *Los Angeles Times,* June 28, 1979.

Pages 322–23:

Food and Drug Administration Pesticide Monitoring Crop Reports for Fruits and Vegetables, 1985–88, Washington, D.C.

Masterson, Mike. "Most Mexican Crops Unchecked." *The Arizona Republic,* February 1, 1989.

Pesticides: Better Sampling and Enforcement Needed on Imported Food. Washington, D.C.: General Accounting Office, September 26, 1988.

Pesticides: Need to Enhance FDA's Ability to Protect the Public from Illegal Residues. Washington, D.C.: General Accounting Office, October 27, 1986.

Pages 323–24:

Hansen, Michael. *Escape from the Pesticide Treadmill: Alternatives to Pesticides in Developing Countries.* Mount Vernon, N.Y.: Institute for Consumer Policy Research, Consumers Union, 1987.

Pages 324–26:

Dunsmoor, Joseph (president of Organic Farms, a national wholesale retailer). Interview with author, May 1989.

Acknowledgments

I would like to thank the following persons: my literary agent, Madeleine Morel, for invaluable and much appreciated help certainly in the beginning and at all times since; Mike Masterson, former director of the *Arizona Republic* special projects team and presently Kiplinger professor at the Kiplinger Public Affairs Reporting program at Ohio State University, for his enthusiasm and encouragement and for bringing me aboard the *Republic*'s special projects team and basing much of the *Republic*'s series "The Poison Within" on what would become *Diet for a Poisoned Planet;* Michael Pietsch, senior editor at Harmony, whose contributions to this book went well beyond the call of duty; Dr. Farid Ahmed, Senior Program Director of the Institute of Medicine at the National Academy of Sciences, for his extremely valuable assistance for my work at the National Academy of Sciences; and Jan Jessie Jocoy, whose love and friendship gave me so much for so long.

Index